'*Attack Warning Red!* effectively pull
from this unsettling aspect of British history and we
them in a way that will alarm and entertain'
BBC History Magazine

'Superb . . . a lucid, totally compulsive read from beginning
to end, chilling as well as profoundly empathetic'
Mick Jackson, director of *Threads*

'[A] frightening but also rather funny book . . .
I found this book so entertaining'
The Times

'Julie McDowall has made the unreadable compulsive and
the unthinkable thinkable. But, above all, this is a book that
cherishes humanity in all its absurdity, intelligence, vulnerability,
courage and, against all odds, belief in hope and survival'
Juliet Nicolson, author of *Frostquake*

'Captivating, chilling, and at times darkly humorous.
A fascinating insight into Britain's preparations for
surviving Armageddon, and the ghastly reality of what the
aftermath of a nuclear war would actually be like. Based
on the Cold War, but with renewed urgency today'
Lewis Dartnell, author of *The Knowledge*

'Fascinating'
Sir Lawrence Freedman, author of *Command*

'Julie McDowall has written the best exploration yet of how
successive British administration grappled with the challenge
of living under the shadow of nuclear war, with depth,
compassion and very necessary dark humour'
Mark Galeotti, author of
The Weaponisation of Everything

JULIE McDOWALL

Julie McDowall is a freelance journalist and book critic specialising in the nuclear threat. Her writing has appeared in *The Times*, *The Economist*, *Spectator*, *Guardian*, *Times Literary Supplement*, *Prospect* and *Independent*, and she also hosts the *Atomic Hobo* podcast in which she reveals findings in the nuclear archives and reports on her travels to nuclear bunkers and other Cold War sites.

JULIE McDOWALL

Attack Warning Red!

How Britain Prepared for Nuclear War

VINTAGE

1 3 5 7 9 10 8 6 4 2

Vintage is part of the Penguin Random House group of companies whose
addresses can be found at global.penguinrandomhouse.com

Penguin
Random House
UK

First published in Vintage in 2024
First published in hardback by The Bodley Head in 2023

penguin.co.uk/vintage

Printed and bound in Great Britain by Clays Ltd, Elcograf S.p.A.

The authorised representative in the EEA is Penguin Random House Ireland,
Morrison Chambers, 32 Nassau Street, Dublin D02 YH68

A CIP catalogue record for this book is available from the British Library

ISBN 9781529920017

In memory of my Gran, May Boyle
1929–2022

Every morning, six days a week, I leave the house and drive a mile to the flat where I work. For seven or eight hours I am alone. Each time I hear a sudden whining in the air or one of the more atrocious impacts of city life, or play host to a certain kind of unwelcome thought, I can't help wondering how it might be. Suppose I survive. Suppose my eyes aren't pouring down my face, suppose I am untouched by the hurricane of secondary missiles that all mortar, metal and glass has abruptly become: suppose all this. I shall be obliged (and it's the last thing I'll feel like doing) to retrace that long mile home, through the firestorm, the remains of the thousand-mile-an-hour winds, the warped atoms, the grovelling dead. Then – God willing, if I still have the strength, and, of course, if they are still alive – I must find my wife and children and I must kill them.

What am I to do with thoughts like these? What is anyone to do with thoughts like these?

Martin Amis (*Einstein's Monsters*)

Contents

1 The Family That Feared Tomorrow

In 1957, in the quiet village of Langho, Lancashire, three young sisters were found dead in bed. Sandra, 10, Yvonne, 9, and Moira, 5, had been dressed in their pyjamas and laid on the mattress beneath a carefully arranged canopy of sheets and blankets. Under the bed, a floorboard had been lifted and the gas pipe fractured. The police found the bodies after a call from their grandmother, who had received a frightening letter from her daughter saying, 'The children are sleeping peacefully', before warning her, 'Please Mother don't go upstairs by yourself.'[1]

With the house empty apart from the three dead girls, a huge police hunt swung into action for the absent mother and father. 'Find these parents', cried the front page of the *Daily Mirror*. 'All-Britain search after three sisters die'.[2]

The hunted pair, Elsie and Andrew Marshall – he a textile weaver and she a nurse – were last seen quietly leaving their village on an early-morning bus, and could be traced as far as Fleetwood, about 30 miles away, on the Lancashire coast, as their final letter to Elsie's mother bore the seaside town's postmark.

Police flooded into the town, from where ships to the Isle of Man sailed. The flurry of summer passengers was watched, and the steamer *Mona's Isle* was searched in the hope that the fugitives might try to make their escape by mingling with the August holiday crowds, but there was no luck.

Elsie and Andrew were located a few days later in another tourist town. Mr Stillings, a holidaymaker out for an early-morning stroll, found them floating in the shallows by Blackpool's North Pier, fully dressed and roped together at the waist. He called for assistance from nearby bathers, who helped in hauling the bodies ashore. The inquest at Blackpool declared the parents' death to be manslaughter by means of a suicide pact, with the girls' inquest a few days later delivering a verdict of murder.[3]

For those who kept an eye on current events, these were anxious times. Cold War fears expressed themselves in the lingering paranoia of McCarthyism. The shocking launch of Sputnik, the world's first satellite, later that year would badly shake Western confidence, as had the previous year's events in Suez and Hungary. Adding to a creeping sense of unease were constant news reports of nuclear tests, including several huge explosions in the Pacific as Britain obtained the terrifying new hydrogen bomb, a weapon thousands of times more powerful than the atomic bombs dropped on Japan in 1945. The papers called these tests 'a dress rehearsal for the death of the world' and described the new bomb as it burst in the sky as 'a boiling red and yellow sun, low above the horizon. It was an oil painting from hell, beautiful and dreadful, magnificent and evil.'[4] Meanwhile, the US was conducting its 'Plumbbob' series of nuclear tests in Nevada, which consisted of 29 explosions and saw 719 pigs tethered to the ground or placed in cages to assess the effects of the bombs' heat flash on their bodies, pig skin being chosen for its similarities to human flesh. In one test, in order to see what protection a US soldier's uniform would offer against a nuclear explosion, little jackets were made for the captive animals. Neatly dressed, they were then forced into wooden cages to await the blast.[5] More nuclear testing took place in the Pacific as the Americans sought to perfect the new hydrogen bomb.

The public had been introduced to the true horror of nuclear weapons in August 1946, when *The New Yorker* devoted an entire issue to John Hersey's harrowing report from Hiroshima. If some of the atomic bomb's impact had been lost in the euphoria of VJ Day, here was the reality, stark and fresh, blaring from the magazine's pages in the post-war lull. Hersey told the stories of several survivors who had witnessed the nuclear attack, including that of a German priest, Father Kleinsorge, who, when making his way through the ruined city, encountered a group of men seemingly frozen in time who had been looking skywards when the bomb exploded. 'He saw there were about twenty men and they were all in exactly the same nightmarish state: their faces were wholly burned, their eye sockets were hollow, the fluid from their melted eyes had run down their cheeks.'[6] Another survivor of the blast recalled that there were

> hundreds and hundreds who were fleeing, and every one of them seemed to be hurt in some way. The eyebrows of some were burned off and skin hung from their faces and hands. Others, because of pain, held their arms up as if carrying some-thing in both hands. Some were vomiting as they walked. Many were naked or in shreds of clothing. On some undressed bodies, the burns had made patterns – of undershirt straps and sus-penders and, on the skin of some women (since white repelled the heat from the bomb and dark clothes absorbed it and con-ducted it to the skin), the shapes of flowers they had had on their kimonos. Many, although injured themselves, supported relatives who were worse off. Almost all had their heads bowed, looked straight ahead, were silent, and showed no expression whatever.

The Marshalls, a working-class couple from a small Lancashire vil-lage, were unlikely to have read that dreadful issue of *The New Yorker*, but the British press carried constant reports of nuclear testing and anxiety. In the months leading up to the family's deaths, their local paper, the *Lancashire Evening Post*, featured pleas to halt nuclear tests for the sake of future generations,[7] and warned of 'the destruction of civilisation by the hydrogen bomb'.[8] A group of women dressed in mourning protested at Downing Street as they called for an end to the tests, their letter to the prime minister declaring, 'Our survival as a nation, perhaps as a species, depends upon nuclear disarmament.' As one protester explained, 'We are wearing mourning for the thousands of people already affected by H-bomb explosions and for the thou-sands who will be in the future.'[9]

This threatening future was discussed frequently in the press in 1957, both nationally and locally, and the phrase 'the next war' was used with bleak certainty. The *Lancashire Evening Post* said 'In the next war, this country will be flattened by Horror-bombs anyhow so what is the use of worrying?'[10] But many people could not help worrying, such as parents like the Marshalls, as lots of these articles stressed the vulnerability of children. The *Daily Mirror* described the new threat of nuclear fallout:

> What happens when the big bang goes off is as nothing compared with what follows. The 'global fallout', as it is called, pours down a radioactive dust called 'Strontium 90' . . . [It] is absorbed into everything living, animal and vegetable. From grass, it goes into milk and so into bones and animals and human beings – especially into children. Strontium 90 causes aplastic anaemia, leukaemia, and blood and bone cancer.[11]

The earlier atomic weapons had provoked terror with their awesome blast power and agonising heat flash, but the silent killer of fallout became obvious with the arrival of the massively powerful hydrogen bomb.

Fallout is dust and debris that is sucked up after the explosion into the mushroom cloud, where it becomes radioactive before falling back to earth. Its destination cannot be easily predicted, as it will move, drift and descend with the weather. It is often invisible, adding to its terror, but sometimes it falls back to earth as perceptible dust or ash, as in the case of the *Lucky Dragon* fishing boat, when in 1954 a group of Japanese fishermen in the Pacific were showered with fallout from an American nuclear test, code-named Castle Bravo.[12] The explosion was far greater than the scientists had predicted, and it pulverised the small island where the bomb was detonated, as well as the surrounding coral reefs, and heaved all the shattered remnants high up into the mushroom cloud. Hours later, this peculiar dust began to rain down, far beyond the exclusion zone. It fell as soft, crunchy powder, and where it touched the skin, it caused itching and pain. When the fishermen got back to shore, doctors found that this powder contained spectacular levels of radiation. Dizziness, blisters, diarrhoea and hair loss followed. One of the men died. Another developed liver cancer, and his first child was stillborn, showing severe birth defects. It was clear to many that in the new age of the hydrogen bomb, another war would be one of unimaginable horror.

It was dread of this future war that provoked the tragedy in Langho, prompting the *Daily Mirror* to label the Marshalls 'The Family That Feared Tomorrow'. Elsie Marshall's final letter to her parents read:

> This is going to be a great shock for you both and this is really the last thing we would have desired. But in view of all the things that are happening in the world and the talk of new wars which would mean the extermination of masses of people and especially children we decided we couldn't allow this to happen to our children. Sandra, Moira and Yvonne are outside all this and no harm can reach them now as they lie forever peacefully together in bed. Andrew and I did this because we love each other and our children and would hate the very idea [that] our children would be left to have to face in the future what other children faced in the last war.[13]

The nuclear bomb had revealed itself to the public in brittle newspaper stories, but then came longer journalism and deeper revelations, like the plight of the Hiroshima Maidens, a group of young women who had been terribly disfigured by the atomic bombing and were taken to the USA for plastic surgery in 1955; and the horrible discovery that fallout from nuclear tests was depositing its particular poisons in the teeth and bones of American children. The Baby Tooth Survey, started in Missouri in 1959, studied over 300,000 American baby teeth to measure the presence of strontium-90, a radioactive isotope, in the human body. The nuclear threat was spreading and unfurling like some unstoppable leathery weed, no longer confined to war zones or test ranges. It began appearing in popular culture too, with early Cold War cinema and pop music often likening the bomb and its explosive power to female sexuality in films such as *Gilda* (1946) and songs like 'Fujiyama Mama' (1957) and 'Thirteen Women' (1955), in which Bill Haley & His Comets ponder the benefits of being the only male survivor in a post-apocalyptic world full of women:

> Well, thirteen women,
> And me the only man around.
> I had two gals every morning,
> Seeing that I was well fed,
> And believe you me,

> One sweetened my tea,
> While another one buttered my bread.

Even when early Cold War pop music dealt directly with nuclear war, it tended to use distancing humour rather than realism, the classic example being Tom Lehrer's witty 'We Will All Go Together When We Go' (1959).

This salty, confident tone mirrored the fact that the bomb was – for a short while – the sole and proud possession of the Americans, and the popular discourse was that it had ended the war swiftly and decisively, and would now pivot from conflict to scientific advancement. President Eisenhower's 1953 Atoms for Peace speech to the United Nations called for a move to atomic energy, and the popular phrase of the day crowed that the feisty little atom would soon give us energy 'too cheap to meter'. For every person worried and protesting and sending a rattling jar of baby teeth off to the lab, there was a pop song or a film about our dazzling new future – it was the era of bombshells and bikinis and bravado where America was on top, the goodies had won the war and all would be well.

But the boasting and goofing of the 1950s gradually faded and reality took over. By the time the 1980s arrived, jaunty atomic pop had been replaced with haunting songs like 'The Earth Dies Screaming', '99 Red Balloons', 'Enola Gay', 'Two Tribes', 'Breathing' and 'Two Suns in the Sunset'. Those fifties tunes seemed like a drunken uncle at a party trying desperately to whip everyone up into cheer. Three decades later, he had retreated to a corner and the morbid relatives had the floor.

In the anxious eighties, pop culture aligned perfectly with the public mood, being associated with doom and dread rather than sex and science, and this was where it found me, in September 1984. I first encountered Armageddon on an autumn evening on BBC2. I was three years old when, at 9.30 p.m. on 23 September, my dad settled down to watch *Threads* (1984), a grim and realistic portrayal of a nuclear attack on Sheffield. I should not have been allowed to watch it. I should have been tucked up safely in bed by this hour, but instead I was left to play quietly by the television set as the credits rolled, and soon my toys lay abandoned on the carpet as I became transfixed by the nightmare on the screen. The experience scarred me for life, and it is the reason you are reading this book. I was traumatised by *Threads*: old enough to absorb the horror, but not old enough to make sense of it.

That evening, 6.9 million people watched *Threads*. The adults amongst them could have sought comfort in denial, or they might have shrugged off the horror with the help of booze, sex, a good meal or thoughts of the to-do pile awaiting them in the office the next morning. But there was no such respite for the toddler who knelt close, far too close, to the TV that September night. I saw milk bottles melt in the nuclear heat, blackened fingers claw out from the rubble, and a traffic warden with a hideously bandaged face, and there was no hint that what I saw was merely an imagined future. To me, this was real life. This was what the important men on late-night telly were saying when we children were supposed to be in bed.

Besides gifting me a life's worth of dread, the film also left me bewildered. I couldn't understand why this was happening. Why didn't the adults put a stop to these terrible things? Why didn't they fix it? I fretted and felt sick but could not speak to anyone about my fear because I had no words for it. I knew the terrible threat came from the air, but what was it exactly? Was it a bomb or a storm? Was it lightning or fire? Who made it? Was it God? What was this thing hanging in the sky?

Years later, in my late twenties, I would find myself stricken with panic attacks and agoraphobia. For weeks I was confined to my flat, and when I was eventually able to go outside, slowly setting one foot in front of the other on the arm of an ex-boyfriend, I found I didn't dare look up. After weeks indoors, the sky was so sudden and stark, so big and wide and appallingly white. Shuffling along the road, I ducked under its glare and wanted shelter. It was 1984 again, a September evening, and danger was everywhere.

The early 1980s were a particularly frightening stretch of the Cold War. The Soviet Union had introduced the momentous decade by invading Afghanistan on Christmas Eve 1979, and tensions, disasters and dangerous misunderstandings followed fast. Ronald Reagan upset the delicate balance between the USA and USSR with his ambitious Strategic Defense Initiative, nicknamed Star Wars, a futuristic plan to shield America from incoming Soviet missiles by zapping them from space. Scientists on both sides of the Cold War divide doubted such a plan could ever work, and some calculations suggested that even if it was 99 per cent effective, enough Soviet missiles would still get through to kill 20 million Americans.[14]

But even though Star Wars was questionable – even though it was doubtful that such a plan could ever come to fruition – it still threatened the balance between East and West. The Soviet Union was made to feel vulnerable, something Reagan worsened by introducing a relentless campaign of PsyOps, in which US planes would fly directly at Soviet airspace, peeling away at the last minute, testing the enemy's readiness and fuelling their paranoia. These psychological games had a dreadful result in September 1983, when the Soviets spotted a plane in their airspace and, assuming it was another American, shot it down. Sadly, this was a civilian plane, Korean Air Lines Flight 007, and all 269 people on board were killed. The incident sparked a wave of revulsion towards the Soviet Union. Reagan called it a 'massacre' and a 'crime against humanity', and sought to position 'civilised' nations against the 'savagery' of the USSR.[15] Soviet newspapers declared the threat of nuclear war to be at its highest since 1945, and the Soviet ambassador to Washington, Anatoly Dobrynin, said, 'Both sides went slightly crazy.'[16]

But three months remained of 1983, and it was about to get worse. NATO began its annual war games, playing out a scenario where Blue Forces (NATO) had been sent to defend Western Europe after Orange Forces (the Warsaw Pact) entered Yugoslavia and then Finland. The games culminated in the Able Archer exercise in November 1983, in which NATO practised its nuclear launch procedures. Although no actual weapons were moved around, the exercise, and the communications chatter that accompanied it, was highly realistic, and this unnerved Moscow, who wondered if NATO might be using the war game as cover for a first strike. The Soviets readied their nuclear weapons in response, fitting planes in Poland and East Germany with nuclear bombs and placing missiles on heightened alert. The exercise ended without incident and the tension defused, but MI5 later called Able Archer 'the most dangerous moment since the Cuban Missile Crisis of 1962'.[17]

In Britain, this alarming year ended with the controversial arrival of American cruise missiles. Intended to balance the recent introduction of Soviet SS-20 missiles, the weapons caused huge controversy and public anxiety, as there was no 'dual key' system, meaning the Americans could choose to launch them from British soil without British consent.

Never had it so good

But let us step back to the optimistic 1950s, the era when you could sing about atomic themes with a cheeky grin rather than dread. While the first deep chill of the Cold War was settling on Britain, Prime Minster Harold Macmillan exclaimed that the British had 'never had it so good'. Rationing had ended, jobs were easy to find wages and production were rising, and there were gleaming new consumer goods on which to splash out. Compared to the Hungry Thirties, and then the hardships and sacrifices of war, things were looking rosy. For a 1956 article in *Encounter*, entitled 'This New England', the author called at Wigan to assess the changes since Orwell's famous visit. He found the town 'full of brisk buying and selling', and thought that it had 'changed from barefoot malnutrition to nylon and television, from hollow idleness to flush contentment'.[18] The concept of the 'teenager' was born, advertising boomed, and hire purchase and mail order were becoming increasingly popular, putting new and impressive products within easy reach of the ordinary family.

Peace, coupled with rising wages and consumerism, turned people's attention to making their homes comfortable. In 1956, the housebuilder Taylor Woodrow advertised 'the house every woman has dreamed about'. It was elegant and spacious, with modern stylish built-in shelves to hold 'a few cherished books, a choice ornament, treasured knick-knacks, or one of those delicate trailing indoor plants'. There was also 'a dream of a kitchen' done in scarlet Formica, with a drawer lined in green baize for the cutlery and 'a space for the washing machine. Yes – this too is included in the price, and, believe it or not, so is the electric clock on the wall.'[19] There was a new passion for DIY, and Dulux paint and Black & Decker tools appeared in the shops. Into these frilled and painted homes, the walls wiped clean of coal dust, the drawers emptied of ration books and the cupboards cleared of the stodgy wartime staples of Woolton pie and the National Loaf, more and more families were proudly introducing a TV set. 'The tellie keeps the family together,' one dad remarked. 'None of us ever have to go out now.'[20] The home was becoming a place to cherish, in which the family could relax, and modern appliances eased slightly the relentless domestic labour of the housewife.

Yet the joy and luxury promised by adverts in Britain's post-war press seemed tenuous when read alongside some of the news stories at the time. It is jarring to see a stern article declaring that the hydrogen bomb spelled the end of Western democracy sitting beside a dress advert for 'High Summer cottons' in 'clear pastels or sharp shades like lime and lemon';[21] or the story of those women at Downing Street dressed in mourning for millions of victims of a future nuclear war appearing beside an advert for facials declaring, 'You'll look lovely after a Cyclax treatment', which would 'erase taut little lines and leave your skin radiantly alive'.[22] All this charming consumerist clutter in 1950s newspapers – adverts for gin, electric cookers, cars, linoleum, export beer, cigarettes, Ovaltine biscuits, Guinness, tinned pineapple chunks and margarine that tasted like butter ('Oh! What a beautiful flavour!') – was offered alongside warnings that the 'Hydrogen Bomb May Hasten World's End'.[23]

These shiny new things suddenly seemed fragile. If the British exhaled a sigh of relief at the end of the Second World War, they drew their breath again at the cold clang of the Iron Curtain. A new world had arisen, and this world was nuclear. Former allies became enemies, and these enemies had weapons that could kill millions in minutes. The atomic bomb soon developed into the even more terrifying hydrogen bomb. Britain's proud long slog of the Second World War was fast redundant. The 'finest hour' shrank to a four-minute warning. Everything was vulnerable and nowhere was safe – not a single street, village or hamlet; no forest, field or valley. The new bomb didn't care for homeowners' prized possessions. It would jerk the curtains from the rail, sweep the clock from the mantel, hurl the car across the street. It would ignite the newspaper, melt the milk bottle and shatter the teapot. And where its fires didn't blaze, the fallout would creep, getting under the door and through gaps in the window, reaching every nook and cranny and touching children's foreheads as they slept. As the nuclear arms race began, the British people learned not just fancy new words like *Formica* and *Tupperware*, but also *megadeath* and *overkill*.

In the nuclear age, possessions offered no protection. Neither did social class. The rich family with the car and the country retreat were just as dreadfully stuck as the poor in their inner-city high-rises where the imaginary shadow of a target loomed across them every day as they hung their damp washing on the balcony. The Blitz had been survivable: the Luftwaffe couldn't strike everywhere, and with a bit of luck, or a bit of cash, people could get out of harm's way. Now there was no such comfort. The air raid shelter at the bottom of the garden that had shielded homeowners in the last war was useless now. Neither money nor reason nor prayer could buy you an escape.

Yet as Britain entered the nuclear age, the Second World War remained the main point of reference. The good old Blitz spirit was summoned again and again. Civil defence groups held meetings in village halls, ironed their uniforms, stored ladders and armbands and tin hats, and carried out drills and rehearsals. Just like in the days of the Blitz, they practised heavy rescue, and in mocked-up bomb sites they lifted stretchers, bandaged arms and cheerfully bundled volunteers into waiting ambulances. A training film released in 1958, *Atomic Attack*, presented a replica bomb site created for such training exercises, complete with rubble and smashed phone boxes. 'Yes, this thing could happen,' says the narrator, as a civil defence worker pats a survivor on the back. It will be just like the Blitz, was the naïve message.

Alongside the civil defence workers, the ladies of the Women's Royal Voluntary Service (WRVS), founded in 1938, trained and rehearsed so they might look after the welfare of survivors if the bomb dropped. They practised how to cook hundreds of emergency meals in a field kitchen. They lectured housewives on fortifying the home against nuclear attack, and taught them how to do first aid and how to calm hysterics. They had well-meant plans to provide post-apocalyptic blankets, books and jigsaws. In *Atomic Attack*, they offer survivors 'nice cups of tea, give them a good old warm-up'.

Meanwhile, doctors and nurses agonised over a post-attack NHS, and were forced to admit that millions would be abandoned to a dreadful death without even the mercy of basic painkillers. Civil servants made plans for forced-labour crews to be equipped with shovels to clear corpses from the streets. Cities would be evacuated. Ice cream vans would bump across the radioactive wasteland to deliver medicines, and nightclubs and hotels would become emergency hospitals.

We shall see in this book that what seemed unthinkable to most at the time – the nuclear holocaust, the collapse of civilisation, the possible extinction of the human race – was actually being considered and planned for. Politicians and civil servants, charities and voluntary groups, doctors and nurses, priests and teachers across Britain were wondering *what if?* They were forced to confront the dreadful *maybe*. The hideous *just in case*. While others were intent on making tea, getting home before the rain came on, applying for that job, breaking up with that bloke, trying out that new restaurant or booking that big holiday, all engaged and engrossed in pleasingly humdrum life, there were men and women who stayed late at work to quietly make plans for the end of the world.

2 Four-Minute Warning

In the hills above Largs, the air is warm and the cows don't bother to lift their heads when we step out of the car. Far below is the sparkling Firth of Clyde, offering the type of splendid view that makes you want to spread a picnic blanket. But we're not here to enjoy the view. We leave the road and step onto the grass verge, approaching a gate wrapped tight with a chain. Frank jingles a bunch of keys, and there's a struggle with the heavy padlock. Finally it snaps open, and he ushers me through.

There's no monstrous installation here, no hideous apocalyptic blight. All I can see is a glossy green concrete block, as though someone has left a large Lego brick on the grass. As we trudge towards it, other little signs appear that show this is no ordinary field: sturdy pipes and boxes protruding from the grass. We arrive at the Lego brick, its surrounding grass neatly trimmed. Here, hidden in the hills high above the bustling seaside town below, with its candyfloss, ten-pin bowling, and strawberry fudge in crinkly cellophane bags, is a bunker designed for nuclear war.

This is the Royal Observer Corps 23 Post Skelmorlie, to give the site its proper name. At the height of the Cold War, there were hundreds of these tiny bunkers across Britain, built to shelter the volunteers of the Royal Observer Corps (ROC) in the event of nuclear war. From here they'd deliver attack warnings and monitor the subsequent explosions and fallout. Each post would feed local conditions to its group HQ, which would analyse the data, assess the damage and the likely path of fallout, and send a report higher up the chain. Sector HQ would then assemble a picture of the destruction: which cities had been hit, which airfields were gone, which roads and bridges were impassable, and where fallout was likely to descend. The result would be a ghastly jigsaw of post-nuclear Britain.

At their peak, there were 1,563 monitoring posts, with the number reduced to 869 after government cutbacks of 1968. They were usually sited on high, empty land, but could also be found in parks and housing estates. Although the ROC was disbanded in 1991, its tiny bunkers have remained. Though most are now abandoned – rusted shut, vandalised, filled in with concrete, flooded to the brim with rainwater – some have found a second life as wine cellars, storage space, even a secure location for the stockpiling of veterinary drugs. You might pass one each day on your way to work but dismiss it as something to do with the electricity board maybe, or the council. Certainly nothing to do with the end of the world.

When we think of the Royal Observer Corps today, most of us will imagine a scene from the Blitz, picturing a man in a tin hat scanning the sky with binoculars, watching for German planes. Maybe he's on the roof of St Paul's. Maybe he's on a hillside in Kent with white con-trails printed fresh on the blue sky. He clocks the planes, lifts the heavy black phone and calls in his report. His chums in HQ plot the raiders' likely course. The RAF scramble. The siren sounds. Then he can climb down from his perch, take off his hat and have a cuppa. It's his finest hour.

This is the nostalgic image of the ROC: the selfless guardians who watched the skies to keep the British people safe. 'Forewarned is fore-armed' was their motto, and their logo a figure from the Elizabethan era holding aloft a burning beacon, the method once used to give warning of approaching invaders. They played a vital part in Britain's air defence during the Second World War, where they were known as 'the eyes and ears of the RAF', but they weren't airmen or soldiers; they were volunteers. Some might have been retired from the RAF, or were aviation buffs, but most were just ordinary men with some spare time on their hands; from 1941, women were also allowed to join. That same year, the Observer Corps was granted the title 'Royal' by the King, in recognition of its essential work during the Battle of Britain.

The Corps was stood down in May 1945. Not only was the war end-ing, but the jet age had come roaring in, and a chap with binoculars was no match for these new planes. Had he glimpsed an incoming jet, it would have vanished over his head before he'd been able to reach for the phone. But only two years later, as the chill of the Cold War came creeping in, the ROC was resurrected. It had a new enemy, as Britain faced an increasing threat from beyond the Iron Curtain, and when the Soviets acquired their own atomic bomb in August 1949, the threat rose higher still. In 1955, the ROC was given the nuclear monitoring role, and told to swap hills and rooftops for tiny bunkers underground, where they'd no longer be watching for planes, but for the sudden flash of a nuclear burst and the deadly drift of fallout.

Going underground

Frank served in the ROC and is now spending his retirement rescuing and restoring his old monitoring post. He twists a key in the bunker's metal hatch and lifts it open. I place my hands on the edge and peer down into a whitewashed shaft with a steel ladder fixed to the wall. Cold air drifts up. A thick rope dangles like a noose. Frank goes first, expertly swinging his legs over the edge and scampering down the ladder. Then I descend, rung by rung, hand over hand, like a frightened old lady, though I soon realise I needn't fear falling: the shaft is so snug that even if I did lose my grip, the walls would immediately 'catch' me. Nonetheless, I'm glad to hear Frank's voice drift up through the gloom: 'You're nearly there!'

I step off the ladder and stamp my feet gratefully on firm ground. Frank has flicked a switch, and the tiny space is filled with a weak aquarium light. I look back up the shaft to the distant square of perfect blue sky. At least I can scoot back up the ladder at any point: had the observers been sent down here for real, the hatch would have been clanged shut, sealing them in here for nuclear war.

These bunkers would have been a nightmare for claustrophobes, containing only a cupboard and a larger room, and if you dwelled too much on the grubby white walls, it might cause you to become dreadfully aware of the damp earth on top of you. Frank gives me the tour. The little cupboard functions as a loo, with the Elsan chemical toilet taking up much of the space. Next to the toilet cupboard is the workspace, a dinky little office equipped to measure the end of the world. It holds a set of steel bunk beds and a desk with various instruments, ring binders and communications equipment. Maps and charts cover the walls, and shelves are filled with ration tins, instruction manuals, tiny pots for cooking, candles and a green plastic first aid kit. There is also a locked red box labelled *TRANSITION TO WAR INSTRUCTIONS*. With the weak light, low ceiling and stacks of clutter, the thought of being confined here while a nuclear war roared above is almost unbearable.

Some of the ration packs contain set meals, their frayed edges held together with masking tape. Frank shows me a very ambitious meal designed to keep the observers in tip-top shape during nuclear war. With the appetising name Menu D, it offers a breakfast of Baconburgers and Beans in Tomato Sauce. Dinner is Oxtail Soup, followed by Chicken Curry with Rice and Carrots, and there are snacks of Luncheon Meat with a Biscuit and Jam. There are also battered little tins, faded to a dull bronze colour, with descriptions of the contents stamped in black print on the lid, such as *Chocolate Sweets Type A*. These nifty ration packs also included a tiny tin opener, scratchy toilet paper, matches and tea bags.

The subject of ROC rations was always a favourite of former observers. David Shaw, of Carlisle, described nicknames for the rations. 'There were other delights, such as Biscuits Brown AB. Never found out what the AB stood for, but "alimentary blocking" was a common suggestion.' The rumour went that this was indeed the purpose of those biscuits – to avoid the need for the toilet in such a confined space. 'Occasionally there would be a treat such as a bar of very nice chocolate or a packet of Spangles. There always seemed to be something no one liked. I found the chicken supreme ghastly.' Other observers recall 'babies' heads' as a nickname for the bulbous steak and kidney puddings, and 'possessed cheese' for a particularly unpalatable processed cheese spread.[1]

And how would an observer wash their hands after such a delectable meal? While the sector and group HQs had proper facilities, those working in the posts had to endure the Elsan chemical toilet, which resembled a large plastic bin with a strong blue chemical sloshed around inside it. During exercises, 'The male observers never used it because every so often you had to empty the wretched thing somewhere. Slight problem with the female observers who, for biological reasons, cannot pee quietly, and so the male observers would sing quite loudly while the ladies used the Elsan.' Some men would indeed pop above ground to answer a call of nature, but others stuck rigidly by the rules requiring them to stay in the post for the duration of the exercise. A consequence of this obedience was the nasty job of hauling the toilet up the ladder so it might be emptied. One observer recalls how his colleague, Gilbert, was manoeuvring the bucket up the narrow shaft when its lid came loose 'and the Sani-Lav fluid, this awful blue stuff, came over the top and Gilbert was covered in rusty water and fluid from the chemical toilet. He was in a great deal of pain, as you can imagine. We put him in one of the chairs and put his head back and flushed his eyes out with some of the liquid we kept in the post for this occurrence.'[2]

Despite being summer, the air in the bunker was chilly. In winter, it must be dreadfully cold, so at no point in the calendar would the observers have been cosy and comfortable down here. Of course, the posts were never used for real, but lengthy training exercises were regularly held, and maintenance had to be done, so some observers tried to spruce up their bunkers, developing clever ways to make them just a little more homely and comfortable by introducing dartboards, scraps of carpet, curtains to screen off the beds, and even, in one case, a portable TV hooked up to a battery. Remembering his time in the ROC, Frank tells me: 'There was a certain degree of autonomy with what you could do, as long as you didn't turn it into a boudoir!' One observer, not content with the official seating arrangements, even managed to manoeuvre an armchair down the shaft. Others invented clever methods for combating the chilly air. 'The main problem was cold and damp,' said Mark Rogers, who served in Horsham. 'We had sacks of polystyrene beads to put our feet into to try and insulate them. We were one of the few posts with an NBC air filter, which we had to hand-crank for ten minutes every hour. Inevitably, it pumped freezing air around the post. It was a great place to retreat if you had a migraine though!'[3]

All the former observers I spoke to recall the great camaraderie between them, and when you consider how they were thrown together in close quarters in such odd circumstances, it's easy to see why strong friendships were forged. 'The long stint when I did the whole 48 hours flew by! It's not like office work. It was fun,' Berny Male, who served in Worcestershire, tells me. 'We had a radio that worked down there, books, magazines, card games, and I remember an epic Monopoly game that seemed to go on for a very long time. Lighting was always a problem. We had a battery that we charged but this failed regularly, and I remember when the lights went out on one exercise scrabbling about for matches and the rest of the exercise was done by candlelight.'[4] Those in charge must have recognised the need for comradeship, as there was a strong social element to life in the ROC, such as the annual training camps held at various RAF bases. 'It was extra special when we went to annual camp, when we all got together from all over the country,' said Joan Blanch-Nicholson, who served in Durham. 'We were one big family who shared the same interests.'[5] Even the small local groups would have a social calendar jammed with summer barbecues, quiz nights, discos and raffles. After training exercises, or meetings to paint the posts and mow the grass, teams would often head to the pub.

It could be liberating for some of the female observers. As Margaret Peacock, who served in Durham, remembered: 'Times were different back then and a woman didn't go in pubs, but as an ROC we could.'[6]

Sounding the siren

So what was it all for, the camaraderie and trips to the pub, the carpet squares and dartboards? What were the observers supposed to do in those chilly little bunkers? During the Second World War, the ROC was associated with the air force, but in its second life in the Cold War, it was paired with a new creation, the UK Warning and Monitoring Organisation (UKWMO). Formed in 1955 and run by the Home Office, this was responsible for Britain's network of warning sirens, monitoring posts and, most famously, the 'golf balls' at Fylingdales on the North York Moors: huge radars sheltered within gigantic spherical coverings to protect them from birds, weather and vandals. Fylingdales was one of the West's three massive radar systems that watched the skies for nuclear missiles; the other two were in Alaska and Greenland. Together they formed the Ballistic Missile Early Warning System (BMEWS). As its name suggests, UKWMO was in charge of both watching the horizon for an incoming attack and issuing the warning to the population. After the bombs had dropped, it would then monitor the destruction and the shifting fallout. It included meteorologists amongst its staff, as the weather would dictate where the fallout drifted, descended and killed.

If the Fylingdales 'golf balls' detected an incoming attack, they'd pass the warning on to government and military bodies, but also to

UKWMO officers, who'd send it down the warning chain for dispersal to the BBC, the police and the ROC observers, who would be waiting in their little monitoring posts across the country. This was the infamous 'four-minute warning', the understanding that the British people would have just four minutes between the sounding of the siren and the impact of the bombs.

The BBC's role in passing on the warning was to interrupt its TV and radio broadcasts, while ITV and Channel 4 would be coupled to the BBC network so that those watching the independent stations would also receive the warning. A special cassette marked with a red spot held the prepared message, which in 1991 was: 'Here is an emergency announcement. An air attack is approaching this country. Go to shelter or take cover immediately.' This frightful warning, interspersed with the wailing sound of a siren, would be repeated 12 times, running for a total of two and a half minutes.[7] A red telephone sat on the desk of the BBC technical manager; should it ever have rung, it would have been the UKWMO on the line issuing the order to make the announcement.

The warning would also be issued to 250 police stations across Britain, each of which was equipped with a bank of telephones known as a Carrier Control Point (CCP). This was a clunky device with three handsets and various lights, keys, alarms and switches. It looked like a child's toy: the four-minute warning, brought to you by Fisher-Price. If one of the phones rang, the duty policeman lifting the handset would receive the verbal message 'Attack Warning Red!' With the turn of a key, he'd switch on the sirens in his area, then, using another handset on the CCP, would issue his own verbal warning – 'Attack Warning Red!' – to the ROC posts and various operators of hand-cranked sirens who were linked to his device.

The alarm signals were sent across the telephone system, piggybacking on BT's Speaking Clock Service, but there were fears that the network would be overloaded if an attack was expected and an anxious population was trying to contact family and friends. For that reason, the Telephone Preference Scheme was introduced, which allocated a category to every single phone line in Britain. In a national emergency, all Category 3 lines, the huge majority, would be automatically cut off, while those designated as Category 1 were of prime importance and could never be disconnected. Category 2 lines were supposed to remain connected in peacetime civil emergencies but were to be cut when war broke out. However, if you were just an ordinary person and found that your phone was somehow still connected even after the Telephone Preference Scheme had been activated, this was no cause for celebration: it meant that your home or premises had been secretly earmarked for official use.[8] You could expect an insistent knock on the door very soon.

So, in the event of an imminent nuclear attack, the police, through their chunky CCP, would pass the warning on to hundreds of ROC posts and remotely trigger local sirens, usually found on top of schools, hospitals or fire stations. The streets of Britain would be shrieking. But what of rural areas and isolated communities who'd be out of earshot of the howling sirens in the towns and cities? In these places, the ROC posts were equipped with a portable siren, which the observers would have to haul up the shaft on a thick rope, assemble on the ground above their bunker, and then begin cranking by hand. Areas with no ROC post in the vicinity may have had to rely on other methods.

There were 11,000 'warning points' across the country, and many were intended to sound the alarm to those who couldn't reliably receive the four-minute warning via the usual urban sirens. A designated warning point would be fitted with a small grey box on the wall, known as a carrier receiver. This constantly ticked, indicating that it was working and that all was well. The receivers would be issued to volunteers in the rural community who were known and trusted – perhaps the local vicar, doctor or pub landlord, who would also be given a hand-cranked air raid siren. If the receiver ever ceased its reassuring tick and instead broke out into a wailing sound, before delivering the verbal warning 'Attack Warning Red!', it meant the vicar had to drop what he was doing and rush outside into the churchyard with his siren, just as the observers in the rural ROC posts would be doing. He would give the handle five quick turns, followed by five slow ones, and then repeat the procedure: this produces the siren's distinctive rising and falling note.

Things would not always have gone smoothly in the countryside. In the early 1980s, the BBC interviewed Derbyshire publican Deccio Tatoni, who had agreed to host a warning point in his pub, the Bull's Head, in the village of Monyash. The little bleeping box was installed behind the bar, but he was never given the accompanying siren. Tatoni told the BBC that if he ever heard 'Attack Warning Red!', he would leap onto his bike and go pedalling through the quiet village streets, shouting, 'The Russians are coming!'[9]

The system for sounding the alarm certainly wasn't foolproof. British newspapers reported sirens being triggered by mistake and causing either panic, confusion or total indifference. A false alarm in Devon, coming shortly after the Chernobyl disaster in 1986, left people 'terrified. Many suffered from shock. Some were physically sick.'[10] In Coventry, a city that suffered badly during the Blitz, there was a false alarm in February 1984 when a policeman dialled the speaking clock at 6.30 a.m. and accidentally triggered the siren, which wailed for 30 horrible seconds. While police switchboards were inundated with calls, it seems that most people simply turned over in their beds and went back to sleep. A local fireman told the *Daily Mirror*, 'It's a good thing it happened by accident because it shows how ill-prepared we are.' 'It put the fear of God in me,' admitted one resident, 'but as I couldn't do anything about it I just stayed in bed.'[11] But another resident, writing to *The Guardian*, called it an 'unforgivable nuclear alarm scare' and objected that media coverage of the incident was insufficient and treated it as a joke: 'The people of Coventry who went through 30 or 40 seconds of sheer hell deserve widespread publicity to prevent a similar occurrence in Coventry or elsewhere, and a ministerial apology.' But his letter also raised a wider question: what is the point of telling people they have but four minutes to live?[12]

It seems, however, that the usual reaction to false alarms was indifference and inaction. In October 1981, the villagers of Great Wakering in Essex heard the dreadful wail of the siren, but there was no panic. 'We're not easily frightened in Great Wakering,' one parish councillor declared. He, like the rest of the village, listened to a nuclear warning siren for 40 minutes without taking action. 'If it'd been the real thing some of them here would have said a quick prayer but the others would just have had a pint at the pub.'[13]

Context is everything of course. During the Second World War, the sirens blared with such wearying regularity that they became known as Moaning Minnies, but when they began their banshee wail, everyone knew what it meant, and what response was required. After all, there was a war on and everyone was aware that the bombers were approaching. But for the pub-goers in Great Wakering, the siren's cry came out of the blue: nobody was expecting a nuclear attack. The news that day reported an IRA bomb at a Wimpy restaurant in Oxford Street, the threat of martial law in Poland, and reassurances from Vice President

George Bush that America aimed to reduce its nuclear forces. The general unease of the Cold War rumbled on, but with nothing that day to indicate a direct threat to the supping locals at Great Wakering's two pubs, and so they just remained at the bar when the siren blared. 'It wasn't very dramatic,' said the local policeman. 'Nobody ran into fields or hid under tables.' It was the same placid behaviour that was initially on display when the *Titanic* began to sink.

In 1968, a study in the *International Encyclopedia of the Social Sciences* of human responses to disaster warnings revealed that

> It is difficult to secure public acceptance of warning messages. People tend to seize on any vagueness, ambiguity, or incompatibility in the warning message that enables them to interpret the situation hopefully. They search for more information that will confirm, deny or clarify the warning message, and often they continue to interpret signs of danger as familiar, normal events until it is too late to take effective precautions.[14]

A siren bursting through the hazy sunlight of an autumn afternoon might be harder to perceive as genuine than one that blares whilst a family are crouched by the TV, receiving the dreadful news of imminent nuclear attack whilst Dad hammers boards over the window and Mum fills the bath with water.

And yet, in the approach of nuclear war, the government may be reluctant to hint at what can be expected, as it might elicit a response that would be undesirable from the authorities' point of view. Ample warning would trigger fear, anger and despair. People would flee the cities in spontaneous and chaotic evacuations. They would stockpile food, medicine and other essentials, leading to massive shortages, which would further fuel panic. It would give anti-war activists time to organise protests, inciting rebellion and discord. It would not be in the interest of the government to give too much advance warning, and yet it doesn't benefit the public if they receive too little. It will come as no surprise to learn there is no good way to announce nuclear war.

If the dreadful event had happened and the four-minute warning had sounded in Britain, country policemen, BBC staff, pub landlords and vicars would have helped deliver it, as would the ROC observers in their tiny bunkers. Having sounded the alarm, the observers would clang the steel hatch shut, climb down the ladder and sit tight, waiting for the bombs to drop. In the HQs, their colleagues would wait for their reports to start coming in so they could assemble a picture of the ruined country and plot the path of the subsequent fallout. The next four minutes would surely be agonising as everybody waited for the nuclear holocaust to begin.

Sketching Armageddon

How would the observers know when it had started? People in the towns and cities targeted by the enemy would see the flash and feel the scorching heat. They would be whipped away by the blast wave, scoured and killed by flying debris and hot hurricane winds. But the observers, if they were secure in their bunkers and some distance away from the target area, would be shielded from much of this, so how would they know the end of the world had begun?

Arranged on their desks were three instruments for monitoring and measuring the nuclear attack. The first indication that war had begun would come from the bomb power indicator (BPI). This is a kind of nuclear barometer, connected to the surface by a long pipe that can detect changes in air pressure. When a nuclear bomb exploded, the pipe would feed the pressure change down to the indicator. At the silent swing of its needle, the observers would get to work. They'd note the time and take a reading from the dial that indicated the strength of the detonation. They'd contact their HQ to confirm the blast using the code word 'Tocsin Bang', and give their location, the time of the explosion and its indicated strength. The HQ would be receiving similar reports from across the region, and by using triangulation they could get a pretty accurate picture of where the bombs had fallen and how powerful they were. Observers in the HQs would be marking the location of the bombs on a huge Perspex map, gradually assembling a picture of their region. Once the locations were known, the meteorologists could start working out where the subsequent fallout was likely to materialise, and warnings could be issued.

But the HQs would need more precise information. Crucially, they'd need to know if the bombs had exploded in the air or on the ground, because these two types of detonation produce hugely different effects. A burst in the air creates more physical damage, as there is nothing to impede the blast, whereas with an explosion on the ground, much of the bomb's power goes into gouging a crater out of the earth and the resulting debris will be sucked up into the mushroom cloud, later to descend as deadly fallout. Again, the observers in the monitoring posts would be able to confirm the type of explosion, thanks to a very basic pinhole camera known as the ground zero indicator (GZI). It is stunningly simple in its design: it's merely a cylindrical drum with a tiny hole, through which pours the awful light of the explosion, burning a scorch mark onto the photographic paper within. A burn mark high on the paper indicates an air burst, and a low mark confirms a detonation on the ground. That's straightforward enough. The only problem – and it is quite a big one – is that the camera is outside, and someone has to leave the safety of the bunker to collect the paper.

Fallout doesn't descend immediately, so there'd be no risk of contamination to the unlucky person who had to go up, but the thought of climbing that steel ladder and entering the post-nuclear world alone would have been a test for anyone's nerves. They'd don protective layers of clothing and put a satchel across their shoulder containing fresh photographic paper so they could restock the camera after removing the scorched contents. While they were up there, working quickly on the camera, they would make a swift visual assessment of any mushroom clouds, noting their size, elevation and location. Having completed their task, they'd dive back down the hatch to hand over the scorched paper to their colleagues, who'd interpret it and make another report. HQ personnel would be receiving this information and sketching out mushroom clouds, weather patterns and fallout plumes on the huge Perspex map of the region. The reassuringly familiar outlines of the geographical map of Britain would gradually become obscured beneath alien patterns, lines and symbols. If a fallout plume was sketched on the map, all the settlements in its ghostly path would have to be evacuated – *if* they were still standing, *if* conditions allowed, and *if* the resources, manpower and will to conduct such an operation still existed. These are big *if*s.

When sketching Armageddon, a picture of the region would soon emerge that would allow HQ to estimate which areas would be free of fallout and which had avoided the worst blast damage. The authorities would be able to deduce where the roads were still passable and the bridges still intact, so they could plan safe routes for the military and any medical, supply or evacuation transports. While there were just three staff in the tiny posts, the HQs housed hundreds of people in large semi-sunken bunkers. They included ROC staff, UKWMO officers, meteorologists, scientists, technicians and critical support staff. They had dormitories, toilets and canteens, and so were palatial compared to the tiny monitoring posts.

Fallout

After the bombs had dropped and a dreadful nuclear silence had fallen over the land, the ROC would turn to their final task: measuring the radiation levels and issuing fallout warnings. Each post also had an instrument called a fixed survey meter (FSM). Like the bomb power indicator, it was connected to the outside world by a long pipe. Indeed, the pesky protuberances of the BPI and FSM were often responsible for observers tripping and taking a tumble in the grass. This was one reason why the grass around the posts was always neatly trimmed. The FSM pipe would measure the radiation levels in the air, and the ROC posts across the country would report their local readings. At HQ, this information, combined with weather reports, allowed each region to assess where the fallout was heaviest, and where it was likely to drift and descend. Warnings could then be issued to the surviving population.

Every region had a huge nuclear government bunker for hundreds of people, including politicians, civil defence staff, council workers, and representatives of the emergency services. Each bunker also had a small BBC studio, which would issue official information, advice and warnings for the area. These little studios would now broadcast local fallout warnings, but they would be supplemented by warnings from police and ROC staff, as not every survivor would have access to a working radio. So the small ROC teams in the affected areas would once again have to climb that steel ladder and venture outside, this time to issue a fallout warning. This was done by firing maroons, which are like huge fireworks, only without the pretty dazzle and light. Instead, they simply take off into the air and release an almighty bang. Three such bangs served as a warning that fallout was soon to descend, and that any survivors must immediately take cover.

It might seem absurd to imagine people emerging from their shelters in this window between detonation and the descent of fallout – usually believed to be about an hour – but official advice encouraged them to do so. The 1980 public information booklet *Protect and Survive* was clear: 'After a nuclear attack there will be a short period before fallout starts to descend. Use this time to do essential tasks.'[15] These included tending to fires, turning off the gas, replenishing water supplies, and seeing to any family members whose clothing had caught fire. Simply 'lay them on the floor and roll them in a blanket, rug or thick coat'.[16] Survivors should also attend to any structural damage to the house and 'do minor jobs to keep out the weather – using curtains or sheets to cover broken windows or holes'.[17] 'Weather' here can be taken to mean 'deadly fall-out'. Finally, 'If there is time, help neighbours in need.'[18] This is the only reference in the booklet to helping others, and it contrasts sharply with its predecessor from 1963, *Advising the Householder on Protection Against Nuclear Attack*, which was far more compassionate, reminding people to care for their pets and asking them to 'give shelter to anyone caught without protection near your home'.[19]

While the fallout warning would generally be delivered by three bangs fired from maroons, *Protect and Survive* informs readers that it may also be issued by three blasts on a whistle or three bangs of a gong. If the latter sounds quaint to you, then consider that some rural survivors might have been alerted by the pealing of church bells.

Having issued the fallout warning, the observers on the ground would return to their posts, where they'd continue to record radiation levels, constantly feeding reports to their HQ, where, on those huge Perspex boards, an ever-changing picture of post-holocaust Britain would emerge from estimates of blast damage, weather reports, fall-out readings and scorched bits of paper.

'My kids thought it was a game . . .'

The ROC saved lives in the Second World War and would surely have done so again in a nuclear war, but in peacetime it represented the enemy for many anti-nuclear activists. Although the observers were volunteers, local people who wanted to 'do their bit' or maybe just take on a weekend activity that offered something more stimulating than an art class or choir practice, many political activists linked them with the military establishment. Their navy-blue uniforms, similar to the RAF's, heightened that belief. Indeed, some ROC volunteers serving in Northern Ireland during the Troubles were advised not to wear their uniform on the streets. Many posts became targets of anti-nuclear protests, much to the bemusement of the observers. 'They treated us as the enemy,' one volunteer told me. 'It's a bit like blaming the fire brigade when there's a fire.'[20] They discovered their locks had been glued, the hatch cemented shut, or they arrived for duty to find their post picketed by members of the Campaign for Nuclear Disarmament (CND). 'We once had a visit from CND who thought we had missiles in the post,' recalls another observer. 'It convinced us that even if they had good intentions they were stupid and misinformed at best. They refused our invitation to look around as they thought we'd shoot them as intruders!'[21]

Other protests saw observers verbally abused or splashed with urine, though some incidents were rather more absurd, such as the occupation in 1981 of the Alexandra Palace monitoring post. As *The Guardian* reported: 'Painting themselves red to resemble blast victims the dozen peace people sat down on the bunker's steel trapdoor and fastened plastic bags over the air vent. They then refused to move, in response to rather bored requests from the local police, while [the protesters] made air raid noises through a loud hailer.'[22]

CND were opposed to the idea of preparing for a nuclear war, as this implied that the holocaust would be survivable, but some managed to bridge the ideological gap between activists and observers. 'I'd been a member of CND a few years before joining the ROC,' Mark Rogers told me. 'My rationale for being in the Corps was that if a nuclear incident happens, regardless of the cause or politics, I'd like to give people a chance of taking shelter, or for the government to be able to move people out of the direction of fallout. Sure, our data would have been used by the government for other purposes to which we are not privy, but that didn't worry me.'[23]

With so much antagonism, it is easy to understand why the ROC volunteers developed a strong camaraderie. Not only were they keeping one another's spirits up during long stints underground, they were also uniting against political attacks and those who ridiculed them in the media as a nuclear 'dad's army'.[24]

This kinship amongst observers also extended to their families. One of the first questions I ask when I meet a former observer is: 'What about your family? Would you have said goodbye to them and turned up for duty on that fateful day?' If the order came, the ROC would be relying on its volunteers to leave their families in the most frightening situation, and even those dedicated to their job might find themselves unable to do so at the crucial moment. As one observer put it: 'A young bloke with a young family, is he going to leave home and leave his wife and kids? I always felt the initial manning of the posts should be done by older men who had far less responsibilities at home.'[25] There was no easy solution to this dreadful dilemma. 'That was the great unknown question,' Frank told me at the Skelmorlie post. 'If it ever happened – and thankfully it never did, or we wouldn't be talking here today – just how many people were going to turn out?'[26]

If war approached and the order was given to man the posts, the observers allocated to each post would be placed on a rota. Three would attend for duty and spend 12 hours in the bunker, waiting for the bomb to drop. If nothing happened, they came off duty and were relieved by another three, who stayed down there for another 12 hours, and so on. If the war started while you were down there, that was obviously where you stayed. It was like Russian roulette: no one knew when the bomb would drop, or if you'd be on duty when it did.

To cope with this fear and uncertainty, many observers made plans to look after one another's families. One ROC volunteer had a large farmhouse: 'All families in the event of nuclear war would come to my place so the three who were down below when the attack started would know that their families were with their friends and colleagues and would be looked after. I can't imagine anything worse than not knowing what happened to your family.'[27] And his wife gallantly told him, 'At times like that you do your duty. If I've got 15 to 20 people here I'm going to be so busy looking after them I'm not going to have time to worry about you.'[28]

Not every post made communal plans, and indeed it may have been futile or impossible for those living in urban areas. Joan Blanch-Nicholson's group of volunteers had no such arrangements. Instead, she made a fallout shelter for her children in the event she had to leave home in a nuclear emergency. 'My kids were OK about it. I suppose they didn't think anything would really happen . . . It was quite terrifying for me to think of leaving them, but I would have done so.' She went on to describe assembling the shelter. 'I did discuss certain stuff with them, but I didn't want them to worry unduly, and to be quite honest, making a shelter for them in the event of a nuclear strike was a family affair. My kids thought it was a game, and I was happy letting them think that, until such time as it became a possibility.'[29]

In preparation for that dreadful trip to the bunker, observers were supposed to have a small bag of essential kit packed. Some kept this ready; others would have prepared it quickly at the first sign of an emergency. Family photos, clean pants and chocolate seemed the most popular contents, although Joan Blanch-Nicholson told me her bag also contained a personal stereo with her favourite Iron Maiden music, plus some make-up. However, despite those luxuries, she wasn't especially optimistic about the prospects for her and her colleagues. '[We] discussed this at length, and the outcome was that there would be nothing left after the expected three weeks from bomb burst to radiation decay, so we probably wouldn't survive anyway. We would carry on doing our job until such time as we became ill through lack of uncontaminated food or water.'[30]

In fact, the idea of the ROC simply carrying on is accurate: there were no specific plans for the observers to stop work or stand down after the nuclear attack. Such a catastrophe simply couldn't be planned for. It was impossible to know which posts and bunkers would survive, and which would be located in areas where some kind of post-nuclear life was possible. There could be no instruction to 'emerge from the post after three weeks', because the area might still be heavily contaminated, although observers were expected, if possible, to conduct some 'mobile monitoring' – that is, to explore the area by car or on foot to measure radiation levels and to make visual assessments of the state of roads and bridges. In the end, the ROC, particularly those observers in isolated posts, would have to use their own initiative. It's reasonable to assume they would emerge when three things had occurred: when they had done all they could in terms of monitoring; when the fallout in their area had decreased to an acceptable level; and when their food and water supplies had run out. At this point, with their role fulfilled, they would be free to try and make their way home, though some might choose to try and link up with any surviving civil defence teams. Indeed, that might have been preferable to going home, where no happy result could be expected.

The end of the ROC

When the Cold War ended, observers prepared themselves for changes to their role, but nobody expected that the ROC would be disbanded altogether. For most volunteers, the news came out of the blue when it was announced in the House of Commons on 10 July 1991. A statement issued the following day by the commander of No. 6 Group spoke of a 'body blow',[31] but expressed the belief that 'the spirit of the Corps will continue' and the hope that 'volunteers will seek to continue their service to the country in other ways'.

Almost every ex-observer I talked to spoke of shock and a sense of betrayal at the sharp, sudden and brutally impersonal end to the Corps. 'I was totally gutted. As a single mam, the ROC had become my life, and I had made many friends,' said Margaret Peacock. 'The way we were told was a total shock. They had been recruiting and someone even had the uniform delivered the day before. There was no lead-up to it. Nothing – just all of a sudden it was over.'[32]

Many believed that the sudden stand-down was a waste of talent and training. As Ann Smith, who served in Bristol and Yeovil, put it, 'When the ROC was stood down, I was absolutely devastated. I felt my world had come to an end. We were a well-disciplined body of 10,000 men and women who could have been put to use in some sort of civil protection, but we were just thrown on the scrap heap.'[33]

The Corps tended to attract people of energy and imagination, and although many ex-observers recall their period of service fondly, outsiders may feel their efforts were wasted, as preparation for nuclear war is quite futile. Nonetheless, those in society blessed with the desire to be active and useful will naturally find a home in such organised voluntary groups, and whilst there was no question of the ROC reliving their glory days of the Blitz had nuclear war broken out, their efforts in triangulating bomb bursts and helping track the path of fallout would certainly have saved some lives. Whether the survivors would have been grateful for that, we cannot know.

3 Evacuation

Summer in the fields. Berry-picking in the hedges. Glad little hands reaching for fresh milk and apples. These images are part of Britain's comforting folk memory of evacuation in the Second World War. The removal of children from cities under threat from German bombers to rural safety continues to be celebrated as a huge success. In fact, it was largely a failure.

In Operation Pied Piper, almost 1.5 million people were evacuated from Britain's cities in just three days, from 1–3 September 1939, and it was all accomplished without a single accident. The packed trains whistled in the distance, and the evacuees were safe from Mr Hitler and off to enjoy hay rides and apple-picking. But the sun-kissed schoolboy roaming the fields and growing tall and strong on fresh vegetables was not the typical wartime evacuee. Instead, the vast majority were upper- or middle-class children and adults who were able to privately evacuate themselves and didn't have to be bundled onto trains and scattered in villages. Instead, they stayed in seaside hotels or second homes in the country, or left Britain altogether for the safety of America, Canada and Australia. Alongside these private evacuees, many public schools, universities and charities left the cities in an unofficial evacuation. The official evacuee scheme removed 1,437,000 children and their escorts, but private evacuation was estimated at about two million. In Devon, these privileged evacuees outnumbered the official ones by seven to one.[1]

In Southampton, a 'horde of satin-clad, pin-striped refugees poured through for two or three days, eating everything that was for sale, downing all the spirits in the pubs, and then vanished',[2] off to safety in America. Others were able to purchase a relatively comfortable war in exclusive seaside or country hotels, and newspapers were crowded with adverts offering luxurious rural retreats for the rich. You might decamp to Fuidge Manor in Devon, where it 'would be hard to find a more suitable spot remote from war. Every modern comfort abounds in this charming old manor. Nor need one be dull for there is tennis, squash, billiards and 180 acres of rough shooting.'[3] Torquay's Headland Hotel offered 'Peace – and protection';[4] or you might 'Feel safe in the Highlands' at the Grant Arms Hotel, where 'the bracing air of Strathspey will tone up the most jaded nerves'.[5] But there was resentment against those who relaxed in hotels whilst British cities burned, and they were scorned in the press when suspicion arose that surplus food stocks were being delivered to posh hotels to feed these 'Mayfair idlers'.[6]

The divide between rich and poor was obvious in the official evacuation too, with many rural residents appalled to receive dirty urban children who had never been shown how to take a meal at a table or sleep in a bed. City poverty differed from the rural kind, and there was dismay when children infected with head lice arrived at country stations. 'There were scenes of horror in the village street,'[7] said a Department of Health report on lice amongst evacuees. Some children were dressed in threadbare clothes, and shoes that might withstand a city street soon fell apart when their owner tried to climb trees, run across fields or help out on the farm. Other evacuees emitted an awful smell because they had wet or soiled themselves on the train ride to the country. The journeys could be hours long, with frequent halts on the line to let military trains pass, and often there were no toilets available on board. One teacher escorting children endured a twelve-and-a-half-hour journey that he later called 'the most depressing, deplorable and disgusting journey I have ever had the misfortune to make'.[8]

For these anxious, soiled and cranky children, things only got worse when they arrived in their rural redoubts. There was no neat register of names matching little Tommy with the cheery farmer and his wife, or young Susan with the nice people at the vicarage. Instead, hordes of children were often corralled into a village hall and the country folk entered to scrutinise them and make their selection. 'Scenes reminiscent of a cross between an early Roman slave market and Selfridges' bargain basement ensued.'[9]

Farmers often chose strong-looking boys, while ladies opted for little girls, and there were reports of billeting officers being forced, as darkness fell, to go door to door with the unwanted children, trying to unload them. In some cases, no home could be found, as one diarist noted:

> Went to Guildford to see the house taken over by the Town Council for child evacuees who could fit in nowhere else. The desolation of the place inside is unutterable, no floor covering of any kind, bare boards of a poor wood, a steep, dismal staircase, of course, bare with marks of former carpets. Dreadful black-grey blankets on the camp beds, and only one sheet on each. Everything gloomy, uncared for, big windows dirty – and in dirt, a scandal for rich Guildford.[10]

Many country folk, used to a more placid pace of living, were nervous of inviting strangers into their home. There were fears of broken crockery and trashed furnishings. There was particular reluctance to host a mother, either expectant or accompanying a toddler. These young women, fresh from the big city with its cinemas, bars and bright lights, were often struck with deathly boredom in the countryside. Mrs H., who interviewed evacuee mothers in the Surrey village of Shere, said, 'Poor things, they stand in the street and cry, and say their homes will never be the same again, and what have they to do with this village?'[11] The uncomfortable feeling of being an invader in another woman's home, plus the maddening boredom, drove many mothers to pack up their children and head back to the city.

Besides the tales of misery, discomfort and humiliation, evacuation also failed in its primary aim: getting children out of the cities. Only half of eligible London children were evacuated, only 42 per cent of Glasgow's went, as did 25 per cent of Bradford's and a tiny 15 per cent of Sheffield's.[12] We now know about the death and destruction brought by the Second World War. But if we skip back in time to sunny September 1939, many people would have felt removed from threats of gas and bombs, particularly in the very early days of the conflict that soon stretched out into the long 'phoney war', where the expected aerial bombardments did not come.

'We want them out of the way'

Although evacuation was not the jolly and spirited success it is often portrayed as, Britain's post-war governments still reached for it as a way of trying to protect the bulk of the population if nuclear war came. Huge questions hung over the suitability of evacuation in a nuclear war. Would there be sufficient notice to implement the plan? How could the authorities know which areas would be safe from fall-out? Which groups would be chosen for evacuation and which would remain in the target areas, and what social tensions might that cause? Would there be a need for supplementary evacuation once the path of fallout plumes was established? How could the authorities feed and supply the newly crowded reception areas? These nagging questions could have no satisfactory answer, but the concept of evacuation was recognised and generally trusted, and it also seemed a natural instinct to try and remove the vulnerable from an obvious place of danger. But the main reason the government clung to evacuation was money. The Second World War had drained Britain financially, and she entered the Cold War as a country significantly reduced. The cost of providing shelters for everyone would be ludicrously expensive. Evacuation, by contrast, was cheap and seemed an easy solution for a cash-strapped country facing a new aerial threat.

So the Blitz evacuation plans were dusted down, tweaked and recycled. The first Cold War plan was published in 1950 and kept very close to the Second World War model, although we must remember that when it was being drafted in 1948–49, the Soviet Union did not yet possess the atomic bomb. The country would be divided up into evacuation, neutral and reception areas, essential workers would stay at their posts, whilst 'priority classes' –schoolchildren, pregnant women, and children below school age accompanied by their mothers – would leave the cities. Given the huge unofficial evacuation during the Second World War, the government were aware of the dangers of an uncoordinated mass flight. Not only would such chaotic travel clog the roads and overload the transport network, but it might prompt essential workers to flee. During the war, many men had been conscripted but this time around it would be difficult to uphold strict discipline, and an enemy might use the constant state of threat to wreck Britain's economy. If workers were ready to down tools at the slightest hint of war, an adversary could cause havoc without dropping a single bomb. The 1950 plan stated that it was 'essential in the national interest that in wartime all persons with work of national importance to do should remain at their posts unless the government advised them to move'.[13] The authorities believed that these workers needed to be assured that their loved ones were being cared for in an official and orderly evacuation.

As the 1950 plan was published, planners began work on a new one, known as Phase III. The Soviet Union had become a nuclear power the previous year, so updates were already required. Phase III spoke of the need to disperse essential industry and its workers from target areas and scatter them in the so-called neutral areas, leaving the reception areas free for evacuees. (These neutral areas would also receive the disabled and the elderly: 'We want them out of the way,' said the new plan.)[14] Industries that could not easily be moved would have their key workers commute to and from work each day – they would be sleeping in accommodation in the neutral areas and would be transported daily into the danger zone.

This plan not only assumed a massive degree of cooperation from Britain's workforce, it also came with its own difficulties. Every business would have to be scrutinised so that it could be designated as essential or not. What was more, dispersing some industry away from target areas was an obvious admission that those still living and working in these locations were in danger. Would workers willingly stay or commute there while they saw others being moved to relative safety? Then there was Britain's persistent north–south divide: how would the people of Sheffield feel if London was being dispersed but not their own city? It would, as one historian put it, have 'dire consequences for industrial production and social harmony'.[15] It seems likely that in reality, dispersal would have caused anger and resentment.

The complexity of human nature was always a problem for the government planners, so they often chose to ignore it. Just as their schemes permitted a generous period of attack warning, skipping the fact that as technology advanced, nuclear weapons could be delivered in a matter of minutes, meaning a so-called 'bolt-from-the-blue' attack was a horrible possibility, so they tended to dodge the difficulties of human behaviour. But as one senior civil servant acknowledged, 'We are not dealing with pawns who can be moved across the chess board to the whims of officials.' Evacuation, he concluded, would not be a 'glorified Sunday School picnic'.[16]

The contagion of panic

Before war broke out in 1939, there had been many dreadful warnings in Britain that the population would panic under aerial bombardment, and that the overwhelming strain it put on people would lead to outbreaks of mass hysteria.[17]

While the soldier on the battlefield had training, discipline, weaponry and the prospect of glory, the untested civilian was expected 'to risk death to fulfil some quite inglorious task, like keeping the firm's ledger up to date or tightening bolts in a factory'.[18] It became a major concern for the authorities to contain wartime panic, because plummeting morale would lead to calls for an end to the war, perhaps pushing the government to negotiate, even surrender. After the Great War, in 1923, the military theorist J. F. C. Fuller predicted that in the next war, Britain would see its cities

attacked from the air, and that a fleet of 500 aeroplanes, each carrying 500 ten-pound bombs of, let us suppose, mustard gas, might cause 200,000 minor casualties and throw the whole city into panic within half an hour of their arrival. Picture, if you can, what the result will be: London, for several days, will be one vast, raving Bedlam, the hospitals will be stormed, traffic will cease, the homeless will shriek for help, the city will be in pandemonium. What of the government at Westminster? It will be swept away by an avalanche of terror. Then will the enemy dictate his terms, which will be grasped at like a straw by a drowning man.[19]

Thus the little guy in the street had to maintain a stiff upper lip for the greater good.

The expectation in the 1930s that the British would panic under German aerial attack came from the experience of the – relatively few – Zeppelin raids in the First World War, and from studies of crowd behaviour in disasters, notably those following the terrible fire in

Chicago's Iroquois Theatre in 1903, which killed 600 people. These studies spoke of the 'contagion'[20] of panic: how one person's terror may spread through a crowd and infect perfectly rational individuals, reducing a collection of thinking people to an unthinking, panic-stricken mass.

In 1938, the authorities were told to expect 30,000 casualties every day once the bombing began, but were warned that psychiatric casualties would outnumber the physical ones by three to one.[21] There was clearly little confidence in the fortitude of the ordinary population. Happily these predictions were proved wrong. The British people did not collapse into panic, but showed themselves to be unexpectedly resilient. When the Blitz started in September 1940, the relentless raids were soon accepted as a tiresome and predictable fact of life, with one wartime diarist writing, 'A Warning went while I was walking. But I have become so blasé that I persevered; and though I could hear Nazi bombers overhead, I had a feeling they were not going to drop bombs where I was. Two or three weeks ago my heart would have been pounding away, and I should have rushed apprehensively into the nearest Shelter.'[22]

A Mass Observation survey in 1941 showed that the majority of people were not emotionally affected by the war at all, and 20 per cent of women were actually made happier by it.[23]

Project East River

The British people's surprising resilience during the Second World War meant that the authorities, at least at the beginning of the Cold War, were less concerned about panic and plummeting morale in a future conflict than they had been ten years earlier. The Americans, on the other hand, were not so relaxed. They realised that the destructive power of the nuclear bomb posed a unique threat to public morale, and because the Cold War was an ideological battle, public perception and emotion mattered hugely. The West had to foster the idea that it represented freedom and righteousness, and that it would prevail over the sinister creep of communism. The optimism needed to underpin this message would be sapped if the population lived in constant dread of the nuclear bomb and expected to die in a holocaust, and so in 1951, Project East River was founded to look at 'emotion management'.

Organised by Associated Universities, a think tank sponsored by the big US universities, the project examined how to change American society's perception of the nuclear bomb, and so deter panic and uphold morale. One strategy was 'conventionalisation': to make the nuclear bomb seem normal. Instead of speaking of this awesome new weapon as, in the words of one of its creators, J. Robert Oppenheimer, 'a destroyer of worlds',[24] the idea was to try and act cool and casual. Hey, it's just a bomb after all. We saw bombs used in the war, didn't we? Well, this is a bomb too, only it's bigger! This was the trivialising message put forward in 1950 in the US public information booklet *Survival Under Atomic Attack*.[25] It suggested that the horrors of the new bomb had been exaggerated: 'You can live through an atomic bomb raid and you won't have to have a Geiger counter, protective clothing, or special training in order to do it.' In fact, the nuclear weapon was 'just another way of causing an explosion'.[26] Radiation was likened to sunburn, and as long as you stayed indoors, 'there is little or nothing to fear'.[27]

A further strand of the conventionalisation argument was to remind the public that the worst single bombing raid of the Second World War, in terms of body count, was not the nuclear attack on Hiroshima or the one on Nagasaki, but the conventional raid on Tokyo on 9–10 March 1945, in which 83,793 people were killed when incendiary devices caused a firestorm.[28]

Another clumsy attempt to trivialise the threat came from the atomic scientist Ralph Lapp, who argued that 'burns from an atomic blast are no worse than those resulting from other forms of modern weapons'.[29] He added: 'Who can say that the victim of an atomic attack suffers more than the victim of a flamethrower or a person who has broken down mentally under the stress of combat?'[30] He seemed to be suggesting that war had myriad ways to destroy human beings; nuclear warfare was simply one more method on a very long list.

If Project East River was anticipating panic from the American people, many British Cold War studies expected apathy to be the main psychological affliction after a nuclear attack. The small but detailed York Experiment of 1965 asked three women to live in a fallout shelter for 48 hours and report their experiences. The results suggested that people penned inside a shelter might experience a terrible dragging lethargy rather than raging claustrophobia. Of course we might panic when the four-minute warning starts to wail, but the panic response would quickly die away and be replaced with euphoria at having survived the cataclysm. This could later develop into 'disaster syndrome', in which complete apathy would take over. In reception areas dealing with hundreds of thousands of evacuees, the emergency services could expect to be faced with listless, helpless crowds. Survivors, as one psychologist put it, would be 'paying for their period of terror by emotional and behavioural exhaustion'.[31] Apathy 'could be a form of wishful fantasy – "if I don't react then nothing has happened". Or it could be that people feel helpless in the face of the massive damage and the impossibility of repairing their shattered world.'[32]

Technology and the futility of evacuation

As efforts were made to manage the public's Cold War fears, nuclear technology continued developing, and was brutally unconcerned with our little human anxieties. Weapons and their delivery systems got keener, sharper, more efficient and more terrifying, which began to suggest that there was no point in a mass evacuation scheme. Perhaps in a small island like Britain there was no safe place to run?

As the Cold War heated up, Glasgow, once 'the second city of the Empire' and full of clashing, smoking, hammering industry, was entering its sad decline. The Clyde yards, which had built famous ships like the *QE2* and the ill-fated RMS *Lusitania*, were starting to die. Old communities were demolished, their residents decanted to ugly highrises on massive council estates whose names – Castlemilk, Pollok, Easterhouse – would soon come to represent urban deprivation. Glasgow was taking a post-war beating, shedding its majesty and its importance. And then, in the early 1960s, something happened that put the struggling city into the nuclear spotlight.

During the Second World War, Britain and the US had worked together to create the first atomic bomb. The top-secret Manhattan Project at the Los Alamos laboratory saw British physicists working in the dry heat of New Mexico alongside Americans and an array of first-class brains from Hungary, Italy and other nations. The project was a truly multinational effort, but the Americans quickly became protect-ive of the nuclear baby born on their soil, and after the war they froze out any foreign scientists. The McMahon Act of 1946 ensured that Brit-ain would no longer have access to nuclear expertise, technology and cooperation from its ally, and so Prime minister Clement Attlee decided that the country must build its own atomic bomb if it was to continue as a global power. On 3 October 1952, in a nuclear test code-named Operation Hurricane, Britain exploded its first atomic bomb, off the coast of Western Australia. The UK had joined the nuclear club. It now needed modern bombers to deliver the new weapon to enemy territory, without which the bomb was just a badge of pride rather than a credible threat.

The result was the creation of the V Force. Three British nuclear bombers were built – Victor, Valiant and Vulcan – entering service in 1955, and it was clear their missions would follow new rules that hadn't applied to the pilots of the huge lumbering Lancasters during their raids on Nazi Germany. Had V bomber pilots ever taken off on a real nuclear mission to Soviet territory, they would have departed with the almost certain knowledge that there would be no recognisable United Kingdom to which they could return. One Vulcan pilot's memoirs sug-gested that they would have tried to 'keep going east and settle down with a nice warm Mongolian woman'.[33] The cockpit of the Vulcan bomber had tiny windows that aimed to minimise the impact of blast and flash. The pilots were given an eye patch, to be worn during their bombing run, so they would be left with one working eye if the other was blinded by the nuclear flash. They would have had to navigate their way to Mongolia with one eye only.

But if the V bombers were sleek, modern and effective, the same could not be said of Britain's nuclear missiles. The bombers could be armed with free-fall bombs, but from 1963, missiles were also used. The Blue Steel missile could be launched from a V bomber but had a very low range, having to be fired about 100 miles from its target, and it quickly became obsolescent given advances in Soviet air defences. The British began working on improvements, but they cherished hopes of acquiring the US's far superior Skybolt missile. In 1959, when the Americans enquired about establishing a British forward-operating base for their nuclear submarines, prime minister Harold Macmillan was keen to open up talks that would unpick the McMahon Act. After discussions at Camp David, it was agreed that the Americans would be given a British submarine base, and in return, the British would get Skybolt.

Finding a suitable base for US submarines proved difficult, however. The preferred site for the Americans was Holy Loch on the west coast of Scotland. A sea loch with the required depth, it was close to Prestwick airport and had easy access to the Atlantic. Crucially, it was also close to civilisation, with the Americans wanting housing and facilities for the crew and their families who would be required to start new lives at the base. But for Macmillan, Holy Loch was rather *too* close to civilisation, being only 30 miles from Glasgow. He told President Kennedy:

> It would surely be a mistake to put down what will become a major nuclear target so near to the third largest and the most overcrowded city in this country . . . From a security point of view a robust population of three or four thousand Highlanders at Fort William [Loch Linnhe] is much more to my taste than the rather mixed population of the cosmopolitan city of Glasgow.[34]

In the end, the Americans got their way and arrived at Holy Loch in 1961 to set up their Polaris submarine base. Submarines were beginning to eclipse the bomber as a delivery system, being mobile and able to glide, almost undetectable, beneath the waves. They also had the benefit of putting nuclear weapons, which were themselves a huge target, out to sea. As Admiral Arleigh Burke, US Chief of Naval Operations, joked, 'Move deterrents out to sea, where the real estate is free, and where they are far away from me.'[35] While bombers sat on airfields, and missiles crouched in silos, a submarine was able to move and hide in the vast oceans. But the Americans had no intention of sharing their new Polaris submarines with the British, who would have to be content with the promised Skybolt missile. So it was a dreadful blow in December 1962 when the Americans cancelled Skybolt, leaving Britain with nothing but free-fall bombs and its outdated Blue Steel missiles.

Macmillan bristled – he had agreed to the Holy Loch base in exchange for Skybolt – and later that month, he and his advisers set off to the Bahamas for crunch talks with Kennedy. The tall, sad-eyed British prime minister, who had fought in the trenches in 1914, gave a soulful speech that reminded the young American president of Britain's role in defending freedom in 1940, and spoke of the great partnership that had created the first atomic bomb. It was a powerful address, and 'there was not a dry eye in the house'.[36]

Would America leave such a close ally without a nuclear deterrent? Kennedy was moved, but seemingly not quite moved enough to hand over Polaris. Instead, he offered to continue the Skybolt programme, but Macmillan now haughtily refused. As he would note in his memoirs, 'I observed that although the proposed British marriage with Skybolt was not exactly a shotgun wedding, the virginity of the lady must now be regarded as doubtful.'[37] Eventually Kennedy agreed to give Macmillan Polaris, but with the proviso that Britain make the weapons available to NATO. This was unacceptable to the British. Macmillan insisted that the UK retain an independent nuclear deterrent. In the end, they agreed a compromise: the weapons could be handed over to NATO as long as they could be returned to British control at a time of national peril.

So Britain got Polaris, but if an American submarine base at Holy Loch had made Glasgow vulnerable, now a British submarine base was to be set up next door, at Gare Loch, creating two massive nuclear targets just 30 miles from the city.

Nuclear strategists might have told nervous Glaswegians to relax, as by now the new doctrine of 'counterforce' had emerged, which held that nuclear war was likely to be limited, with the belligerents only attacking one another's military installations and sparing cities and civilians. In reality, though, many military bases were dangerously close to populated areas, and a counterforce attack on a military installation would create heavy fallout. So even in such a limited nuclear confrontation, Glasgow was in hellish danger. The city authorities prepared detailed evacuation plans, but these could not contend with the facts of Britain's geography. As the weapons grew more awesome, the country seemed to shrink: there was simply not enough space in which to run and hide.

'Now I am become Death'

While civil servants scribbled in smoky rooms, tinkering with the evacuation policies – increasing the numbers, changing the categories, stretching the boundaries, altering the terminology, trying desperately to make a Blitz policy fit the nuclear age – something was bound to prove once and for all that such policies were futile on a small and crowded island like Britain. Enter the hydrogen bomb.

There had been surprisingly few moral concerns over whether it was right to build an atomic bomb. The physicists at Los Alamos could quell their worries by convincing themselves that they were in a nuclear race against the Nazis; or that their new bomb would secure a faster end to the war; or that they were building a device so frightful it would end conflict forever, as no sane person would dare use it. Still, J. Robert Oppenheimer, the creator of the atomic bomb, felt deeply uncomfortable as he watched his invention explode in the chilly dawn of the New Mexico desert. 'Now I am become Death,' he wrote. Overall, however, the atomic bomb was created with the minimum of moral agonising. Its bigger brother, the hydrogen bomb, was a different story.

An atomic bomb works via nuclear fission: the splitting of atoms. The hydrogen bomb instead seeks to fuse atoms, a process that can create, in theory, limitless energy. Therefore the hydrogen bomb could be as big and as devastating as its creator wished. This was new and alarming territory for some scientists, but others, such as the Hungarian physicist Edward Teller, were eager to get started. The US government pondered whether to proceed with this new bomb, nicknamed 'the super', and in October 1949, the top atomic physicists of the day gathered in Washington to discuss the new weapon. They would advise the Atomic Energy Commission, which in turn would advise the White House. Oppenheimer was the chairman of the advisory group. The question of whether to be satisfied with the existing nuclear bomb or to push ahead with the super had gained new urgency with the explosion of the first Soviet atomic bomb, code-named First Lightning, in August 1949. This was a nasty shock to the Americans, who had not expected the Soviets to catch up so quickly. Suddenly the US was no longer the sole nuclear power, and in order to regain dominance, some argued it would have to scamper further up the nuclear ladder.

Today we tend to think that post-war America was gung-ho, keen to invent and produce anything that would boost its military might and to hell with the consequences, but the atomic scientists at the Washington meeting in 1949 were sombre and worried. Some argued that by creating the super, America would lose her hard-won moral superiority. Having just helped the world defeat the Nazis, did she want to sully her reputation so fast with this monstrous new bomb? Others believed that there was no need for agonising: the super was just an atomic bomb, only bigger (a variation of the conventionalisation argument we encountered earlier). Having created the atomic bomb and dropped it on Japan in 1945, why worry now about morality? It was merely a question of scale. Strong moral objections came from the scientists Isidor Rabi and Enrico Fermi, who said:

> The fact that no limit exists to the destructiveness of this weapon makes its very existence and the knowledge of its construction a danger to humanity as a whole. For these reasons, we believe it important for the President of the United States to tell the American people and the world that we think it wrong on fundamental ethical principles to initiate the development of such a weapon.[38]

Some feared that proceeding with the super would render the US military 'gadget-minded' – making it think that every crisis could be solved by reaching for a bigger and better weapon. More practical voices in the room argued that the super would be, literally, useless: it would simply be too powerful and destructive to be used. Indeed, its power was such that it could only be a weapon of genocide, and which country, after the horrors committed by the Nazis, wanted to be the author of another Holocaust? And if the super could never be deployed, then its effect could only ever be psychological – so was it worth jeopardising America's name and reputation for an unusable weapon?

While these agonising questions continued to resonate, the decision to proceed with the super was pushed along when scientist Klaus Fuchs was arrested in January 1950 and admitted passing nuclear secrets to the Soviets. The alternative seemed simple: if the Americans did not build the super, the Soviets would. Again scientists and politicians felt the need to keep climbing the nuclear ladder. After the US government's decision to proceed with the hydrogen bomb, Albert Einstein issued a stark warning:

> successful radioactive poisoning of the atmosphere and hence annihilation of any life on Earth has been brought within the

realm of technical possibilities. The ghostlike character of this development lies in its apparently compulsory trend. Every step appears as the unavoidable consequence of the preceding one. In the end, there beckons more and more clearly general annihilation.[39]

So far the hydrogen bomb only existed in theory, but could the scientists make it work? The model for the super was nothing less than the sun. The reason why the sun has not burned itself out is that it constantly renews itself via nuclear fusion, thereby creating new atoms. The scientists now had to harness the same spectacular power here on earth; the computer used to make the necessary calculations had the fitting acronym MANIAC.[40]

The world's first hydrogen bomb was exploded on 1 November 1952, in a test codenamed Ivy Mike. The detonation took place on Elugelab, in what is now the Marshall Islands. Sailors removed to a distance of between 35 and 50 miles from ground zero lined up to watch, wearing tinted goggles. Those without goggles had to turn their backs on the explosion. As one eyewitness recalled:

All at once the whole sky [was] just like the sun had come up all at once; a brilliant flash. I mean *brilliant*. Even with the goggles on, I had to turn my head because it hurt my eyes. And the tremendous flash. No noise, but the flash. Pretty soon then you heard the rumble, the ship moved, the wind, the heat. It was tremendous – the most spectacular thing I've ever seen in my life. You just couldn't believe, the whole sky, the whole horizon lit up. We all just stood there, our mouths open, and couldn't believe what we had just witnessed. Still we didn't know what it was. We knew it wasn't an atomic bomb. It was much, much bigger than an atomic bomb.[41]

Afterwards came the fallout. 'Then they announced over the loudspeakers, everybody down below. You had to go down below the ship. Batten down all the hatches. Everybody down below. *Everybody*.'[42]

Nothing remained of the island of Elugelab. After the steam from the evaporated ocean around it had cleared, there was nothing left but a crater, 185 feet deep, which had swiftly filled with seawater. The island had been pulverised and its fragments hauled up into the huge mushroom cloud, later descending in a poisonous pitter-patter of radioactive coral. In his laboratory in California, Edward Teller, 'the father of the H-bomb', watched a seismometer needle swing into life, detecting the shock waves in the Pacific and proving that his bomb had worked. He sent a telegram to a colleague: 'It's a boy.'

The Lucky Dragon

Two years later, another hydrogen bomb test would run dangerously out of control, spewing lethal radiation far beyond its exclusion zone and showing the world how dangerous this new weapon really was. The infamous Castle Bravo test on Bikini Atoll in the Marshall Islands on 1 March 1954 was supposed to have a relatively low yield of 6 megatons but instead yielded 15, making the various safety precautions useless. The explosive force was about 700 times as powerful as the Hiroshima bomb. One eyewitness recalled that he was given dark goggles to wear, so dark he likened them to black welder's goggles. He then turned his back on the direction of the detonation and covered his goggles with his arms. Even so, the light was still so intense he could see the bones in his arms:

> Several of the guys looked up and they could see a guy right through a guy standing in front of them. The light is so bright and so hot that I really felt that it was all over as far as my vision [was concerned]. I said *there's no way*. Because I'm closing my eyes, brighter and brighter and brighter, with black goggles on, and I mean I just can't take it any more. And then the heat was *horrible*. Now the heat, it was like somebody with a blowtorch, I guess, and just getting closer to your back. And I thought *geez, I can't take it much more*, I thought. And the Marine Officer said, *If one god-damned Marine moves, you'll answer to me*. Now in the meantime, the other people on the ship are running all over the place. You could hear their feet. And you were saying, *Oh my God, we're going to die*.[43]

Gradually, the heat and light began to lessen, and the PA system on the ship declared that those wearing goggles could now turn around and look directly at the bomb. As the witness recalled:

> I thought way over on the horizon I was going to see this little white cloud coming up with the mushroom on top of it. And when I turned around, I looked straight up and all around us and we were *in* that cloud, but it wasn't white. It was every [colour] of the rainbow and just *boiling* . . . How can anything that beautiful be so deadly?[44]

The scientists in the firing bunker on the island of Enyu, just twenty miles from ground zero, could also tell something had gone badly wrong with Bravo. Just ten seconds after the detonation, the chief scientist, Bernard O'Keefe, felt the walls of the bunker, which were three feet thick, begin to move.

'Is this building moving, or am I getting dizzy?' another scientist asked.

'My God, it is,' O'Keefe said. 'It's moving!'

He began to feel nauseated, as though he were seasick, and held on to a workbench as objects slid across the room. The bunker was rolling and shaking, he later recalled, 'like it was resting on a bowl of jelly'. The shock wave from the explosion, travelling through the ground, had reached them faster than the blast wave passing through the air.[45]

The scientists emerged after fifteen minutes to find the bomb had turned everything upside down: much of the sea floor and the coral reef was now up in the sky. Bravo had gouged out 200 billion pounds of matter and hauled it upwards, where it now spread and drifted in a mushroom cloud sixty miles wide, later to descend as fallout. 'A light rain of white ash that looked like snowflakes began to fall. Then pebbles and rocks started dropping from the sky.'[46] The men retreated to their bunker, and were eventually rescued by air, having first wrapped themselves in the thin protection of bedsheets for the dash to the helicopter.

Others were not so lucky. A Japanese trawler, *Lucky Dragon*, was in the water fishing for tuna when Bravo detonated. The boat was about 100 miles from ground zero and supposedly outside the exclusion zone. As dawn broke, one of the fishermen, Matashichi Oishi, saw a vast alien light suddenly bloom on the horizon. There was no flash; instead he noted that the weird light seemed to flow. It remained in the sky for a few minutes, then died away. The crew were unsettled and decided to move off after breakfast, but as they sat down to a meal of rice, miso and fish, the dreadful thunderclap of the blast struck them:

> When we heard the sound everyone dived to the deck and crawled into the cabins and hid themselves. It was a huge rumbling that came up from the bottom of the ocean. Everyone was stunned by the sound. It was not a bang, like the explosion of a bomb. It was the earth rumbling, from the bottom of the ocean to the surface. I couldn't tell from which way this big sound was coming. Everyone was stunned by it. Something extraordinary was happening, and we wondered what would happen next.[47]

What came next was far worse. As Oishi and his crewmates hurriedly began to pull in their lines so they could flee the area, they noticed a thick white cloud on the horizon where the weird light had been, which seemed to be speeding towards them. It was heavy with lethal fallout:

> Stark white powder started falling. On the southern ocean, there was no way it would snow and we wondered what this white stuff was, but I didn't feel any danger, because the white powder was falling all over my face but it didn't leave any mark. We picked it up, licked it and nibbled it. If it had been snow it would have melted in our mouths, but it didn't melt – it was crunchy like eating sand.[48]

Sailing fast now for home, the crew began to notice blisters erupting on their skin where the strange ash had touched it. They started to be sick. One man took to his bed. Others had diarrhoea. Four days into the long journey back, their hair started to fall out. Handfuls could be tugged out easily, without pain. When scientists at Tokyo University checked their hair, skin and clothes and the 800 pounds of tuna[49] they had brought home, they discovered it was bristling with radioactivity. The men were taken to hospital and given urgent blood transfusions, but it transpired that the blood was infected with hepatitis C. One man,

Aikichi Kuboyama, the ship's radio operator, developed liver failure and died, becoming the world's first H-bomb fatality.

The story of the *Lucky Dragon* made headlines around the world, bringing to public attention the terrible new threat of nuclear fallout. It seemed likely that fallout might even kill more people than the hydrogen bomb's massive blast and heat. At the time, Britain did not yet have hydrogen bombs – she wouldn't test her first thermonuclear device until 1957 – but it was clear where the arms race was heading. In the House of Commons, former prime minister Clement Attlee declared that the new bomb represented 'a grave threat to civilisation'. The current prime minister, Winston Churchill, admitted that the earlier atomic bombs, despite their obvious horrors, 'did not seem unmanageable as an instrument of war', but the new hydrogen bomb 'carries us into dimensions which have never confronted practical human thought and have been confined to the realms of fancy and imagination'.[50] Churchill was sufficiently concerned about the new weapon that he commissioned a detailed report on what a hydrogen bomb attack on Britain might look like, and in what state it might leave the country.

The end of innocence

The report was to be compiled by the eminent civil servant Sir William Strath. But before his committee began their work, they requested a report from the Joint Intelligence Committee (JIC). The resulting document, 'The H-Bomb Threat to the UK in the Event of a General War', was blunt and horrifying, concluding that the Soviet Union would aim to disable the UK for a long period and that it would 'not hesitate to destroy great parts of the UK to achieve this aim'.[51] It delivered this chilling warning:

> To render the UK useless as a base for any form of military operations the simplest and most effective form of attack would be by surface bursts, effected in suitable meteorological conditions. These, besides causing local damage, would cause very considerable areas of the country to be affected by fallout. We are advised that something like ten 'H' Bombs, each of a yield of about ten

megatons,[52] delivered in the western half of the UK, or in the waters close in off the western seaboard, with the normal prevailing winds, would effectively disrupt the life of the country and make normal activity completely impossible.[53]

The top-secret Strath Report, which was only declassified in 2002, was delivered to the government in 1955, and although written in the measured language of the civil servant, it revealed conclusively the futility of Britain's plans to defend itself from nuclear attack. It opened with a warning that 'fallout, combined with the vast explosive power of the hydrogen bomb, presents problems of a revolutionary character for the defence of this country and a threat of the utmost gravity to our survival as a nation'.[54] It went on:

> Hydrogen bomb war would be total war in a sense not hitherto conceived. The entire nation would be in the front line. Life and property would be obliterated by blast and fire on a vast scale. An attack of the size assumed would unleash an explosive force equivalent to 100 million tons of TNT. This is forty-five times as great as the total tonnage of bombs delivered by all the allies over Germany, Italy and occupied France throughout the whole of the last war. It is equivalent to 20,000 'one-thousand-bomber' raids of the last war. A single 10-megaton bomb could destroy any of our cities (except Greater London) and all, or nearly all, its inhabitants. While much could be done to reduce the number of casualties, loss of life on a massive scale would be unavoidable.[55]

The report believed that 'the aim of the enemy will be to eliminate us from the contest'. This was because Britain was not only a nuclear power in its own right, but also provided a home to American nuclear bombers and airbases. It envisaged that the Soviets would target these airbases and major cities, but with Britain being a small and densely populated island, the resulting blast and fallout would spread and drift across the entire country. The attack would most likely come at night, when the nation's defences – or at least those of the civilian population – would be lower. Strath estimated that a successful night attack with 10 hydrogen bombs would kill 12 million people and seriously injure or disable another 4 million. In addition, he believed that a further 13 million people would be confined to their homes or shelters for at least a week, waiting for the radiation to subside.

The Strath Report was the first big official study to consider the new threat of fallout, and the conclusions were terrifying. It effectively killed off any hopes of a widespread evacuation plan, because 'no part of the country would be free from the risk of radioactive contamination'. What would life be like in these contaminated areas? 'To remain in the open during fallout would be suicidal,' the report concluded, and to survive would 'demand a high degree of self-discipline': 'survivors in such areas would for a period be isolated not merely from the less contaminated areas but from one another. The household would become the unit of survival. Individuals would have to subsist on such stocks of food and water as they had got ready in advance in their individual places of shelter.'

Although Strath still saw a use for evacuation, in terms of 'levelling out the risk, wherever the bombs may fall', the report killed the previous assumption that rural areas were inherently safe. If a Second World War-style evacuation were to be enacted, Britain would also have to provide fallout shelters in the receiving country towns and villages. This would be a huge and massively expensive endeavour. Besides, removal of everyone, not just the priority classes, would bring the economy to a standstill. 'Nothing approaching complete evacuation could, therefore, be contemplated,' he believed. He advocated three measures: the local dispersal of essential workers, evacuation of others, plus the building of shelters – and the report stressed that all three would be required. For the workers subject to dispersal, he envisioned 'spreading the risk' by having them do a shift in a high-risk area then commute to a safer suburb at night. This approach would 'provide some prospect of reducing the risk of casualties on an appalling scale without bringing production and essential services to a standstill'.

The conclusion was stark: this new weapon made every area of the country unsafe and broke apart Britain's civil defence plans. The Strath Report made clear that if civil defence in Britain was to have any meaning in the thermonuclear age, it needed massive investment. And indeed, money determined the reaction to the report. Yet Britain did not embark on a massive shelter-building programme. Instead, the response was to invest in 'offensive measures' in the belief that nuclear bombs would deter the enemy. And so successive governments focused on two priorities: to build up Britain's nuclear arsenal to prevent an enemy attack; and to ensure continuity of government if nuclear war broke out. The state had to survive, even if most of its people did not.

Evacuation in the 1980s

The weight of the hydrogen bomb wore evacuation plans thin, so in the latter half of the Cold War, the notion of evacuation was turned upside down. In the 1970s and 80s, the public would be told to stay at home in the event of nuclear attack. The household, rather than the countryside, would be your place of safety.

That message was clearly conveyed in the *Protect and Survive* public information booklet, first published in 1980, which advised the British people that the home was the safest place – though it failed to address what to do if your home was right in the target area. If the Strath Report had defined the household as the key 'unit of survival', *Protect and Survive* took this message to the extreme, placing all responsibility for survival on the householder, who should not look to the state for evacuation, shelter or provisions. It was a suitably Thatcherite response to the nuclear threat. And why flee to the irradiated countryside or die in a traffic jam on the M1 when you can fortify your home by blocking the windows, and strengthening the walls with boxes of earth, sand-bags, stacks of books and tangles of heavy furniture? In 1982, a Home Office official explained: 'It was judged best to advise people that their prospects of survival were greater if they stayed where they were part of established communities and made the best protection they could in and about their own homes, and best use of whatever of their personal resources had survived the attack.'[56]

There was some logic in that advice. If you did not live within a target area and had the time and means to buy adequate supplies, then it would make sense to hunker down in your own home. To reinforce this message, the *Protect and Survive* booklet contained a politely worded threat: 'If you leave, your local authority may need to take your empty house for others to use. So stay at home.'[57] Although with the guidance so obviously aimed at able-bodied, can-do nuclear families with a house and garden in a relatively unscathed suburb, a nuclear attack might still have prompted those less equipped or fortunate to flee.

But just like the issue of public shelters, the topic of evacuation would never vanish completely, and continued to preoccupy the planners. After the Home Defence Review of 1980, which pledged more money for civil defence, civil servants were asked yet again to turn their thoughts to making evacuation work. It was recognised that there was an innate human desire, which no amount of public information campaigns could quell, to flee danger. This insistence on evacuation was exacerbated by anti-nuclear protesters, who pointed to the government's provision of bunkers for themselves whilst the public was offered no protection other than what people could scrape together with boards and sandbags. But if protesters might have urged evacuation, they were also the reason why the government was reluctant to revive its plans:

While moves towards an evacuation policy might enhance the credibility of the civil defence programme as a whole, they would almost certainly be characterised by the anti-nuclear movement as an indication that the Government believed war, and particularly nuclear war, was becoming more likely. This would be highly damaging, particularly as the date for the scheduled deployment of cruise missiles to this country approaches.[58]

So the Home Office were in a jam: they realised that a new and neat evacuation policy would silence the 'mischievous'[59] activists, who used 'stay put' to attack the government, but the timing was problematic. '1983 will be an especially difficult year for the government and NATO generally over nuclear defence issues,' the report stated. 'The public debate will have to be managed carefully and is crucial to the success of the initial deployments.'[60] To introduce an evacuation policy at the same time as cruise missiles arrived in Western Europe would be a nightmare, making people think the missiles' arrival made war more likely.

The dreaded 'doodlebug', or V-weapon, of 1944 was an early version of a cruise missile: a small unpiloted aircraft that could be programmed to fly straight to its target and explode. Cruise missiles could carry several nuclear warheads and fly so low they'd be undetectable on radar, but unlike the big intercontinental ballistic missiles (ICBMs), they were painfully slow. Still, this sluggishness allowed the Americans to argue they could never be used to launch a first strike upon the enemy, because an effective first strike required a rapid bolt-from-the-blue attack. The argument was that cruise missiles would only ever be useful in retaliation, so how could anyone object to them? Their other advantage was that they were mobile. They didn't have to be stored in a silo, making them a known target, but could be put on trucks and tucked in a forest where spy satellites couldn't spot them. So cruise missiles were low and slow, and they could run and hide. They were devious and dangerous. It's not surprising that anti-nuclear campaigners in Britain and elsewhere loathed them.

They now arrived in Britain in response to new Soviet SS-20 missiles, which were medium range, meaning they could not threaten America but instead targeted Western Europe. NATO's collective defence policy meant in theory that if a country in Western Europe was hit by a Soviet missile, then all NATO members must treat it as an attack on their own soil. But if a few SS-20s were launched at Europe, would the US really go to war and endanger New York or Washington? Would America wade into a global nuclear conflict if the Soviets demonstrated they were willing to keep the horror strictly contained in Europe? Unsurprisingly, Western European countries felt unprotected, so the US decided to provide them with missiles on their own soil to match and deter the SS-20s. Britain, West Germany, Italy and the Netherlands were all set to receive cruise missiles in 1983. Protesters cried that this made Britain a target for the SS-20s, but arguably Britain had been a nuclear target since the 1950s.[61] Another aspect of the debate was control: who would get to decide whether to launch the missiles? The official stance was that it would be a joint US–UK decision, but the fact remained that the Americans could turn the key and launch the missiles without Britain's knowledge or consent. Britain merely hosted them. In theory, the US could start nuclear war from British soil.

4 School's Out

Escaping to the moon

Moving thousands of children across the country in an evacuation scheme would have been challenging for the authorities, but arguably their parents faced a more difficult task in having to explain why it might be necessary. Parents were often reluctant to talk about nuclear war, not only because they too were afraid, but because it was not something that could be easily explained. Formerly, if children had fretted about a ghost in the attic or a monster under the bed, parents could tell them such fears were just in their heads or a bad dream, but the threat of the nuclear bomb curtailed their power to soothe and pacify. Mum and Dad were now just as helpless as their children. As one child psychologist noted: 'Since 1945, there's grown up a generation which sees that a nuclear war is a real possibility. They've even seen nuclear weapons travelling along the roads. You can't reassure a child about it. You're just as powerless as he is.'[1]

By the 1980s, 70 per cent of young people in Britain thought nuclear war was inevitable.[2] Most other fears could be guarded against, but not this one. Every child knew the risk of talking to strangers, but the danger of abduction could be minimised by not walking alone, or by refusing to engage with a person you didn't know. It was dangerous to cross the road, so children had the Green Cross Code and the lollipop lady to help keep them safe. Don't wade into 'dark and lonely water', they were told. Don't retrieve your stranded kite from an electricity pylon. Don't return to a lit firework. All these fears were confronted in fairy stories, public information films, school lectures and whispered urban legends that usually had a dark lesson to impart: this is what happens to bad children who don't listen. But not so with nuclear war.

This was the one appalling threat that could not be neutralised by a creepy tale and a stern talking-to. It was just too big. It ballooned beyond words, warnings and a child's understanding.

For parents, the nuclear threat seemed to be mocking their most basic duty: that of keeping their child safe and seeing it into adulthood, where it could then produce its own children and so keep life going. The creation of the nuclear bomb in 1945 marked a terrible break: for the first time, this endless and obvious unfolding of life was threatened. Ironically perhaps, the children born into the new nuclear age were the healthiest and sturdiest there had ever been. The creation of the National Health Service in 1948, with its vaccinations, vitamins and antibiotics, plus state education, the safety net of welfare benefits, and increased living standards had pushed most British children into relatively rosy health. The new NHS brought better health and well-being; but it also chivvied death out of the house and into hospital, leaving the home as a place of relaxation and leisure. But just as the British people were becoming acquainted with the new concepts of home and health, the mushroom cloud arose and threatened every aspect of their lives.

The nuclear threat pressed hard on the soft children of the Cold War, who, unlike earlier generations, tended not to have routinely gone hungry or seen their siblings die in infancy and psychologists were keen to study the effect the nuclear threat was having on young minds. In a British survey of children's thoughts on the bomb in the 1980s, one child likened it to the sun: something distant and yet constantly present and with the ability to burn, devour and kill. Another drew a picture in which he imagined himself in 'a dangerously polluted sea, surrounded by dead fish, with an aeroplane dropping bombs directly onto him'.[3] It seemed that in their imagination, the forces of nature and the basic elements of life on earth – the sun, light, water, animals – were all caught in the nuclear snare and turned foul and dangerous. Other children sought relief in fantasies, with some dreaming of being free of the nuclear threat by escaping to the moon with bags of oxygen on their heads. Another child suggested writing a letter to the Queen, clearly regarding her as the ultimate mature and sensible adult who could order that a problem be resolved. For many, their anxieties were focused on school. This was the place where they spent most of their days, but it was also, crucially, where they were separated from their parents and home. In an American study around the same time, children spoke frequently of their fears of their school being bombed: 'The school can fall down when the bomb comes and it can come straight down on it, it can!'[4]

Duck and cover

It is no surprise that American children's fears of the nuclear bomb were often pinned to school, as this was where many of them endured frightening experiences in the early Cold War. If American parents were dutifully following US civil defence advice of the 1950s and early 60s, Dad would be digging a backyard shelter, Mom would be stockpiling the kitchen and learning home nursing skills, and the kids would play their own part by participating in the atomic air raid drills at school. Civil defence seeped into every part of post-war American family life, and getting ready for the bomb was seen as the wholesome and patriotic thing to do. It meant you were keeping the family safe by securing it not only against atomic blast but against a communist takeover. Every soup can placed on the shelf was an act of defiance. Sweat broken in the building of a backyard bunker was good patriotic sweat. These civil defence measures were not just practical, but also had huge psychological significance. Civil defence planners developed a theory of 'emotion management', which figured that being engaged hands-on in civil defence would help transform the American public's nuclear terror into a more manageable nuclear fear.[5] *Terror* is wild and frenzied, and its heightened emotional state might exhaust a person and push them into apathy and defeatism. *Fear*, on the other hand, can be controlled or guided with willpower and reasoning. It is useful because it keeps us alert. Fear is also motivating and makes us want to protect ourselves. Nuclear fear is therefore desirable. Terror is not.

As the Project East River concluded:

> Civil defense education must make people aware that a considerable degree of fear under attack is normal and inevitable. As with the development of healthy attitudes among combat troops, civil defense must, in effect, tell people: 'You will feel afraid when the first attack comes. So will everyone else, for attack is dangerous. There is no abnormality and no cowardliness in such justified

fear. It is not whether you feel afraid, but what you do when you are afraid that counts. The fear you experience will make you more alert, stronger, and more tireless for the things that you and your neighbours can do to protect yourselves.'[6]

But if adults could channel their nuclear fear into work, children could do little with it but be distressed. Atomic drills were introduced to American classrooms in 1950. The teacher would suddenly cry, 'DROP!' and everyone would have to throw themselves from their chair and huddle beneath their desk with their head bowed and hands clasped behind the neck. This was the 'duck and cover' method, popularised by the cartoon figure of Bert the Turtle, who taught America's post-war youth, via a maddeningly catchy song, what to do on seeing the nuclear flash in the sky:

> There was a turtle by the name of Bert
> And Bert the Turtle was very alert
> When danger threatened him he never got hurt
> He knew just what to do
> He'd duck and cover!
> Duck and cover!
> He did what we all must learn to do
> You and you and you and you
> Duck and cover!

In 1951, a jaunty *Duck and Cover* booklet and film appeared, and preparation for nuclear attack took its place beside familiar childhood lessons like crossing the road safely and knowing what to do in case of fire. Being ready for the bomb was just another thing for kids to learn: 'We must get ready for [nuclear attack], just as we are ready for many other dangers that are around us all the time.'[7] When the reassuring narrator talked of the danger of fire, he was quick to assure his young audience that there were fire departments and well-practised drills. Cars were dangerous too, but there were traffic lights and road laws and policemen. The film showed soothing images of traffic policemen wearing neat white gloves, of mothers herding kids safely across the road, and of brave firemen sprinting into action. For every problem there was a solution! 'Now we must be ready for a new danger,' the narrator told his young viewers, as though nuclear war was just another typical childhood fear that mothers could soothe and simple rules keep at bay. But the 'duck and cover' drills frightened many children rather than instilling a sense of preparation and control. 'The teachers would tell everybody to get under the desks,' one child recalled. 'You could feel the tension in the air, fear. The kids are fidgety and jumpy . . . then there would be absolute silence. You never knew if it was a drill – a test – or the real thing.'[8] During one drill in Queens, New York, the principal entered the classroom, pointed at a little boy who hadn't adopted the 'atomic clutch' position correctly and shouted: 'Your right arm is burned off! And half your face is burned away!'[9]

Duck and cover would be the classroom's response to a nuclear attack that arrived without warning – a sudden hot, blinding burst in the sky – but if the incoming attack had been detected and the siren sounded, this would allow time to react and seek shelter. In this scenario, schools would have to decide what to do with their children: should they let them run for home, or try to gather them into the basement? With the arrival of the hydrogen bomb, it was clear that ducking under a desk would be quite useless as a defence. Pupils who lived close to school were made to practise that dreadful dash home to see if they could get there within fifteen minutes. In this way, for some children, even the route to and from school acquired a patina of horror: it was where you practised your last run home before the bombs hit. It all had a devastating effect on these young minds: 'Kids were reminded constantly by civil defense drills that any day, while they were sitting at their desks or playing kickball in the schoolyard, their world could be destroyed by a country thousands of miles away.'[10]

Schools could also choose to send children into basements or corridors if the siren sounded. In these drills, they would gather in the dimness, far from windows and exterior walls, and learn how to hunker down and press themselves against the concrete, waiting for the blast wave. The protest singer Joan Baez traced her first act of resistance back to her refusal to participate in these drills. As another student recalled, 'In many ways the styles and explosion of the 1960s were born in these dank, subterranean high school corridors near the boiler room where we decided that our elders were indeed unreliable.'[11]

Many American schools issued steel dog tags to their pupils with their names and addresses engraved on them, so that in the chaos of an attack; children who got lost could be reunited with parents. It also meant that bodies burned in the attack might still be identifiable. In poor areas, where schools could not afford to issue dog tags, parents were invited to sew fabric labels into their children's clothes. Some states issued free dog tags; others looked at issuing plastic or cardboard tags as a cheaper alternative, although they were unlikely to endure.

If the duck and cover exercises sparked acts of rebellion in some students, for many younger kids, the swinging, clinking dog tags quickly became a plaything. Teachers reported that children swapped tags or played for them, as they did with cards and marbles.[12] But to parents who waved their children off each morning fearing that the worst might happen that day, they offered a sense of security. To some, the tags might have seemed like an amulet placed round the neck for luck or to call down a blessing upon the child. Indeed, religion featured on some dog tags, with certain states stamping them with an initial to indicate the child's religion, such as 'P' for Protestant, so that the body of its wearer might be given an appropriate burial.

Britain had also considered issuing nuclear ID tags for the population, but the idea never took off. For one, there was natural aversion to such a scheme, as remains today with opposition to ID cards or COVID vaccine certificates. But there was also no agreement on what to stamp on the tags. Should it be a person's National Insurance number? Not everyone had one – and children certainly didn't. Perhaps their address? This would be meaningless in case of evacuation, of course. Then there was also a post-war steel shortage, which quashed the prospect of steel tags, while plastic and cardboard would be quite useless. Some planners suggested discs made out of tough fibre, secured with a nylon loop. The Home Office were scrambling to find ways to do it on the cheap, as is revealed in this memo from October 1953:

[The Ministry of Supply] asked whether we wanted something that would stand up to incineration of a body, or merely something that would still be legible if the body were charred, the clothing burnt, and face unrecognisable. I said the former would be what was really wanted but that the latter would do if there were insuperable difficulties in the way of the former.[13]

A letter in the archives from the Save the Children Fund, dating from 1957, argued that any such ID scheme would be of 'dubious worth' due to the devastating scale of hydrogen bomb warfare. Common sense might be found in a 1955 memo, which seemed to settle the debate by stating, 'We may be obliged to think in terms of a roll-call of the living after the attack and making a presumption of death in respect of the remainder.'[14]

So with no ID scheme and no atomic drills, in Britain there were no specific rules for schools on what to do if the bomb dropped. Councils were left to their own devices and measures were local, piecemeal and random. In 1983, pupils at Cliffe Woods Middle School in Kent wondered what was going on when workmen arrived to install a siren on the roof. Their teacher rang the police to ask what the school should do if the thing ever went off, but was chastised for his enquiry: 'They told me I was acting irresponsibly and had no business telephoning.' Kent County Council were of no great help either, saying that if the siren ever sounded, 'We rely on the good sense of teachers to take the necessary action. Presumably, it's for the Home Office to tell people what to do if it goes off.'[15]

Readying the schools for war

If the outbreak of nuclear war was preceded by a period of international tension and therefore didn't come as a surprise, schools in Britain would have been closed. There were three steps in preparing British schools for nuclear conflict. At the planning stage, local authorities would quietly earmark which of their schools would play a wartime role – serving as rest centres, emergency feeding venues or medical hubs – and civil defence duties would be allocated to their staff. As international tensions increased, the government would move to the precautionary stage, at which point war planning would become painfully visible. Equipment and supplies would be brought into the previously selected schools and kept in storage. Then, at the final stage, when a nuclear attack seemed imminent, all schools, whether earmarked for wartime use or not, would be closed. Towards the end of the Cold War, such closures would fit nicely into the government's preference for keeping everyone locked down at home as war approached.

There would have been no prospect of a quick return to organised education after the bombs had exploded. As a Ministry of Education circular put it in 1964: 'The Government have come to the conclusion that education could not be continued in the sort of conditions expected to follow a nuclear attack. These conditions would require every effort to be concentrated first upon life-saving and survival and secondly upon physical reconstruction.'[16]

In its depiction of nuclear war, *Threads* took viewers into the future and portrayed the generation of children who had been born since the attack as they reached adolescence. They had received no education and could barely use language, communicating in alien sounds and jerky one-word sentences. When a TV set was hooked up to a generator and a crackling old children's programme called *Words and Pictures* was played to them, they simply stared at the screen, glum and blank. There were no teachers, because every able-bodied adult was engaged in physical labour. Learning had become a luxury. The alphabet had to wait and would perhaps be forgotten in time.

Peace studies

Yet schools were already becoming a battlefield in peacetime. One of the biggest nuclear controversies in Cold War Britain was a teaching issue. Peace studies arose as an academic discipline in the 1960s, and began appearing in many British classrooms in the 1980s. Despite its name, it caused heated debates and rows in political and academic establishments. Those in favour of the new subject insisted that it was teaching pupils about conflict, war and violence, but opponents alleged left-wing brainwashing and political indoctrination. The controversy began with the subject's name: if maths taught maths and history taught history, wouldn't peace studies teach peace – and peace at any cost, for that matter? What if the cost was appeasement of an aggressor? What lesson then for children studying Hitler in their history class who then trooped down the corridor for 50 minutes of peace studies?

This was the complaint of the strident education minister Rhodes Boyson, previously a headmaster and someone who was exuberantly Victorian in both his physical appearance and his teaching philosophy.

He declared that allowing peace studies in the classroom was 'an encouragement to lay down our arms and let anyone walk over us and destroy our society . . . an open invitation to the Soviets to take control of the world by threatening nuclear war'. He suggested that parents should have the right to 'withdraw their children from something they may consider as corrupting as the excesses of unpleasant sex education'.[17]

Peace studies opened itself to accusations of being a 'trendy' subject, as some of its lessons had a distinctly non-academic quality. Mrs Marguerite Courtney, head of history at St Veronica's in south London, spoke loftily of her role in teaching peace studies as 'the opening of young minds to issues rather than just providing them with answers'. 'Teachers must act as animators,' she declared. 'It is no longer a question of handing down knowledge from on high.' In her role as animator, she conducted a peace studies class where the pupils were shown slides of 'various items ranging from flowers and fountains, through land and seascapes, to mothers and children suffering from the ravages of war and asked to categorise them into peaceful and violent scenes'.[18]

But aside from the question of academic worth, opponents argued that the emotional nature of the subject changed the role of the teacher as dispassionate educator. For Professor Ian Lister, an expert in political education, peace studies placed the 'teacher as preacher, trying to persuade students of a particular point of view rather than enabling students to make decisions for themselves'.[19] This left teachers open to accusations of indoctrination, or of denting the respect of their profession, and there were angry scenes at teaching conferences in the 1980s, with one speaker calling CND supporters 'legions of hot-eyed Ayatollahs crowding at the school gates'.[20]

Unsurprisingly, the letters page of *The Guardian* saw anger at the pretence that a teacher could equate the bomb with 'prickly issues such as sex, religion, violence and race'. As one writer put it: 'If educationalists are supposed to deal with this delicate subject as a sort of intellectual exercise – getting the facts, having both sides of the argument etc. – we are all surely doomed.' Another said that young people were undeserving of their youth if they didn't question and rebel: 'What they need in the classroom – and everywhere else for that matter – is somebody to fight . . . On this issue I should like to see the classroom explode with wrath.'[21]

The philosopher Roger Scruton warned that the subject was planting notions of unilateralism into minds still too young for critical evaluation. Other people swapped stories of tactics by politically engaged teachers. One school chose to ignore a Remembrance Day service and instead held a 'peace assembly'; at another, a teacher organised a trip to an open-air disco in London that was in fact a CND meeting.[22]

There was alarm about the size and influence of CND in the 1980s. Launched in 1957, its support reached a peak in the early 1960s, when it would attract tens of thousands to rallies and its iconic Aldermaston marches between the Atomic Weapons Research Establishment in Berkshire, and Trafalgar Square. The marches, held each Easter, drew a remarkable cross-section of British society and campaign groups. In the crowd could be found vicars, students, mothers, musicians, professors, communists, Labour MPs and, in his teenage years, a young Rod Stewart. The 1961 gathering had a small group carrying a banner reading: *Even some Etonians support the march.*

The peaceful resolution of the Cuban Missile Crisis in October 1962, followed by the Partial Test Ban Treaty in 1963, which banned all nuclear tests except for those underground, meant a significant relaxation in nuclear anxieties, after which many peace activists turned their attention to the Vietnam war. CND's prominence began to wane, and the detente era of the 1970s weakened it further. The movement needed fear in order to flourish. Historian Dominic Sandbrook, in his survey of Britain in the early 1980s, *Who Dares Wins*, says that by 1979 CND 'had declined to the point of outright irrelevance' and had just four employees and about 2,000 members.[23]

But the infamously anxious eighties began, and CND's fortunes changed. In Britain, and across Western Europe and the USA, peace groups and the public were rediscovering nuclear anxiety, and as the controversy over the release of *Protect and Survive* showed (see p.91), there was widespread concern that the nation was not prepared for nuclear war, and that people did not know how they might protect themselves if it happened. The historian E. P. Thompson, a star of the nuclear disarmament movement, wrote in *Protest and Survive* that the government's advice might save some lives, but for others who had obeyed the guidance to stay at home and burrow into a 'cubbyhole', a horrible fate awaited:

within a certain distance of the centre of the detonation all houses, cars, clothes, the hair on dogs, cats and persons, and so on, will spontaneously ignite, while at the same time the blast will bring the houses tumbling down about the cubbyholes. We must envisage many thousands of nuclear families listening to [the BBC] on their portable radios as they are baked, crushed or suffocated to death.[24]

CND's membership soared. The movement had huge clout within the Labour Party, whose new leader in November 1980, Michael Foot, favoured unilateral nuclear disarmament, and thousands were again flocking to protests across the country. As 1981 dawned, CND's popularity was at 'unimaginable' levels, with tens of thousands estimated to be joining every month.[25] In October of that year, it held a rally in London's Hyde Park. *The Guardian* said it was the biggest demonstration the city had ever seen, and that instead of the old CND image of activists with duffel coats and earnest opinions, this demo was noisy with punks, performers, penny whistles, purple hair, and music by The Jam.[26] CND had become trendy. But just as the trend for purple punk styles would fade, so would the movement's popularity. The Labour Party remained stuck in opposition for the rest of the Cold War, with the majority of the British electorate repeatedly saying no to the party that had favoured nuclear disarmament. Pursuing this rigid policy also made CND an easy target for criticism, with many commentators claiming that unilateral disarmament would be of huge benefit to the Soviet Union, and the movement was always dogged by the suspicion that it was manipulated from Moscow.

Teachers fought back against allegations of bias and brainwashing in 1987, when Fred Jarvis, the General Secretary of the National Union of Teachers, accused the education secretary, Kenneth Baker, of slandering the profession,[27] but the controversy was largely neutralised by the introduction of the National Curriculum for England, Wales and Northern Ireland in 1989.

School dinners

While noisy educational battles raged about peace, the authorities made their quiet plans for war. In the heat and horror of nuclear conflict, the notion of dinner and a cup of sweet tea might seem impossibly luxurious, but the government knew that food in the after-math of the bomb would be literally priceless. With the economy destroyed and money having lost its value, food would be the ultimate reward, and therefore the means with which to control and direct the surviving population.

The authorities recognised that school cafeterias would be an excellent resource for feeding in wartime, bolstered by the passage of the 1944 Education Act, which placed an obligation upon every school to provide meals for its pupils. By the time the Cold War arrived, therefore, every school in Britain was a potential emer-gency feeding centre. In the early days, the School Meals Service gladly accepted the role of feeding the post-nuclear masses, and even drew up generous sample menus: breakfast would consist of porridge, followed by biscuits with marge or jam and tea. Dinner included such luxuries as shepherd's pie, followed by steamed fruit pudding, and there would be a light supper of tomato soup and bread.[28] As the Cold War progressed and reality kicked in, the naïve prospect of such nourishing meals was replaced with shrunk-down feeding plans that reflected the idea that food should only be doled out to those who could work or were of some service to the state. This went hand in hand with the broader change in civil defence planning from a focus on rescue and welfare facilitated by the authorities to the idea that people should stay at home and look after themselves.

But even with school canteens prepared and dinner ladies at the ready, where would the post-nuclear grub come from? The supply of food was a major concern for war planners, particularly as Britain in peacetime imported half of its foodstuffs. After nuclear attack, imports would cease and there would be no quick prospect of them resuming any time soon. Neither could the authorities expect to receive much of a bounty from farmland, given the likely destruction wrought by fire and fallout. As the Ministry of Agriculture noted:

> There would be heavy casualties in the more heavily contam-inated areas amongst livestock left in the open or housed in buildings affording poor protection; and an even greater hazard

to cattle and sheep would arise from eating contaminated grass. Nearly all our milk might be too dangerous to drink for a number of weeks. Growing crops would also be seriously affected, not merely by external contamination with the radioactive dust but through absorption of certain of the fission products through their roots and leaves.[29]

Many animals would be suffering from radiation sickness and would have to be slaughtered fast, but their meat would be unfit for human consumption. Britain would be at risk of starvation, especially if the nuclear attack happened in spring or summer and destroyed or contaminated growing crops. If we were lucky, nuclear war would break out in the autumn, after the harvest had been safely brought in.

To mitigate against shortages, the authorities were stockpiling essential foodstuffs in huge warehouses known as buffer depots, which were stacked high with sugar, fats, flour, yeast, biscuits, boiled sweets and milk powder. But these provisions came with their own problems. In 1988, a group of schoolchildren from Adwick Comprehensive in Doncaster broke into one of the depots and feasted on boxes of biscuits and sweets. Unfortunately, some of the biscuits dated from 1943, so they soon began to feel sick. The chairman of the emergency planning department at the local council remarked, 'You would have thought kids would have enough problems in World War Three without being made ill by ancient sweets as their post-holocaust treat.'[30]

In the event of a nuclear attack, each region in Britain would have an official in charge of food supply who would assess what food was available in shops and supermarkets, take control of it, and distribute strictly rationed amounts to the various emergency feeding centres. Once these supplies were exhausted, the big buffer depots would release their stockpiles. Of course, the emergency feeding could only begin once fallout had decreased to a safe level, so for an initial period after the attack each household would have to fend for itself. The advice was to obtain a 14-day supply of food and water, although it would be difficult for families to find the required amount if the announcement to prepare for nuclear war provoked panic-buying.

Python

All planning depended upon Britain being supplied and fed. A post-nuclear government, already battered and dislocated, could not hope to exert control over a population who were starving. To maintain authority, the state would need to procure food and then carefully control its distribution and allocation.

In 1970, the Ministry of Agriculture decided to nominate trade advisers, who would be drawn from key areas of the food industry – meat, cereals, oils and fats, and groceries – and after a nuclear attack would advise the authorities on how to procure and distribute food. Staff at the ministry considered potential candidates, exchanging notes and memos as they whittled down the numbers. Mr J. A. Sainsbury seemed an obvious choice as adviser on meat, but doubts were raised: 'He is surely too old and gentle.' Mr K. W. Spreckley was mooted as the post-nuclear cereals tsar, but one civil servant objected: 'I am very doubtful about Mr Spreckley. He is not a "doer".' And Mr A. O'Reilly of Heinz was struck from the groceries shortlist 'on the grounds that he is a strong Irish Republican'.[31]

In the event of a nuclear attack, these food experts would become members of UKSA, the United Kingdom Supply Agency, whose job it was to assess post-war Britain's food stocks, procure supplies from overseas and organise their distribution. This essential task would be implemented under the top-secret Python plan, drawn up in 1968. Crucially, it decreed that central government, instead of decamping to its secret 'Burlington' bunker in Wiltshire,[32] would instead be divided up into small teams, which would scatter across Britain prior to the attack and take shelter in various types of protected accommodation, such as castles, army barracks and universities. The hope was that some of the groups would survive the initial attack and then reunite to resume the work of government. Under the Python plan, three of these groups would form UKSA. One of them, code-named Whiskey, would endure nuclear war in the Scottish sea lochs.

In the early 1960s the Secretary of State for Scotland ordered three special ships to be built that could hide out in the vast and empty sea lochs if nuclear war came. However, until the dreaded day arrived, these ships were to be put to use lest they rust, so the government leased them to the Scottish ferry company Caledonian MacBrayne, which painted them with their red and blue livery, gave them the pretty names of *Clansman*, *Columba* and *Hebrides* and put them to use as ordinary car ferries, taking passengers between the Scottish islands and the mainland. They did look unremarkable: the features that made them usable as floating nuclear bunkers went unnoticed by the majority of passengers. Only real maritime nerds might have wondered why three of the ferries in the CalMac fleet had huge airtight doors that could seal the car deck, decontamination chambers with showers, and sprinklers able to wash the exterior clean of fallout; and why the air pressure could be altered to repel external contamination.

These strange ferries glided through the cold Scottish waters without ever being called up to their horrible purpose, but if they had been summoned, one of them would have gone to either Oban or Mallaig, where it would have received the Whiskey group and taken it to the lochs, hoping to survive the worst of the war. Mystery surrounds the purpose of the other two: only one was needed for UKSA. There is speculation that one was intended to receive the Queen and sail her to safety. Plans for the royal family's nuclear escape, known by the code name Candid, have never been made public, but it has been a popular assumption that she would have sought safety at sea on the Royal Yacht *Britannia*. Yet recent research has revealed that *Britannia* would have been reserved for use in the Python plan, so might Her Majesty have been ushered to safety aboard one of the CalMac ferries? There is a royal connection with the *Columba*, the only one of the three nuclear ships still active, which is now owned by a luxury cruise company. She sails as the *Hebridean Princess* and previously received the Queen as a passenger. However, had nuclear war broken out whilst Her Majesty was aboard, she would have offered little protection as the ship's nuclear features were removed prior to its sale in 1988.

'Real cloak and dagger stuff'

While the supermarket tsars sailed the Scottish lochs, survivors back on land would have been crowding the feeding centres in schools, where exhausted dinner ladies would have been supplemented by an army of female volunteers who had trained for this scenario as members of the Women's Royal Voluntary Service (WRVS). The ladies were ready to lend a hand in many crises and were often called out by police and local councils to provide warm clothing, hot drinks and meals at the scenes of disasters, floods and fires, but one of their main roles was to be ready to provide welfare services after a nuclear attack.

The WRVS had been formed to utilise the millions of housewives and mothers across Britain who were willing to help with civil defence in the Second World War, and they did spectacular work in accompanying evacuees to their new homes, tending to the welfare needs of bombed-out families, and setting up rest centres and first aid posts in the ruined streets.[33]

During the war, fleets of lorries known as the Queen's Messengers had been loaded with food supplies and emergency cooking equipment and stationed around the country, ready to swoop into badly damaged areas and feed those who had lost their homes. Each local authority was obliged to instigate their own emergency feeding plan after an attack, but until that swung into action, the lorries could bridge the gap. The Queen had paid for the first convoy of lorries, and she handed them into the care of the food minister, Lord Woolton, in the grand quadrangle of Buckingham Palace, where the minister suggested their motto might be 'Food and Kindliness'. Later renamed Food Flying Squads, these convoys were revived in the Cold War, and would be staffed by trained volunteers from the WRVS. Intended to be the 'shock troops' of emergency feeding, 11 Food Flying Squads would be strategically positioned around the country, ready to get out on the road and rush to where they were needed. This was the theory, but there was a catch. After a nuclear attack, no movement would be permissible for perhaps 14 days, until fallout had declined, so the shock troops would have to wait until it was safe to go into action. They could no longer roll into the street and instantly start dishing out tea and soup, as they had done during the Blitz.

After the Second World War ended, many WRVS volunteers may have felt rather deflated at the sudden change in the nature of their work. While they had once raced lorries through rubble-strewn streets under the sweep of searchlights, they were now crocheting blankets for refugees and escorting the elderly on seaside trips to Margate. The Cold War seemed to give them another chance at thrilling civil defence work and a return to their former wartime vigour. But if the ladies often seemed to relish the revival of civil defence, this opened them to anger and ridicule, with many people suspecting that they failed to appreciate the reality of a nuclear war, assuming it would be just like the Blitz.

At a press conference in March 1981, Lady Pike, the organisation's chairman, spoke of their determination to continue their treasured 'meals on wheels' service after a nuclear attack, saying that they would hope to supplement it with a 'jigsaw on wheels' service. 'We intend to provide the same service we have always provided in peace time,' she told the WRVS annual meeting, seemingly in blissful ignorance of the reality of nuclear war. 'We shall provide rest homes for the injured, emergency clothing from our depots, and emergency food to stranded people.'[34] This blind confidence provoked some furious letters to *The Guardian* in the following days, with one correspondent asking if Lady Pike's comments were an early April Fools' joke. Another was angered by her words:

> She is not a dear old member of the aristocracy with centuries of taking hot soup to hovels behind her; but a politician of many years standing . . . she must have a very clear understanding of nuclear war and my reaction to her address to the WRVS is one of cold fury. What she said I would define as obscenity, and it is time we stopped being polite to such people whose remarks bring an appalling future ever closer.[35]

Others despaired that the WRVS's 'naïve and sheep-like acceptance' and 'pathetic misguidedness' was splendid fuel for chauvinists, who would gladly snigger at women's involvement in civil defence work. There were sarcastic remarks about the WRVS post-nuclear 'meals on wheels' being slightly overcooked in the fire zones, and declaring that 'drivers must remember to be on time, properly attired, and still alive'.[36]

But these attacks didn't stop the WRVS ladies from sharpening their skills for rapid cooking under pressure during peacetime emergencies. After terrible flooding in Nottinghamshire in 1972, the local WRVS were asked to provide food for 12 families who had been temporarily made homeless, and so in the local church hall they served up steak, potatoes and peas, followed by strawberry tart and evaporated milk. Their report stated that the only difficulty on the night was 'several cut and bruised fingers due to not being able to use the old type of hand-operated tin opener'.[37] And when the WRVS ladies of Keighley were asked by the local Scout group to provide food for the annual Fellsman hike, they managed to serve 836 meals of 'shepherd's pie with peas, fruit with rice and custard, cheese, biscuits and tea'.

In this way they trained for the ultimate emergency call-out: feeding the survivors of nuclear war. While they waited for that horror, they were ready to attend to any other crisis, and were often summoned to real emergencies. A report from the Kidderminster branch in early 1970 described one such incident and proudly spoke of 'real cloak and dagger stuff':

Late on Monday, January 12th, 1970, through the County Emergency Officer, WRVS Emergency Welfare Organiser was alerted that 2 blocks of flats in Kidderminster had been declared by Consultants to be unsafe and were to be evacuated. No details of how or when were available, but strict secrecy was imposed. Two days later (still strict secrecy) the EWO was called to a meeting of the Chief Officers named in the 4 County Emergency Plan, briefed fully and asked what WRVS could do to help. She offered help at the evacuation end in the way of a Canteen from early morning till late in the evening – also cars to aid in the evacuation of the elderly or specially difficult cases, and at the reception end to help the County Welfare Emergency Officer at the Families Camp which was to be set up at a recently evacuated Army Camp at Witton, Droitwich. D-Day was fixed for 8 a.m. Thursday – January 15th, 1970. Strict secrecy was still imposed so that teams had to be called out and told not to ask why . . . The Camp was prepared for its new occupants and in all accommodated 33 families (61 persons) – ages ranging from a 3 week old baby to one or two over 80s. Each family had a small, medium or large room, and once installed this was their private domain to which they had the key. We arranged a large room as a Rest Room – with easy chairs and a television set lent to us by the Mayor of Droitwich, and decorated it with lovely pot plants which were loaned to us by Droitwich and Kidderminster Parks Dept (each family had a flowering plant in their own room). We arranged evening entertainments – films (3

times), a concert by a local folk group, and finally a Party before
the last families left.

Such reports read like cartoonish capers, but the ladies clearly felt
well prepared to feed the nation after a nuclear holocaust. However,
their optimism and chirpy demeanour made them easy targets for ridicule. Even if they had proved their mettle during the Second World
War, and subsequently by attending peacetime disasters such as Lock-
erbie, the Clapham rail crash, the Dunblane massacre and the IRA
bombing in Manchester, they did not exactly project an image of themselves as hard-edged warriors ready to haul an irradiated Britain back
from post-nuclear starvation. Yet during the Blitz and at various
moments of national horror and grief after the war, these good ladies
had been able to ease people's distress and, as Lord Woolton suggested
at Buckingham Palace back in 1941, offered 'food and kindliness'.

5 Protect and Survive

President Eisenhower was proud of the American interstate highways built during his term in office, and boasted of them in his memoirs, writing that his great road-building project had consumed enough concrete to build 'six sidewalks to the moon'.[1] These wide, straight roads kept the US economy booming. They also allowed the post-war picket-fenced dream of the nuclear family to flourish, as Father could work in the city and then speed home to the wholesome suburbs, where Mom, Junior and Sally waited with dinner on the table and an apple pie cooling on the windowsill. State was linked to state and city to suburb, on smooth paths of grey.

But these new highways were not just about big bucks and an easy commute. When the hydrogen bomb arrived in 1952 and showed itself capable of destroying a city, the Eisenhower administration prepared to evacuate key urban areas in the event of a nuclear attack, because, in the words of a Federal Civil Defense Administration (FCDA) official, 'The only 100% defence against it is not to be there when it goes off.' Val Peterson, the head of the FCDA, added, 'The alternatives are to dig, die or get out; and we certainly don't want to die.'[2]

Running with the idea of utilising the new roads, in 1955 Peterson suggested digging trenches along these highways. If the bomb dropped while the cities were still being emptied, people could leap from their cars, duck into these handy roadside holes and pull a board over their heads to shield themselves from fallout. Another suggestion was to lay fat concrete pipes by the roadside so evacuees might crawl inside. A jaunty red booklet was issued that same year, optimistically entitled *Four Wheels to Survival*, which showed how the trusty American car could be used to zoom the family to safety as long as the sensible motorist made sure his boot was stocked with food and water, the fuel tank topped up and the tyres inflated. The car, properly prepared, would act as a 'small movable house. You can get away in it – then live, eat and sleep in it in almost any climatic conditions.' The car radio would keep the family connected to the outside world. But the motorist was reminded to drive politely in a nuclear evacuation: 'If traffic gets stalled, don't lean on the horn. Your impatience may become someone else's panic. That can cost lives!'[3]

As tempting as it is to believe that the concrete criss-cross of these highways offered an escape route, nuclear fallout could not be evaded with a fast car and an open road. It would have produced a colossal game of thermonuclear whack-a-mole, with hundreds of thousands of cars scattering across the country, some reaching safety and others not. Some would be vaporised by the fireball, and some perhaps obliterated by a missile that had overshot its target. Others might be ravaged by a plume of fallout that reached across the sky and then bent its eerie ghost down into a cornfield. It would not be enough merely to 'get out'; people needed fallout protection when they reached their destination.

Thus in 1958, Eisenhower announced a National Shelter Policy, which advised the American people to make plans for their own safety and consider building a personal shelter; then, under Kennedy, these individual efforts gave way to a public fallout shelter building programme. But the all-American idea of using the car to escape the nuclear catastrophe never quite died, and highway evacuation tips were still being offered by the Reagan administration in the 1980s. Now the public were reminded to pack their car with stocks, bonds, wills and credit cards, and if they were caught in the vehicle when the siren wailed, they could turn it into a shelter by digging a trench and then parking the car overhead – cynics might say they were digging their own roadside grave, with the car serving as the coffin lid. In Washington DC, motorists would be told to evacuate on a regimented basis, with those who held even-numbered licence plates leaving first, while the rest were expected to sit quietly and wait their turn. If this seemed like an unlikely scenario, some saw the futility of any highway evacuation scheme. As the governor of California, Jerry Brown, remarked, 'Los Angeles cannot even evacuate itself on a Friday afternoon.'[4]

Kitchen patriots

Evacuation by road would not have worked in a small and crowded country like Britain, so instead of promoting motorways as escape routes, the British authorities took the opposite approach and denied the public access to these roads. In the last days before nuclear war, Britain's motorways would be declared essential service routes and guarded by police. This would keep them clear for vital traffic and help suppress any chaotic unofficial evacuations. If panicked civilians tried to flee, they would have to resort to minor routes and back roads instead, and it was assumed that these would quickly be gridlocked. The idea that there was no viable escape route from the cities via the road network fitted nicely with the government's official advice in the later Cold War that people were safer in their own homes and should stay there.

Civil defence had entered the home in the Second World War, when the responsible wife and mother was expected to stockpile food, water and medical supplies, and use rations carefully. There had been plenty of spirited talk of women as 'kitchen patriots', who would help secure victory by not wasting food and in utilising their domestic skills to transform glum ingredients into tasty meals to keep the family fed and strong. Women were told to use less bread in order to reduce Britain's demand for grain imports, thereby creating valuable space on incoming cargo ships for essential war materials. 'Food brought with it the reek of battle into the kitchen',[5] according to The Times, and food minister Lord Woolton declared that 'Any woman who helps in this work is to me the modern Helen of Troy.'[6] When rationing began in January 1940, it was a matter of both housewifely and national pride to feed your family on the reduced assortment offered. Meat became scarce, but offal was abundant, and Woman's Own published recipes for repulsive dishes like brain soufflé, while the Daily Express helpfully suggested sheep head in caper sauce.[7] A mother who could keep the family from unpatriotic grumbling when she placed before them a bowl of wobbling brains was a kitchen patriot indeed.

The famous Dig for Victory campaign asked people to turn parks and gardens into vegetable patches. In Nottingham, the famous rose grower Harry Wheatcroft uprooted his precious shrubs to make way for tomatoes, lettuces and onions, announcing: 'Pigs now wander about where our Polyantha roses bloomed. There's wheat and barley where acres of Hybrid Teas covered the land – even the humble cabbage stands where our standard roses once held majestic sway.'[8] (Incidentally, after the war the flamboyant Mr Wheatcroft introduced the French-bred Peace rose to Britain. The pale rose with a yellow tint became a sensation in the horticultural world and was presented to the Soviet ambassador on his visit to Harrogate in 1955.)

The simple things women should know about nuclear warfare

In 1938, Britain had begun recruiting ARP (Air Raid Precautions) volunteers, who would enforce blackout regulations, be trained in smoke drills and gas detection, and learn how to put out a flaming incendiary bomb with a stirrup pump. It was hoped that this type of civil defence work would appeal to women, as the ARP were required to know the domestic arrangements of every household on their patch – how many people were at home, whether there were any children, elderly or infirm, and what their shelter arrangements were. This was invaluable information if the street was hit, as it allowed them to direct the rescue teams. They would also nag and chide and tell off, shouting, 'Put that light out!' and badgering people into their shelters as the siren wailed. They aimed to be 'the chartered "good neighbour" of the Blitz'.[9]

But despite the local nature of ARP work and its obvious welfare aspect, recruitment among women was slow. Some ARP posts had a positively raffish air, which deterred middle-class women who were looking to get involved in war work. As one female ARP worker recalled:

owing to the fact that race-tracks, boxing rings and similar chancy means of livelihood closed down at the outbreak of war, there was a considerable percentage of bookies' touts and even more parasitic professions in the CD [civil defence] services, together with a collection of workers in light industry, 'intellectuals', opera singers, street traders, dog fanciers etc. In the early days the Control Rooms were crowded with chorus girls. There was also an ex-burglar, a trade unionist, and two men who hoped that joining the ARP would defer their call-up papers.[10]

That was where the WRVS came in. It tapped into that huge reserve of well-meaning women, offering them a path into civil defence work that was not seen as too male-dominated, grubby or physically danger-ous. Plenty of women signed up for more daring or arduous roles in the WRNS (Women's Royal Naval Service), WAAF (Women's Auxil-iary Air Force) or ATS (Auxiliary Territorial Service), or went off to work as Land Girls, but for those ladies who felt more comfortable in local welfare and relief work, the WRVS had endless jobs: accompany-ing evacuated children, feeding exhausted rescue teams, setting up rest centres, arranging shelter and clothing for bombed-out families, and manning incident inquiry points at the scene of bombings, where they would work to reunite scattered households and, all too often, break the news of deaths. A fragrant cloak of femininity was cast over civil defence work by the respectable ladies of the WRVS when it might otherwise have seemed like a man's job. Their reassuring presence on the bomb site and the dusty street corner was a reminder that this was also women's work.

The WRVS was too big and too useful to be disbanded after the war, and in the 1950s, the threat of nuclear conflict claimed them again. Besides helping stressed mothers, lonely old folk, sick children and borstal boys, they were now asked to prepare the women of Brit-ain for nuclear war.

In 1956, the WRVS launched the One in Five campaign to reach those women who were detached from civil defence: those who were unconcerned by it or who simply didn't think there was anything they could do in the face of the nuclear threat. It aimed to teach them small practical skills and offer tips on protecting the home and nursing the family under nuclear attack. The campaign took its name from its intention to reach one fifth of British women with its little lectures. The hope was that a woman who had heard a One in Five talk at her local church hall, community centre or workplace canteen would be converted to the cause of civil defence. She would not only be eager to stockpile tinned food, practise wrapping bandages and whip up a mix-ture of borax and ammonium sulphate in case the roof of her thatched cottage caught fire; she would also pass on her newly acquired knowledge to her female friends at drinks at the tennis club or during neighbourly chats over the garden fence. So, the WRVS hoped, feminine gossip would spread the One in Five message across the land to every woman in Britain.

The lectures were careful not to scare people by presenting the horrifying, unvarnished truth about nuclear holocaust: you would hear no talk of charred skin, severed limbs or wretched radiation sickness. Instead, the prim and dainty instructors spoke of 'the simple things women should know about nuclear warfare'. The campaign literature appealed not to patriotism and civic duty but to a woman's presumed natural concern for her home and family:

> There is so much talk about nuclear weapons these days that most women must be wondering what would happen to their families should Britain ever be attacked. As you watch your children playing or think of the elderly people and others who seem so dependent on you, you may be worrying about whether there is anything you should know or could do to help them if such a terrible disaster should ever come. You have heard of many dangers which might affect even an unbombed house, but do remember that by knowing what to do your family could be made much safer.[11]

The underlying message of the campaign was that women should be galvanised, prepared and trained to take on the care, rescue and welfare duties of the post-nuclear state. Just as their domestic skills had made them 'the modern Helen of Troy' during the Second World War, so the nuclear threat called upon them to once again become everyday heroines – and by doing so, reduce the burden on the state. During the Blitz, they had been saviours with wooden spoons and whisks; now they would once again go into action with hoarded tins, toilet rolls and bottles of Dettol.

The talks were delivered in workplaces or community halls; some even took place in the sitting rooms of dedicated WRVS members who were able to round up enough interested ladies. The leaflets advertised their convenience: the meetings would be friendly get-togethers, free of charge, and last just half an hour, The women were assured that there was plenty they could do as housewives, carers and mothers to protect home and family if nuclear war came. Yet it is obvious that the One in Five talks were delivered from a position of privilege. Lady lecturers advised housewives to stock up on things such as butter, veal, sausages, stewed steak, jam, honey, cordial and biscuits, but such a well-stocked larder would have felt luxurious to many households in 1950s austerity Britain. They were told to assemble a 'nursing chest' and stock it with bandages and antiseptic, talcum powder, hot-water bottles and Air Wick room deodorisers. While all this suggested post-nuclear comfort, the idea of filling hot-water bottles seems ludicrous when water would have to be severely rationed after a nuclear attack. The One in Five talks were careful not to deliver hard nuclear truths, but instead created a reassuring image of the middle-class home, over which mother could preside as normal in a warm, fragrant fug of talcum powder.

When the campaign began, the ladies working on it were largely the same volunteers who had come through the Blitz; and yet, reading the coy material of the One in Five lectures, you would be forgiven for thinking they had never experienced war. This was a retreat into denial, with its focus on keeping women calm and keeping them at home, to stop them running into the street in panic and overwhelming the social services and the NHS. It is hardly surprising that the government was pleased with the WRVS's work. A grateful Home Secretary told them in 1963: 'I simply cannot thank you enough. I hope those engaged in One in Five talks realise that they have the gratitude of the government.'[12]

Marion Yool trained as a One in Five instructor and recognised that part of her role in delivering the talks was 'trying to put a positive skew on a very unpleasant subject'. Nuclear attack was 'a terrifying prospect so you had to be very careful how you presented it'. She told her audience

> how to prepare their house and to make a safe little sanctuary within the house, sort of under the stairs sort of thing. If there was a warning, to get as much food and blankets and medical kit, everything that you might need to sustain you for as long as it would take perhaps. It was a very grim prospect but, you know, it was better than nothing and you have to give people hope that there is something they can do.[13]

But there can only be hope if you survive the nuclear attack. Afterwards, your prospects depend not on a nation of capable housewives, but on the country's leaders being able to emerge from their bunkers and implement some kind of order and organisation to provide shelter, treat the injured and distribute food stocks – and on the dreaded nuclear winter not becoming a reality. Without all of that, hope is futile.

Advising the householder

In 1963, a booklet titled *Civil Defence Handbook No. 10 Advising the Householder on Protection Against Nuclear Attack*, offering practical advice on how to fortify and defend the home against nuclear attack, inched slightly closer to the realities of war. The booklet, and the series of short films that accompanied it, was intended as training material for civil defence and emergency workers, although it was also put on sale to the wider public. The moment nuclear war threatened, it would have been reproduced in every national newspaper, and the short films broadcast on TV.

The films were shot in sombre black and white, each beginning with funereal theme music that makes you expect the announcement of a royal death or that thousands of lives have been lost at sea. Instead, the Scottish actor Robert Urquhart, dressed in a neat black civil defence uniform and perched on the edge of his desk with arms folded in a no-nonsense manner, speaks to the camera like a stern headmaster who has seen all the trouble in the world – and here is yet more.

The seven short films complement the seven sections of the *Advising the Householder* booklet, and could have been lifted straight from Blitz newsreels: we see civil defence workers blowing whistles, checking on neighbours, making notes and organising rescues. They are capable and unruffled and wear the tin hats so familiar from the war. The householders are docile and efficient. There is not a hint of panic or distress as the housewife stocks her kitchen cupboards with the recommended tinned foods, and the husband, equally calm, starts piling sandbags and boarding up windows. There is no nervous chatter or questioning: the civilians merely obey the advice of the civil defence worker. Post-war Britain is still a deferential society. Everyone trusts authority, and everyone does as their betters bid them, and does it meekly. What's more, the advice we see being enacted in the films and advised in the booklet worked well enough in the Blitz, so why not trust in it again? When the nuclear attack occurs, everyone remains unruffled. The civil defence worker is able to calmly note the local fall-out readings with an elegant fountain pen.

The guidance also assumes a great deal of DIY know-how from the obedient civilians, expecting that householders will be able to whip out window frames and brick up windows, or alternatively fill the window space with boards and tightly wire them together; and that they have stirrup pumps and garden syringes for domestic firefighting. Questions were asked in Parliament about the practicality of these home defence instructions by the Labour MP Emrys Hughes, who remarked that the 'elaborate measures would tax the ingenuity of a very good general contractor'.[14] And if everyone was advised to procure the recommended materials, wouldn't it prompt a run on building supplies? Where were all the planks, bricks and sandbags to come from? (This question was still being raised in the 1980s, when the journalist Duncan Campbell, in *War Plan UK*, calculated that the sandbagging requirements of Hull alone would exhaust the entire national supply of sand.)[15] What was more, Hughes represented a working-class constituency where many families lived in overcrowded conditions and did not have the luxury of a spare room that could be packed high with the paraphernalia of survival.

The booklet recommended that the following be taken into the fall-out room:

Mattresses, pillows and blankets, tables and chairs, plates, cups, knives, forks, spoons, tea-pot, tin-opener, bottle-opener, kettle, saucepans, portable stove and fuel, portable radio set and spare batteries, torches, batteries, candles, matches, face flannels, towels, sanitary towels, soap, tea towels, rubber or plastic gloves, clock, books and magazines, toys for children, notebook and pencil, box containing personal papers, e.g. NHS medical cards, savings bank books, birth and marriage certificates, first aid kit.[16]

It also advised householders to store three days' worth of drinking water and provide 'large receptacles with covers and with improvised seats for use as urinal, and for excreta', plus 'a dust bin with a well-fitting lid'. Despite all that stuff in the room, there was still supposed to be 'enough space to move about in'.[17]

Clearly the advice was better suited to those with the luxury of a spacious house, and who had the financial resources to buy the necessary building supplies and assemble 'an emergency reserve of tinned or other non-perishable food'.[18] The film shows a housewife prettily dressed in an apron and earrings as she stocks her fallout-room cupboard with reassuringly familiar items, such as Farley's Rusks and a tin of mock turtle soup. The latter had been a larder essential during the Second World War, with the grocer Thomas Wallis of Holborn Circus offering for sale in 1939 a sturdy wooden case containing 19 food tins, one of which was mock turtle soup, and calling the package 'ARP Storage – Your Duty to Your Family'.[19]

Another nod to typically British notions of home and family was the reminder to care for one's pets in the event of nuclear war. Many in the 1960s would have remembered 'the great cat and dog massacre' in the first week of the Second World War, when 400,000 animals were euthanised in London alone.[20] This 'holocaust of pets'[21] was not ordered by the government, nor advised by vets, and it was abhorred by animal charities. Nonetheless, many owners chose to have their pets put down before Hitler's bombs started falling. Various reasons were offered for this decision: evacuated families could not take pets with them, crippling food shortages were anticipated, or the pet might be driven mad with fear under aerial bombardment and become a danger to itself and others. But it was an irrational act that contradicted the British people's wartime image of themselves as resolute and steadfast in the face of the Nazi threat. Not only was the killing unnecessary, it was undesirable, with the dearth of cats leading to a horrible rise in vermin in some urban areas, whilst the sudden loss of the family dog meant the removal of 'man's best friend' that would otherwise have brought comfort and joy during the strain of war.

In order to prevent a similar panic reaction, in 1950 the RSPCA (Royal Society for the Prevention of Cruelty to Animals) drew up sombre and practical advice on caring for animals under atomic attack. With the approval of the Home Office, they issued a booklet called *First Aid and Fire Precautions (Including Animals and Air Raids)*, which showed on its pale blue front cover a cat and a dog perching prettily on a first aid box and water bucket.[22] This cute image belied the booklet's horrible contents. Having learned lessons from the Second World War, the RSPCA warned that the biggest danger to animals was fire, caused either by conventional or nuclear bombing. The booklet tried to apply old wartime measures to the new atomic threat, advising householders to keep sand and water buckets ready to smother fires; a small blaze might even be doused by using a siphon of soda water. The suggestion of soda water as a defence against a nuclear firestorm sits awkwardly alongside the warning that pets might be so badly burned they would require 'prompt destruction'. The reality of an atomic attack was only slowly sinking in.

Even if the home was not directly damaged in a nuclear attack, there was always the risk that a pet would be driven into a frenzy of fear by the alien sounds of war: the wail of the siren, the drone of the planes, the roar of the bombs, the crash of the blast wave and the cries of dying neighbours through the walls. There was advice on how to calm a frightened dog during an attack, with diagrams showing how to fashion a makeshift muzzle from a strip of bandage so he wouldn't harm anyone in his panic. He might also be sedated with aspirin. The booklet told readers how to behave in front of a distressed animal:

> Nothing communicates itself to an animal quicker than human fear or apprehension. A quiet calm approach with soothing tones does wonders with a hysterical animal in pain. The voice is of the greatest value and if the speaker is the owner and the voice is known this is an advantage. Hysterical outbursts of sympathy are the worst possible environment for patients.

Here we can detect again the nanny-ish tone of wartime Britain, ordering people to pull themselves together in front of Fido, but any reassurance they might have drawn from that comforting tone of voice would have withered when they turned the page and got to the 'Cat Grasper'. Resembling a riding crop with a loop at the tip, this could be used to extricate a pet from a pile of debris after an air raid. It could also be deployed to restrain an animal, holding it utterly still so it could be shot in the head. With the loop around the animal's neck, the person administering the bullet presses on the length of the Grasper with his foot, forcing the animal's head to the floor and rendering it unable to rear up or wriggle. Diagrams show where on the head a captive bolt or gun should be placed. This section of the booklet was aimed at vets and farmers, and featured cows, pigs, sheep and horses as well as family dogs and cats. The advice on how to kill is horribly detailed: 'Fix the instrument [the gun] about a finger's width above the level of the eyes, halfway across the forehead, aiming well up into the head . . . To avoid any risk from the bullet place a pail of water or a thick piece of wood under the head to receive the bullet in case it goes through.'[23]

But there were animals other than dogs, kittens and sheep in Britain, and their behaviour and security under aerial assault had to be considered. In the early 1980s, the nuclear survivalist magazine *Protect and Survive Monthly* ran a series of articles on the risk posed by captive animals if they broke out of their compounds in the chaos of nuclear war. Every zoo and safari park, and every eccentric with a tank of tarantulas in the bedroom or a pet puma in the grounds, was just another threat to be added to the great list of dangers. The magazine explained that nuclear survivors needn't fear wild animals, as they were accustomed to fending for themselves and would know how to obtain prey. Instead, they should be concerned about tame or captive animals that were suddenly set free. 'They have not been taught to hunt for themselves and when they do escape, hungry and frightened in strange surroundings, they are far more likely to act out of character. Food will be one of their first priorities, whether it be farm animals or humans trapped in buildings or just the badly injured. The smell of blood will not help matters.'[24]

More advice on how to prepare farms and their animals for nuclear attack was provided in 1961 by an information film called *Home Defence and the Farmer*. The message was that the farmer had a responsibility not only to himself and his family but also to his herd. The animals would be essential, as nuclear conflict would most likely bring Britain's food imports to an end. The farmer must therefore protect his animals, and humanely dispose of those desperately injured or made sick by fallout. The film showed the countryside after nuclear attack being as lush and green as it ever was, perhaps playing on the popular perception of war as something that affected only cities, industrial areas and key infrastructure, with the enemy unlikely to show interest in meadows and orchards.

Propaganda in the Great War had urged men to enlist and fight to defend a Britain that was portrayed on the recruitment posters as bucolic and arcadian and littered with thatched cottages that seemed to come straight out of a Thomas Hardy novel. 'Your country's call. Isn't this worth fighting for?' the poster asked – even though the majority of fighting men were from poor urban areas and would never have eaten fruit freshly plucked from the tree. Yet they were told that this was the real Britain: here was the ideal they had to defend and preserve. In a similar way, while *Home Defence and the Farmer* spoke directly to farmers, there was the implication that they were the custodians of an idealised Britain that was wholesome, pure and untouched by the corrupting forces of modernisation.

On the face of it at least, the rural idyll seems untouched by the bomb. 'The countryside looks much the same,' the film's narrator tells the viewer, before warning, 'Nonetheless there is danger in every place where fallout has come down.'[25] The farmer is told that he can eventually emerge from his shelter to get on with his jobs, but he should wear a hat and scarf and tuck his trousers into gum boots. He might also wish to plug his ears with cotton wool and wear a pair of goggles. Thus the pastoral beauty of the countryside is spoiled by the nightmarish vision of the farmer stalking the fields muffled and plugged.

But the central message of the film is work, and even though he cuts an apocalyptic figure, the farmer is still out on the land, labouring and producing and providing for the urban survivors, who are told to 'stay in their homes' and who, when they do emerge, will be desperate for food. It seems that the planners envisaged the urban survivors as either a burden on the state or, if they managed to leave the city, a zombie-like horde of refugees descending on small towns and villages in search of sustenance. On the other hand, *Home Defence and the Farmer* appeals to the old-fashioned notion that country folk are made of hardy stuff and will not riot or panic but will instead tuck their trousers into their boots and get to it.

Protect and Survive, 1980

As the Cold War progressed and it became obvious that the Second World War no longer offered a model for future conflict, public information advice on nuclear war became more realistic and impersonal.

The reassuring, nanny-ish voice of the home front, still detectable in the booklets and films of the 1950s and 60s, had vanished by the time the Protect and Survive campaign was launched in 1980. There was not a scrap of comfort here. The old certainties were gone, replaced with something cold and forbidding. The campaign reflected the new era of individualism.

In 1987, prime minister Margaret Thatcher, ridiculed the notion that the government should always lend a helping hand:

> I think we have gone through a period when too many children and people have been given to understand 'I have a problem, it is the Government's job to cope with it!' or 'I have a problem, I will go and get a grant to cope with it!' 'I am homeless, the Government must house me!' and so they are casting their problems on society and who is society? There is no such thing! There are individual men and women and there are families and no government can do anything except through the people and people look to themselves first.[26]

Protect and Survive, the updated official advice on 'how to make your home and your family as safe as possible under nuclear attack',[27] displays a similar ethos. The films would have been broadcast to the nation in the last few days before an expected nuclear attack, and the booklet distributed to homes and reproduced in newspapers. Gone are the instructions we saw in *Advising the Householder* to wait calmly for an orderly evacuation, look after your pets, offer help to strangers and remember your raincoat. As if to match Margaret Thatcher's notion that there is no such thing as society, *Protect and Survive* zooms in on the individual and the small nuclear family unit, who are encouraged to secure their home and endure the war without the expectation of help from either neighbours or officialdom. No one is coming to rescue you. No one is coming to feed you. Close the door to your neighbours. Look to yourself.

Advising the Householder stressed the value of community. In the accompanying films, neighbours were portrayed as familiar and friendly faces who could be relied upon if the electricity went off or the tea bags ran out. In the *Protect and Survive* films, neighbours barely make an appearance. Most of the scenes show empty rooms and silent stacks of furniture waiting to be assembled into a fallout shelter, or piles of tins, blankets and bottles. There are no human faces. There is no community. The suggestion is that viewers should forget outside help, whether from a neighbour, the council, the police or the government. Indeed, neighbours are cast as sources of threat, with the warning given that 'if you leave your home, your local authority may take it over for homeless families'.[28] Your neighbour is your competitor, the films suggest, a rival who is clutching at the same scarce resources as you, and who will grab your house if you dare let your guard down. Even the campaign's logo suggested isolation, portraying a faceless nuclear family enclosed in a sealed circle.

Public information materials of the 1980s were generally frightening. They warned about rabies and drink-driving and Christmas trees going up in flames. They showed what might happen if children retrieved a frisbee from an electricity substation, or played with fireworks, or trespassed on the railway tracks for the sake of a shortcut home. Many children were haunted by eerie images from TV public information campaigns, like the tombstone warning people about AIDS, or the hooded 'Spirit of Dark and Lonely Water', voiced by Donald Pleasence, who tried to deter children from careless wild swimming. *Protect and Survive* fitted perfectly amongst these official horror shows.

As with *Advising the Householder*, it came in the form of a booklet and a series of short films which focused on how families could fortify their homes against nuclear attack and then endure the subsequent 14-day fallout period penned inside. It stressed the absolute importance of the family home: householders had to make it as safe as they could. They were told that if they fled, the authorities in other areas 'will not help you with food, accommodation or other essentials'.[29] Exposed and alone and with no expectation of aid, families would be at risk from fallout, exposure, hunger and lawlessness, so the only possible hope of safety would be to stay in their own home, behind barricaded doors and windows, where they could rely on a supply of stockpiled food, medicine and water.

The instructions for fortifying the home were far simpler than those formerly criticised for their complexity in *Advising the Householder*, with the advice being to 'block up windows' and increase the thickness of exterior walls by simply stacking bricks, timber, bags of earth and sand or books in front of them. Heavy furniture could be dragged across the room to provide yet another layer of protection. A fallout room should be selected that was furthest from the roof and any exterior walls, and inside that room an 'inner refuge' must be constructed. This was a tiny reinforced area into which the family must squeeze themselves and remain for the first 48 hours after nuclear attack.

The advice for building this inner refuge was simple – and its simplicity left it open to ridicule. 'Making a refuge is not difficult,' the film's narrator informed viewers. 'The main things you will need are shovel, boxes, cartons or large plastic bags, earth or sand.'[30] To assemble the refuge, the householder was advised to take off interior doors and prop them against the wall in the designated fallout room, forming a diagonal. He should then stack bags and boxes filled with 'sand, earth, books or rolled-up clothes' against the slant of the doors. For good measure he might also wish to throw a mattress on top and lash it all down with rope. He should then stack boxes and furniture around each end of his construction, leaving a little gap for the family so they could wriggle inside. They would be expected to hunker beneath the slanted doors for 48 hours. A cupboard under the stairs might also make a suitable refuge as long as the staircase was similarly piled high with boxes and mattresses. Perhaps recalling the earlier criticisms about obtaining building supplies, *Protect and Survive* suggested that 'If you cannot get hold of sand bags or boxes try travel bags, haversacks, suitcases, pillowcases or anything that will hold sand or earth.'[31]

In 1980, the BBC's *Panorama* programme asked a Yorkshire family to build a refuge according to the *Protect and Survive* advice. We are told the family would need 'one hundred plastic bags or similar containers, access to a garden, the strength to dig and carry over a ton of earth, and floor joists strong enough to bear that sort of weight'.[32] The family piled their refuge with bags, mattresses and golden-bronze sofa cushions before squeezing inside with their dog. The camera peered into their den of chintzy claustrophobia and they were asked what they imagined conditions would be like in their refuge after a few days. 'Pretty grim I would say,' the pragmatic father admitted, 'but what can you do?'[33]

The narrator of *Protect and Survive*, Patrick Allen, who later found more light-hearted work on BBC2's *Shooting Stars* with Vic Reeves and Bob Mortimer, talked slowly and in short sentences, as though he was speaking to children who were home from school and keen to build a den in the living room. Still, the simple tone, supplemented by animated churning mushroom clouds and cartoon speckles of fallout descending on a doll's house, gave the films a nightmarish quality, as it gradually dawned on viewers that something hideous was being concealed by these bright colours and childish instructions and the pretence that they might protect themselves with kitchen doors and pillowcases.

The submerged horror only rose like a nuclear Kraken in the final short film, and a section of the booklet entitled 'Casualties'. Here, delivered like a hasty afterthought, we find terrible honesty at last. Having spent the earlier films telling viewers that home is a haven, a place of safety, a refuge to be stocked and fortified, where the family will have their bottled water and Heinz soup, and their snakes and ladders set, the narrator finally gets to the point by speaking of the ultimate horror:

> If anyone dies while you are kept in your fallout room, move the body to another room in the house. Label the body with name and address and cover it as tightly as possible in polythene, paper, sheets or blankets. Tie a second card to the covering. The radio will advise you what to do about taking the body away for burial. If however you have had a body in the house for more than five days and if it is safe to go outside then you should bury the body for the time being in a trench or cover it with earth and mark the spot of the burial.[34]

In modern society, many people die in hospitals and bodies are dealt with by professionals, but the notorious *Protect and Survive* advice on how to bury the dead forced viewers back in time. It was clear that if one of their own died, there was no one they could summon: they had to deal with the corpse themselves. In a campaign devoted to making the home a haven, this was the ultimate desecration: the garden shall become a graveyard.

The *Protect and Survive* guidance sparked suspicion and unease when a rumour arose that it was being kept secret from the public. This was not strictly true. Over 2,000 copies of the booklet were made available to politicians, fire and police bosses, and attendees of the civil defence colleges, although when a member of the House of Lords tried to test how easy it was to obtain one, he found it 'rather difficult to get hold of. I rang the Home Office to ask them about it and they told me I could not have a copy.'[35] The reason it was not distributed en masse was not secrecy, but because it was intended as advice at a time of imminent nuclear threat, at which point it would be posted to households, printed in the newspapers, and the films broadcast on TV. Releasing it in a calm period without any obvious cause might provoke panic, or suggest to the enemy that Britain was preparing a nuclear attack. It might even be counterproductive: if it was distributed when the public were not overly troubled by the nuclear threat, the advice might vanish quickly from people's minds, and they would soon lose the booklet at the back of the cutlery drawer. Home Affairs Minister Leon Brittan told Parliament in February 1980 that *Protect and Survive* 'has not been published for the simple reason that it was produced for distribution at a time of grave international crisis when war seemed imminent, and it was calculated that it would have the greatest impact if distributed then'.[36]

So the booklets were never distributed and the films only appeared on television briefly when they were leaked to the BBC in 1980. Short clips were shown on the *Panorama* programme in an episode called 'If the Bomb Drops'. 'These films are secret,' presenter Jeremy Paxman explained, 'but we have managed to obtain copies of them. They've never been seen before and won't be seen again until nuclear war is imminent.'[37]

But the government's intention to keep *Protect and Survive* under wraps until a war crisis erupted was foiled by the frightening surge in international tension between East and West in the early 1980s. Clamour grew for official guidance on how Britain might protect itself in a nuclear war, and the suspicion that the government was hiding information from the public made things worse. A hard-hitting series of articles about civil defence in *The Times* in January 1980 spoke of the government's duty to provide such official advice:

The most obvious need is for a programme of public education. The image of civil defence in Britain remains quaint and outdated, a hazy distillation of middle-aged memories and the television persona of Captain Mainwaring. Yet even those who are sufficiently interested to educate themselves receive scant encouragement, with little material for them to read. Other countries persuade members of the public to enlighten themselves on the means of survival in the unlikely event of nuclear attack. In Britain, a Home Office booklet, *Protect and Survive*, remains unavailable.[38]

Under pressure, the government finally released the booklet in May 1980, not posting it free to every home as was the original intention but placing it on sale for 50p, and making 150,000 copies available in post offices and libraries. A year later, 81,000 booklets had been sold – to appear decades later on eBay as faded, curious reminders of a very British approach to Armageddon.

Collapsible coffins

The dreadful notion of having to bury your own dead emerged in the later Cold War, but in the 1950s, when the spirit of the Second World War still lingered and the implications of the hydrogen bomb were not yet obvious, there persisted hopes of burying the nuclear dead with some dignity. A batch of black and white photographs in the National Records of Scotland show waistcoated staff of the Scottish Office proudly showcasing a 'collapsible coffin', complete with tassels and ornate handles, which would allow for speedy but dignified mass burials after nuclear attack.[39]

The question of coffins regularly arose in British civil defence planning. It might have seemed an unpleasant topic to many genteel civil servants in a country that had recently known war, albeit not to the apocalyptic degree of Germany, Poland or the Soviet Union, for example. When large losses of life occurred in Britain during the Blitz, there had always been the manpower and resources to bury the bodies with the necessary ceremony and dignity. There had been prayers, coffins and flowers. But the nuclear age took the prospect of mass death beyond anything experienced in the Blitz. In London, there were proposals to use Wanstead Flats and the Oval cricket ground as mass burial sites, both being wide and flat and relatively removed from a water source, but planners were reluctant to imagine corpses being tossed into a mass grave, so their plans frequently tried to allow for coffins, dignity and ritual of some description.

In the early Cold War, the Home Office considered 'a coffin with a hinged bottom, as we saw being demonstrated in Edinburgh, which would be used for lowering the body into the grave. The body, lying on a wooden tray, would be released by opening the hinges with a cord and the coffin shell could then be pulled out of the grave and used over again.'[40] This would preserve the above-ground ceremony of burial and provide a smidgen of comfort to any members of the public who might catch sight of the strange goings-on at the freshly dug park, nature reserve or golf course. Containers made of strong fabric were also suggested, although 'this type of covering looks, as it is, cheaper than a coffin; on the other hand there seems to us no reason why it should not lend itself to a dignified ceremony'. The dignity of the coffin maintained a connection to civilised behaviour, and that connection held a promise of national recovery: the British people had not been reduced to the status of brutes.

Painted heads and boiled rivers

But as the Cold War progressed, brutal reality could no longer be concealed. In South Yorkshire, the local authority in the 1980s had declared the area 'a nuclear-free zone', part of a wave of protest from left-wing councils who objected to Whitehall's demand that they plan for nuclear war. Manchester started the trend in November 1980, and others followed, declaring they would not engage in the futile act of planning for nuclear survival, nor would they allow nuclear weapons to be transported across their boundaries. The rebels were told that if they failed to make civil defence plans, the Home Office would send someone to do it for them, and then charge the council for the privilege. In response, South Yorkshire, in what some might say was admirably blunt Yorkshire style, prepared the plans but did it with such lurid detail that Whitehall might have preferred their silence.

Having completed their planning in December 1988, South Yorkshire Fire and Civil Defence Authority immediately shared it with the media and the public, declaring that the electorate, in line with the council's policy of 'honest and realistic plan-making', had the right to know every awful detail. Its chairman, Councillor Frank White, said: 'These plans have been meticulously prepared – but I am still left with the gut reaction – why bother? The best indications are that the death and destruction following a nuclear war would be so vast that no amount of planning would make coping any easier.'[41] The council presented copies of the finished plans to the libraries in Sheffield, Doncaster, Rotherham and Barnsley for public consultation, and invited the media and photographers along for a press conference at Barnsley library.[42]

The planners had not minced their words, writing in the introduction of 'disposing of dead relatives in black plastic rubbish bags' and of plans to dig up local beauty spots such as Cannon Hall country park and the nature reserves at Thrybergh and Ulley Park so they could be used as mass burial grounds.[43] And whilst *Protect and Survive* had simply asked people to wrap their dead relatives in polythene, the South Yorkshire guidance described the ghastly logistics of that procedure, advising that 'the bag should not be too tightly sealed as pressure of the gases produced by a body decomposing is likely to rupture the bag and the resulting smell is likely to create unnecessary offence'.[44]

There was more distressing detail when it came to the disposal of bodies. When they were eventually collected by the authorities, South Yorkshire's corpses would be buried with a cross or other grave marker, and at the foot of the grave a bottle or can would be placed, half buried and with its open side pushed down into the soil. Inside would be a piece of paper bearing the name of the deceased ('if known'), their sex ('if determinable') and the date of burial. A white cross would also be painted on the heads of the corpses to indicate that they had been identified and their death recorded. To facilitate useful recording, 'parts of bodies should be treated as whole bodies except for statistical purposes when recovered heads should be used for counting'.[45] It would be hard to imagine a more powerful anti-nuclear protest.

In Glasgow, also a nuclear-free council, corpse disposal plans were equally plain and realistic, with the planners declaring that there were no solutions to the lack of plant, fuel and equipment for this dreadful job, and so 'the only realistic policy would be to abandon these areas along with the dead which they contained. These areas would certainly be rapidly abandoned by most mobile survivors.'[46] The Glasgow authorities also produced, as did many other nuclear-free councils, leaflets describing in detail the reality of nuclear war. Many councils distributed such leaflets to residents' homes – and this perhaps accounts for some people's false memory of having received a copy of *Protect and Survive*.

South Yorkshire's leaflet was titled *You and the Bomb*.[47] Printed in black, white and orange, like *Protect and Survive*, it was posted to 500,000 homes and described 'What a Nuclear Attack Would Do to South Yorkshire', based on advice from doctors and scientists, and the government's own conclusions from their various planning exercises. Here is a description of the horrors in Zone A, the ground zero of the attack:

> John is on his shift in a Sheffield engineering works when the bomb explodes. In seconds, the works are totally devastated by the blast and intense heat of the explosion. His wife Katie and their children are at home in Burngreave. They too are killed instantly. The whole area is unrecognisable. Roads and railways are obliterated, cars melt, and the River Don and River Sheaf boil dry. Eight of Sheffield's hospitals are destroyed. No help can be provided for the few survivors and they are left to die.[48]

Things are only marginally better in the outer zone of destruction, Zone D:

> Doris is elderly and lives alone in Armthorpe, Doncaster. The doors and windows of her house are blown in by the bomb at Finningley, and she is badly cut by flying glass. In the garden, a tree is uprooted by the gale-force winds which follow the blast. Doris knows that broken windows and doors let in radiation, but she is unable to repair them. Within an hour, deadly radioactive fallout begins to blow into her house. A fortnight later, her food and water have run out. Radiation has made Doris sick. Her hair has fallen out and she has diarrhoea. Bewildered by it all, she sits weak and shivering in a corner.

When it came to collecting the corpses, the leaflet drew on similar scenarios from history:

In Manila in 1945, about 39,000 people died after the US invasion against Japanese marines who refused to retreat or surrender. In the intense heat, the corpses rotted quickly. They were soon covered in flies and became a danger to health. Meat hooks were used to handle the bodies as they started to disintegrate. Mass burials were organised. But US troops were unable to participate for more than a week before being overcome by anorexia, nausea, vomiting, depression and insomnia. When they could sleep they had nightmares.[49]

But the rebels of South Yorkshire offered a bright side for those condemned to corpse disposal duty:

> Of course, not all bodies would require disposal because individuals close to the epicentre of a nuclear detonation would be vaporised, thousands would be buried beyond recovery under rubble or in areas of high radiation, and many more would be so mutilated by the effects of blast and fire as to no longer be recognisable human remains.[50]

It is easy to imagine the rebellious authors taking grim delight in such gruesome detail as it allowed them to comply with London's demands for war planning while still describing the horror of nuclear war. South Yorkshire's 'obedience' delivered a far more powerful protest than any anti-nuclear demonstration, badges or banners.

Councils across the country were forced to plan for the collection and disposal of potentially millions of nuclear dead. If the householder reading *Protect and Survive* was forced to imagine wrapping his mother in plastic and digging a shallow grave in the garden, at least the civil defence workers – made up of volunteers, council staff and forced labourers – who would have had to retrieve bodies from the rubble of a ruined Britain would be better equipped. The archives provide lists of what the corpse disposal squads would require:

> Rubber gloves
> Oilskin Jackets and trousers
> Rubber boots
> Face Masks (gauze)

Triangular bandages or cloth as Neckerchief
Towel and Soap
Haversack
And for the squad as a whole:
Picks and shovels – one for each manual worker
Disinfectant – drum per vehicle
Disinfectant – drum per disposal site
Sack coffins – 10,000[51]

Some authorities planned to get rid of the corpses quickly, with speed rather than dignity being the key concern. The thinking was that the sight of so many dead on the streets would utterly crush morale and diminish any hopes of post-war recovery. There were suggestions to tip heaps of corpses into abandoned quarries or mines, or pile them onto barges to be sunk at sea.[52] Mass burial or cremation were unlikely options due to the lack of fuel, machinery and manpower.

6 Taking Shelter

Nantwich in Cheshire is a pretty town, with cheery pubs and tea shops, hanging baskets and cobblestoned streets. There are polite signs by the road asking drivers to beware of ducks crossing. If you drive past the River Weaver and head out onto French Lane, the road takes you past hedgerows and meadows before narrowing into a single track. The glowering oaks bend their branches to inspect, and the bushes prod at your car window. You spot antennae spiking the horizon. Steel fencing flashes through the trees, with barbed wire on top. Here is where pretty olde England ends.

Just a few minutes' drive from charming Nantwich, the road has taken you to Hack Green nuclear bunker. The quick switch in the landscape is befuddling, from sunny countryside to brutal concrete. It feels like stepping into another dimension. You wonder what would happen to that idyllic town if the bomb went off. How would the cows in the field fare in the white nuclear flash? What would happen to the town's scarlet geraniums bobbing in their baskets? Would the river bubble? Would the cobblestones crack? What about all the people holding pint glasses in the Talbot and the Black Lion? I doubt anybody in the town I had just passed through was spending a moment's thought on that bunker at the end of the lane, calling you into a dreadful other world.

Most bunkers invite you down – down a steel ladder, down a spiral staircase, down a chilly sloping tunnel – but this one beckons me *up*. I walk up a concrete ramp, then step over a sleeping cat on the threshold. I click through a turnstile and immediately enter a cheerful café and gift shop: Union Jack bunting, glass cabinets and clinking crockery. A coffee machine hisses behind the counter. This is not how nuclear bunkers are supposed to look. I buy a coffee and a Crunchie and sit down, but it feels odd to eat a chocolate bar in a nuclear bunker. It almost seems disrespectful. The bunting bobs above my head in an air-conditioned breeze fragrant with espresso, and I unwrap my guilty snack quietly. No other tourists are here today at Hack Green Secret Nuclear Bunker, where I was led by toffee-coloured English Tourist Board signs. The gift shop offers fridge magnets, dosimeters, some model planes, a yellow civil defence armband and a pair of 'Russian Radiation Goggles'. The Crunchie lies uneaten on the table. It feels strange to be indulging in sweets, gifts and coffee when below me lie three floors of nuclear bunker. It would be like laughing in church.

Hack Green was a bomb decoy site during the Second World War, designed to draw the Luftwaffe away from the railway at Crewe, and in 1941 it became an RAF radar station. In the Cold War, it was equipped with advanced long-range radar to detect incoming Soviet bombers, trying to give Britain time to scramble her defences. Then, in 1976, the site was sold by the Ministry of Defence to the Home Office so it might be reshaped as a seat of regional government if nuclear war came. At that time, planners had provisionally divided the country into civil defence regions, and if the bomb exploded and London was destroyed, each region would be governed independently from local bunkers until central government was able to take control again. There would be no bunkers for the people – only for the politicians, civil servants and experts judged necessary to keep Britain functioning. Whereas in the earlier days of the Cold War the emphasis had been on the rescue and welfare of survivors, continuity of government was the post-nuclear priority when Hack Green took on its new role in the 1970s. The people would now be expected to look after themselves, while the authorities and experts in the bunkers tended to the essentials: maintaining law and order, restoring facilities, providing health services.

Other countries, notably Switzerland, Sweden and Russia, continued to provide nuclear shelters for their populations. One of the world's largest nuclear bunkers is located inside the Sonnenberg motorway tunnel outside Lucerne. Seven storeys deep, it can hold 20,000 people for a fortnight and supply them with clean air, water and electricity. It has a 328-bed hospital with intensive care facilities, two operating theatres and a mortuary. Soothing music can be piped throughout the tunnels, but for survivors who refuse to be pacified, the bunker also has a small jail. In Moscow, the splendid and cavernous metro stations would have doubled as nuclear shelters, with the population expected to pour down the escalators on hearing the siren before massive blast doors would seal the entrances and the citizens would hunker on the platforms beneath the trembling chandeliers.

There were no such plans for Britain's population. During the Blitz, people had sought shelter in the Tube, at the bottom of their garden, in the basements of department stores and in caves and church crypts, but in the Cold War, no provisions were made. Bunkers such as Hack Green were reserved for officialdom, as was the enormous bunker beneath the Wiltshire countryside known as Burlington, which was like Hack Green on a massive scale.[1] Originally a limestone quarry, it had housed a huge underground aircraft factory in the Second World War. When the Cold War began and Whitehall was looking for a place of safety far from London, the cavernous spaces and vast corridors of the old factory seemed ideal. It was to Burlington that central government would relocate in the last days before nuclear war, with 4,000 selected politicians, scientists, analysts, strategists, clerical staff, technicians, cooks and medics being rushed to the West Country to be joined at the last moment by the prime minister,[2] and there they would remain for weeks.[3]

Burlington had 800 offices, dormitories, a medical wing, a BBC studio, a laundry, and a huge telephone exchange to connect it with the world above. Storerooms were stuffed with wooden crates holding 11 million sheets of copy paper, 10,000 ballpoint pens and 400 typewriters, some fitted with Cyrillic keys. There were 4,600 mattresses, and stacks of steel-legged office chairs, still in their dusty paper wrapping.[4] There was provision for underground religious worship too, with plans to supply altar cloths, prayer books and candlesticks,[5] but persistent rumours that the bunker housed a pub, the Rose and Crown, were false. There would be praying, but no drinking. People might seek comfort in food, however. There was a huge canteen and a vast kitchen to feed the 4,000 staff, and the latter was generously equipped with industrial cake-mixers and bread-makers, automatic potato-peelers and coffee machines. There was even a nifty device on the shelves called a ButtaPatta, so that butter put out on the canteen tables could be nicely shaped – a nod to British propriety at a time when nuclear war would be blackening the limestone above.

With its dormitories, medical wing and canteen, Burlington seems like a spartan boarding school, a setting with which many of Britain's top politicians and civil servants would have been familiar, and the travel arrangements for getting there in a nuclear crisis do have the ring of a nightmarish school trip. The staff selected for duty wouldn't know their names had been added to the list of the post-nuclear chosen until one dreadful day when their boss would hand them written instructions. They had been carefully chosen, not just on the basis of their skills but for their lack of claustrophobia, mental illness or any physical impediments. Of course, you cannot properly predict a person's ability to face Doomsday, but those with a troubling HR file would have been instantly omitted. Still, if younger men were picked who had wives and young children at home, could they be depended upon to leave them in a crisis and scramble to the West Country? There was simply no way of knowing. To ease the separation of families, the selected staff would be able to draw an advance of £25 on their wages, and have all subsequent monies paid directly to the spouse. It was anybody's guess, of course, if banks and supermarkets would still be functioning normally in these dreadful final days, and indeed, if they would still be there after the attack. This was little more than a bureaucratic conceit, then, a comforting measure rather than a practical one.

The letter handed to the lucky civil servant was short on detail, telling them they'd been 'selected for duty at an important wartime headquarters' and 'so far as anyone can say you may be there for about one month'.[6] Brief instructions followed. They were to go home and pack a small bag, then return immediately to the office. 'You should not reveal to anyone beyond your immediate family that you are going to the headquarters and you should not be drawn into speculation as to your future whereabouts.'

In an oddly comic tone that shades the whole exercise as an apocalyptic school outing, they were also advised to bring 'pocket money', 'chocolate and biscuits' and a book for entertainment. Then they must 'keep together' as they made their way from their Westminster offices to designated pick-up points at Horse Guards Avenue, Marsham Street and Gresham Street. Buses would take the nervous groups to Kensington Olympia station, where special trains bearing the decoy destination of Taunton were waiting to evacuate them to the West Country. The trains would take them to Warminster, where they would be fed in a barracks on the edge of the town before army trucks delivered them to the Burlington bunker. When they finally arrived at their secret destination, they might have felt a little underwhelmed. 'Dust,' remarked a Cabinet Office official when he visited in the early 1970s. 'I couldn't believe that such a scruffy place would be the last seat of what government would be left.'[7]

Gimme shelter

As scruffy as Burlington was, there would be no such refuge for the British people. The issue was often debated privately in Whitehall, and publicly in Parliament and in the media, but public nuclear shelters were never built. The main reason, of course, was cost. In 1981, the civil defence minister spoke of the 'enormous expense . . . we're talking about billions and billions and billions of pounds'.[8] A Home Office assessment the previous year estimated that it would cost £70 billion to shelter every person in the country – at a time when total government spending amounted to £100 billion per year. The second reason was geography: Britain is a small country, so if hydrogen bombs struck its military, civilian and industrial targets, much of it would be wiped out by the ensuing blast, fire and fallout. Against this furious destructive force a public shelter at the end of the street would be useless.

Instead, Britain relied on deterrence, with politicians arguing that if the country possessed nuclear weapons, it would discourage the enemy from launching an attack, so there would be no need for shelters. This was the sinister logic of mutually assured destruction (which has the fitting acronym MAD): if East and West both possessed awesome nuclear firepower, then neither would be foolish enough to launch a nuclear attack, as it would merely assure their own destruction via retaliation in kind. But anti-nuclear campaigners despaired of MAD logic, which drove the arms race at a furious pace and claimed that the only way to be safe from nuclear weapons was to amass more and more of them.

However, when British politicians explained why shelters would not be built, and spoke to the press about sombre details like cost, they didn't take into account Britain's shelter nostalgia. The Second World War was still a relatively recent memory, and many believed that public shelters had protected them from the German bombs. Popular culture presented sheltering as a cheerful, defiant collective experience, with Londoners singing 'Roll Out the Barrel' and sticking two fingers up at Hitler as they hunkered down on the Tube platforms. Yet folk memory of the Blitz ignored the more unpleasant aspects of that experience. A *Times* report from November 1940 was horrified at the lack of toilet facilities in some public shelters: 'The sanitary arrangements are utterly inadequate and so placed as to ensure the minimum of privacy and the maximum of filth and stench for numbers of men, women and children who are forced by overcrowding to spread their bedding close by.'[9] The *British Medical Journal* reported that in one shelter for 300 people, the only toilet was three buckets behind a curtain,[10] and highlighted outbreaks of diphtheria and laryngitis, plus the easy transmission of the common cold.

But even with the smells, the coughs and sneezes and the crying babies, there was some comfort in the shared experience of sheltering. Hearing the roar of the bombs or the dreadful whistle of the doodlebugs whilst huddled with friends and neighbours was, for many, preferable to enduring it alone in the gloom, and so when the nuclear threat arose, it was natural that people looked to the government to once again provide them with public shelters. But even if the money and will had existed, it would have been a hard task. Many shelters had been dismantled or repurposed as soon as the war was over. By 1948, most of the domestic Anderson and Morrison shelters had been sold off for scrap metal.[11] There was no spare cash in austerity Britain to build new shelters, let alone construct massively reinforced ones that might stand a chance against the new atomic bomb. Rebuilding and repairing bombed houses was the priority for the post-war Attlee government, and this ate up most of the available steel supply. Money was also needed for founding the 'New Jerusalem' of the welfare state. As early as October 1946, the Home Office said it would need £260 million to build shelters for 11 million key workers – a sum exceeding the entire NHS estimate for 1949–50.[12] Unsurprisingly, the idea was rejected.

Shoot thy neighbour

America had no such shortages of steel and cash. Its post-war economy was booming, and companies began offering fallout shelters to the flush consumer, an easy expansion for businesses who were already building tornado and hurricane shelters for Americans in the Midwest and coastal regions. But if money and space were no hindrance in America, there was one little niggle: the question of 'shelter morality'.

If the British would have welcomed nuclear shelters, some US media commentators were appalled at the idea of red-blooded American patriots hiding from a communist assault. Sheltering underground was evolution in reverse, 'a reversion to cave man barbarism',[13] they cried. But beside the churlish argument about whether shelters would reduce gutsy Yanks to creeping moles was the more troubling debate on how to protect your shelter, not from the bomb, but from your own friends and neighbours.

American fallout shelters were largely individual enterprises. Families were urged to buy and build their own protection under the lawn or in the basement, but this raised an uncomfortable question: if the shelter is on your property, and was built with your own muscle and your own hard-earned dollars, with space and supplies only for Mom, Pop, Junior and Sally, what do you do when your friends and neighbours – those who chuckled at your nuclear paranoia and laughed at all your peaceful Sundays lost to building your shelter when you could have been golfing and barbecuing – come pounding on the door begging to be let in? Perhaps only a true Christian, faced with terrified townsfolk in distress, would swing wide the door and let everyone inside – even if that means there is no space for him. More realistic was a 1961 episode of *The Twilight Zone* called 'The Shelter'. Bill, a jovial and beloved local doctor, has built a shelter in his basement, a DIY project for which the neighbours have affectionately mocked him, but when the sirens sound, they plead for entry. When the good doctor refuses, these wholesome small-town Americans turn savage and start battering their way inside. When it's revealed that the siren was a false alarm, the embarrassed neighbours are forced to face one another with all their civility stripped away.

In 1959, the authorities in Los Angeles realised they could not put a number to the fallout shelters that existed in the city, as people were building them in secret because they didn't want the neighbours to know they had one tucked at the bottom of the garden. Some tried to conceal the building work by having a swimming pool installed at the same time, or by pretending they were having improvements done to the basement.

And so the question of shelter morality entered US public debate. Should you allow your vulnerable neighbour into the shelter even if by doing so you deny food, space and safety to your own children? Should responsible families who display the lauded Protestant work ethic accommodate those who couldn't be bothered to prepare themselves for nuclear war? Is it right to bar the door to friends? And what does a God-fearing American do when those friends and neighbours resort to violence to try and force their way in?

For some people this was no question of morality: it was a simple, no-nonsense matter of defending your property. One man from the Chicago suburbs put it bluntly:

> When I get my shelter finished I'm going to mount a machine gun at the hatch to keep the neighbours out if the bomb falls. I'm deadly serious about this. If the stupid American public will not do what they have to to save themselves I'm not going to run the risk of not being able to use the shelter I've taken the trouble to provide to save my own family.[14]

Meanwhile, a man from Texas boasted of his guns and tear gas and the shelter's thick wooden door: 'This isn't to keep radiation out. It's to keep people out.'[15]

A civil defence meeting in Hartford, Connecticut, in 1961 produced some brutal honesty from a local resident named John, who owned a shelter. When his neighbour and good friend asked what he'd do if she and her baby begged to be let in, John replied: 'It would be too bad. You should have built a shelter of your own. I've got to look out for my own family.' What if we had built one, she said, but the blast blocked the entrance with rubble. What then? Would you let us in? He'd still refuse was the answer. 'Suppose I wouldn't go away and kept trying to get in?' the neighbour asked. 'Would you shoot us?' John replied that if the only way he could keep her out was by shooting her and her baby, he would have to do it.[16]

As the population agonised, squabbled and readied their guns and gas canisters, religious ministers tried to offer advice. In a 1961 article in *Time* magazine, a reverend from Atlanta was unequivocal: 'If someone wanted to use the shelter then you yourself should get out and let him use it.' He admitted that 'That's not what would happen, but that's the strict Christian application.' In an article entitled 'Ethics at the Shelter Doorway', a certain Father McHugh disagreed. He believed it was absurd to preach that you must love your neighbour more than your own family, as this stance showed Christian teaching running directly against the natural human instinct for survival. He argued that it was 'the height of nonsense to say a man should thrust his family into the rain of fallout when unsheltered neighbours plead for entrance'.[17]

With guns and God cluttering the debate in the early 1960s, the public discourse became so heated that President Kennedy withdrew his former warm encouragement for Americans to build shelters in their homes. Attention now shifted to public fallout shelters, which removed the thorny issue of private property and its gun-wielding defence. America organised thousands of communal fallout shelters in cities across the country, usually in the basements of large public buildings. The federal government would supply the rations, but it would be the responsibility of local authorities to physically stock and maintain the shelters. The main ration was 'survival biscuits', although the allowance would be sparse. In 1962, for example, it would allow a calorie intake of just 714 per day For this reason, some states aimed to supplement the federal ration supply with their own.[18]

The idea was that, as had happened during the Blitz in Britain, people would make a dash for the nearest shelter as soon as the siren sounded and would remain there until fallout decreased. While the location of the shelters in the basements of large, sturdy public buildings offered a decent chance of protection against fallout, they were not fortified bunkers so could offer no special protection from nuclear blast, heat or firestorm. Each was marked by a distinctive yellow and black sign on the building's exterior, some of which still remain to this day.

'What could be safer than a stout medieval fortress?'

The presence of these public shelters soothed America's conscience and cooled the debate about shelter morality, even though simple arithmetic showed there would never be enough fallout shelter space for everyone. In 1966, British civil defence planners discussed the merit of public fallout shelters and what supplies, food and medicines they would need. They envisaged a ration of biscuits and boiled sweets with a similar calorific value to the American allowance, but it never became official policy,[19] and it seems obvious that by 1980, the message had sunk in among the British population that there was no escape from the nuclear holocaust, and that sheltering would be futile. Members of the public interviewed that year for the BBC's *Panorama*, and for the Tyne Tees show *Check It Out* were resigned both to a lack of official shelters and to certain death if the bomb dropped. Asked what they'd do if they heard the nuclear siren, they replied:

'Go home and get my kids. Drive out to the countryside somewhere.'

'Waste of time, innit, going anywhere. You've had it, ain't ya?'

'Well, what could you do? They haven't built shelters for anybody, have they? You wouldn't stand a chance. All you'd wind up with is a lump in your trousers.'[20]

'I'd get down a drain, out the road.'

'Go outside and welcome it . . . let's end it all.'[21]

Even if the tentative plans for British public fallout shelters had been put into practice, they would have been drastically different from the shelters of the last war, because they could not protect you from a nuclear blast. Arguably, no structure can. Even the USA's massive Cheyenne Mountain complex, hidden beneath 9,000 feet of pink granite, would not be able to withstand a direct hit.[22] It is obvious that Britain's little Anderson shelters would be useless under nuclear attack; even under conventional bombing during the Blitz they offered no guarantee of safety. Neither did the deepest parts of the London Underground, with Balham station taking a direct hit on 14 October 1940 that killed 66 people. The only defence against nuclear blast was avoidance of nuclear war.

The communal fallout shelter, therefore, would merely receive survivors of the blast, offering them a hiding place within thick walls where they could dwell with strangers for a fetid fortnight until radiation levels decreased. It was a very different scenario from the Blitz, when people simply hunkered down for the night before slipping back into relatively normal life and fresh air the following morning. In a nuclear war, they would be confined for many days, raising awful concerns about hygiene, food, water, ventilation and mental health – and what they would find when they emerged again into the outside world.

In the early Cold War, when the government was quietly considering public fallout shelters in Britain, planners naturally thought about the London Underground, and in 1950 the Ministry of Works was asked to identify suitable stations for this purpose. A handful of stations had been built especially deep and so might offer reasonable protection from blast, flooding and fallout. These stations were Belsize Park, Camden Town, Goodge Street, Stockwell, Clapham North, Clapham Common, Clapham South and Chancery Lane, the latter becoming the heavily protected Kingsway telephone exchange in the 1950s. As a legacy of the Blitz, each had an air raid shelter built beneath the platforms, and so could be stocked and prepared without impeding the smooth peacetime running of the trains. There was room in each shelter for 8,000 people, sleeping in three-tier bunks. But the main problem was access, with the stations having just two entrance shafts, served by two narrow spiral staircases and a lift that could only take six people at a time.[23] There were concerns about a crush on the stairs as panicked people rushed for cover, as had happened at Bethnal Green Underground station on 3 March 1943, when 173 people lost their lives through crush injuries or suffocation.

Some enterprising Brits were looking elsewhere for shelter. Castle Acre parish council in rural Norfolk wrote to the authorities in November 1980 seeking permission to turn the ruins of their local castle, dating back to the eleventh century, into a nuclear shelter. With its thick gnarled walls and hiding space tucked beneath a gargantuan mound of grassy earth, it seemed a wise choice, but a tart reply from the Ancient Monuments Secretariat snuffed out their plans:

> We do not share your view that the castle is suitable for such use; there are no cellars in the castle and although as you say the walls are very thick and would probably withstand blast waves, the

Castle would offer no protection against fallout. It would cost a great deal of money to put a roof on the Castle and even if this money were available, we could not consider carrying out such a measure to this very important ancient monument. It would also presumably be necessary to provide adequate sanitary arrangements in such a public shelter – again this is unacceptable from an ancient monument point of view.[24]

The council's letter was part of a small wave of enquiries to the government requesting permission to transform Britain's castles into shelters, and it prompted the Department of the Environment to issue guidance on how to politely decline these anxious requests. *The Architects' Journal* offered gentle mockery: 'What could be safer than a stout medieval fortress? Just pile the ratepayers into the local dungeon until the coast is clear.'[25] The 'ancient monument point of view' certainly got full consideration, though some may have wondered what the point of great heritage was with no one left alive to appreciate it. Indeed, this strong desire to protect things rather than people played a key role in Britain's nuclear war preparations: Operation Methodical would have seen the evacuation of London's art treasures to Manod quarry in Wales and the limestone quarries near Bradford on Avon in Wiltshire.

The dangers of boiled sweets

Deep in the quarries and mines, the artworks wouldn't require food, medicines or water, but when British planners toyed with the idea of introducing public fallout shelters, it was recognised that the inhabitants would need all those items and more. It was expected that people would bring their own food into the shelter, and as they would have been encouraged to stockpile in the last weeks before war, when tensions were building, the hope was that each would arrive with rations of their own. But in the chaos of a nuclear attack, this was hardly a certainty, and it would be an ugly prospect to have some people tucking into their packed lunches whilst those next to them went hungry. It was decided, therefore, to stock the shelters in advance with basic rations, including boiled sweets, special hard biscuits, and milk powder.

Every person seeking shelter would be fed just 700 kcals per day, instead of the recommended calorie intake of 2,500 for an adult male. This pitiful amount was justified on the grounds that the people would not only be 'almost totally inactive' inside the shelter but would be able to supplement their ration with the food they had brought themselves. Even in this grim scenario, strange little worries made their way into the documents. Planners knew that sweets would be a quick and easy way to deliver carbohydrates to survivors, but there were concerns that 'continual sucking of boiled sweets could cause mouth sores'. Following US practice, therefore, sugar lumps would be stored in shelters; unlike glassy lemon drops, these would dissolve easily on the tongue.[26]

The shelters would also be stocked with tranquillisers to treat those who suffered breakdowns or bursts of claustrophobia, and there would be drugs to deal with the ugly early effects of radiation poisoning. Home Office papers discussed a device called an Autoject: a disposable syringe that could be used to quickly deliver fast-acting sedatives like paraldehyde or chlorpromazine. According to the Chief Scientific Officer, 'These could be used to knock out quickly people threatening violent behaviour, including epileptics. The alternative would be to use strong tranquilliser tablets crushed in water and administered by mouth but this would not only be more difficult to administer without spilling but would also take a much longer time to become effective.' He also noted that hospitals would have been largely emptied of patients in the countdown to nuclear war, and this could mean that psychiatric patients suddenly without their usual care and medication might find themselves amongst the people confined in the shelter.[27]

Despite these worries about panics and breakdowns, we might expect, if the policy had ever become official, that people would be relieved that public fallout shelters existed. Even if it was doubtful that they could offer much protection, would they not be a sign of a benevolent government trying to protect its people? CND would have disagreed. They argued that the existence of fallout shelters – indeed the existence of any civil defence measures – implied that nuclear war was survivable, and that it was therefore an acceptable political risk. A representative of CND wrote in *The Guardian* in June 1981 that 'a nation with nuclear weapons which attempts to protect its civilian population in nuclear shelters is condemning them to incineration, asphyxiation, or emergence to an irradiated, empty land, deprived of resources – a dead civilisation whose few survivors would fight it out for the bit of food left over. Nuclear war is not, in any meaning of the word, survivable.'[28]

Plans for communal fallout shelters were occasionally discussed in Whitehall, but never came to fruition. The official government advice was always for the public to fortify their homes if war threatened – and if they wanted a shelter in the garden or basement then they would have to pay for it themselves. In the 1980s, plenty of companies and enterprising individuals popped up offering all manner of domestic shelters, including toughened tents and hi-tech tubular steel contraptions to be buried deep in the garden soil. There were even proposed underground communities for a carefully chosen few. In Chippenham, a company called Rusepalm Shelters claimed to be constructing 2,500 'family units' in an old MoD ammunition dump:

> Among the apartment owners will be doctors, nurses, social workers, craftsmen, sportsmen, teachers and experts in many fields but, most of all, responsible people with families and the will to survive a nuclear war. This main shelter is constructed to provide safety for you, your children, and your children's children. That the human race is meant to survive is proved every time a child is born.[29]

Meanwhile, there were plans for the well-to-do of Peterborough to take shelter in a maze of steel tubes at a cost of £2,000 per head. The tubes were to be sunk beneath the town's industrial area, Fengate; in the end, the council refused planning permission, worried about the flood of traffic that would ensue as people rushed to their steely shelter, but also because it was concerned that the tubes could become flooded with sewage.[30]

Money and class did of course play a major role in Britain's shelter debate, as the construction of a private shelter was an expensive endeavour and required a sizeable garden or a spacious home in which to assemble it, as well as the privilege and security of home ownership. The old antagonism between town and country was also relevant. The people of Somerset may have already grumbled about wealthy Londoners buying up rural properties for use as second homes or weekend retreats, but in 1981, the *Central Somerset Gazette* reported that some disused railway tunnels near Shepton Mallet were to be transformed into 'holocaust havens' for wealthy Londoners. The newspaper spoke of 'survival for the rich' and joked that nuclear warfare was turning into class warfare: 'No one opposes a rich person from London buying some of the area's beautiful but expensive (exclusive, elitist!) country houses and estates. All things being equal, that's life. It's when we face death that our finer, or baser, feelings of equality are roused.'[31]

If nuclear hope could be purchased by the rich, what of those who could not afford it? As shelter building was a private initiative, there were some who believed that the government should step up to help those who lacked the funds. In 1984, an Aberdeen man, John Sangster, who was living on benefits, asked for extra money so he might build himself a nuclear shelter. He applied for a benefit known as the 'single payment', which was intended for one-off items like a cooker or furniture if it was judged that the item was needed to avoid 'serious damage or serious risk to the health or safety' of the claimant. In support of his claim, he pointed out that his local council, Grampian, were spending £50,000 on upgrading their own shelter, and argued that 'Social Security claimants have as good a right to protection as anyone else.' His claim included spare ground on which to build; digging equipment; reinforced concrete; steel beams and sandbags, plus a stove, saucepan, cutlery, tin opener, map, compass and toilet rolls.[32] It was quickly rejected on the grounds that it represented his personal view of the future rather than an existing need. A similar claim was lodged in Derby by a Mr Bill Mooney, a bus driver who intended to build a shelter in his garden in the perhaps appropriately named Deadman's Lane. As with Mr Sangster's claim, it was rejected.[33]

Had their claims been successful, what kind of shelter might they have built? In the 1980s, plenty of companies were offering to design and assemble smaller shelters for the cellar or back garden. Dafal, based in Hastings, offered shelters with the patriotic names Churchill, Bulldog and Kingdom, and displayed them in 1980 'with a flash of razzmatazz'[34] at a launch event attended by the beauty queen of Kent, followed by a slap-up buffet lunch at the Old Golden Cross inn. It was the go-getting 1980s, and the threat of nuclear war was another business opportunity that was too good to miss.

Protect and Survive Monthly

There was no need for lunch and beauty queens for the companies who advertised their shelters in *Protect and Survive Monthly*. This was an eccentric British magazine published in 1981–2 and aimed at what we might today call 'preppers': people who were convinced nuclear war was coming and were ready to splash the cash to protect themselves. In typical style, its editor wrote, 'Dear Reader, Do you dream, like me, of green pleasant lands?' before going on to warn, 'ARMAGEDDON IS SURELY COMING . . . and if we do nothing our utopian dreams will die with us.'[35] The magazine came with lurid front covers, often resembling sci-fi comics, and featured articles with titles like 'Wartime Food Stores', 'Evacuation via Tunnels?', 'Living with the Aftermath', and 'Survival Without Doctors'. There was a particularly memorable contribution from a clergyman asking whether we might turn to cannibalism after nuclear war.[36]

Yet it often seemed that these articles were just an excuse for the true purpose of the magazine: advertising. Its pages were jammed with countless adverts for air purification systems, freeze-dried food, specialist radio equipment, light sticks, Geiger counters, NBC suits and 'Survival Kitty Gold' (consisting of 'official Fractional Kruger-rands'). You could send a cheque for £3.50 and receive a neat 'Survival Tie', which showed a radiation symbol surrounding a phoenix rising from the nuclear ashes – 'an attractively designed, well-made tie for those who'd like to identify themselves as a survival enthusiast'.

But the most numerous adverts were for fallout shelters. Readers were offered nuclear havens that were 'completely pre-assembled and ready for instant DIY installation'. 'Low on cost, low on space and high on protection', they were said to provide 'truly amazing capacity in a sensible size'.[37] Or you could splash out on a nicely timber-lined 'self-contained luxury survival module' that claimed to be 'designed on facts and research' and came with six beds, water tanks, toilet and shower and a useful escape hatch. The shelter, readers were told, 'can be used as a home in the aftermath of nuclear attack until conventional homes have been repaired or rebuilt'. Alternatively, if you weren't tempted by timber-lined luxury, the savvy Mole Shelters tried to flog their hideout by pointing out that it could be used as a music room, sauna, cinema or cellar until the dreaded day arrived. 'Extension Now . . . Shelter If!' announced their optimistic ad.[38]

Other companies sought to indulge readers in dreamy sci-fi coolness. Biosphere Corporation offered the Egg, a futuristic ovoid shelter made of white fibreglass with a rigid foam core that was designed to nestle snugly underground, with any nasty blast waves simply gliding over its eggy curves. If you wished to shelter with friends, several Eggs could be buried in the soil together and made to interconnect, like some apocalyptic maze. 'The Egg is ahead of its time!' declared the advert.

The manufacturers claimed it could double as a holiday home: 'We visualise the Egg as much more than a fallout shelter. Here is a bug-free, rodent-free, vandal-free vacation home . . . The Egg can be enjoyed year-round because it is buried well beneath frost levels.'[39] It could be kitted out with carpet and cushions, a TV and radio/cassette player, a vacuum-assisted toilet, a freeze-dried food assortment, as well as, ominously, some shovels. The clever little thing even offered reassurance to potential buyers who might 'fear entombment'. Above the Egg's escape hatch (pun intended?) sat a cylinder filled with dry sand. In an emergency, when the Egg-dwellers opened the hatch, the protective sand would fall into the shelter, allowing them to scamper up through the empty cylinder to the surface. The Egg's creator, John G. Brodie, told *Protect and Survive Monthly*: 'I am devoting all my time and energies to the business. In fact, I describe myself as one who has all his baskets in one Egg.'[40]

These shelter adverts made some bold and confident claims, with Blair Engineering of Chesterfield announcing that their shelters 'in the event of a nuclear war would save the occupants' lives'. 'Saves Money. Saves Worry. Saves Life', declared Bentall Simplex.[41] The Advertising Standards Authority had to intervene when one manufacturer claimed, 'You can assure your own family survival with a nuclear shelter.'[42] And it wasn't just shelters that were being touted as a way to dodge the holocaust. The editor of *Protect and Survive Monthly* described one less reputable vendor: 'Someone is going round with a lead umbrella which you wheel around behind you until the time of attack when you open it up.'[43]

Obviously, nuclear protection could not be properly tested until the time came, when there'd be little chance of consumer justice or a quick refund. There were fears that in a relatively consequence-free business, 'nuclear cowboys' were using the shelter fad to make a quick buck, 'going to the more expensive parts of town, putting the fear of God into old ladies, and selling them useless shelters at outrageous prices', as the *Observer* put it.[44] By late 1980, at least 300 firms were offering shelters to British households, and the lack of regulation meant that many of the models on sale were indeed useless. *The Guardian* reported that 'some of their design features were actually lethal. There are shelters which use combustible materials or lead linings which, combined with inadequate heat insulation, would melt and burn the occupants; others recommend the use of naked flame cookers, a totally pointless way of using up your oxygen, or suggest storing highly flammable fuels inside the shelter.'[45]

In 1981, the government was prodded into action and issued its own nuclear shelter recommendations. In the Home Office booklet *Domestic Nuclear Shelters*, it set out approved designs, ranging from the basic Type 1a – 'easily constructed improvised garden shelter using household materials' such as shovels, tape measure, blankets, pillowcases, pegs, string and doors – up to the complex and expensive Type 4, which was a reinforced concrete shelter that had to be constructed by a professional builder under the guidance of a chartered civil engineer.[46] But this attempt at bringing clarity and standards to the new shelter-building industry caused problems on another level. Local authorities argued that current building regulations required them to treat such shelters as a 'habitable room', which meant they were obliged to have a window – a fatal flaw in any underground shelter.[47]

Worried residents who were stuck in a high-rise or didn't have the space or means to dig a shelter in their garden might have taken comfort from a portable 'commuter survival pack'. Sold by a company called Aftermath, costing £115 and no bigger than a collapsible umbrella, it contained 'a silver foil protective blanket, iron rations and medical supplies, a radiation dose meter and a miniature radio'.[48] Yet nuclear survival in Britain was really always pegged to having spare cash and a big garden. Indeed, some shelter-builders leapt on the 1980s DIY craze by comparing the addition of a shelter to the installation of central heating or a nice conservatory in that it would bump up the value of your home. *The Guardian* reported that one Londoner had built a £15,000 shelter in his garden thanks to a mortgage from the

Abbey National, whose secretary, in response to media enquiries, primly replied, 'One gets all kind of strange requests. We don't want to poke our nose too much into people's affairs.'[49]

A Guide to Armageddon

In 1982, the BBC broadcast *A Guide to Armageddon*, a short documentary that offered a grim consumer guide to the nuclear shelters on the market. Two ordinary London couples were asked to assemble various types of shelter, some home-made and others purchased and built according to manufacturers' instructions. Joy and Eric lived in a sturdy Victorian terrace in Finsbury Park, three miles from St Paul's, where viewers were asked to imagine a nuclear bomb had burst. How could they prepare themselves? In one scenario they were advised to keep buckets of water around the house with which to fight fires, and to paint their window panes white to deter the heat rays. They were then to hunker under the stairs surrounded by a little fortress made of heavy luggage, bags of clothes and unscrewed doors. 'Joy and Eric should survive,' viewers were told, 'at least, for seventeen seconds.' But then the blast wave would arrive and demolish their home, taking with it their carefully arranged buckets and bags.

The couple then tried to build the various shelters recommended for construction in the back garden, and soon encountered a maddening host of problems. Digging a trench, they reached the water table and the hole was flooded with eight inches of water. ('Bloody hell,' sighed Eric.) Flooding aside, did they have the necessary materials? asked the film's narrator. Did they have the money to buy them? Was their garden big enough? They found it was too small to yield the required earth with which to cover their shelter, and so had to order an extra four and a half tons of soil to give them the necessary protection. The problems continued. How do you dig if the ground is frozen in winter? Will you strike sewage pipes below? Crucially, of course, to be able to embark on a building project that, the narrator told viewers, took 'a long hard weekend', Joy and Eric needed sufficient advance warning.

Next they attempted to assemble another shelter, an indoor steel box like the wartime Morrison shelter. They put it together in the living room and piled bricks around it to offer extra layers of protection. Surprisingly, this 1940s solution might well withstand the house falling down on top of it – but could there be any guarantee of a rescue party to dig them out, or had Joy and Eric constructed their own steel coffin? This scenario also didn't take account of firestorms – after all, their house sat in the middle of the fire zone extending out from St Paul's. 'Inside your shelter you might not only be roasted, but suffocate,' said the narrator. The film revealed that the various steel, concrete or fibreglass constructions offered for sale by private companies, while beyond the pocket of most ordinary consumers, were little more than death traps. But if you were fortunate enough to be able to afford a top-of-the-range shelter, pumped with filtered clean air, kitted with a proper toilet and soft bedding, and with shelves bursting with tinned spaghetti and noodle soup, would you have the courage to defend it against desperate friends and neighbours?

In an early experiment with what we would now call reality TV, the second couple, Kenneth and Elizabeth, from Shepherd's Bush, were given the challenge of constructing a shelter in their back garden and then living inside it for two weeks with no contact with the outside world – a fortnight being the period expected for fallout to decrease to acceptable levels. If Joy and Eric had struggled with the physical aspects of shelter building, Kenneth and Elizabeth were to reveal the mental and psychological strain. The camera showed them fidgeting and dozing inside their tiny shelter, 36 inches wide. Kenneth reported to the camera that they were restless, stiff and unable to sleep. With a cigarette between her lips, Elizabeth carefully removed her trousers below her blanket, and then used the toilet bucket off-camera. The film was brave enough to ask viewers how they would cope with using the bucket in such close quarters with no ventilation when they might be suffering from panic or radiation sickness, both of which could provoke diarrhoea and vomiting.

Toilet training

In 1984, a similar shelter experiment was carried out in Limehouse, in east London, by a CND activist who was aiming to show how futile the project was. Ben Hayden built the Home Office-recommended

A selection of *Protect and Survive Monthly*, a British magazine, published 1981–82, which sought to prepare its readers for nuclear war. 'Armageddon is surely coming,' wrote the editor, C. Bruce Sibley.

The vandalised and fire-damaged interior of Barnton Quarry, a bunker in the Edinburgh suburbs. It is undergoing careful restoration and will re-open as a museum.

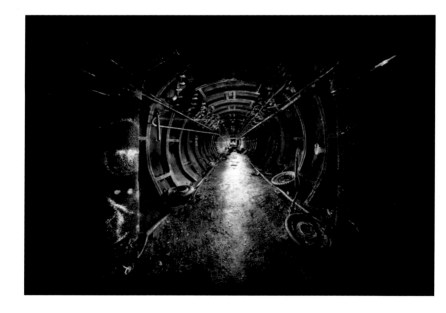

At the end of a pretty country lane outside Nantwich in Cheshire lies Hack Green bunker. Originally used as a decoy site to protect Crewe railway junction during the Second World War, it is now a museum.

The tiny Royal Observer Corps Monitoring Post in the hills at Skelmorlie, North Ayrshire. Closed in 1991 when the Corps stood down, it has been carefully restored by ex-observer Frank Alexander.

The *Columba*, one of three specially designed ferries commissioned by the government in 1964 for use in a nuclear war. She now sails as the *Hebridean Princess*, having mercifully never been called to her nuclear role.

An advert from *Protect and Survive Monthly*. The magazine featured many others, advertising nuclear shelters, freeze-dried meals, dosimeters, respirators and short courses under 'realistic conditions' at the School of Atomic Survival.

Only appearing on screen for 20 seconds, and with no name or speaking role, the traffic warden has nonetheless become an iconic image of *Threads* and graced the cover of the *Radio Times* in September 1984 to promote the film.

A scene from *The War Game*, showing the aftermath of a nuclear attack on Kent. Many of these dreadful scenes were informed by the wartime firestorms in Germany.

Collapsible coffins are demonstrated for the camera at the rear of St Andrew's House in Edinburgh. Designed to lend dignity and ceremony to hasty mass burials, they would have been futile in a nuclear war.

At home

All at home must go to the fall-out room and stay inside the inner refuge, keeping the radio tuned for Government advice and instructions.

Stay in your refuge

The dangers will be so intense that you may all need to stay inside your inner refuge in the fall-out room for at least forty-eight hours. If you need to go to the lavatory, or to replenish food or water supplies, do not stay outside your refuge for a second longer than is necessary.

The government's infamous *Protect and Survive* booklet from 1980 with its advice to burrow under the stairs and bury your own dead.

A Carrier Control Point. 250 were placed in major police stations across Britain and would have alerted specially trained officers to incoming nuclear attack. They would then use it to activate local sirens and alert the warning points, cascading the alarm across the land.

domestic shelter called Type 1b, which was an A-frame of scaffolding poles arranged over a trench. The tent-shaped frame was then covered with layers of plywood and heavy polythene – the addition of straw or a few mattresses was recommended for extra fallout protection – before the apocalyptic Wendy house was covered with about 18 inches of earth, with only a little pipe poking out for ventilation. While he was trying to recreate the darkness, despair and boredom of shelter life for a fortnight, the media interest in his experiment meant that Hayden did not have to experience the total isolation that survivors of nuclear war would have to endure. TV crews were camped outside and local kids scampered over the roof of his shelter and crowed down the ventilation pipe.[50]

He kept a diary, which provided a bleak and honest account of what happens to the human body when forced to live in airless gloom for two weeks. Besides the expected boredom, aches and cramps, dampness added to the physical discomfort: 'The place is damp now – there's water coming up through the floor and it's also coming in at the sides and creeping up the walls. There's mould growing in the corner by the food and everything smells of piss and disinfectant.'[51] A few days later, he wrote: 'Condensation is the main problem now – it's on everything. This paper I'm writing on is all clammy and my skin's wet all the time. The damp's still gradually creeping up the sides of the shelter.'

Mould and rust started to appear on his food tins and he worried that he might be at risk of food poisoning. Black flies began buzzing around in the damp, dim light and he discovered a fat white worm in his clothes ('It made a very loud crunching noise as I pulped it into the floor, and kept wriggling for ages'). Soon he found it difficult to light a candle as the shelter's oxygen levels were getting dangerously low. Before long, the 'piss bucket' in the corner was full to the brim and he had to store his excrement in little plastic bags. But things soon got worse: 'My shit bags talk. After I'd been in for about two days, I started hearing this weird farting noise, and at first I thought it was gas leaking from the little camping stove. The other day I realised what it was: as the shit begins to decay, the air in the bags expands and leaks out: PFFFFFFT!'

The indelicate matter of toilet use in the fallout room was discussed briefly in *Protect and Survive*. Survivors were told to line a bucket with a plastic bag and slosh some disinfectant inside. By placing a seatless chair over it they could create a makeshift toilet, the waste from which could be securely tied up in its plastic bag. For the first 48 hours after nuclear attack, people would be strictly forbidden from leaving their shelter, so would have to sleep, eat and live in the immediate vicinity of buckets of human waste. Afterwards, these bags could be placed outside the door of the fallout room to await more rigorous disposal in the garden when radiation levels had declined.

The primary aspect of maintaining and promoting post-war environmental health was solving the problem of the safe disposal of toilet waste. While in their homes survivors were expected to use buckets and bin liners, they were to dig outdoor communal latrines at refugee camps and rest centres. 'Some communal facilities would be essential in all areas for living conditions would not be conducive to bowel control,' said the Government circular *Environmental Health in War*.[52] It was suggested that these latrines be placed in the vicinity but at the greatest possible distance from rest and feeding centres.

In 1980, Surrey County Council produced a lengthy document called *A Guide to Communities for Survival in War*,[53] which featured detailed instructions on how to prepare such communal latrines. It too warned that the maintenance of hygiene would be 'absolutely vital if survivors are not to be overwhelmed by the diseases which a primitive level of existence could well bring'. Yet while the document states that 'high standards of personal cleanliness are essential', it does not indicate how this might be achieved when clean water, soap, shampoo and disinfectants might be scarce – as might be the motivation to keep one's body clean. One symptom of disaster syndrome, which was expected to befall most survivors, was terrible apathy and depression, something that had been witnessed in Hiroshima, Nagasaki and Dresden.

For the communal latrines, deep trenches should be dug, and for the sake of dignity, the latrine should be covered. The preferred option was corrugated iron sheeting, but if this was not available, trees would also be suitable. The best tree cover would be given by saplings 'reinforced with twigs and branches and thatched with grass and straw'. When the latrine had reached capacity, it had to be abandoned, but should first be clearly marked as 'Foul Ground'. A further reminder of the difficulty in maintaining hygiene after nuclear war was the suggestion that survivors try to do their bit to quell disease by indulging in 'vigorous fly-swatting campaigns'.[54]

7 The Doctor Won't See You Now

Aberdeen's Beach Ballroom is a pearly-white art deco building on the seafront that looks directly out to the chilly North Sea. This is the Granite City, a place of cold winds and hard frosts, but inside the Beach Ballroom there is a softly twinkling glamour. A grand staircase leads to a sprung dance floor surrounded by graceful columns and balconies. The venue was opened in May 1929 with a spectacular masked ball, with a thousand dancers whirling, waltzing and foxtrotting in their finery. Next morning's newspaper reported that

> The scene was the most fantastically wonderful one of a marvellous evening. Much of the charm of the ball was the mask-hidden identity of one's neighbours. One wondered who was the tall gentleman who made such a handsome courtier of Charles II's time. Who was the Sioux Indian who looked so ferocious that people trembled at the sight of him? Here a languorous Creole consorted with an Admiral of Nelson's day. Malevolent Mephistopheles, in his flaming crimson, foxtrotted with a demure Dresden shepherdess, and a daringly dressed Follies' girl gaily vamped the kirk elder with whom she danced.[1]

Over the years, and despite the often brutal weather, the Beach Ballroom has clung to its glamour by hosting The Beatles, Pink Floyd and The Who, while on more humdrum evenings, locals have enjoyed musical talent like Joe Daniels and his Hot Shots, Jimmy Shand and his Old-Time Band, and Dr Crock and his Crackpots.

Aberdeen had a good number of nightclubs and dance halls, and during the Second World War they helped to boost morale. A local paper reported how a band at the Central Hall in Skene Street boldly continued playing during an air raid. 'They did it while the *Titanic* sank, and they did it while Aberdeen was bombed during the big Blitz of April 21, 1943 – the band played on . . . Even with the siren sounding, the bombs falling, and the lights flickering, the show always went on. The Master of Ceremonies, in his white gloves, kept all the dancers going.' When the band's accordionist finally emerged from the club, he saw 'desolation and devastation everywhere. Buildings were burning and there was glass and debris all over the street.'[2] Despite their home town acquiring the nickname 'Siren City' because of its frequent raids, the people of Aberdeen would not be deterred from a drink and a dance, with some venues open six nights a week during the war. But the revellers were denied a twirl at the Beach Ballroom, as the building was commandeered by the military to serve as accommodation for soldiers and would not reopen until the freezing Christmas of 1946.

In the council archives, a folder of thin crinkled papers from 1965[3] reveals that if nuclear war had threatened, the Beach Ballroom would have been commandeered again by the Aberdeen authorities. As required by central government, the city was planning for nuclear war by assessing its hospitals' capacity, totting up the estimated number of patients they could hold if extra beds were jammed in under 'drastic crowding-up' arrangements, and if stretchers were laid in corridors, day rooms and recreation areas. Yet needing more and more bed space, the planners also looked beyond the hospitals.

Cleared of furniture and decoration, and with its big dance floor, the Beach Ballroom would offer plenty of space to accommodate the sick and injured, and so joined the list of other entertainment venues in the city to be taken over, such as the Palais de Danse, the Gaiety Restaurant and Donald's Ballroom. Schools and colleges were also chosen, as classrooms and gym halls could be quickly cleared to make way for stretchers and medical equipment; they had the added advantage of having canteen facilities that could be used for feeding the patients. Various hotels were also earmarked, but while their beds, lifts, kitchens and long, straight corridors made them ideal for use as overflow hospitals, it seems perhaps a little absurd to select ballrooms and nightclubs. The idea of hundreds of dreadfully burned and injured people bundled onto the dance floor and left to scream for pain relief beneath the ornate cornicing, the stained-glass panels and the dead glitter ball is a hideous one.

And yet transforming ballrooms into hospitals was not the most absurd plan for the post-nuclear NHS. Although the government held medical stockpiles at five secret depots, in 1986 a report warned that these would be 'totally inadequate'[4] after nuclear war, and it was for that reason that the East Anglia Regional Health Board in 1981 considered what they would do when the drugs ran out and there was no longer a pharmaceutical industry to issue replacements. They realised they would have to look at 'obtaining medicaments from crude sources'[5] – by scouring trees, hedgerows, parks, gardens and fields. They sought the expert advice of Cambridge University's Botanic Garden and a Suffolk company called Thornham's Herbs, and drew up guidance for East Anglian NHS staff on which local plants could be gathered and safely utilised as medicines – with the obvious proviso that they could not know what debilitating effect radiation might have on the plants' efficacy.

The guidance explained how locally sourced plants might be used to treat illness, but unfortunately none of the recommended leaves, twigs and berries would be useful in tackling massive burns, violent radiation sickness or the excruciating pain of crush injuries. Instead, NHS staff were told that the dried leaves of the foxglove found in coastal areas might help with an irregular heartbeat, and leafy twigs of mistletoe could ease high blood pressure: 'Collect young twigs in spring and dry at 45°C' was the advice.[6] A nuclear winter, however, caused by massive amounts of smoke generated by nuclear explosions, might mean the end of predictable seasons. It might also deny survivors the use of mistletoe by killing most plants. In fact, the outlook for East Anglia in any nuclear conflict was dreadful. Secret government projections placed the region in a Z zone, meaning it was predicted to come under heavy attack due to its many airbases, and so it would be smothered in lethal fallout. A Home Office map of Britain from 1961 showed East Anglia, Greater London and the Home Counties lost under filthy black streaks. In the deadly Z zones, there would be no gathering of mistletoe twigs in spring.

Unaware of that grim prospect, East Anglia's advice for the NHS continued. For a sedative, seek lime trees, to be found in local parks and gardens, and add its flowers to hot water. Chew bruised juniper berries for cystitis. Soothe boils with burdock. Roll the seeds of the thornapple with leaves of coltsfoot into a cigarette to relieve asthma. Mustard seeds can be made into an ointment for muscle pain. Oats might be an antidepressant; hops a hypnotic. Instead of morphine and antiseptics, put your trust in witchy concoctions of black horehound, horsetail and skullcup.

Even if their staff were able to harvest a crop of potent plants, the NHS would be largely forbidden from treating the sick and injured in the immediate aftermath of an attack. Official guidance declared, 'Medical staff, who would be irreplaceable except in the long-term, should not be wasted by allowing them to enter highly radioactive areas to assist casualties', and 'for the first 48 hours after an attack therefore, little or no life-saving activity would be possible except on the most limited, self-help basis'.[7] Afterwards, fallout would have reduced and short essential excursions might be permitted, although the public were warned to expect to largely stay at home, living off their own supplies, for the next two weeks.

It is hard to believe that a frightened population, with many in great pain and distress, would have been content with the family first aid box. Still, survivors were told to rely upon their household stock of plasters and paracetamol before dragging themselves across the ash, the leathery corpses and the deformed swirls of melted glass to reach the medical relief of the dock leaf and the marshmallow root. East Anglia's health board recommended people keep a full first aid kit at home containing painkillers, treatment for stomach upsets, anti-nausea pills, water purification tablets and 'a contraceptive, if appropriate'.

East Anglia also planned, if nuclear conflict drew near, to seize extra drugs and medical supplies from local chemists and corner shops instead of relying on a potentially thin allocation from the national stockpile. They identified four groups of drugs that should be given priority in stockpiling – painkillers, tranquillisers, anti-nausea drugs and the contraceptive pill[8] – and advised their staff that shortages would be so dire that 'commandeering becomes necessary from stockists, chemist shops, suppliers, wholesalers, supermarkets and industrial/research organisations'.[9] 'Foraging parties' would therefore descend on towns and seize what they could before the bomb dropped. They would primarily target dispensing GP practices, where they could hope to find drugs plus a good supply of disinfectants, vitamins and surgical dressings; they should also raid local grocers and supermarkets to strip their shelves of toilet paper, general drugs like antacids and painkillers, plus scissors, thread, and 'alcohol and spirits in all forms'. In a nice touch of politeness, the raiders would have to issue receipts so that the disgruntled shopkeeper could – one day – claim compensation.

This scenario was also portrayed in the 1965 civil defence film *Care of the Homeless*, where in the last days before nuclear war, a van stopped at a chemist's and a clothing shop and the team politely introduced themselves to the shopkeepers as a 'civil defence requisition party'. The fashionable shopkeeper in the dress shop simply nodded her sixties beehive and the men scooted behind the counter and started stripping the shelves. Having emptied the shop, they delivered their load to the civil defence stores, where one of them cheekily announced: 'We can do you a nice line in ladies' jumpers!'[10] The squads were also advised to target industrial and university research laboratories to obtain good quantities of bleach and laboratory apparatus. The loot would be placed under the care of appointed pharmacists in secure locations, but even when every little corner shop and chemist had been scraped bare, and all the booty counted, the stockpile would still be inadequate and with no possibility of fresh supplies being manufactured.

Blood, bulbs and burgers

Blood would also need to be stockpiled, and with tension building in the run-up to nuclear war, the National Blood Transfusion Service would make a nationwide call for donors. In the early 1980s, the Soviet leader, Yuri Andropov, ordered his spies in Britain to carefully monitor the price of blood. He believed that a huge demand for blood would precede nuclear war, so if the price rose, it would surely indicate that the West was planning a strike against the USSR. He did not realise that blood donors in Britain are unpaid and are rewarded with nothing more than a thank you and a digestive biscuit. Ben Macintyre mocked Andropov's misunderstanding in his espionage book *The Spy and the Traitor*, writing that the Kremlin, 'assuming that capitalism penetrated every aspect of Western life, believed that a "blood bank" was, in fact, a bank where blood could be bought and sold'. Operation Ryan, a plan to detect signs of an imminent nuclear strike against the Warsaw Pact, also urged Soviet spies to check if lights were burning late into the night in various Whitehall buildings, and to monitor abattoirs, because if there was an increase in the amount of cattle being slaughtered, it could be an indication that Britain was stockpiling hamburgers in anticipation of war.[11]

It was reasonable to assume that nuclear war would be preceded by international tension, and would perhaps enter a period of conventional war before escalating to a nuclear exchange. The National Blood Transfusion Service would need to boost its stocks because it might have found itself supplying military and civilian war casualties from the initial round of hostilities, as well as dealing with the usual everyday demands, before facing a further onslaught from the escalation to nuclear attack. It was estimated that during the period of conventional bombing, 'there would be a need for roughly twice as much blood as is normally collected in one week'.[12] It was therefore suggested that the Transfusion Service set up collection points in local factories and commandeer suitable buildings for donations, all backed up by 'a crash programme of public appeals'. Still, that campaign would have to be fighting for attention with news of the coming war, as well as the public information campaigns about protection against imminent nuclear attack that would be on air and in the papers at the same time. With a fearful population focused on survival, would many Britons be charitable enough to make time to donate blood?

The stockpiled blood would be dispersed around the country, and due to its need for refrigeration it was suggested that the nation's ice cream vans be requisitioned, as their chilled compartments would make them excellent choices for transporting blood, medication and food.

'It's grand to feel you're wanted'

It was obvious to planners that in the event of nuclear war, the NHS needed more staff. In 1948, the National Hospital Service Reserve had been formed. It was a voluntary organisation that created a register of retired nurses, and those who had otherwise left the profession, who could be summoned to help their local hospital in a time of dire national need. As a supplement to this emergency workforce, people without nursing qualifications were also asked to join the Reserve, for which they would be trained by the local Red Cross in peacetime, quickly turning them into auxiliary nurses ready to be called into service if war broke out. The recruitment campaign adopted the tone of wartime propaganda:

> What use are YOU in an emergency? Do you stand back, pale and helpless, hoping that someone else will know how to cope? Are you one of those people who make matters worse by losing their nerve completely? Or do you come forward, with cool head and steady hands, to do quietly and without fuss whatever ought to be done?[13]

The Reserve was open to both men and women, but the campaign was largely aimed at housewives who were keen to do something useful outside the home. 'What a wonderful spare-time interest the Hospital Reserve could give you!' one recruitment leaflet exclaimed.[14]

Many of the women targeted for recruitment from 1948 until the Reserve's demise twenty years later would have served in voluntary civil defence roles in the Second World War, and now the authorities called them to help their country once again. Ladies in the Reserve, one 1950s newspaper advert promised, will 'meet so many people, make good friends, find a new interest . . . No more boredom. No more loneliness . . . They'll make better wives and mothers, too.'[15] 'It's grand to feel you're wanted and useful and welcome amongst these jolly and capable people,' declared another. There was also the appeal of an 'attractive' uniform and an enamel badge.[16]

Uniforms and badges and the promise to make new friends: joining the Reserve seemed like a return to school. There were even competitions that set the Reserve ladies of one hospital against their local rivals. In 1963, four teams of Reserve nurses from hospitals in the south-west gathered at Mendip Hospital for a 'nuclear test',[17] in which they had to pretend that the bomb had dropped. Each team was given an 18-bed ward of patients and told no doctor was available, 'and until one arrived the nurses had to cope in the best way possible'. The ladies were awarded points and the winners were the team from Keynsham Hospital. It was all very jolly and good-natured, like school sports day. Indeed, it's hard to find a hint of unpleasantness – or an acknowledgement that all this was being done in anticipation of nuclear war.

Armageddon in Victorian splendour

In addition to the boosting of nursing staff in preparation for nuclear war, doctors and NHS administrators – alongside policemen, politicians, civil servants and fire chiefs – were sent on training courses at the government's civil defence colleges at Easingwold in North Yorkshire and Taymouth Castle in Perthshire. Both colleges were housed in stately homes in lush countryside, so the participants could learn how to plan for Armageddon whilst enjoying splendid lunches and strolls on the lawn.[18]

The country house at Easingwold, The Hawkhills, had been built for a Victorian mining millionaire, and a convivial atmosphere lingered into the Cold War, as though the grand old house could not accept it was no longer home to Victorian splendour and fine living. When *The Guardian* sent a reporter to the college in 1987, they were welcomed by a jovial chap who recommended the quality of the stabling and tempted the guests with the prospect of cigars and 'rum-soaked shag'.[19] Mick Jackson, researching his 1984 nuclear war film *Threads*, attended the college as an observer and recalled it as 'a very pleasant place . . . very bucolic setting, and rather nice rooms and you could walk in the grounds and then you had breakfast with everybody, and then you did your role-playing and exercises for a bit, and there were breaks and a rather excellent lunch . . . Nothing in that was anything like what it would be in reality.'[20]

The highlight of the training at Easingwold was a war game called Hot Seat, in which participants assumed control of the fictional English county of Naptonshire in a nuclear war. Reporting in 1981, *TV Eye* described it as 'a life or death game that's played out every month by chief officers from local authorities across the country . . . The task of the players is to ensure that those who survive are fed, clothed, and that law and order is maintained.'[21] The programme showed a room full of chairs and blackboards, where middle-aged men in gold-rimmed glasses open their ring binders to make their 'life or death' plans, regularly interrupted by fake news flashes from a TV set in the corner that reports on the deteriorating international situation. When war breaks out, the men move into another room, where the blinds are drawn and the easy chairs have been replaced with hard-backed seats. They take off their suit jackets and roll up their sleeves. This is their bunker for the imaginary war.

A typical session of the game focused on how the various teams might feed the county's survivors. In one scenario, nervous food officers direct them to a communal feeding centre. At first, their daily meal is a relatively generous dish of beef or chicken stew, meat being in plentiful supply initially as thousands of cattle fall ill from radiation exposure and are sent for quick slaughter. The same largesse applies to poultry, as hundreds of thousands of fowl have lately died in broiler houses without electricity.[22] As the initial glut of meat wanes, rations go down to 1,200 calories a day, then are reduced even further, with the harvest still months away. At the evaluation session, the exhausted food officers are asked, 'Did you realise that, from then on, everyone was starving?' The journalist observing this game wrote of its 'breath of nightmare'.[23]

There were also lectures on the health service after nuclear war, attended by NHS staff and representatives from the voluntary medical organisations who would be involved in the aftermath, such as the Red Cross, the WRVS and the St John and St Andrew's Ambulance Associations. But there were many within the medical profession who refused to attend Easingwold, and who ridiculed the notion that the NHS could be prepared for nuclear war. 'We regret that money is being spent on planning the unplannable,'[24] said one doctor and British Medical Association member. Further criticism was that the training received at Easingwold was being implemented by NHS emergency planning officers, who were also trained to prepare for scenarios like . plane crashes, motorway pile-ups and terrorist attacks. This implied that nuclear war was 'just another disaster', a dangerous approach to take because not only would a nuclear attack dwarf all other disasters in its scale and horror, but the plans assumed that the country's infrastructure would survive unscathed and the injured could be rushed to a high-technology, fully functioning hospital. Easingwold tried to deflect these criticisms by using a chart that suggested there could be many different stages of war before the total destruction of an all-out nuclear exchange, and so there was a place for their civil defence lessons: 'We're concerned that if there are damage and casualties, there's a job to be done.'[25]

After the gruelling and upsetting training sessions, Easingwold's Victorian comforts were much appreciated. A *Guardian* journalist who visited in 1989 wrote: 'It had been a hell of a day. They'd had all the mass burials to organise, and the dissidents to round up, and they hadn't even started to find billets for the refugees from the tower blocks. No wonder the bar was packed after dinner and the cash register chiming at a demented pace.'[26] One of the participants that day confided: 'I'd been issued with an allowance for the bar from the council before I went, and I thought "this is immoral, I shouldn't be given this money to spend on drink" but, by golly, I didn't half need it . . . On the first night I was getting quite pie-eyed. It was all the tension I was under.'[27]

The courses at Easingwold were often distressing, not merely for their content but also because they represented a terrible break with the certainties of the past. The harsh lessons delivered made it painfully obvious that a nuclear attack would be nothing like the Blitz. As *The Guardian* put it, 'Middle-aged councillors who could remember the last war were horrified to discover that old notions of mucking in and smiling through were chillingly obsolete . . . Calmly discussing the termination of radiation-sick babies was a world away from Vera Lynn, the Second World War, and digging for victory.'[28]

The Scottish civil defence training college at Taymouth Castle could be just as traumatic. One lecture on the state of nursing after nuclear war was delivered by a Miss Macnaughton. The text of her speech indicates that she was an indomitable, stern figure: just the type the country would need after nuclear war – and just the type to send attendees rushing to the bar for a shot of courage. She began her lecture, 'Nursing Under Disaster Conditions', by chiding the population for its apathy and pessimism in the face of the nuclear threat, declaring that 'much could be done to relieve human suffering if a nuclear explosion should occur'.[29] Pull your socks up, she told her audience, and once the worst has happened, be prepared to deal with it:

> In the shambles that will ensue the first phase is life-saving and this will create many breaks with tradition. Adequate screening may be difficult but at all costs the skilled help available must be kept only for those who would die without immediate care. One of the most painful aspects of this period will be that many who are painfully but not dangerously injured will have to be left, as will those who are so grossly injured that surgical help would have no effect. It may be possible to bring some comfort and help to those groups through the voluntary bodies or by making use of the less seriously injured.

Not giving up hope and keeping a clear head were essential:

> It has been said that one of the most essential qualities during this time will be to go on hopefully in the face of apparent defeat. To have the capacity to assess the situation, no matter how appalling; to assess staff and equipment available no matter how inadequate, and thereby to make the best plans possible under the circumstances, will be the only way to cope . . . The importance of calm cheerfulness on the morale of all concerned in such circumstances cannot be overestimated. Accepted standards of nursing care will not exist, all energy being channelled into life-saving activities. There will be no place for grumblers.[30]

'Grumblers' seems like an odd choice of word in the circumstances. It is a chiding term, but with a knot of affection snagged in it, and it seems to have leapt straight from the Second World War, along with other nagging-but-kindly home-front slogans like 'Turn That Light Out!' 'Make Do and Mend' and 'Dig For Victory!' And just like those old phrases, Miss Macnaughton's advice for postnuclear grumblers feels hopelessly out of date. Here was a woman who understood the horror of nuclear attack but chose to deliver her warnings in the language and tone of the last war. Little wonder then that many people regarded civil defence as a bit of a lark – or simply a waste of time.

Emptying the hospitals

Having readied as many drugs, bandages and extra staff as possible, the next step in preparing the NHS for imminent nuclear attack was to empty the hospitals. Official guidance stipulated that in the last days before war, hospitals should discharge all their convalescents, 70 per cent of their maternity and sick children cases, half of their non-active infection and chest patients, and 15 per cent of their psychiatric patients.[31] Sending these groups home, and keeping only those too ill to be moved would allow hospitals to disperse most of their staff and equipment around the region to areas of relative safety.

We can assume that many patients would not be happy at being turned out of their hospital beds, especially if they had no family or carer to receive them at home, so the guidance insisted this was a benevolent move, and that patients would be safer in their own homes rather than in a big city hospital. In fact, the opposite was true. Experts recognised that there was not much safety for those who lived in tower blocks or bungalows, both of which offered little protection against blast or radiation. Indeed, a typical Victorian hospital building, with warrens of corridors and vast basements, would offer far greater protection than most ordinary dwellings. The guidance was unequivocal, however: patients should return home to a safe environment conducive to their recovery, but that 'discharge should not be held up merely because home conditions were not ideal or could not be checked and it must be accepted that the crisis would entail hardship'.[32]

Those who were being sent home would be collected by family and friends, but even this might prove difficult in the countdown to nuclear war, as by now the Telephone Preference Scheme would have clicked into place. Designed to keep phone lines clear for official use, it meant that most of the public would no longer be able to make calls. To evade the communication obstacle, it was suggested that Scouts and Girl Guides be brought in to act as a messenger service and to escort vulnerable patients home. Taxis, ambulances and other hospital vehicles would also be used. After this great exodus, the hospitals would accept emergency cases only.

Patients who were too sick to be discharged would be relocated inside the building to an area deemed to offer greatest protection from the coming blast and fallout. This would be somewhere deep in the core of the hospital – a basement, a windowless ward or a corridor furthest from the exterior walls. There, attended by a skeleton staff, they would await the bomb.

As the guidance document reminds us, 'trained staff are the most valuable asset possessed by the Health Service'. A makeshift hospital could be hurriedly set up in a ballroom, but you couldn't easily train a new doctor or nurse. It was paramount that staff be kept as safe as possible. Even after the bomb had exploded, when they would be most needed, they would be forbidden from assisting survivors until radiation had decreased. They must not be 'wasted'. Some lives were worth more than others.

But in the early Cold War, when there was still a belief that any future conflict could be meaningfully endured, the health service would have been kinder to survivors. If you found yourself injured in an area of heavy fallout – the so-called Z zones – you would not be abandoned and told to hunker down and hope for the best. There were plans for 'the transport of war casualties and the evacuation of patients from "Z" belts';[33] and instead of ruthlessly emptying the hospitals and cramming the remaining patients into basements, fleets of special trains, ambulances and buses would be engaged to evacuate the sick to hospitals in safe areas, with the medical equipment following the lengthy caravan in hired furniture vans and lorries.[34]

Crucially, there was no rule that doctors should not be 'wasted' by attending to casualties immediately after the attack. The threat of fallout did not become clear to government until 1955, so plans from the early 1950s saw medics and rescue squads dashing to try and reach survivors as they lay injured or trapped in the atomic rubble. Members of the Civil Defence Corps would dig them out and then hand them over to stretcher-bearers, who would carry them to a forward medical aid unit (FMAU). These plans cheerfully insisted that 'most of the serious cases would arrive at hospital without unnecessary delay'.[35] The FMAUs would be located in the epicentre of the catastrophe, set up in the midst of the chaos like an army field hospital. Each would have four doctors, four nurses, forty auxiliaries, and teams of drivers and stretcher-bearers.

In the aftermath of the Strath Report, in 1959 health service planners began to talk of hopeless cases, seeking to determine who was beyond help – the 'moribund' – and so should be 'filtered off'. There was a loose guide to the types of injury that would condemn a casualty to that status:

Serious injuries to head and neck involving the central nervous system
Severe crush injuries to the chest
Multiple injuries with extensive burns
Multiple perforated abdominal wounds[36]

As a guidance booklet explained in 1961:

For the majority of them it will be possible to do little beyond the administering of pain-relieving drugs and warm drinks, and attention to physical needs. The condition of these casualties will be constantly watched however and those who subsequently show promise of responding to treatment will be transferred to the treatment area. Those who die will be moved to the temporary mortuary.[37]

Comfort and support would still be given to people who were beyond help, but that was no longer the care and kindness that had been in evidence during the Blitz. There were also warnings that after a nuclear attack, survivors could pose a danger to the emergency services. After a 1961 FMAU training exercise, code-named Rawhide, it was noted that

When an FMAU is set up during operations it will need some protection from unwanted visitors. The site occupied by an FMAU is likely to be near where the main streams of homeless will be expected to flow. Many homeless may be prompted, for one reason or another, to attempt to enter the FMAU and must be prevented. Local volunteers may come forward offering help but should be 'screened' before being employed to be sure they can be of real help and are not prompted only by curiosity or a morbid desire for sensation.

'A small unit of uniformed persons' should therefore be attached to each FMAU to keep the desperate population away. Here too we can detect that shift from protecting people to maintaining the state. Instead of the authorities rushing to help, the concern becomes how they might be shielded from the population.

Correspondingly, civil defence planning was nudged forward to meet the new hydrogen bomb horror, with policy shifting from 'we'll rescue you' to 'look after yourself'. As we have seen, this new and more realistic outlook meant the abandonment of evacuation. Yet while the new official advice for people to stay in their own homes might have helped to control and contain the population, the threat of widespread fallout placed a huge burden on the NHS. If every area of the country was declared to be equally in danger, then every single hospital needed to plan for nuclear attack. A small hospital in Newquay or Barnstaple was as much at risk as Barts or the Royal London. 'No part of the country could expect to avoid the effects of an attack,' explained Cambridgeshire Area Health Authority's war plan. 'Those areas not directly attacked might suffer from radioactive fallout and would certainly feel the effects of the destruction and disruption elsewhere of supplies, services and transport, and might receive an influx of refugees. All health authorities must therefore plan to meet the consequences of an attack on any part of the country.'[38]

'How can you sleep?'

The British Medical Association (BMA) believed that the NHS would not be able to cope with a single Hiroshima-sized atomic bomb, let alone full nuclear war. And indeed, while the government bullishly insisted that the NHS get ready, we can detect a spasm of hopelessness in the key policy to keep most of the sick and injured firmly out of hospital. Even with the extra capacity created by 'crowding up', and by setting up beds in ballrooms and restaurants, it seemed clear that the NHS preferred not to see you after the bomb dropped. From the late 1970s, therefore, survivors were advised to resort to self-help, tending their own wounds with basic first aid and relying on the assistance of family and friends.

Various voluntary organisations, like the Red Cross, the St John's Ambulance Brigade and the St Andrew's Ambulance Association in Scotland, began offering first aid training, and it was these same organisations who would swing into action after nuclear war, trying to prevent crowds from besieging their local hospital. After the attack, if your injuries were too severe for the flimsy first aid kit, you would be directed to your local first aid post (FAP). These were to be set up across the country, in every village, suburb and district. They would be the first port of call for every survivor, where volunteers would administer first aid and refer the injured onwards if deemed necessary – and worthy. But these little FAPs would be poorly resourced. Not only would there be no doctors or nurses present, but much of their equipment would have been scavenged from their surroundings: 'The equipping of the post may have to be from local resources, sheets torn into bandages, splints from floor boards, "scrounged" sterilising outfits, or improvised ones etc. Local vans to act as ambulances in area etc.'[39] It was hoped that the posts might receive a share of the stockpiled medicines and kit that had been previously requisitioned from shops, GP surgeries and chemists, but with every hospital crying out for supplies, we can easily imagine that the FAPs might be forgotten. In 1978, the government guidance *Medical Supplies in War* advised that

> Health Directors with requisitioned medical equipment and supplies in their area should bear in mind that these are national assets . . . It may be a very long time after attack before any significant quantity of medical equipment or supplies could be manufactured or imported and all items, however plentiful locally, would have to be treated as scarce nationally.[40]

Having received first aid at the FAP, you would either be sent home or directed to a nearby rest centre. The latter may sound luxurious but would effectively be just a room filled with the sick and injured, who would be allocated a stretcher, or a space on the floor, whilst they recovered. Any nursing you required would have to be carried out by your family, under the harried supervision of a volunteer trained in first aid. If you were seriously sick or injured, the FAP could refer you upwards through the post-nuclear medical chain to a casualty collecting centre (CCC). These would have 'strict admission priorities' and you would only be permitted entry if you had a decent chance of survival: only the hopeful casualties would be admitted. The CCCs would be manned by a group of GPs working with trained volunteers, although dentists might also assist. The doctors could perform minor surgery, but patients would still be expected to provide basic nursing care for themselves and others, as far as their condition allowed. Besides this enhanced level of care, the purpose of the CCC was to sort its patients into categories, deciding who was well enough to be passed back down the chain to a rest centre, who could go home, and who merited the gold star of a hospital admission.

But CCCs had another, more sinister purpose, and that was to 'hold' patients. Even if they had been deemed worthy by the FAP, there would naturally be a number of survivors who could not be helped further as their sickness or injury was too severe. The painfully scarce resources were not to be squandered on difficult or hopeless cases. The doctors at the CCCs were instructed to be 'ruthless' in their decisions and advised to favour the lightly injured over the desperate. We need to remember that this is a post-nuclear NHS so stripped of medicines that it has been forced to consider treating people with mistletoe, mustard seeds and marshmallow root. The condemned patients referred to as 'moribund' – meaning at the point of death – would be moved to a separate section of the CCC known as the holding area, where they would be left to die. 'Those suffering from multiple injuries or severe deep burns, the treatment of which would be wasteful of time and supplies, would come into this category,' the guidance specified. 'Also included would be those suffering from abdominal wounds, some of whom might survive without an operation. All these would be held in an area separate from the other groups.'[41]

However, an advisory document suggested that staff at the CCCs refrain from using the word 'moribund'. These patients should be referred to as 'expectant', a word normally associated with the bloom of a pregnant woman. Clearly the term was regarded as being bad for morale: 'The word to use is not *moribund* – expecting to die – but *expectant* meaning expecting to get away to hospital just as soon as possible.'[42] To lift the morale of both the staff and the condemned patients, and perhaps to fend off rage and despair from their relatives, the word suggested that they would soon be cared for in a more suitable environment, perhaps a necessary deception to avoid chaos and threats from desperate family members.

It might seem futile to try and lift morale in such a desperate place as a CCC, where conditions would have been atrocious. Unlike hospitals which were at the top of the medical chain and would only be receiving a limited number of patients, consisting of those hopeful of recovery, the CCC, stuck in the middle of the chain, had the worst of it. They might not even have power or running water. Here the hopeless cases would be laid out and left to die, with the ailing lying next to the freshly dead, while more and more people with hideous burns, appalling crush injuries and raging radiation sickness would be constantly brought in. A CCC might have looked like the Red Cross hospital in Hiroshima described by John Hersey:

> Plaster, dust, blood and vomit were everywhere. Patients were dying by the hundred, but there was nobody to carry away the corpses. Some of the hospital staff distributed biscuits and rice balls, but the charnel house smell was so strong that few were hungry. By three o'clock the next morning, after nineteen straight hours of his gruesome work, Dr Sasaki was incapable of dressing another wound. He and some other survivors of the hospital staff got straw mats and went outdoors – thousands of patients and hundreds of dead were in the yard and on the driveway – and hurried round behind the hospital and lay down in hiding to snatch some sleep. But within an hour wounded people had found them; a complaining circle formed around them. 'Doctors! Help us! How can you sleep?'[43]

We can imagine all the medical facilities – FAPs, CCCs, hospitals – as places of absolute horror. Here there would be no room for traditional comfort or care. They would be nothing more than medical repair shops where people were processed, and the dud ones scrapped.

Liars and actors

In 1983, the British Medical Association published a book-length report called *The Medical Effects of Nuclear War*, which delivered its verdict on how the NHS would cope with nuclear attack:

Civilised life as we know it, and the human values and ethical standards upon which the practice of medicine is based, would cease to exist in vast areas of these islands. It would be impossible to run even a basic medical care service without minimal standards of law and order. Survivors would be preoccupied exclusively with the search for food and shelter. They would be unlikely to devote attention to the care of the sick and dying.[44]

The report imagined a single one-megaton bomb exploding over St Paul's Cathedral. This would create 26,000 major burns casualties alone, and yet Britain in peacetime had beds for only 106 burns patients. Many of the dead would have been instantly vaporised, although 'vast numbers would still remain to be buried and would be a continual reminder to survivors of the horror that they were experiencing'. But the central, and most stinging, criticism of the BMA experts was that the government were being utterly naïve in assuming nuclear war would be similar to conventional war, only a few degrees worse. 'We do not wish to underestimate any part of the damage, destruction and loss inflicted in the course of World War II,' they said. 'However there is no doubt that experience of conventional warfare is *irrelevant* to the scene that would confront whatever survivors remained after a nuclear war.'

It was this naïvety that set Sir John Stallworthy bristling. An emeritus professor at Oxford, and a former chairman of the BMA's Board of Science and Education, he had compiled the report, and fumed that he could not understand why the Home Office, prime minister Margaret Thatcher and defence secretary Michael Heseltine persisted in planning for survival. 'Either they are very good liars, or they are very good actors,' he snapped (and perhaps they were both).[45] 'The Home Office chappies came to us when we were preparing our report,' Sir John recalled,

and we told them, 'Imagine you come up from your bunkers and all the buildings are gone, the streets are running with water and sewage, they're piled with the corpses of people and animals, some of the people are still alive and the rats are eating them. There's no one to come to your rescue. Your food supplies are going to run out and they're probably contaminated.' And you know, they seemed surprised. It was as if they really thought they'd come up from the shelter and call for the Rolls and go down and get a hamper from Harrods and all would be well with the world . . . oh dear. You have to keep a sense of humour dealing with these wallies.[46]

At a press conference on the report's release, Professor Stallworthy was met with similar naïvety from journalists, with one reporter asking if people would go to the doctor after the bomb dropped to beg for a suicide pill. The professor despaired: there would be no popping to the GP surgery after nuclear war.[47]

The Royal College of Nursing (RCN) issued their own highly critical report that same year, dismissing the government's plans for a post-nuclear NHS as 'totally inadequate':

> The inescapable fact is that in the context of a nuclear attack, the skills and training of any surviving nurse would be rendered virtually irrelevant. In the absence of fundamental essentials, such as a radiologically clean environment, uncontaminated water supplies, energy, public utilities, basic drugs, dressings and equipment, nursing as it is generally understood would be impracticable.[48]

In fact, in this situation the special skills of a psychiatric nurse might be more useful, while due to the lack of equipment, a general nurse 'would have little to offer, apart from basic hygiene and words of comfort for the dying'. The report concluded:

> The post-nuclear war picture is occasionally painted, somewhat cosily, as a return to medieval living and medicine. Even that, in our opinion, is a highly optimistic and dangerous view. Survivors would lack various factors which made life possible in the Middle Ages: a 'clean' environment, uncontaminated food supplies, stable social structure, and the basic knowledge and skills necessary for survival.

It ended with the stark warning that 'all the adjectives of doom in the English language would hardly do justice to the effects of a nuclear strike involving one major weapon'.

Individual doctors also took a stand against the government's NHS survival plans. Dr Peter Sims of Leighton Buzzard wrote a leaflet called *The Dilemma*, which told patients the blunt truth about what nuclear attack would mean for their family doctor: 'I would be unable to look after children, the chronic sick, the old and the handicapped; they would be last in the queue. I would be obliged to practise euthanasia; rapid and pain free death would be envied. I would be able to care only for people expected to recover within a few days; with limited medical care anyone else would have to be left and most would die.' He felt compelled to paint a realistic picture: 'Nuclear war is the greatest single threat to the health and survival of humanity. I must forsake the security of my profession and speak out. I don't wish to practise post-nuclear medicine and must strive so that it should never become necessary.'[49]

In the small village of Congresbury, near Bristol, a public meeting was called by another GP, Dr Richard Lawson, which showed its overwhelming support for his plan to distribute suicide pills before a nuclear attack. The doctor, a CND member, had arranged the meeting after learning that some of his patients intended to kill their children rather than have them endure a slow death from radiation sickness.[50]

A more spiky and darkly comic approach was adopted by Dr B. J. Williams of Chippenham, who issued a leaflet to his patients advising them that in the event of nuclear attack the surgery would be closed until further notice. He then delivered some advice, blending blunt truths with black humour:

1. If you are severely injured please arrange to die where you will not pollute water supplies or cause disease. You will not require a death certificate.
2. Severe pain and radiation sickness are best treated by getting someone to hit you on the head with a LARGE stone.[51]

Another doctor, John Gleisner, after attending a conference at Imperial College about post-nuclear health care, wrote a caustic newspaper article that described the event as naïve and foolishly optimistic. With 'feminine attendants in tight T-shirts bearing the slogan "Don't Panic", it was as if we were being seduced away from realistic analysis . . . It had something of the comfortable reassurance of a long episode of *Dad's Army*.' There were some glimpses of the horrible reality when the conference spoke of the need for special training so that doctors might become 'hardened'. After a nuclear incident they must be compelled to 'ignore the dying and the injured' and to provide quick care to the relatively well. 'Perhaps doctors can be "hardened" as others can be hardened,' Dr Gleisner wrote. 'Some doctors survived working in concentration camps. Psychopathy lurks in all of us. If, in the end, in this terrible context of nuclear aftermath, "survival of the fittest" becomes "survival of the most psychopathic", even in the caring professions, then it seems unlikely that those professions will ever be trusted again. Do you wonder that I am frightened?'[52]

8 Civil Defence is Common Sense

After the grey of the war years came strawberry pink and bright blue. In 1951, the Festival of Britain opened in London on land cleared of Blitz debris. A national celebration of British industry, science and creativity, it would be a tonic for the exhausted nation, representing a 'milestone between past and future, to enrich and enliven the present. A diverse place of serious fun and light-hearted solemnity, reclaimed from the bomb wrack and the decay of years.'[1] Enjoying the fountains and boating ponds, carousels and acrobats, fantastic murals and sleek futuristic buildings of curving steel, austerity Britons strolled through the grounds in their Sunday best, stretching limbs and taking the sun after long years of war and those anxious nights stifled by the blackout, getting accustomed once again to colour and pizzazz. The Festival offered science and candy floss, combining engineering with streamers and teacakes. It was a thrilling peep at what Britain would look like now the war was over and the world was beginning anew. 'Whole walls of decoration are made of squares of coloured canvas pulled taut in geometric shapes and triangles, to be lit with a variety of colours,' wrote Cecil Beaton. 'A screen is made by hanging Miro-like coloured balls against the distant chimney pots of the city. Arches underneath the railway are painted strawberry pink or bright blue.'[2]

The King opened the Festival with a lavish ceremony on 2 May, and every day thousands flooded through the gates to marvel at the shiny display of post-war Britain. The huge Dome of Discovery hosted demonstrations on everything from the achievements of Newton and Darwin to jet propulsion and nuclear physics. There was the new Festival Hall and the futuristic 300-foot 'Skylon', the Exhibition of Science ('as you go in, you watch a pencil lead growing to ten thousand million times its normal size')[3] and exhibits of British craftsmanship and culture from fine china to *Alice in Wonderland*.

Although local papers advertised cheap train fares to the capital so their readers might visit the heart of the Festival, there were hundreds of regional celebrations held across the country. York Minster had special performances of choral and chamber music, and the city held a grand river carnival and Georgian masked ball. There was a display of fine Scottish crafts and architecture in Edinburgh, and a special Festival ship, the HMS *Campania*, painted a brilliant white and strung with bunting, called at the river cities of Plymouth, Glasgow, Newcastle, Bristol and Liverpool. (Just a few months later, the *Campania* would find herself in Australia, participating in Britain's first nuclear test.) And there were more homely celebrations, such as the gathering in Roundhay Park, Leeds, which featured donkeys and sandpits, or in Bridlington, where there was a 'quite bewildering profusion of bowls tournaments and sand competitions'.[4] Coatbridge had a performance by the band of the Scottish Gas Board, and Chichester held an 'ankle show'.

While sandcastles and ankles might detract from the original idea of the Festival, Corby in Northamptonshire might have been accused of lowering the tone even further by devoting one day of its programme to the grim, unglamorous act of preparing for nuclear war. The local Civil Defence Corps joined with the fire brigade on playing fields to demonstrate how they'd save the good people of Corby after a nuclear attack. They had to tone down their performance when concerns were raised about potential damage to nearby housing if they began hosing water and tossing smoke bombs, so they focused instead on a demonstration of their rescue skills. Four local schoolboys ran up to the roof of a block of flats and were then 'lowered by pulley from the top of the flats, much to the excitement of dozens of onlooking children, together with the Festival Queen, Miss Rita Crawford'.[5]

It might seem odd to remind people of the nuclear threat at festivities celebrating the future, but the Corps, formed just two years earlier, was eager to recruit volunteers, and its campaigns, with their hints of adventure and dashes of national pride, were not out of kilter with the spirit being drummed up by the Festival on London's South Bank.

The Civil Defence Corps was a voluntary organisation that aimed to recruit hundreds of thousands of Brits in the event of nuclear war. They would be trained in first aid, rescue work and welfare tasks; they would form ambulance squads and become wardens. Civil defence of a similar type had worked well during the Blitz, but the prime minister, Clement Attlee, was sceptical that it would be useful in the new kind of war. After the atomic bombings of Hiroshima and Nagasaki, he told the House of Commons on 19 August 1945, 'We have been living through great events, and we have got to realise we are living in a new world. We have seen in action a new force, the result of scientific discovery, the far-reaching consequences of which, I think, we find it difficult to grasp.' A few days later, in a private address to ministers, he warned that using Blitz-style civil defence against atomic attack would be a 'futile waste'.[6] But in the absence of any alternative ideas, Britain passed the Civil Defence Act of 1948, which saw the formation of the Corps the following year and required local authorities to form and train their own divisions.

The Battle of Priory Row

Many councils, particularly those run by Labour, resented this instruction from Whitehall. The earliest and loudest dissent came from Coventry, which was still scarred from its dreadful bombardment in the war, when it had suffered 1,000 dead and firestorms devastated the city centre. After the horrors of the Blitz, Coventry council was in no mood to entertain the idea that another war, this time with weapons far more powerful and destructive, could be survived with the same old civil defences. While many local people answered the recruitment call and joined Coventry's newly formed branch of the Civil Defence Corps individually, the council rebelled in 1954 and announced that it would disband the new Civil Defence Committee and play no part in the formation of the revived Corps. Neither would they send delegates to civil defence courses or permit training exercises on the city streets.

The council leader, Sidney Stringer, argued that civil defence was a waste of time and money, and a defiant letter was sent to the Home Secretary. However, the testy councillors weakened their stance by admitting that one of their aims was to 'strengthen the hands of those who want to outlaw the bomb',[7] leading some critics to question whether this was actually a dignified rebellion in defence of a wounded city or just another disarmament protest by the political left. A spiky argument broke out between London and Coventry, and matters came to a head when the government announced that a large civil defence training exercise called Priory was due to take place in Coventry right beside the ruined cathedral that had been attacked by the Luftwaffe. There could not have been a more symbolic location, nor one more deliberately designed to rile the council that had forbidden civil defence events on their turf.

The exercise was set for 1 May 1954, and would see civil defence teams out on the streets practising their rescue skills by attending a mock disaster. The exercise could have taken place on moorland, or on an army training ground, but its main purpose was display; the public were supposed to take notice. The smoke bombs, the shouted commands, the rushing and dashing – it was amateur dramatics on the street corner designed as a big smoky open-air advert for the Civil Defence Corps. With the sulky council refusing to cooperate, the Home Office had rewritten the script of the exercise pretending that the (non-existent) Coventry team had 'withdrawn to rest',[8] and so a team from Birmingham was attending instead. The battle between London and Coventry had escalated, and London was going to ensure that civil defence uniforms would be seen on the city's streets.

The setting for the exercise was a wrecked building in Priory Row. Enthusiastic locals had volunteered to act as casualties for the day and were told to scream and moan and lie askew in the carefully arranged rubble, allowing the Birmingham team to rescue them by strapping them onto stretchers, lowering them from windows and getting them out of the danger zone. The city councillors were furious. They had managed to obtain a copy of the script that was to be read aloud to the public watching the exercise, and they took particular offence to a passage that implied they would rather see Coventry folk suffer in agony than permit civil defence training:

> The public-spirited volunteers of Coventry are disappointed by this action of the council, and many of them have come forward as individuals and are taking part in the role of casualties etc. The council's attitude has deprived us of organised local forces, however, and we must now appreciate that if this were the real

thing, and there were no local workers, a long time would elapse before those sufferers you can see and hear, together with those too badly hurt to move, could be rescued. We must therefore now imagine that some hours have passed. We will not keep you waiting as the sufferers would have to wait. The rescue teams are near so that you can see how they set about their task, but remember as you see them come, unless Coventry were prepared it would be a long time before help could arrive. Some of your own relatives or friends might be among those trapped in agony waiting through seemingly endless hours before the vehicles you now see could really be here.[9]

Sidney Stringer strode into Priory Row in the midst of the exercise and began shouting his complaints through a loudspeaker, intending to cause maximum disruption. This prompted the civil defence teams to yell their script and instructions even louder, and the squawking racket rose higher and higher. As the *Manchester Guardian* reported:

From opposite sides of the street rival loudspeakers blared away at each other while between them Britain's first hydrogen bomb civil defence exercise was carried out in Coventry today. Members of the Labour group controlling Coventry City Council held a counter-demonstration to the Home Office exercises because they objected to passages in the official script for the Home Office commentator. As the official read his script, the demonstrators tried to blot out his words by speeches from their side . . . As he spoke, the volunteer 'casualties' surged out from the bombed house which was being used for the exercise, screaming and hysterically wandering about between the loudspeakers.[10]

If the Home Office was irritated by Coventry's defiance, it endured it quietly, but there was no such restraint from angry locals, who expressed their feelings in letters to the *Coventry Evening Telegraph*:

Never have I experienced such a shameful exhibition.

These crazy and contemptible caperings by the [council] will have utterly disgusted all sane and decent people in this city and have again made Coventry a national laughing stock.

Had the people of Britain been led by such as the present Coventry Socialists in 1940, none of us would be here to witness this interesting but sickening exhibition on the part of the chosen representatives of this gallant city . . . If we listen too long to our councillors here we might as well throw in the sponge![11]

There was also anger on the streets during the exercise when one elderly lady, dressed as a bleeding casualty, took exception to the shout-ing council protesters. 'It was a strange scene for a Sunday afternoon, in the shade of the quiet cathedral ruins and the stately trees in the churchyard,' reported the local newspaper. 'When the band of slight-injured "casualties" ran screaming from the bombed building they were led by an elderly woman who carried a canary in a cage. She ran towards the Labour speakers and tossed a bundle into the loud-speaker.'[12] Reports of the flying birdcage reached Prime Minister Churchill, who was annoyed at the bad publicity for the new Civil Defence Corps, writing, 'I hope there isn't going to be any more of this sort of thing at Government expense,' and adding, 'The Coventry City Council of course behaved as badly as they could.'[13]

Yet the often lurid theatrical display of civil defence exercises – the local people dressed in bandages and splattered with fake blood, the wailing and crying, the eerie setting of the ruined cathedral – drummed up publicity and helped recruit volunteers, whilst reinforcing the sense that the Corps was bold and active, and not just a relic from the Blitz. The drama – and the risk of farce that came with it – was necessary to pique public interest in a weary post-war society that was in no rush to get back into uniform.

Coventry's punishment wasn't long in coming. The Home Office decided to impose its own civil defence organisers on the city and then charge the rebellious council for the service. Three advisers descended from London and restarted recruitment to the Coventry Civil Defence Corps. They did so with vigour in door-to-door campaigns that increased the Corps' visibility, but the organisers knew civil defence was a prickly topic in Coventry and so 'each canvasser has been instructed to refrain from entering into arguments with householders on the value of civil defence against hydrogen bombs'.[14] London had won the Battle of Priory Row, but the Home Office knew better than to gloat. They realised that opposition to the new Civil Defence Corps was born not just of left-wing politics, but of war-weariness and a sense of futility in the face of the terrifying new hydrogen bomb.

'The fire that has started in Korea may burn down your house'

A volunteer from Coventry signing the recruitment forms for Britain's new Civil Defence Corps could have chosen to join one of five different sections:

> *Headquarters* – staffing the control centres, handling information, operating and maintaining communications equipment, science and technology and reconnaissance
>
> *Warden* – dealing with the public under attack, offering organisation and guidance: 'acting as guide, philosopher, friend, and leader of the public'[15]
>
> *Welfare* – arranging accommodation and food for those made homeless by the attack
>
> *Ambulance* – first aid and transport to hospital
>
> *Rescue* – rescue, demolition and clearance of debris[16]

The Corps recruited women over the age of 18 and men over 40. Although the male age restriction was lowered in 1952, the limit existed because young men would be called up if war came, so there seemed little point in training a large body of them only to see them all vanish into active service. Besides, it made good sense to recruit older men who were likely to have served in civil defence during the last war and so would come to the new Corps with relevant experience and knowledge. In addition, the Corps could draw on war veterans now too old to be conscripted again. Thus the Second World War provided a ready pool of recruits, and much of the new Corps' initial recruitment was done through wartime Civil Defence Associations, where former volunteers met to share their memories of the Blitz; indeed, 80 per cent of the new Corps' early recruits were Blitz veterans.[17]

Yet the recruitment adverts of the early 1950s didn't emphasise courage, heroism and the drama of nights spent under attack as they had during the Blitz. Instead, people were asked to volunteer because in 1945 they had won for themselves decent, peaceful lives and now they had an interest in preserving that pleasantly ordinary existence. Perhaps they had fought in the war like George Maggs, a 42-year-old retired soldier who appeared on a Civil Defence Corps recruitment advert. George looked like the sturdy and brave type, but the advert suggested that he now wanted a quiet life: 'In the rest of his spare time he gardens, follows football, and wins cups at skittles.' Here was a man with the required mettle and physical courage to come through the war but who was now happy to enjoy the small pleasures in life; a decent and wholesome chap but also someone who could step up to the task when needed. George was the ideal candidate for the Civil Defence Corps. If you want a bit of action, join the services, the adverts seemed to imply. If you want to keep things nice and steady, join Civil Defence.

Another such ideal volunteer was Mr Philip B. Dingle, who was Manchester's Town Clerk and took the minutes at his local civil defence meetings. His notes reveal the unadventurous nature of the new Corps. There is a remarkable absence of any kind of warlike glamour or excitement; instead, the minutes summarise the plodding, ordinary transactions that made up much of Cold War civil defence activity. 'With a view to making the premises more attractive to volunteers who attend for training,' he wrote on 13 April 1954, 'the Town Clerk suggests that curtains be provided for the four windows which overlook Hyde Road.' Things got a bit more lively when he reported on a quiz between the Manchester and Oldham civil defence divisions. In a thrilling match, the score was Manchester 69, Oldham 69½. There were some light refreshments followed by a coach ride home.[18] Men tired from the war and women bored at being stuck again in the kitchen gathered in meeting rooms above shops, in church halls and community centres, their work summed up by the splendidly humdrum slogan of the Corps: 'Civil defence is common sense'.

A recruitment advert from 1954 showed a group of people, one of whom had joined the Corps. The ad asked: 'Which of these is a good neighbour? They're more or less like the rest of us. They all cherish their wives, pay their taxes, are kind to children and the cat. But the good neighbour takes a wider view. He's helping to make the world a safer place for the rest of us.' The same message was delivered in recruitment films, which were often shown in cinemas before the main movie. In 1951, a film called *The Waking Point* portrayed a decent bloke called Joe who served in the civil defence during the war, and so is tempted to join the new Corps but is blocked by Gwen, his complaining wife, who quashes his small ambition. 'Now look here, Joe, I've had enough,' she says. 'It was bad enough during the war when you had to do it night after night. When you did have an evening off I was up to my elbows in nappies, babies' bottles, and I don't know what else. There was no end to it. Now when the kids are older and we could enjoy an evening off you want to stick a tin hat on your head again! Honestly, you make me tired, really you do!' But then one day his son becomes trapped in a landslide and Joe rushes to the rescue. His meek persona is completely transformed: he is suddenly commanding, keen and alert, recalling his old civil defence training from the war. With Joe having rescued their son, Gwen collapses at his feet in a grateful heap – never again to be a nag. He immediately joins the Corps and all is right with the world. The film suggested that the Civil Defence Corps was about so much more than preparing for nuclear attack: it trained you to be a useful member of society who could take charge and rescue small boys from crumbling hillsides – and you could repair your brittle marriage at the same time.

This emphasis on how the Corps' training would be useful in ordinary life allowed it to appeal to a wider section of society. Numbers were boosted, but never to a spectacular degree, although the outbreak of the Korean War in 1950 provoked a surge, especially when Clement Attlee appealed for volunteers by warning, 'The fire that has started in Korea may burn down your house.'[19] This increased membership fivefold, climbing to a total of 147,464 by June 1951.[20] But although the Korean War might have sparked a rise in numbers, a 1951 Home Office briefing told the prime minister that Britain's civil defence would not be able to cope with an attack on the scale of the Blitz, let alone a war with nuclear weapons. The British Chiefs of Staff concluded that eighteen months' warning would be needed to equip Britain properly for war, yet 'It was clear from events in Korea that it was more than possible there would be little, if any, warning. In these circumstances, the peace-time forces maintained by the United Kingdom were hardly more than bluff.'[21]

'Some of them think we're crazy.'

The poor state of the Civil Defence Corps was revealed in an October 1960 episode of the BBC current affairs programme *Panorama*.[22] Presenter Jim Mossman visited civil defence stores in Stafford that he described as being full of 'homely equipment of the sort that served so well in the last war . . . picks, hammers, emergency food containers and cooking pots'. The embarrassing perception was that the Corps had no resources other than dusty crockery and some tools grabbed from Grandpa's shed. He then interviewed the county civil defence officer, Colonel Marshall.

> MOSSMAN: How many air raid wardens – how many civil defence workers would you need in a nuclear war?
>
> MARSHALL: In the borough of Stafford – something of the order, perhaps, of a thousand.
>
> MOSSMAN: How many have you got today?
>
> MARSHALL: Active – about a hundred. But there are many more who have undertaken some training – although they don't attend training classes now.
>
> MOSSMAN: How many air raid posts have you got for wardens in Stafford?
>
> MARSHALL: The borough has planned for twenty-four warden posts.
>
> MOSSMAN: How many are in existence?
>
> MARSHALL: One at the present time, but of the others quite a number are earmarked premises.
>
> MOSSMAN: Assume that an H-bomb had dropped ten miles away from here, what could your people do about it?
>
> MARSHALL: Very little, if it's fallen ten miles away – until we've had time to get our senses together.

So what would they do? Mossman repeated the question four times. 'At this moment, little or nothing,' the colonel eventually replied.

When Mossman then interviewed some civil defence volunteers, he asked about the public perception of the Corps.

MOSSMAN: Do you find that people that aren't in [civil defence] think you're a bit funny?

FEMALE VOICE: Well some of them think we're crazy.

MOSSMAN: Why do they think that, do you think?

FEMALE VOICE: Well I don't know. I think it's wasting our time, and wasting the people's money . . .

When the interviewer spoke to members of the public, many were scathing about civil defence. 'A waste of time – absolute waste of time,' said one.

Mossman's dramatic conclusion was that the Civil Defence Corps should change its name and drop the word 'defence', as there could be no defence against the hydrogen bomb with such shoddy preparation. Instead he proposed that it call itself the Civil Emergency Corps, and that in the event of some great disaster or war, this reformed Corps should restrict itself modestly to 'some mopping up afterwards'. He ended his report with a stark conclusion: 'I think it's obvious that some sort of emergency organisation must exist, and it's equally obvious that in Britain at the moment the present organisation is not up to the job. It's not big enough. Indeed from our survey of just one town I think it's become fairly clear that not many people take civil defence in this country very seriously.'[23]

The Corps was furious. The civil defence college at Easingwold wrote to the Home Office, blaming it for giving the BBC access to the Corps, which as a result had been 'publicly ridiculed'. 'The whole tone was sneering, defeatist, and calculated to discourage recruiting throughout the country,' one Corps member from Devon complained; the leadership should 'arrange another programme immediately, to undo the harm'. A representative in the south-west wrote: 'I am very much afraid that the programme has done a tremendous amount of harm, particularly amongst the more thinking people who have probably got the impression that they wouldn't want to belong to a rag, tag and bobtail organisation such as Civil Defence if what was shown on the BBC was a typical example of how Civil Defence was run. I felt that I must let you know that a real storm of protest has been coming to me from the ground.'

The BBC's director general, Hugh Greene, responded to the storm by saying that he had watched the programme and did not agree that it was negative or unhelpful to civil defence: 'My own personal reaction to the item was that it gained enormously through not being obvious propaganda for Civil Defence but a truthful presentation of the situation in one particular town. I should have thought that it would be more likely to help in obtaining recruits in the Civil Defence Corps than any overt appeal.'[24]

While hard truths were being told by the BBC, out on the playing fields, show grounds and meadows of Britain, the Civil Defence Corps continued its recruitment campaign. Its members polished their buttons, straightened their caps and rolled out their trucks and equipment to put on a show to attract volunteers, creating an image of action and endeavour. They would regularly appear at carnivals, flower shows and county fairs, being listed on the bill alongside firework displays, Morris dancing contests, dog shows and tennis tournaments. The local newspaper described Reading's Civil Defence Sunday in 1958:

> While an air of seriousness was generally prevalent, there was also a gala spirit present. This was emphasised by the hundreds of youngsters who between eating 'hot-dogs', prepared by the mobile kitchen staff, and licking ever popular ice lollies, were allowed to 'play soldiers' at the Army's different exhibitions . . . During the afternoon a helicopter arrived and with almost uncanny manoeuvrability delighted the crowd by dancing in the air.[25]

Yet, the paper continued, 'the horrors of war, with its tragedy and suffering, were forcibly stressed':

> There were several demonstrations, but the one which focused most attention was the simulation of a bombing raid on an ammunition store in an Army depot in which Army personnel and civilians worked. With the aid of recorded sounds of an actual bombing raid, it was easy to conjure up a realistic picture of what could and what has actually happened, as Civil Defence wardens rescued seemingly badly-injured persons from the imagined blazing building and rushed them away for treatment.[26]

In another piece of nuclear street theatre, in west London in 1956,

> a once familiar sound, the air raid warning siren, sounded over
> Wormwood Scrubs on Monday evening and air raid wardens were
> seen ordering people to shelter. Suddenly there was a loud explo-
> sion! It was the beginning of a Civil Defence demonstration . . .
> Monday's demonstration was lit by searchlights and the centre-
> piece was a mock-up house . . . Wardens reported to Headquarters
> by walkie-talkie radio sets and then a column rescue vehicle and
> its crew were seen rescuing casualties from the damaged house.
> Then came the welfare section who were instructed to construct
> a fore and cross trench cooker which they did by collecting deb-
> ris from the same house. At the same time, appliances of the
> Auxiliary Fire Service entered the arena and demonstrated the
> drill of fixing hoses, starting their pumps and directing jets of
> water.

Display, showmanship and amateur dramatics had always featured
strongly in civil defence, both in recruiting the public and in training
volunteers. But because nuclear war was almost beyond imagination,
the Corps literally had to put on an act. Yet entertaining tableaux,
scripted lines, cries and sirens, and old ladies with birdcages being
pulled from rubble skirted over the reality of nuclear attack. The volunteers were recreating scenes from the Blitz rather than Hiroshima.
They helped fake casualties with bruises and sprains. Nobody was suffering from radiation sickness and there was no talk of those who
would have simply vaporised in the flash, leaving nothing but a shadow
on the wall.

Some Civil Defence Corps exercises were hidden from public view,
such as Exercise Dovetail, held at Old Boston Colliery in Lancashire in
1953. The RAF laid on some Canberra bombers, which made dummy
runs over the area, including realistic diving manoeuvres, as smoke
bombs were detonated on the ground. In Bristol two years earlier, the
theatrical element had reached a new height in Exercise Medusa, with
one volunteer, who was also the president of a local opera company,
calling on his friends to use their remarkable voices and make-up artistry skills, the fake casualties 'screaming in almost unearthly manner as
the soldiers cleared away the debris above the void'.[27]

But the exercises were not all about play-acting amid the rubble. In November 1964, Exercise Dustbath focused on the role of the BBC in communicating nuclear warnings and information to the public. A radio script was created for the exercise, complete with fake place names:

> This is the BBC Regional Service for the counties of AYSHIRE, BEESHIRE, CEESHIRE and the West Riding of DEESHIRE. Alvan Fiddell reporting. Between one o'clock and three o'clock this morning a number of attacks were made on this country by nuclear weapons. The main attack has been directed against London and the Home Counties but this region has been subjected to attacks on West Middlepoole, Nottington and Darlingham. Serious fires are raging in these places and there are very many casualties. Civil Defence and other rescue services are doing everything they can to rescue survivors. Immediate retaliatory measures were taken by our own forces and there have been no further attacks since three o'clock. Radioactive fallout already affects part of our region and will affect other areas later. If you have not already been warned to get to your refuge room, listen for the public warnings.[28]

The fictional towns of Nottington and Darlingham had an eerie ring of reality, but despite the neat uniforms, the roaring trucks, the heaps of rubble and the passionate commitment of their volunteers, the Civil Defence Corps was only ever faking nuclear war. Like Nottington and Darlingham, it almost seemed real, but every civil defence exercise had a huge hollow at its heart, what Professor Tracy Davis in her study of public civil defence exercises called 'the deferred event'. It was perhaps not that dissimilar to an office fire drill, where bored workers grab their coffees and file out of the building, glad to have an excuse for a chat and a cigarette. There is no panic, as it is just a rehearsal for the real thing and so can never recreate the terror and horror of a real fire. It's the same for all such training exercises: it can only ever be acting. What made these nuclear war games different was that the Civil Defence Corps was re-enacting the last war. It failed to imagine the reality of the nuclear holocaust.

'In hell, it is not only hot, but loud'

Those who sought a more specific role should war come were able to join the Auxiliary Fire Service (AFS), which was re-formed in 1949. Its volunteers would supplement the regular fire service in the event of nuclear attack, mainly by transporting and pumping water, although they could be summoned to do actual firefighting too, having received basic training.

Bombing in the Second World War had introduced a new horror: the firestorm. When bombs are dropped, fires start. If enough fires meet on the ground, they create a conflagration that produces super-heated air, which then rises. As the hot air ascends, it leaves a vacuum below that pulls in cooler air from the surrounding area. This new air is filled with oxygen, which feeds the fire, so that the flames surge higher and hotter, sucking in even more air. This creates violent winds on the ground as the air is swept into the fire's howling heart: the fire has slipped loose from the control of man and is creating its own weather.

A survivor of the 1943 Hamburg firestorm recalled the dreadful noise. 'What a sound it was! It was hell. It was hell's fires. In hell, it is not only hot, but loud. The firestorm was screaming!'[29] Another likened the fiery scream to someone pressing all the keys on an old church organ, a deep, incessant grinding drone. There was no escaping the churning hellscape of the city as the roads started to soften and bubble:

At some point in the night I ran on once more with the dripping wet jacket of [a] dead man over my head. In this whirling fire I had lost all sense of direction. On my way out of the chaos I came across a burned-out tram. The windows had melted in the heat. Dead bodies lay stacked on top of one another in the carriage. Their clothes had disintegrated into embers. The people had tried to shelter there from the firestorm. In Eiffestrasse they struggled for survival. Sinking into the hot tarmac they had tried to support themselves with their hands and lay now on their knees. They ended their lives screaming with fear and pain.[30]

Firestorms also occurred in Dresden, Tokyo, Hiroshima and Naga-saki in 1945, but it wasn't until the Strath Report a decade later that the British authorities were presented with the reality of what a nuclear firestorm on British soil would look like. Although written in the spare and detached prose of the civil servant, the 1955 report is one of the most fearsome documents ever produced by government:

> The fire hazard from nuclear attack dwarfs all previous experi-ence to insignificance. The heat flash from one hydrogen bomb would start in a built-up area anything up to 100,000 fires, with a circumference of between 60 to 200 miles. Conflagrations might develop and sweep downwind until they burnt themselves out or encountered a natural fire break, but the risk of this in a British city is hard to assess. If the bomb were ground-burst, radioactive debris and fallout from the explosion might soon make the downwind half of the fire zone inaccessible from outside.[31]

The report recommended whitewashing windows in an effort to deflect some of the heat of the flash, and using 'flash-resisting curtains and the removal of combustible material which could act as tinder if left lying about'. But this sits awkwardly alongside the official advice for the householder at the time[32] to pile the refuge room full of such material by barricading windows with chests of drawers packed with books or similar heavy items, and reinforcing thin outer walls with 'pieces of heavy furniture and stacks of books'. Strath reached the sobering conclusion that the fire services would be helpless in the face of this apocalyptic scenario: 'Many fires would have to be left to burn themselves out.'

The terrible conclusions of the Strath Report were disseminated and discussed secretly in Whitehall; they were not disclosed to the Brit-ish people for fear of causing public despair and a rise in support for nuclear disarmament. Thus, in ignorance of the reality of nuclear war, each fire station across the country continued to organise its band of new AFS volunteers, who would attend once a week for training.

Transporting water would be the AFS's main task in nuclear war, and for that they were supplied with chunky Bedford fire engines, offi-cially called the RLHZ Self Propelled Pump, but popularly known as the Green Goddess. Painted in the British armed forces' favoured shade, bronze green, these had a siren and a ladder and hoses like ordinary red fire engines, but their chief purpose was to transport water, and then to pump it to where it was needed by the regular firemen. Dave Smith, a former AFS man who served in Wareham, Dorset, in the 1960s, recalled a training session where fifty Green Goddesses were connected to one another in a long conga line:

> That's what you trained to be part of. Your big aluminium hose pipes just connecting and connecting from one appliance to another and the pumpmen would feed the water up the line, and at the other end of the line there could be a fireman, not necessarily an AFS person, because you neither had the gear nor the experience to be helping with fires. So that wasn't your main job, your main job was to get it [water] to them.

The Green Goddess deliberately lacked the sophisticated gear of a modern fire engine so she could be easily maintained and repaired in a war situation. With her chassis set high off the ground to enable her to barrel across rough war-torn terrain with her heavy load of water, she did not make for a smooth ride. Dave recalled: 'If you had the Green Goddess today, coming after what we drive today, wow, it's like getting on a train with wooden slat seats, but fifty years ago we didn't take any notice of it. Being out in the Green Goddess was brilliant! Great fun.'

Whilst there were some complaints from AFS men about not being taken seriously by the regular firemen, Dave never encountered any animosity. There were complaints that the AFS were not properly protected, as they were not kitted out like regular firemen but wore the old wartime tin hats. One Middlesex AFS man remembered that he had not attended a single fire where members of the public had not made jokes about his helmet. However, Dave had no complaints about the kit.

> We were AFS. I don't think any one of us moaned that we didn't have the posh helmets that the firemen had . . . I think if we were doing serious firefighting I'd say the gear we had was maybe too heavy when it was wet. The coats, in particular, if they got wet you'd wish you didn't have them on, and if you were out in the sun you'd really melt in them, but I don't think any of us thought, 'wish we had their gear'.

The end

While Dave and his AFS colleagues were shifting water and the Civil Defence Corps continued its recruitment campaigns, warm memories of the Blitz were gradually replaced with the cold reality of nuclear war. In the late 1950s, CND arose as a serious force and exploded into the news headlines with their massive Ban the Bomb marches. By this point the Corps was already struggling with its near-impossible task of convincing the British people that nuclear war was survivable. Indeed, the government recognised the Corps' increasingly obvious futility when it axed the redundant Rescue and Ambulance sections in 1966, and from this moment onwards, the weakened Civil Defence Corps was little more than a boost for morale; a signal to the enemy that Britain was in some small way prepared; a means of organising and training a body of people for other national emergencies. The Corps became the 'public face of nuclear survivability which the government knew to be false',[33] at least since the Strath Report had revealed the awful truth.

In 1968, both the Civil Defence Corps and the Auxiliary Fire Service were disbanded. The main reason was the ever-present need to save money. In *After the Bomb*, Matthew Grant writes that the Wilson government had devalued the pound against the dollar in November 1967, and so we had 'a sterling crisis too far and the whole basis of cold war civil defence was swept away and the Civil Defence Corps consigned to history'.[34]

9 Control

Durham Prison in the north of England is one of Britain's most notorious jails. Built in the early nineteenth century, it still looks grimy with the soot of the Industrial Revolution, gloomy and forbidding, a vast stone edifice punctured by hundreds of tiny barred windows, encircled with fencing and coils of barbed wire. Some of Britain's most infamous criminals have been locked up here: Ian Brady, Ronnie Kray, Frankie Fraser and Rosemary West.

The Moors Murderer, Myra Hindley, was serving her sentence in London's Holloway when, due to renovation work at the prison in 1977, she was suddenly sent to Durham. In Holloway she had taken tea with the governor, where they discussed poetry by the fireside; she sang and played guitar, joined a cookery club, decorated her cell with photographs and cards, and was permitted a small TV. Durham offered no such leniency. Breakfast was taken whilst the inmates filed past to 'slop out', a foul smell hanging over the food trays, and she took her exercise in a concrete yard overlooked by the male prisoners, who yelled, 'Hang Mad Myra!' when she appeared. She referred to the prison as a 'concrete submarine' and fell into depression.[1]

Durham was no easy stretch. The local paper, the *Newcastle Journal*, called the jail a 'dungeon'; its H Wing was 'unfit for animals', with '"archaic" sanitation facilities' and 'confined and claustrophobic cells with no natural light'.[2]

Yet in nuclear war, such a dreadful place becomes desirable. The authorities wanted Durham to house and shelter government staff, and there were similar plans for Canterbury and Chelmsford prisons. As with Castle Acre, vast, tough, impenetrable buildings made to keep out invaders and contain people inside were becoming ideal places of shelter under nuclear attack and fallout conditions. But to be of use to the government, Durham and the other prisons would have to be emptied in the final days before nuclear war.

Getting out of jail free

In the dreadful conditions after a nuclear strike, the care and maintenance of prisoners would have been a massive burden on the state: far better to throw the doors wide and allow them to fend for themselves. This would free up hundreds of trained prison officers for war duties, perhaps supplementing the police, and allow the secure buildings to be put to wartime use. The decision to clear the jails was also prompted by the notion that, after a devastating nuclear war, a prison sentence would no longer be an effective punishment; on the contrary, it would be desirable to be in a place of shelter and be given a bed and regular meals. 'Certain people may have to be constrained,' said the Home Office, 'but a prison sentence as a punishment would lose its meaning.'[3]

The prisoner releases would happen during the precautionary stage, the last days before nuclear attack was expected, but a public already tense and fearful would not be asked to cope with an influx of dangerous murderers and rapists into their communities. It was decided that only the more palatable types of prisoner would be released: those in open prisons; those serving less than three years; those on longer sentences but with less than twelve months remaining; and those on remand charged with an offence carrying a maximum penalty of five years. The prison governors would continue to retain 'long-term prisoners and those persons who would be an exceptionally grave danger to the public if set at liberty, i.e. a) the worst type of dangerous criminal, b) persons of dangerous and violent propensities by reason of mental disorder, and c) potential fifth columnists'.[4]

But there was one group of serious offenders whose release into the community might actually be beneficial to reconstruction after nuclear war. Psychiatrists estimated that about 1 per cent of the population could be described as psychopaths, and the Home Office reckoned these people might be of unique value in the chaos of post-nuclear Britain. A psychopath was not expected to be hampered by disaster syndrome and would experience 'no psychological effects in the communities which suffer the severest losses'. Therefore, a report noted,

'They are very good in crises, as they have no feelings for others, no moral code, and tend to be very intelligent and logical. Pre-strike, the only solution for these people is to contain them; post-strike, the authorities may find it advantageous to recruit these people, as they could prove an exceptionally valuable resource.'[5]

Prisoners would be released in haste and expected to slot back into a society that would be in a state of terror and turmoil. There would be no rehab programmes and no guidance from probation officers, no re-employment schemes, no hostels or halfway houses. There might not even be functioning public transport to get them home, as their release would coincide with other emergency measures, such as the closure of petrol stations and major roads. A prisoner released in London would have no easy way of getting home to his mum or his missus in Newcastle before the bomb dropped.

The prisoners who were retained, plus all the subversives who had been rounded up in the countdown to war, would be corralled in one or two prisons or other secure locations. In his book *War Plan UK*, Duncan Campbell thought it was 'tempting to suppose they may have been located in major target areas'.[6] Documents in the Scottish national archive from 1965 suggested putting the retained Scottish prisoners in Peterhead Prison,[7] a notorious maximum-security jail that has been labelled 'Scotland's gulag', a 'powder-keg jail', and a 'hate factory', with a violent history of riots, rooftop protests and the seizure of guards as hostages.[8] In 1987, a riot saw a prison officer dragged across the prison roof in chains, with the siege only ending when the SAS entered with stun grenades and CS gas.[9] At the resulting trial, one of the defendants wrote a letter about conditions in the jail that was read aloud in court by his QC: 'If the prison authorities insist on treating prisoners like animals, then prisoners will continue to act like animals.'[10]

One of the main complaints of the recurring riots was the difficulty of inmates receiving visits from friends and family. Located on the inhospitable north-east coast, Peterhead was far from the central belt of Scotland where most of the prisoners came from, lying 200 miles away from Glasgow. 'TO [*sic*] FAR FOR VISITS' read a message scrawled on a sheet on the roof during the unrest. But its relative isolation would become an asset during nuclear attack. The government's list of probable nuclear targets from 1972 names just a few in the north-east of Scotland, such as the bomber bases of RAF Lossiemouth and RAF Kinloss and the radar station at Buchan, but none near Peterhead. Edinburgh and Glasgow were noted as 'major cities' and therefore likely targets, but there was no mention of Aberdeen, the nearest city to Peterhead.

If this plan had been carried out, prison guards would have been tasked with controlling the very worst and most violent of Scottish prisoners whilst a nuclear war raged. We may wonder whether they would have stayed at their posts under these nightmarish conditions.

Most people would have been unaware that in the event of nuclear war masses of prisoners would be released amongst them, so they voiced no concerns; but the country's chief constables expressed 'general misgivings'[11] about the proposal. A letter from the City of Glasgow Police to the Scottish Home and Health Department declared that senior CID officers were 'most unhappy' and that the plans would allow for the release of 'some dangerous and persistent criminals who would be a real menace if they were liberated at such a time'.[12] They proposed that each criminal be given a category, which would make it clear whether they were safe and acceptable for this type of pre-strike release. Recognising that this would add a layer of bureaucracy and work for a prison staff already under impossible stress and strain in the approach of war, they suggested, quite sensibly, that the categorisation take place in advance of the emergency. However, such a measure came with its own problems. There was the possibility that the prisoners' categorisations might be discovered, leading to unrest and possibly riots by those who learned that they would be confined to a cell during nuclear attack whilst others were set free.

Barnton Quarry

The civil defence authorities for the north of England had earmarked the sturdy, secure building of Durham Prison for their own use in nuclear war. For similar reasons, the north-west region had chosen the Imperial Hotel in Blackpool: a huge Victorian pile on the seafront, well-built enough to withstand fierce storms rolling in off the Irish Sea, and offering living space well away from any target areas. Elsewhere, Scarborough's Grand Hotel, Arundel Castle, Ilkley's Craiglands Hotel, and Welbeck Abbey were all listed as potential hideouts for regional leaders during and after nuclear attack.

After London had been knocked out as the seat of government – which seemed certain – the country would be divided into civil defence regions, each to be led by a regional commissioner, probably a Cabinet minister, who would be given complete power over his region until central government could reassert itself. The commissioners would be in charge of every aspect of life and law-making. With a staff of about 400 drawn from the NHS, the police and fire service, and the BBC, plus scientific advisers and experts in agriculture, transport and distribution, they would set the rules on food distribution, medical aid and the organisation of labour. Kitchen and security staff would be provided by the army. They would all carry out their work from a regional seat of government (RSG). In the popular imagination, these were bunkers but many of the RSGs would in fact be located in a ragtag collection of buildings, from army barracks toughened with sandbags and boarded windows to the Imperial Hotel in Blackpool and Durham Prison. There were plans, always delayed and constantly revised, to build proper subterranean bunkers for each region, but until then, in classic British fashion, each region would have to 'muddle on'.

Still, there was one proper RSG bunker, at Barnton Quarry, which lies in a quiet suburb of Edinburgh. Originally a stone quarry, it had been used by the RAF during the war, and its first Cold War role was in radar operations, housing a team that watched the sky for incoming Russian bombers and processed information from Scottish radar stations. With the arrival of intercontinental ballistic missiles, which moved too fast to be spotted and shot down, Barnton Quarry's role changed yet again. In the 1960s, the huge Barnton Quarry bunker, three floors deep, became an RSG[13] that would house 400 politicians, experts and administrators in a nuclear war, sheltering them for up to 30 days. Until that moment, it lay empty but in constant readiness, with phone lines installed and its water tanks topped up.

It lost this important role in 1983, when ownership passed to the local council but they found it too expensive to maintain. The authority tried to sell it, and a series of entrepreneurs expressed interest. There were ambitious plans to turn it into luxury flats, even a shellfish farm, but the bunker proved impossible to demolish or remodel, so it was eventually abandoned. It soon became a paradise for scrap-metal thieves, who broke in and feasted on the rich copper wire in the site's telephone exchange. Anything of value was stripped and stolen, including the massive blast doors, each weighing a ton and a half. It was also a playground for local kids, who were attracted by this dark, forbidden place. Then someone rammed a truck into the bunker's long, sloping entrance tunnel, and piled various underground rooms high with old tyres, so when a fire was started in the bunker in 1993, it gorged on the rubber and burned for days, reaching temperatures of 800°C. Firemen stood helplessly at the mouth of the tunnel as the fire raged below, and violent explosions could be heard underground as the heat caused metal fittings in the walls to expand, forcing huge chunks of concrete to burst free. The bunker was now burned and black inside, and this was how I found it when I visited in 2016.

My guide was Grant More, who was leading the bunker's restoration. Barnton Quarry was eventually purchased by James Mitchell, who also owns Scotland's Secret Bunker in Fife, and since 2011, a project has been under way to return the site to its Cold War glory, with the intention of opening it as a museum. The work was being done by local volunteers under the supervision of a site foreman, and the funding came from ticket sales at Scotland's Secret Bunker. Grant had real passion for the project and admitted to having played inside the ruined bunker as a child. He knew the place intimately.

Equipped with hard hats and lanterns, we walked down the tunnel as he explained that the first job for his restoration team had been to drag the burned truck from the tunnel entrance and gouge the remnants of the melted tyres from the various rooms. As he strode ahead explaining the bunker's history, his words echoed off the black walls. He leapt nimbly over piles of crumbled brick, hopped down dangerous staircases and vanished round corners. I trotted behind him, out of breath, my lantern bobbing and throwing ghosts on the wall. The place looked like the set of a horror film, everything black and scarred and jagged. Scampering to keep pace with Grant, I stubbed my toe on some strange bumpy swirls on the ground. When I shone my lantern on them, it looked like rough black ice had formed on the floor. He explained that this was melted glass that had dripped from various interior doors and windows during the fire before hardening into black whorls. In fact, these stains were aiding the restoration work, as each frozen pool of glass told the volunteers where there had once been a door or window, and so helped them plot the bunker's original layout.

We passed ladies' toilets with their parade of sooty, vandalised cubicles. I was relieved to see the cubicles had doors, having once visited a nuclear bunker in Prague intended for civilians whose toilets had no lockable doors. My Czech guide had explained that this was aimed at preventing people from killing themselves in the cubicles in an attempt to escape the apocalypse. There had been other suicide deterrents in the toilet block, such as the use of a sheet of polished steel instead of a mirror, so it could not be broken and a shard of glass used to slash the wrists. In the civilian bunkers of West Germany, such as that behind the Pankstrasse underground station in Berlin, the number of toilet cubicles was deliberately insufficient for the many people seeking refuge, so there would always be a long queue – again denying solitude to those who were thinking about ending their lives. I asked Grant if the toilet blocks at Barnton Quarry had been planned with any such suicide deterrents, but the answer was negative. In the event of nuclear war, the bunker would have been staffed with busy people, and we might imagine that their overwhelming duties and sense of purpose might have given them a different mindset to that of a frightened civilian herded into a shelter with just a few minutes' notice.

Spies for Peace

The locations – indeed, the very existence – of Britain's RSGs were to be kept top secret: the government knew that there would be great public anger if it became known that bunkers were being provided for the elite but not for the people. And of course they had to remain secret so they could not be targeted by the enemy. But in 1963, every detail of Britain's secret bunker system was revealed to the public by an anonymous group of activists calling themselves Spies for Peace.

The CND Ban the Bomb marches to Aldermaston had grabbed the headlines since they began in 1958. They were largely peaceful, but one group of protesters called the Committee of 100 (C100) favoured a more disruptive approach, summed up by the slogan 'fill the jails'. They rejected polite middle-class marching for mass disobedience, such as the sit-in in Parliament Square in February 1961, which led to over 800 arrests.[14] Forcing the police to detain large numbers of protesters would not only generate headlines but would threaten to overwhelm the authorities. Yet before long, being bundled endlessly into police vans was no longer good enough either.[15] In early 1963, a report entitled 'Beyond Counting Arses' was circulated amongst C100. It argued that the 'fill the jails' policy had become a repetitive performance, 'a ritual "pas-de-deux" with the police';[16] something new was needed, beyond the self-congratulatory counting of 'arrested arses'.

In February 1963, four activists from C100 broke into the RSG near Warren Row in Berkshire. The bunker had formerly been a chalk pit and served as an underground aircraft factory in the war before it was repurposed as a bunker. A *New Statesman* article written years later by the daughter of one of the activists explained how the group had been able to gain access to the structure, secured with blast doors and designed to withstand nuclear attack:

> They drove for hours over ice-covered roads, and tramped over snow-covered fields. At the east end of a village called Warren Row they found a fenced off hill with a padlocked wooden gate and an unmarked hut. They climbed over the gate to find a brick boiler house and a wide concrete ramp leading into the hillside. Radio aerials stood a little way off, their cables leading into the hill. One of the explorers tried the doors of the boiler house and found them unlocked. The four of them went in. Inside, they tried another door to what looked like a cupboard. This was also unlocked and swung open to reveal a steep staircase leading into an underground office complex. They ran down the stairs, their feet clattering in the silence, and snatched what papers they could from the desks. Then they rushed out, and drove away, hardly able to believe their luck.[17]

When the group returned later to explore the bunker in more detail, they found the door locked. This time they simply picked the lock. They had come armed with cameras and spent hours in the bunker, snapping photos of maps and taking copies of documents. They then produced a pamphlet revealing what lay beneath this Berkshire hillside, entitled 'DANGER: OFFICIAL SECRET!' Three thousand copies were sent from different parts of the country to politicians, newspapers and other activists. The document began:

> This pamphlet is about a small group of people who have accepted thermonuclear war as a probability, and are consciously

and carefully planning for it. They are above the army, the police, the ministries, or civil defence. They are based in 14 Secret headquarters each ruled by a regional commissioner with absolute power over millions of people. In the whole of Britain, only about 5,000 men and women are involved. These chosen few are a shadow military government. Their headquarters are called regional seats of government. Our story mainly concerns RSG 6, which will rule much of southern England. The people in RSG 6 are professors, top civil servants, Air Marshals and policemen. They are quietly waiting for the day the bomb drops, for that will be the day they take over.

The pamphlet blew the secret of Britain's secret RSGs, even publishing their addresses and phone numbers. The story hit the front pages and the hunt was on to find the anonymous spies. Plain-clothes policemen mingled with the crowd at Ban the Bomb marches hoping to catch a bit of gossip, hear a name being dropped or see some of the pamphlets being passed around. A man found handing out copies in Turnham Green in London was arrested. Mr Kenneth Browning, a builder and activist from Clacton, told the court that he hadn't printed them himself, but someone had dropped 14,000 copies at his caravan during the night and asked if he wouldn't mind distributing them. He was charged with assaulting a police officer and remanded on £20 bail. The original spies were never found, although a *New Statesman* article in 2002 named one of them as the late journalist Nicolas Walter.

With every newspaper now aware of their locations, the RSGs became useless, as it could be assumed the Soviets knew them too and would have adjusted their target lists accordingly. The Review of Home Defence in 1965 effectively spelled the end for the RSGs in their current role. The massive bunkers, kept permanently on standby, would no longer be manned in advance of the attack, housing hundreds of people to lead and manage the country after the war; instead, if they survived the blast, they would be occupied as soon as possible *after* the strike. In advance of the nuclear war, groups of nominated people would now gather in smaller scattered bunkers and basements throughout the country. They were the Sub-Regional Controls (SRCs), as explained by Subterranea Britannica, a group devoted to the study of underground places in Britain:

The role of the new SRC was to organise help for any local authority which was overwhelmed, to deploy resources over a wider area than a county and deal with functions such as trade and electricity distribution which were not local authority functions. They would also be essential in the command and control of the armed forces, fire service, police and the maintenance or resumption of power and water supplies, transport, food and other essentials. The Home Office maintained that without them there would be no means of organising any government above the local authority level after a nuclear attack.[18]

Meanwhile, the regional commissioner and his staff, who would previously have been accommodated at the big RSGs, would disperse across the region to various bolt-holes. As soon as possible after the attack, once radiation levels permitted movement, they would emerge and gather at a suitable meeting point to begin their governance of the region, listening out for a call from London that might never come.

Ladies to the rescue

The politicians, experts and planners emerging from the bunkers, basements, prisons and hotels after the nuclear strike could only hope to control the post-strike population, and seek to fend off bubbling threats of anarchy and chaos, if the survivors were clothed, sheltered and fed. There was no chance of maintaining order if the state did not provide that most basic level of relief. So while at the top of the post-nuclear pyramid we might have the regional commissioners and their band of experts, at the bottom, doing the most basic but critical work, would be the indefatigable Women's Royal Voluntary Service, who would offer blankets, tea, soup and shelter at organised rest centres. If their endeavour failed, everything balanced on top would collapse.

Despite the scraps of comfort to be found at a rest centre, it was crucial that survivors were not allowed to linger there. This was a departure from what had happened during the Blitz. Nineteen days after the first attack on London on 7 September 1940, there were 25,000 people still in rest centres,[19] even though these places were intended to be busy production lines: survivors would arrive, give their details, get a space to rest, be given a hot drink, maybe a bowl of soup or stew, before emerging at the other end having been provided with a new address for a temporary billet until their old home could be rebuilt or repaired. There was some frustration in the rest centres among the bereaved and homeless, but these were localised incidents. In a nuclear attack, however, when society had been shattered and the whole nation was enduring terror and disruption, local panics and disputes would quickly escalate. A bombed-out family in the Blitz who grumbled they had not been rehoused would pose no threat to law and order, but millions of desperate people with the same complaint would become a serious threat indeed. Understandably, there would therefore be a heavy emphasis on moving people through the rest centres as quickly as possible.

The WRVS was told how to get people from the rest centres into temporary accommodation. 'A long stay is bad for morale, is trying on the temper and nerves and makes family life strained,' the advice warned.[20] The ladies would be expected to canvass local households – those which were still intact – to judge their suitability for accepting homeless people, and, at the same time, persuade householders to let them into their homes. The guidance suggested a soft, feminine approach: 'The best people for this job are those who understand how to approach the woman of the house, how to present the situation in a way which gains her sympathy and who can also assess quickly the condition of the home being visited.' Recognising householders' unwillingness to open their homes to strangers, the guidance insisted, 'One *must* be a salesman.'

The angry homeless

Despite the name, therefore, rest centres were never intended for 'rest' but for a speedy processing of people. 'Those who are homeless are *angry*,' the Blitz journalist Mea Allan had reported in October 1940,[21] and so it was important to prevent them gathering in groups, because in the close quarters of the rest centre, anger might rise, rumours could spread and gossip would be exchanged, all of which might fuel resentment and fire rebellion. Specific guidance was issued in 1964 on how these people should be handled. In a section bluntly headed 'Dangers of the Homeless in Large Groups', the booklet insisted that homeless people should only be gathered together for as short a time as possible, and that 'every effort should be made to avoid large groups'. Three reasons were given:

1. The longer groups of people are held together the greater is the danger of epidemics.
2. The control of groups and the maintenance of law and order would become more difficult as their size increased and the longer they remained together.
3. The morale of the homeless would suffer the longer they were held in groups.[22]

The prospect of finding safe billets for displaced people would be difficult, if not hopeless. War-gaming exercises and predictions of nuclear attack indicated that in a worst-case scenario, most houses in Britain would be damaged, their windows broken and roofs shattered, leaving the inhabitants exposed to the elements. The relatively small-scale evacuation operation in Britain in 1939 had also revealed the social tensions created by allocating billets. Yet the guidance insisted that this was the goal and end point of rest centres. Telling the refugees that a home was waiting for them was a way to pacify their rage: 'It would be made clear to people in the rest centres that billeting was the objective; the knowledge that a home would be found for them in which they could settle down for the time being would be a powerful factor in raising their morale.'[23]

But imagine the furious drop in morale when stunned survivors came to realise that no safe home awaited. Surely their anger would surge, both at the deception and at the hopelessness of their condition; there would also be resentment that some others had a roof over their heads. The numbed state of disaster syndrome might wear off, and fury would come instead to the fore. The authorities' best hope, at this early stage, was that they would be able to splinter and divide any large crowds, so there would be angry individuals and family groups but no mobs to threaten the state.

The British government's move in the later Cold War to replace evacuation with a 'stay put' policy also sought to prevent the gathering of large and unmanageable crowds. But the focus on individual households as units of survival created resentment as householders competed with each other. Does your neighbour have a trench or shelter? Does he have the know-how to fortify the house? Are his windows nicely boarded up? Does he have the spare cash to stock up his larder? Is it groaning with tins of chicken noodle soup and Carnation milk and plastic bottles of crystal-clear Evian? Are there piles of bandages and bottles of disinfectant and good, trusty painkillers in his bathroom? Does he *have*, and you have *not*? Evacuation creates a mob, whereas 'stay put' divides and discourages collective action.

Operation Vicar Elastic

In a post-nuclear Britain, populated with displaced, homeless and angry people with nothing left to lose, the authorities might enlist the churches to pacify and control them. Home Office guidance suggested that if people were refusing to open their spare rooms to the homeless, the local clergyman might knock on a few doors. He might also remind his congregation from the pulpit of the importance of an orderly and obedient evacuation.[24] These proposals were concrete enough, but the general role of clergymen during and after the nuclear attack was vague. The same guidance suggested that they could be of assistance by 'allaying fear, controlling panic', but the magical methods of doing so were not specified. These naïve proposals date from the early Cold War, and we can see in them once again the long hangover of the Blitz: clergymen might be of assistance at the local rest centre and 'the ladies of the congregation could probably be depended upon for additional help'. This almost paints the post-bomb landscape as a church picnic, with fragrant wives in pastels dishing out madeira cake and Earl Grey with their gloved hands.

By the 1980s, advice on how the churches might assist in calming and controlling the population had become more hard-headed and practical. Just as the emptying of prisons would free up substantial buildings, the many churches in England would be utilised after an attack. Selected clergymen were sent off to civil defence training courses at the Home Office colleges at Easingwold and Taymouth Castle, in the hope that this would make them more than just a comforting presence after the attack. In 1986, a group of vicars joined the Parachute Regiment for a weekend of barrage balloon training, abseiling and a spot of driving tanks across Salisbury Plain. Operation Vicar Elastic had been organised by army chaplains to give their more sedentary colleagues some 'insight into the role of an army chaplain in the nuclear age'.[25] In 1984, the Home Office outlined its views on the usefulness of post-nuclear clergy:

> We consider that the primary role of the clergy in an emergency, both before and after an attack, should be to carry out their pastoral duties. In the face of the threat of attack they would be among those to whom people would naturally turn for information and advice. After an attack they would expect to be with the dying, the injured and the distraught. While each clergyman would be free to do what he thought best, his work might be more effective if he was in touch with the civil defence services and had some knowledge of the dangers and of the action various services were taking.[26]

The Home Office suggested a 36-hour training course to equip clergymen with the necessary knowledge. It also recommended they be given a dosimeter and an armband saying *Minister of Religion*. It was clear that 'survivors would need, *and would expect to find*, spiritual help as well as material assistance [my italics]'.[27] Even if the men of the cloth could do little other than wander the rubble and the rest centres with kind words and feeble blessings, their presence would serve as an extension of the power of the state: it suggested that the authorities were still in charge.

While the local vicar or priest would pull on his armband and see to his flock, a few chosen clergymen would endure the nuclear attack deep in the government bunkers. The Home Office believed that 'there would be an advantage in the Regional Commissioner having the advice of a clergyman available to him . . . Other possible duties which come to mind are acting as chaplain to the staff and broadcasting through the facilities which would be available.'[28] The BBC studios in each bunker would make short broadcasts to the surviving local population: they had to be brief because it was expected that listeners would be tuning in on battery-powered radios, whose life had to be eked out for as long as possible. Broadcasts therefore would be restricted to short announcements on the hour giving essential information and instruction. It is hard to believe they would have made space for the luxury of prayer, but this would have been up to each individual regional commissioner. If he felt a religious broadcast to his region would be of use, then he had the option. Certainly there are plenty of Bible verses on the importance of sacrifice and duty.

As space was severely limited in the RSGs, there would have been no room for representatives of all the main religious faiths, so the Home Office suggested local churches decide amongst themselves who should be nominated. The chosen denomination would then select three clergymen for the job, in the expectation that at least one would be available on the day. It is likely that space would have been cleared in the canteen for any services or communion to be conducted underground. However, the government's cavernous Burlington bunker allowed itself the luxury of the following in its supplies list:

COVERS, altar, frontal, green/purple, reversible 1
COVERS, altar, frontal, red/white, reversible 1
CROSSES, altar, brass, 21x W/O figure 1
CANDLESTICKS, altar, brass, 12x hexagonal pairs[29]

The inclusion of altar cloths of various colours would mean that clergymen were prepared for nuclear war at any stage of the liturgical calendar, with the various shades marking different occasions: green for Pentecost, white for Christmas Day, red for Holy Week and purple during Advent. Interestingly, purple is also recommended on the altar for funerals and for the Commemoration of the Faithful Departed.

Reagan and Armageddon theology

Religion could be used to pacify, comfort and control a terrified population, but in the 1980s, we saw how it could also be used to goad the atheist enemy and raise fears of nuclear war. When Ronald Reagan became US president in 1980, the Americans had elected for themselves a handsome man with a Hollywood smile. 'It's morning again in America', declared the sunny campaign ads of the former actor, but Reagan was, like so many other American politicians, a religious conservative. In fact, he was so religious, and so intent on interpreting the

Bible literally, that it caused alarm. He was fascinated by the end-of-the-world prophecies set out in the fiery Book of Revelation, writing in his diary, 'I swear I believe Armageddon is near.'[30]

For a president to believe in the end of the world was concerning: it suggested he thought nuclear war was inevitable, that it was God's plan, and that to try and avert it would be to meddle with His work. After a documentary called *Ronald Reagan and the Prophecy of Armageddon* was broadcast by 175 radio stations during the 1984 re-election campaign,[31] the president's position on the inevitability of Armageddon caused such consternation that 100 religious leaders from the Catholic, Protestant and Jewish faiths signed a letter expressing their concern and asking him to make a public statement in which he rejected Armageddon theology. Some people worried that a US president possessed of such religious beliefs might 'consider pressing the nuclear button in the Christian conviction that global war was biblically predicted and divinely pre-ordained . . . It is irresponsible to say that war is inevitable because predicted in the Bible. That creates passivity and inertia, resignation and despair. How better to ensure it happens than to say it is going to happen?'[32]

However, the religious right in the US were delighted, and it was in a speech to the National Association of Evangelicals in 1983 that Reagan made one of his most dangerous comments. His address was theatrically religious in its tone and words. 'Yes, let us pray for the salvation of all of those who live in that totalitarian darkness – pray they will discover the joy of knowing God,' he announced, before calling the Soviet Union 'an evil empire' and 'the focus of evil in the modern world'. He had turned from politician to preacher, delivering a fire-breathing sermon that placed East and West as eternal enemies. So while religion could bring comfort after nuclear war, there was also the risk that it would drive the world towards the brink.

The police

The major force of control in the event of nuclear war would of course be the police. Prior to an attack, they would have been steadily expanding their resources. Those who had left the service would be asked to return, young cadets would be swiftly promoted, and all requests for leave, resignation or retirement would be cancelled. The thin blue line would thicken as the countdown to war ticked on. Officers' duties would also change: they would have to roll up their sleeves and start shifting sandbags and boarding up windows, fortifying police stations against blast and fallout. They would likewise have to stock water and food at the station on the assumption that staff would be taking cover there during the attack and would have to remain in place for several days until fallout had decreased. As the approach of war grew closer, they would be sent to guard essential service routes, keeping them clear for use by officials and thereby forestalling any unofficial evacuation.[33]

Officers would guard petrol stations so that fuel stocks could be preserved for official use – another way to stop a frightened population from leaving the cities. They would check and prepare local sirens for use; they would guard town halls, food supply depots and power stations. Perhaps their most troubling role at this point would be to detain any potential subversives threatening to undermine the national defence. As instructions issued to the police in 1977 put it, they would be 'keeping a close watch on any persons of doubtful loyalty employed or living in key points'.[34] Anybody deemed untrustworthy in that respect should be sent to prison without delay. As we have seen, prisons would have been largely emptied at this stage, and the police would be filling some of the vacant space with these 'persons of doubtful loyalty'.[35] Here they would rub shoulders with the most violent and dangerous offenders, who could not be released. 'Subversives' could include dangerous saboteurs or potential terrorists, but in this febrile atmosphere it was likely that the police would also scoop up peace campaigners, disarmament activists and trade unionists – anyone warning about the coming war or critical of the authorities.

When the attack began, policemen on duty would seek shelter in their stations and, like the rest of the population, would not emerge until radiation levels had dropped. Like for everyone else, the days spent penned in the basement of the police station would be hellish. It was recommended that the senior officer 'take steps at an early stage to maintain morale at a high level and to sustain the physical well-being of the men in the refuge room'.[36] If lighting was available, officers should occupy themselves with 'reading, playing cards, or in some other quiet way which would conserve oxygen and energy'.[37] If the electricity was out, they could light candles for essential tasks, but they had to remember that candles burned precious oxygen. In the post-nuclear world, none of the basics of human existence and comfort – breathing air, lighting candles, drinking water – could be taken for granted any more.

Despite the lack of light, the maddening boredom and growing stress, the stink of sweat and toilet waste, the guidance still urged the officers to remain clean and tidy, and instructed senior officers to keep their men in good mental shape, for when the day came that they emerged from their shelter, 'they will have to lead and set an example to the public'.[38]

When the officers did emerge blinking into the dusty light, each would be provided with a personal dosimeter so he could measure his radiation exposure and ensure he didn't exceed the limit. Senior officers must consider the 'need to preserve the radiological lives of the police', because, as with doctors and nurses, they were now an invaluable resource. No officer should be exposed in the post-nuclear line of duty to anything that took him over the war emergency dose (WED) of 150r. This meant that they could only go out for short periods of time and had to be regularly relieved by colleagues.

The police's post-attack duties would be similar to those fulfilled in the days leading up to war: keeping people off the roads so they were free for official use, guarding food and fuel supplies, preventing looting. The main difference would be that they were now trying to control a population that was in various stages of disaster syndrome, displaying distress, shock and grief, as well as suffering from dreadful injuries and the slow and horrible onset of radiation sickness.

Their tasks would be made more difficult due to loss of manpower. The nuclear attack might have wiped out thousands of the new officers who had filled the ranks in the pre-strike recruitment drive. Therefore, the manual stipulated that when it came to controlling the bands of unsettled homeless on the streets, the police should do so 'with any available assistance'.

In the countryside, a bobby on the beat might have been a rare sight even in peacetime – it would be rarer still after a nuclear attack. As the ash drifted on the garden path and the roses faded to grey, it would be obvious to those living in Britain's many small villages that no outside help was going to arrive to protect their homes and belongings. Indeed, they would rightly fear that they might make tempting targets for looters and criminals from urban areas, as their homes were outside the blast zone, with plentiful supplies of food, medicines and clean drinking water. It was conceivable therefore that villagers might create their own law enforcement, erecting roadblocks and barricades to keep out refugees. After all, during the COVID-19 pandemic, some isolated settlements in Britain, free of the virus and desperate to remain so, placed angry signs on their approach roads telling outsiders to 'Go Home!',[39] with local politicians warning that people 'will turn vigilante' if outsiders tried to enter their village.[40]

In the 1980s, a plan to maintain law and order in the small communities of Surrey was drawn up. It anticipated that a surviving rural policeman would liaise with community leaders to select and organise 'a system of streetwatchers to report cases of lawlessness'.[41] Such people might have been called 'nosy neighbours' in peacetime, but after a nuclear attack they would be transformed into auxiliary policemen, patrolling the village streets and safeguarding petrol stations and food stocks. With electronic communications down after an attack, it was expected that these local heroes would be summoned to duty by the banging of bin lids. Yet the streetwatchers were reminded that they were not a replacement for the police and should keep their crime-fighting ambitions in check: 'They must not act on their own initiative, except to protect life and property.' It was important that the surviving local policeman impressed on his ragtag bunch of volunteers that he, and therefore the state, remained firmly in charge.

Forced labour

If there was to be any prospect of law and order being maintained in post-nuclear Britain, the survivors would need to feel some kind of hope. If they saw nothing but rubble, starvation and brutality, with no indication of improvement, why should they cooperate with the authorities? Thus the rubble had to be cleared, corpses buried, food distributed, hospitals rebuilt – these were essential measures to give people a glimpse of recovery. Therefore, a key element of restoring and maintaining order was labour. The authorities would have to show themselves able to organise and deploy labour squads that could be tasked with the post-nuclear clear-up.

In 1953, a questionnaire was sent to all government departments asking them which post-nuclear jobs would need to be done, and whether these tasks would be unpleasant.[42] The Ministry of Agriculture responded that it was concerned about the disposal of the carcasses of animals that had been killed either by the blast or by radiation sickness. The Ministry of Food would require workers to salvage and then decontaminate foodstuffs. The War Office said it would need labour squads to collect and dispose of the dead and to clear rubble from the streets. This was all tough manual work with no prospect of a good meal, a hot bath and a soft bed at the end of the day.

So how could the authorities compel people to step forward to embark on this essential work when they might still be stunned and horrified, unable to come to terms with the new world created by the nuclear attack? The government realised it would have to rely on forced labour: either through impressment, with officials turning up at a factory or other place of work and taking workers away; or via muster, having compiled a register of all able-bodied suitable men, who would then be called up. Forced labour was an unpalatable idea, but the authorities believed the public would agree to it given the severity of the crisis: 'after an atom bomb attack the public will have so much hardship to endure that they will be prepared to stand extreme measures and to tolerate a certain degree of unfairness for a short time'.[43] As long as the awful work was seen as essential for life to continue, it would perhaps be accepted.

The Home Office knew how dreadful the task of corpse disposal would be from what had happened in Germany during the Second World War.[44] It was estimated that in 1945, Germany had 500 million cubic metres of rubble to clear, with many festering corpses scattered within it. During the war, the German authorities had used POWs and concentration camp inmates to dispose of the dead; after the war, in some places, former SS and Nazi Party members were given the task as punishment. But the bulk of the work was done by *Trümmerfrauen* – 'rubble women' – who would toil for hours, forming straggling chains across the ruins as they passed debris from one to another in buckets. Although it wasn't forced labour, it wasn't entirely voluntary. 'Anyone who doesn't come and shovel will get no ration cards!'[45] they were told.

After the Hamburg firestorm of July 1943, 10,000 bodies had to be collected from across the city, many of them lying in public view. One member of the city's civil defence recalled the sight that greeted her after the Allied attack:

> On a little open square near Boonsweg – I shall never forget the sight – there lay hundreds of men and women, soldiers in uniform, children, old people. Many had torn the clothes from their bodies shortly before their death. They were naked. Their bodies seemed unmarked, the faces showed peaceful expressions, like in deep sleep. Other bodies could hardly be recognised; they were charred, torn to pieces, and had shattered skulls . . . And there, a soldier with charred stumps for legs. There a woman with a torn body, on whose bulging-out intestines the flies were feeding. And there a child, clutching a birdcage in his hand. And there, detached from the body, a boy's foot with a black boot; a small brown girl's hand with a blue ring . . . The heart almost stops beating at such sights.[46]

The labourers trying to dispose of the dead, among them SS men and prisoners from Neuengamme concentration camp, recalled that the worst part of their work was not the distressing sight, but the appalling smell of rotting flesh, which provoked violent nausea. Many crews wore gas masks with the filter replaced by a fabric pad soaked in cognac or rum. Most of Hamburg's dead lay beneath the streets in bunkers and cellars, where they had escaped the flames only to die of carbon monoxide poisoning as the firestorm above sucked the oxygen from the air. The smell in these blackened tombs was so bad that some labourers would scorch the interiors with a flamethrower before daring to venture inside.

Jan Melsen, a Dutchman held in the Neuengamme camp, was brought into the city for some of the worst duties:

> Later a lorry came. Then we formed a chain and passed the corpses along until they were laid on the back of the truck . . . After we had carried the corpses out of the cellars we had to start afresh with searching through the rubble for body parts, because they wanted to know approximately how many dead there were. We fetched ourselves bowls and buckets – there were enough lying around – then dug through the rubble and put

whatever body parts we found in the buckets. In the evenings an SS doctor came with his assistants, and then we had to spread the body parts across the ground. From this he would estimate the number of men and women.[47]

The forced labour squads tasked with the disposal of the dead after a nuclear attack on Britain would likely face a similarly gruesome scenario, and the intense horror of the task would arguably provoke disgust, refusal and rebellion, testing the post-war state's ability to control and direct the surviving population.

Rotten fruit and the rope

The instructions to form labour squads by impressment or muster would come from the regional commissioner deep in his bunker and would be announced to the population via a short radio broadcast from the RSG's small BBC studio. Survivors might refuse the instruction for a number of reasons. Some might find the work too disgusting, or be fearful of leaving their shelter unguarded and vulnerable to looters. Others might be too ill or weak to work, or would object to the order as a form of protest.

In a post-nuclear society, food would be the most desired of currencies, so the obvious punishment for those refusing to work was going to be the withholding of food. But what of those survivors who not merely refused orders to work but became looters, thieves, rapists and murderers? How were they going to be punished or deterred? The authorities in their bunkers, ruling their little parcel of Britain, would have to create other punishments and other inducements to obedience and productivity. Government guidance hinted at what form that might take:

In conditions in which death, destruction and injury were commonplace, such penalties as probation, fines or sentences would no longer be effective in dealing with anti-social offenders. Such penalties as communal labour, restricted rations and exposure to public disapproval might be appropriate for all but the gravest offences, but in the case of flagrantly anti-social behaviour there might be a need for harsher penalties than would generally be acceptable in peace time.[48]

The authorities would also be able to administer punishments 'not normally available to the courts'. This suggests not only a return to the death penalty but perhaps also the reintroduction of the pillory. Putting a criminal in the stocks would certainly qualify as 'exposure to public disapproval', and would allow justice to be seen. After nuclear war, there would be no around-the-clock news to reassure the worried public that a feared criminal had been caught and punished, and that the state was still in charge. Whilst more serious crimes would probably be dealt with by a firing squad or a hangman away from public view, punishment for lesser crimes could be turned into public spectacle, which would spread the word that justice was still administered and afford a stressed and furious public some satisfaction.

Locked in the pillory, a wooden frame with holes for his head and hands, the criminal would come face to face with his victims. Indeed, the London historian Peter Ackroyd has noted that the pillory was an especially apt punishment for those who had committed fraud or deceit in trading, since the faulty goods he had sold could be burned before his eyes, or the people he had cheated could stand before him and enjoy his prostration: 'To be identified and paraded in front of neighbours and fellow tradesmen was, for any citizen of London, the cause of extreme shame. It could also be perilous. Some were plied with rotten fruit, fish and excrement, but the most unpopular or unprincipled offenders were in danger of being pelted to death with sticks and stones.'[49]

Once released from the stocks, the post-nuclear criminal would not have the relief of hiding his shame by going home and locking the door. He might be homeless or living in billets, a refugee camp or other shared accommodation, so his shame would continue to be broadcast. Public disapproval would be a powerful sanction indeed.

Besides the withholding of food and the public shaming of the pillory, punishment could extend to floggings and, ultimately, execution. The government guidance, *Briefing Material for Wartime Controllers*, stipulated the appointment of regional 'commissioners of justice', persons who had held any kind of judicial role in peacetime. They could travel throughout the region, like the circuit judges of the past, to set up courts.

> In capital cases, wherever practicable there would be a jury of not more than five empowered summarily, or a court consisting of not less than three commissioners. In other cases, commissioners would sit with or without a jury as they saw fit . . . There would be no appeals but the senior commissioner would make arrangements to review decisions of the emergency courts in his area.[50]

In 1980, the BBC's *Panorama* programme interviewed a former accountant who was designated to be the regional controller in charge of the Humberside area after nuclear war. Keith Bridge was described as 'a man with more power than he could ever have imagined even in his grossest dreams or nightmares'. The programme's presenter, Jeremy Paxman, spoke to him about the prospect of his post-war authority.

> PAXMAN: How much power do you have as controller?
> BRIDGE: As soon as the bomb goes off, total power. Theoretically.
> PAXMAN: That would include power over police, fire brigade, all that sort of thing?
> BRIDGE: Yes. And life and death.
> PAXMAN: Powers of life and death?
> BRIDGE: Yes.
> PAXMAN: What does that mean?
> BRIDGE: That if people were looting it would be within my competence to instruct that they be executed.
> PAXMAN: Do you expect that kind of situation to arise?
> BRIDGE: It's quite possible. It's feasible.
> PAXMAN: Does having that kind of power – total power – worry you?
> BRIDGE: No.[51]

10 'The programme will, of course, be horrifying': Nuclear War at the BBC

The 1967 Oscar ceremony was a feast of classic Hollywood glamour. The set was styled like a sugary musical extravaganza, the men wore white tie, and the ladies had gowns in hot pink, bronze and buttery yellow. Awards were presented by film idols like Omar Sharif, Olivia de Havilland, James Stewart and Audrey Hepburn, and Fred Astaire and Ginger Rogers danced onto the stage to announce the award for Best Screenplay. America was in turmoil, with the escalation of the war in Vietnam and the fight for civil rights making the news headlines, but for one night TV viewers were transported back to America's golden age. Yet any such pretence was rudely interrupted when the actor Richard Harris announced the winner for Best Documentary Feature: *The War Game*. The Oscar ceremony might have fastened the door against the foul and unfriendly night, but *The War Game* kicked it open and brought nuclear war onto the stage, like a dog dragging a carcass. The acceptance speech was polite and brief. It was as though no one wanted to dwell too much on the topic of the film.

The War Game was a hideous portrayal of a nuclear attack on Britain, directed by Peter Watkins, a young documentary film-maker at the BBC who had been championed by the head of documentaries, Huw Wheldon. Watkins had come to his attention in the early 1960s with a brutal reconstruction of the Hungarian uprising of 1956, *The Forgotten Faces*. When the writer Milton Shulman viewed it at Granada Studios, he assumed it was a documentary: 'the violence, the agony, the despair . . . the rough camera work, the crude lighting, the texture of the celluloid, the chaotic shots of fighting, tussling men had that quality of immediacy and involvement reminiscent of the work of cameramen covering the front line during the Second World War at places like Stalingrad and Arnhem'.[1] Amazed, he asked the young director how he had managed to smuggle the footage out of Budapest. Watkins replied that he had filmed it in Canterbury.

When he joined the BBC in 1963, Watkins decided to turn his skill for realistic reconstruction to the effects of nuclear war. This was a spectacularly ambitious project for any new boy in the office, but two things worked in his favour. The first was the changing nature of the BBC. In the early 1960s, under the leadership of director general Hugh Greene, it had begun shedding its old image as the well-meaning but fussy 'Auntie', the guardian of the nation's morals and provider of enlightenment. It was showcasing bolder writers and directors, such as Ken Loach and Dennis Potter, in the *Wednesday Play* slot, which produced the ground-breaking drama about homelessness, *Cathy Come Home*. The bold satire *That Was the Week That Was* mocked the political establishment and came as a shock to what was still a deferential society.

The second factor in Watkins' favour was the support of Huw Wheldon. Yet to start with, Wheldon gently steered his young recruit away from his controversial idea of a nuclear war film, encouraging him to explore other projects. Watkins thought about historical dramas on Nelson, Napoleon, Joan of Arc and Cromwell; he suggested more controversial topics, such as the force-feeding of the imprisoned suffragettes before the First World War or the recent Sharpeville massacre in South Africa. Eventually the young director fixed on the Battle of Culloden, the last pitched battle on British soil, at which the Duke of Cumberland's troops had fought the Highland clans. Wheldon was not entirely at ease with this project – knowing his protégé's commitment to realism, it was clearly going to be a violent film – but he recognised that, having batted away Watkins' original nuclear war idea, he had to consent to one of his projects or risk losing this fine new talent.

In August 1964, Watkins set off for Culloden, near Inverness, with a tiny budget, a cannon, some tartan, a few bugles and drums, plus a cast of 140 ordinary people. To evoke and retain the feel of grubby reality, he did not want eloquently enunciating actors. 'I wanted to break through the conventional use of professional actors in historical melo-dramas,' he recalled, 'with the comfortable avoidance of reality that these provide.'[2] Instead, he used local newspaper adverts and amateur dramatics groups to recruit non-professional actors who were keen to wrap themselves in muddy tartan and pick up a musket. As Wheldon remembered: 'Greengrocers, lawyers, teachers from Inverness, young-sters, he marched them in their clobber through heather, gorse and bog, twenty-three miles, and at the end of it they looked exhausted, and he filmed them, and it was quite brilliant.'[3]

Culloden felt as if a TV crew had joined the battlefield, dodging the fire, skipping over the dead, ducking behind walls, interviewing the combatants, who were filthy, exhausted, dying. Men spoke directly to the camera, almost resentful of the crew for distracting them from bat-tle. It was a shocking production that stripped away all Highland romance from the scene: we see no springy purple heather or misty mountains, only men suffering and dying, falling into the grass and writhing and rolling in their agony. There is no glory, no heroism on either side. War is a hideous thing.

Aired on BBC1 on 15 December 1964, *Culloden* was a spectacular success. 'An artistic triumph,' wrote *The Scotsman*. 'Unforgettable,' said *The Guardian*. 'Compulsively viewable,' confirmed *The Times*. With such a boost to his reputation, the young director thought he should go back into Huw Wheldon's office. He still wanted to make his nuclear war film, he announced, with the provisional title *After the Bomb*. This time it was hard to say no, but still impossible to say yes, so Wheldon said maybe and gave the young director permission to begin research.

'The major fact of this century?'

The BBC had been very coy about nuclear weapons. If the broadcaster was beginning to stretch itself in daring new directions with satire and social commentary, there was no similar bravery in confronting the nuclear threat. In fact, Winston Churchill had prohibited any broad-casts on the topic. When in 1954 he learned that the BBC were considering a programme on the nuclear bomb, he ordered the Post-master General to tell them that unless scripts of any future programmes on the nuclear threat were submitted to the government in advance, and met its approval, they would be banned by ministerial order. Churchill's defence secretary, Harold Macmillan, spoke of the government's concern to retain control of 'the manner in which the effects of nuclear weapons were made known to the public. If these effects were presented too abruptly or in too alarming a fashion, there was a real danger people would adopt a defeatist attitude.'[4] The BBC was not to 'inform and educate', as its mission statement put it, when it came to nuclear war. This shameful ban on the topic persisted well into the 1960s, but was arguably weakened by the Cuban Missile Crisis of October 1962. As people around the world sat watching the creeping approach of nuclear holocaust on their TV sets, no one was left in any doubt about the dangers they would face.

Wheldon was therefore wary of proceeding with a project that aimed to show the reality of nuclear war. *Culloden* had been stark and violent, so wouldn't a film about nuclear attack, taking the young director's same realistic approach, be utterly horrifying? Still, as he confided to colleagues, in order to avoid losing the mercurial young Watkins, 'I must certainly let him get this film out of his system.'[5] He explained in a memo:

> The programme will, of course, be horrifying. It is being worked on with the greatest possible care. We intend to retain counsel on certain security aspects. The build-up, both of the attack and the reaction of the country, is being done well within the bounds of possibility according to the best authorities and the best calculations. That is to say, it is likely to be the more appallingly credible because it is not exaggerated.[6]

But he had given consent to Watkins to start work on the film because 'should we not all be aware of what is after all in some sense the major fact of this century?'[7] Yet every seemingly bold step was tempered with caution, with the firm understanding that 'the film cannot be put out until it is seen, and we must decide later precisely who should see it'.[8]

When Hugh Greene heard of the troubling project, he summoned Wheldon to his office. They agreed to move slowly, one careful step at a time. On seeing the first draft, Greene tried to halt its progress but Wheldon continued to champion his fierce young director, arguing on behalf of the film – now entitled *The War Game* – and securing permission for shooting to begin. Everything was inching forward slowly.

But if the BBC were being painfully cautious, the government were alarmed. They had been alerted to the nuclear project by none other than the young director himself. As part of his exhaustive research, Watkins had sent a lengthy questionnaire to the Home Office, which was in charge of civil defence, asking blunt questions about hospital capacity after a nuclear attack, about stockpiling and about who would be in charge of the state. 'I made formal approaches, realising that I was rather putting my head in the lion's mouth,' he recalled, 'but I thought, what the hell, I've got to try it all ways round. So I went to the Home Office . . . and I said, "I would please like to know . . ." and I gave them a long, long list of questions about civil defence preparation in Britain.'[9] There was an icy silence for several weeks. Then one day Watkins was summoned and told by a Home Office official: 'We're afraid you are not going to get this information, and we believe it's best for you not to push the point.'[10]

The Home Office had in fact sent a letter to the BBC, following Watkins' enquiries, saying they considered the broadcaster and the government to be 'partners' in the realm of civil defence 'and therefore hope that any programme which in the government view could be against the national interest or prejudicial to security should be prepared with the utmost care and responsibility and be controlled at the highest level within the Corporation'.[11] They not only refused to cooperate but forbade all other government departments in receipt of the questionnaire from doing so. 'Sorry, we've been told not to touch you,'[12] Watkins was told. The only body that ignored the order was the fire service, which, Watkins recalled, was 'the weak link in the official "happiness bureau"'. Many of its members had witnessed the incendiary raids during the Blitz, and they knew all about the firestorms of Dresden and Hamburg.

Despite the forbidding response from the government, Watkins went down to Kent to start filming. As with *Culloden*, he shunned professional actors and recruited his cast from local amateur dramatic groups. He began by amassing a few hundred people in a meeting room and explaining his purpose in making the film: to bring the truth about nuclear attack and civil defence to the millions of ordinary people sitting at home in front of their TVs. After his speech, he tried to meet each actor individually, making notes on who would be a good policeman or a suitable looter, and who might do well as a badly injured and quivering old lady.

The filming took place in Dover, Gravesend and Tonbridge in April 1965. *The War Game* begins with the swirling approach of nuclear war due to international tensions over Vietnam that then spread to Berlin, the eternal flashpoint of the Cold War. As news rolls in from the Continent, Britain makes its feeble preparations. Women and children are evacuated from the cities to be billeted upon reluctant householders. ('Are they coloured?' one housewife asks anxiously.) The sirens are tested, their horrible wail rolling through the streets as people stand around confused. What is to be done? Where are they to go? How can they afford the sandbags and building materials to secure their houses? To add to the sense of realism, Watkins included vox-pop-style interviews on the streets, pushing a camera and microphone into the faces of his actors and asking them whether they thought war would come, whether Britain should retaliate and what they knew of nuclear fall-out. The responses seemed utterly natural, because they were: Watkins later said that this was the only part of the film that was not a reconstruction. His cast were asked to give free and honest answers. One day, the unorthodox filming brought the police onto the set. 'There was a lot of trouble,' one crew member recalled. 'We were hanging people on the street, and Peter [Watkins] hadn't got permission to do this.'[13]

When the attack on Britain begins, we witness painful domestic scenes. A family start to panic on hearing the siren and fumble with the furniture, trying to assemble some kind of protection in the four minutes that remain. When the bomb drops, the lampshade swings wildly from the ceiling, crockery is smashed, and a little boy is blinded in the garden. Kent has been targeted as it hosts Manston airfield, which was used by the US Air Force during the Cold War, but the missile has overshot the target and hit populated areas. The father, a big, bumbling man in a crumpled suit, charges across the lawn, scoops up his sightless toddler and runs back into the house, where the terrified family crouch under a kitchen table, cradling the children's heads. They huddle there in silence, staring into the camera, waiting for the shock wave to arrive. The scene shudders as the blast hits, and the emotionless narrator likens it to an enormous door being slammed shut in the depths of hell.

Closer to ground zero, the attack has ignited many fires, which have merged to form a firestorm. Watkins' close collaboration with the fire service is evident here, as this is one of the film's most powerful and merciless scenes. In the midst of the conflagration, firemen struggling to contain the immense wall of flame are fighting for breath, as the firestorm is sucking oxygen from the air, sweeping it into the heart of the fire in hurricane-force winds and using it to feed the inferno. As oxygen vanishes, it is replaced with carbon monoxide. In Watkins' cinematic trademark, we see stark close-ups of the firemen's faces, looking blackened and exhausted. Before long, they collapse one by one, dying of heat exhaustion and suffocation.

Yet the film did not dwell too long on the attack itself; it was the aftermath that chiefly concerned the director. After the bomb, Kent is still Kent; this has been a limited nuclear attack. But even though houses still stand, and country lanes keep their leafy hedgerows, the psychological effects on the survivors are horrendous. Watkins had early on realised that there was plenty of information available about blast waves, heat flashes and radiation – a lot of scientific stuff – but not much about the social impact of the bomb. He wanted to know what it would do to people, to their mood and their manner and their ability to cope. How would they stay clean, care for children, relate to friends and strangers, and remain civilised? Where would they find hope?

The War Game shows us the terrifying disintegration of law and order and a furious contempt for authority. Gentle people are compelled to loot; they seize guns and join a violent raid on a food depot. Others give up and sink into terrible apathy. Some are reduced by trauma to communicating only through grunts and violent spasms. Children have lost all hope for the future: 'I don't want to be nothing,' says a little boy when asked what he wants to do when he grows up. Executions are being carried out on the streets by the authorities. Policemen conduct mercy killings of the injured, for whom there can be no medical care or basic pain relief. In one scene we see the trusted figure of a 1960s British bobby pressing a gun to the head of a civilian. When the film shows a crate of guns being delivered to the police, the local coppers root through the box as though they've received their Christmas presents, eagerly choosing their weapons and tucking them snugly into their belts. It was the sight of the mercy killings that most upset Huw Wheldon: 'I was sure if that was going to be done they'd

have got doctors, nurses or even nuns! Anything other than the police.'
He recalled asking the director to cut the scene, 'and Watkins went
through the roof!'[14]

In this derelict world, viewers were shown the opposite of the spirited and victorious country that had, just twenty years before,
withstood the Blitz and helped defeat fascism. This was Britain seen
through a cracked looking-glass, where everything has been warped
and inverted. It presented people destroyed by war, and a place where
values, manners and respect no longer mattered. It showed, over the
course of a few short days, the total disintegration of an entire world.
It also revealed that British civil defence was utterly futile against the
nuclear bomb. What prime minister Clement Attlee had acknowledged in private to a few men of privilege and power in 1945, Peter
Watkins now intended to tell the entire nation on BBC1. Little wonder
the authorities feared his film.

The final cut

On 2 September 1965, the film was shown to the two most powerful
men at the BBC: director general Sir Hugh Greene and the chairman
of the board of governors Lord Normanbrook. The support of Huw
Wheldon had brought it this far, but now its fate lay with these two
men. Greene was known as forward-thinking, but Normanbrook was
the man the young director would have to satisfy if *The War Game* was
to be safely delivered to BBC1. Before joining the BBC in 1964, he had
been head of the civil service, and having worked on many of the government's civil defence policies, he arguably knew more about the
hideous reality of nuclear war than Watkins himself.

Both Greene and Normanbrook admitted that they were impressed
by the film, but shied away from giving full consent to broadcasting it.
They argued that it was so powerful, and carried such consequences,
that the responsibility for showing it was too great for the BBC to bear
alone. The concern was that the film could be seen as questioning, and
indeed destabilising, the whole notion of nuclear deterrence, and so
Normanbrook suggested they take advice from the government.

Watkins was appalled and threatened to resign. Wheldon tried to
appease him, explaining that 'the BBC's decision to consult further on

this important and powerful documentary arises solely from its responsibility, *which must override all other considerations*, to act in the public interest [my italics]'.[15] But Watkins knew that if the BBC was consulting the government – which had already frozen his enquiries and obstructed his research – then *The War Game* was doomed. He submitted his resignation on 20 September.

Four days later, government officials filed into Theatre 2 of East Tower at Television Centre to view *The War Game*. The distinguished guests included the Cabinet Secretary, the head of the Home Office and representatives from the Ministry of Defence. Lord Normanbrook was present, but Greene was away in Africa, meaning the BBC was wholly represented on this decisive day by an ex-Whitehall man. Years later, Sir Christopher Bland, chairman of the BBC from 1996 to 2001, declared himself horrified at this practice: 'A really bad idea . . . Why don't you show [the government] all our programmes and ask whether they like them?'[16]

The government men's immediate reaction to the screening was not recorded, but Normanbrook noted afterwards that 'It is clear that Whitehall will be relieved if we do not show it.'[17] The government were, of course, too wise to publicly demand that *The War Game* be banned, which would have created an enormous scandal about censorship and the BBC's treasured independence. Instead, as is often the way, hints and careful understatement were deployed. The government made their feelings known, and quietly left the public announcement, the explanation and the responsibility to the BBC.

The Corporation needed to find a convincing reason for its refusal to broadcast *The War Game*, and so they reverted to good old-fashioned paternalism. They stopped trying to be progressive and liberal and instead sought refuge in their reputation as the nation's 'Auntie'. The official stance was that the film was 'too horrifying for the medium of broadcasting because of the indiscriminate nature of the audience'.[18] So they were subtly blaming the British public, who would be unable to tell fact from fiction; too ignorant to realise this was not a true documentary, and too lazy to put their kids to bed before the watershed. Viewers were not to be trusted and needed to be protected. Auntie knew best.

The press release sounded like a hostage statement: 'This is the BBC's own decision. It has been taken after a good deal of thought and discussion, but not as a result of outside pressure of any kind.'[19] Questions were asked in Parliament about whether the government had tried to censor the broadcaster's output. An angry Peter Watkins wrote to Huw Wheldon, '[You] have finally betrayed me.'[20]

Hugh Greene later explained his reasoning, falling back on the excuse that the viewing public were feeble: 'I could not face the responsibility of putting on the air a programme which was so shocking that old people living alone, for instance, or people who were somewhat disordered might be so much upset by it that they could go out of their flat and throw themselves under a bus.'[21] Watkins claimed the BBC privately told him they would expect 20,000 suicides if the film was broadcast.[22] And yet despite the apparent risk of mass suicide, the Corporation decided to show it to their staff before allowing it to be screened in selected cinemas. It seems that BBC employees, and those who attended art-house cinemas, could be trusted with the truth of *The War Game*, but not the masses at home, watching with their tea and biscuits. For Watkins this 'hypocritical elitism' was 'spectacularly disgusting'.[23] The insulting idea that the public had to be shielded from the film persisted even into the early 1980s, when the then director general, Sir Ian Trethowan, said, 'If the film was broadcast, however late at night and with however many advance warnings, there would be not just the likelihood but the certainty that some elderly people living alone would find themselves watching it without warning, and so might some people of limited mental intelligence.'[24]

The BBC might have been thinking of the panic caused by Orson Welles' 1938 radio broadcast of *The War of the Worlds*, but the audience of the 1960s, and certainly that of the 1980s, was surely far more discriminating and sturdy, given that they had lived through the trauma of the Second World War since Orson had stepped up to the microphone to yell of Martians. Indeed, many of the people Trethowan was patronising as feeble and frightened elderly folk would have fought in the war or ducked into an Anderson shelter whilst the ground shook and the sky roared.

When the debate about *The War Game* revived in the early 1980s, sparked by the surge in international tensions, Mary Whitehouse, president of the National Viewers' and Listeners' Association, agreed the film should be banned, and used young children to make her predictable arguments, saying it would 'blow their minds and fill them with destructive terror'.[25] Consequently, she was mocked in *The Guardian's* letters pages for several days: 'We can only hope that in the unhappy event of a nuclear holocaust that good lady will arrange that it takes place only after the kiddies have been put to bed.'[26] Another writer questioned her logic: 'Is she really suggesting that it is crueller to risk young children being disturbed by *The War Game* through pretending that we could survive a nuclear holocaust without too much trouble, than to risk a nuclear holocaust in which the same young children will be burned alive or will die lingering deaths from leukaemia, radiation sickness, bone cancers or other equally horrifying diseases?'[27]

It is easy to understand Watkins' anger at the BBC's treatment of his film, but, you could argue, at least *The War Game* was not completely banned; it was simply not shown on television. On the other hand, while it was made available for those who were determined to see it when the BBC consented to a theatrical release in 1966, you would not have found the film slotted in alongside the blockbusters at the local Odeon. It was distributed to art-house cinemas and film societies, so it was never going to reach a mass audience. However, decision-makers at the BBC might have felt some satisfaction when it was awarded an X certificate, meaning it was deemed unsuitable for audiences below the age of 16.

They would also have been vindicated by the press reviews following a series of private screenings for journalists and politicians at the National Film Theatre, where it was delivered under guard, and police and BBC security were present to keep the public out. Many of the reviewers rushed to agree with the BBC's verdict that it was 'too horrifying' for television – although many papers decided to send their defence correspondent to review it, rather than their film critic. The *Sunday Mirror* was critical of this crafty move: 'Why else did the BBC invite editors, political and defence correspondents, MPs – even a junior minister – but not a single TV writer to its private showing except to get a political blessing for its decision?'[28] The legendary columnist Chapman Pincher launched a fierce attack in the *Daily Express*, calling the film 'so super-horrific that it could not possibly be shown on television'. He praised its artistry but argued that any film that could not be screened was automatically a failure. But if he admired the acting and camera work, he loathed the logic behind the film, writing that it was driven by 'naïve and immature thinking' that prodded the viewer to the 'monstrous' notion that Britain's nuclear weapons were part of a conspiracy against its innocent population that placed them at constant risk of Russian incineration. Instead, Chapman assured his readers, these weapons deterred such an attack, and to argue otherwise was to play 'the CND game', which he suggested should have been the title of the film. He ended by calling it 'repulsive'.[29]

The strongest voice in defence of *The War Game* came from the famously waspish critic Kenneth Tynan, who wrote in *The Observer* that 'It may be the most important film ever made', and that with a wide audience it could change the course of history. As long as suitable warning was provided for the anxious viewer, 'it should not only be televised but screened in cinemas, not just here but everywhere on earth, especially in countries that possess (or would like to possess) the bomb. In refusing to show it, the BBC is like a doctor withholding the truth from a patient who is suffering from a potentially fatal disease; silence may preclude panic, but it also precludes cure.'[30]

Britain's civil defence training schools in Berkshire and Perthshire wrote to the Home Office seeking permission to show the controversial film to their attendees, who of course were not delicate old ladies, but police officers, doctors, nurses and council workers trained in civil defence and emergency planning. Permission was refused. Scotland's chief medical officer was 'anxious'[31] to show *The War Game* at the Taymouth Castle college to an audience of doctors in August 1966. He agreed that although the training staff disliked it, the doctors would 'wish to present the film as containing a highly speculative picture of the worst sort of situation that might befall us in the event of a nuclear attack', and he felt that there would also be value in discussing the various anti-civil-defence views in it. 'With all its inaccuracies the film does provide a background of realism which no other available film and no amount of talking is likely to conjure up in the minds of persons assembled to study hard problems of nuclear war,' he wrote. The Home Office again refused, replying that although the film 'might well have a use as a graphic illustration' of nuclear attack, 'it was plain that we ought not to give the film any official endorsement'. Their letter explained frankly that, 'having so far "weathered the storm" by ignoring the film, we should not now be seen to be taking notice of it'.[32]

When *The War Game* won its Oscar in 1967, Peter Watkins learned that the BBC intended to send their own man over to Los Angeles to collect the statue the morning after the ceremony. He picked up the phone and rang one of his friends in LA, a certain Elizabeth Taylor, and asked her to dash round and collect it before the BBC could snatch it away.

Lifting the curse

A young student at Southampton University was watching the furore over *The War Game*. Later, he would go on to Hollywood fame as the director of blockbusters like *The Bodyguard* and *LA Story*, but in 1966, when Mick Jackson got his first job at the BBC as an assistant film editor, the scandal about *The War Game* was still fresh. He was instantly aware of the wound it had inflicted on the BBC and that the topic of nuclear war was 'a no-go area'.[33] But as he progressed in his career at the BBC and began to acquire some creative clout, he wondered if he might attempt the unthinkable: a nuclear war film.

In the early 1980s, the era of detente, when Cold War tensions had eased, was coming to an end. 'You couldn't help, as a thinking person, be concerned about the state of the world,' Jackson recalled. At Christmas 1979, the Soviets invaded Afghanistan and relations between East and West froze again. Nuclear war loomed closer than it had since the Cuban Missile Crisis. Relations worsened, and neither side could understand the other. The Soviets, recalling the German invasion of 1941, thought a US attack was imminent. Reagan shrugged off their fears, writing in his diary: 'What the hell have they got that anyone would want?'[34] However, although everybody was thinking about nuclear war, very few people knew the precise details of such a conflict – which had been the reason for Peter Watkins to make *The War Game* in 1965. Britain was in a state of nuclear anxiety, Jackson recalled, but 'You don't have any facts, you don't have any images in your head, you just have a sense of dread.'

In the early 1980s, he was working in the science and features department at the BBC, producing respected series like *Horizon* and *Tomorrow's World*, when he was asked to create some thirty-minute episodes for a new popular science series called *QED*. He realised that this new series might offer the opportunity he had been waiting for.

Knowing the BBC would be sensitive, he was cautious and pitched an episode that would be scrupulously non-political and rely wholly on unarguable science and facts. His proposed programme about fallout shelters would mimic a consumer guide. 'If you are doing a consumer test on how you can protect yourself against nuclear war,' he explained, 'then you have to show what it is you are protecting yourself against, and that was the idea of the half hour programme. This is what a nuclear weapon will do: blast, fire, radiation and so on.' A carefully clinical and scientific approach, he hoped, would be liberating for the BBC after the humiliation over Peter Watkins' film:

> Hopefully this might lift the curse of *The War Game*. That stain of shame and humiliation, and really a loss of the BBC's editorial [independence], and the government putting a very heavy thumb on the scales, all hung over the BBC till I thought . . . I'll put a toe in the water, make it very non-political, all about science, this might be the way that we can break this spell.

The finished programme was called *A Guide to Armageddon*. The first half described in clear, painful detail the consequences of a nuclear explosion over St Paul's Cathedral. The BBC retained some of the squeamishness of the sixties, and so Jackson used slabs of meat and a pumpkin on a pole to show the effects of heat and blast: the extreme heat made the fat on the steak bubble and blacken, and when a pane of glass positioned next to the pumpkin shattered, the camera went into slow motion to follow the flying glass as it pierced the soft flesh of the vegetable, transforming it to pulp and tatters. The episode was approved for broadcast. It seemed that finally, 17 years after refusing to broadcast *The War Game*, the BBC's nuclear curse had been broken.

There was only one hiccup as the day of transmission approached in the summer of 1982. The film opened with a one-megaton bomb exploding a mile above the dome of St Paul's. The temperature at the instant of its detonation was 20 million degrees – as hot as the centre of the sun – which was intense enough to melt the huge bronze cross atop the cathedral. 'It vaporises the liquid metal as it runs down the dome,' the emotionless narrator told the viewers. The problem was that prime minister Margaret Thatcher was due at St Paul's on the day of broadcast for a Falklands memorial service, so the episode was hastily pulled from the schedule. Unlike its predecessor, however, it was quickly reinstated, and shown on BBC1 on 26 July 1982. Viewers were entrusted with a frank and honest look at the effects of nuclear war, and this time there was no talk of mass suicide or hysteria. As Mick Jackson put it, 'The earth didn't open and swallow everybody up!' Reviews noted the show's 'self-consciously dead-pan'[35] tone and how it used the 'coolest, most measured terms',[36] and it was this that allowed Jackson to smuggle truth and reality about nuclear weapons onto prime-time television.

Threads

Emboldened, Jackson told his BBC bosses, 'Look, we got away with that. There was no great drama and crisis. What I'd like to do is go further.' He had amassed mountains of research for his *QED* show and now wanted to push on and make a programme not about the physical effects of nuclear war but about what it did to people's psychology and emotions and the concept of civilised society. He suggested a drama.

As with *The War Game*, the BBC's initial response was cool, but they gave the go-head for Jackson to start research. 'I made myself an expert on nuclear war,' he recalled, but to create an effective drama, he wanted a scriptwriter who knew nothing of melting eyeballs and blast radius and flying glass and toilet buckets. He needed someone untainted by such horrible nuclear knowledge, who would be free to create ordinary, authentic characters who could then be thrust into the total horror of nuclear war. He instantly thought of Barry Hines, the Yorkshire writer who had made his name with *A Kestrel for a Knave*, filmed as *Kes* by Ken Loach in 1969. 'You'll write it,' he told Hines, 'and I'll subject these people, almost sadistically, to what nuclear weapons can do.'

Like Watkins, he did not cast stars or easily recognisable actors, but opted for relative unknowns. He recalled a 'tempestuous relationship' with Hines: there were spectacular arguments between the two men about the nature of the film. Hines objected to Jackson's injection of a documentary style, such as the inclusion of data onscreen and the use of a narrator. Jackson remembers Hines crying: ' "What place does this have in a drama?" and I said, "This isn't a drama! It isn't a documentary!

It isn't anything except what it is! It's a one-off thing, and the more oddball it is, the more it will stick in people's memory."'

The film they created is perhaps the most powerful nuclear war film ever made. *Threads* began like a standard kitchen-sink drama, with the title referring to the intricate connections that allow modern society to function. It is set in grimy industrial Sheffield, where a middle-class girl, Ruth, has fallen pregnant to a working-class boy, Jimmy, and the two families come awkwardly together across the class divide as the couple prepare for a hasty wedding, a new flat and the baby. As the star-crossed lovers worry, their parents fret and the siblings bicker, the camera shifts to TV screens flickering in Sheffield's dark pubs and chintzy living rooms, the news presenters reporting of rising tensions in the Middle East. As Jimmy and Ruth scrape the wallpaper in their new flat, Ruth dissolves into tears because the radio is not playing tunes suitable for young lovers but constantly repeated broadcasts of *Protect and Survive*.

The threat of nuclear war is getting closer and closer. Lifting the net curtain, you might see a van delivering stacks of mismatched blankets to the local primary school, a silent parade of fire engines leaving the city, or fleets of ambulances emptying the hospitals for what is to come. Food prices have skyrocketed. In Sheffield's main square, anti-war protesters gather and there are soon tussles with the police. The protest leaders are shoved into the back of police vans, and in the midst of the roaring crowd a man waves a bunch of tin openers for sale: 'Come on, all of you! One pound! Could save your life!'

As the people begin to panic, council staff gather in the claustro-phobic basement beneath Sheffield Town Hall. Yet ordinary life persists. The milk float still trundles down the street, the papers are being delivered, and the shops stay open. The two storylines of young love and nuclear rumblings run in parallel until Thursday 26 May, when the bomb drops and we witness the dreadful burst of thermo-nuclear light in the sky over Sheffield. When the siren wails, the shoppers are milling about in the city's pedestrianised shopping pre-cinct. Mums pushing buggies and old ladies in sensible coats stop and look up to the sky. Then everyone begins to run, seeking shelter in British Home Stores or Woolworths, or perhaps trying to make it home in their last four minutes. A police car speeds past with little chance of reaching its destination.

If Mick Jackson was wary of a blatant portrayal of horror in *A Guide to Armageddon*, there is no such restraint here. He presents a grotesque parade of images. We see a burned hand poking through a gap in the nuclear rubble, each blackened finger tipped with a small wavering flame, a scene described by survivors in Hiroshima. As Ruth wanders through the ruined city to witness the horror, there is no more dialogue; the film becomes eerily quiet. As speech falls away, we hear the ghostly moan of the nuclear wind. A child yells for his mum, and in the rubble, a man gnaws at something. A man with bandaged eyes cowers and shakes. A stiff, crumpled dog shows its stomach to the sky in animal surrender. A sooty corpse bares appallingly white teeth. A staring woman clutches a dead baby to her breast. Leathery corpses lie crimped and twisted in postures of agony. Through these terrible images, Jackson wanted to give the viewer 'a vocabulary in their heads for thinking the unthinkable'. With only a small budget, he conveyed that vocabulary through these carefully chosen scenes, which imprint themselves on the viewers' minds.

After the bomb drops, the kitchen-sink drama comes to an abrupt end. Most of the characters simply disappear, including Jimmy, the working-class hero. We are not even told of their fate. We are left to follow Ruth – pregnant, stunned and alone – across the nightmare landscape. While the film began with the conception of her baby, it ends with a birth from the next generation. Ruth's daughter, Jane, now 13, staggers to the ruined hospital to deliver her own baby, which was conceived in a brutal rape on the moors. Ruth has by now died, her hair prematurely white and her eyes creamy with cataracts. Jane is reluctantly given help by a midwife in the silent hospital. The final image is a close-up of her exhausted face as she is handed a bloody bundle. She unwraps the stained shawl to look at what she has delivered – and then opens her mouth to scream. We don't see what she is looking at. 'You're not really sure what it is that's been born,' Jackson explained.

The film went out on BBC2 on 23 September 1984, when it was watched by seven million viewers. One of the actors, Rita May, recalled the press screening in Sheffield:

When the film finished: total silence. And that's not normal. Normally you get people chatting: 'Ooh it were good weren't it?'

Total silence. And when the film finished, I walked to the back of the room and I stood behind this pillar, and I sobbed. *I sobbed!* And people were crying.[37]

Mick Jackson experienced the same unnerving silence on the night of broadcast:

When *Threads* went out I watched it on TV at home with my wife – and nothing. The phone didn't ring. The phone didn't ring. Phone didn't ring. And I thought, 'Oh. It's landed with a thud. It must be the most awful disaster in the history of television!' And the next day I realised that all over the country – some people called it 'The Night Britain Didn't Sleep' – people had watched it and just sat there slumped in their chairs, and not knowing what to do or what to say, and didn't want to go to bed because of the dreams that would come.

After the initial silence and sleeplessness came the reviews. The coverage was limited as it was a late Sunday-night drama on BBC2, but those who did review it were awed, even if some were confused about what they had seen. Was it a drama, a documentary, a warning, or something plucked from hell? *The Guardian* called it 'an impressive achievement on a very large and chilling scale'.[38] The *Financial Times* described it as 'devastating', writing that 'the BBC deserves our admiration and gratitude' for having the courage to show it, and for finally acknowledging how wrong they were to ban *The War Game*. In fact, it considered *Threads* far more frightening than Peter Watkins' film.[39] Russell Davies in *The Observer* seemed to get exactly what the film was trying to achieve with its terrible spring from the cloying minutiae of family life to the vast emptiness of a world ruined, stripped and smashed, where no comfort could ever be found.

The immediate deaths, mutilations and loss of communications are frightful to contemplate, but almost manageable compared to the subsequent damage to the global environment and human genetics. We saw years pass under the frozen skies [but] any thought of let's-all-start-again was brutally blown away by scenes of savagery: the rapes and looting, the bloody stillbirths, and the breakdown of language as thought itself regressed towards the single syllable 'Ugh'.[40]

Once the threads that connect each to each in a civilised society snap, they cannot be repaired.

'Oh no, they did blow it!'

The BBC's nuclear spell had been broken. When Jackson's boss, Graham McDonald, the head of BBC2, watched the film's first cut, he initially took notes and offered comments on pacing and structure, but then he fell silent and offered no more advice. No one tried to interfere with the film.

But if the BBC were happy with *Threads*, Mick Jackson detected a possible flicker of hostility from the government. In exchange for allowing him to attend Easingwold's civil defence college for research, it had been agreed that the Home Office would be permitted to view the film before broadcast – not in an attempt to censor or stop it from being shown, but so they might get their official response and rebuttal ready. (Home Office correspondence reveals that they were fearful of lending credibility to the film by engaging with it: 'We surely want to play down the programmes rather than adding to the controversy.')[41] So Jackson was taken to meet two officials, who sat at a desk with reams of notes in front of them. Also present were 'two muscular young men who were seated one on each side of me . . . I didn't know whether they were there to grab me by the shoulders and put me in jail, or were there to intimidate me – but I think it was that. It was certainly intimidating.'

The muscular men remained silent, but the Home Office officials started to point out perceived errors in the film. For example, they insisted that there would be no panic buying in reality, as the government would have warned people in advance to stock their cupboards. But Jackson was able to quote scenarios from civil defence plans and exercises that predicted shortages. 'They retreated,' he recalled.

Yet the film almost didn't get shown for other reasons. In 1983, when Jackson was in the early stages of pre-production on *Threads*, he heard that the American TV channel ABC were planning a similar project. While he was working with a small BBC budget, his American counterpart, director Nicholas Meyer, had been given $7 million. Jackson was prepared to abandon *Threads* at this point, believing that if the Americans could create a merciless, realistic vision of nuclear war, there would be little point in him trying to do the same the following year. 'Oh my God,' he thought. 'Please don't let them blow this.'

But when *The Day After* (1983) was broadcast on 20 November 1983, to huge fanfare, media attention and an audience of 100 million viewers across the United States, Jackson's verdict was, 'Oh no, they did blow it!' *The Day After* failed to convey real nuclear horror. It was Hollywood's version of nuclear war: it had rousing theme music, sentimental plot lines and good-looking heroes played by famous actors Steve Guttenberg, John Lithgow and Jason Robards. There was even a scene paying cinematic homage to the famous moment in *Gone with the Wind* where Scarlett O'Hara picks her way through masses of dead and dying at a casualty centre in Atlanta.

The difference in the realism and honesty of the two films is most obvious in their respective post-attack hospital scenes. In the American film, the lights are still working, the place is clean, people are being wheeled around on gurneys, and the doctors are heroic and noble, if a little tired. In *Threads*, Mick Jackson reminds us, 'the hospital is overrun in Sheffield. There's blood and shit on the floor and nobody has any tools to be a doctor with. There's no power. There's no water. No instruments. No anaesthetic. No medication.'

With the magnificent *Threads*, the BBC had redeemed itself after its failure to broadcast *The War Game*. Finally, on 31 July 1985, it showed Peter Watkins' film alongside a repeat of *Threads*[42] to mark the fortieth anniversary of the atomic bombings in Japan.

The Wartime Broadcasting Service

If nuclear war had erupted, the BBC would have come off air. Lighthearted ITV and the punchy newcomer, Channel 4, would also have disappeared. They would have been replaced with the spartan Wartime Broadcasting Service (WTBS), which would go out on the radio, on one channel only. Television had disappeared during the Second World War too, although at the time there were only 20,000 sets in

British homes, so the cultural impact of its loss was far less severe than if the same had happened in the Cold War. A blank TV screen in the corner of the room would have been a constant reminder that normal life had come to an end.

Throughout the Second World War, the BBC had been broadcasting on radio only, reducing itself to what was called the Home Service. The same would happen in nuclear war. The big difference was that during the previous conflict, BBC radio had provided not just news and information, but also morale-boosting music, comedy and entertainment, when shows like *It's That Man Again* and *Workers' Playtime* provided much-needed distraction. The WTBS would offer no such light-hearted comfort: there would be nothing but hourly announcements and instructions. If you wanted a morale-boosting sing-song, you would have to organise it yourself.

There were practical reasons for this, as survivors would be listening on battery-powered radios, and so should not waste their precious charge by tuning in for songs and skits. The Second World War had also been a very different conflict, which required high morale among workers in the factories, farmers in the fields and ingenious mothers in the kitchen keeping everyone in tip-top health on rations. The Home Service offered a jaunty soundtrack to keep spirits high throughout all this work. In nuclear war, the last thing officialdom would want was an energetic and organised population. A silent, weary obedience would be preferable so that survivors might begin, without too much protest and revolt, the slow, back-breaking, dangerous and often repulsive work of national recovery. This time there would be no patriotic striving to win, no putting up two fingers to the enemy, only a gradual creep back from defeat. There would be no lyrics for such a desolate song, and certainly no sweetheart to sing them.

N-Hour

The BBC's Cold War planning intended to keep television on air until the last possible moment. This would project a sense that normal life was persisting and so might help quieten any panic at the worsening international situation. It would also allow the *Protect and Survive* films to be shown repeatedly in the last days before nuclear war.

The moment at which the BBC vanished would be known as N-Hour, with N standing for National. Prior to it, there would be A-Hour, with A standing for Announcements, when a voice would read out the local radio frequencies to which the British people should now tune their battery-powered receivers so they might get regional WTBS bulletins after the bomb. These frequencies would also have been printed in the newspapers in the preceding days, but here was the last chance to note them down before the BBC receded into nuclear silence. There would also have been a list of cities and towns that might now be doomed; it would have seemed like a long goodbye to familiar places, with each place triggering personal memories among listeners – of an old home town, a holiday resort or a school trip. It was a slow recitation of what was about to be lost.

Despite the name, A-Hour was only half an hour long, and would be followed by S-Hour, also 30 minutes long. The eerie S-Hour would consist of total silence as radio transmitters across the country changed their wavelengths and readied themselves for the switch to the WTBS. A script had been prepared to introduce the frightened population to the new service:

> This is the Wartime Broadcasting Service from now until further notice. All broadcasting in this country will be part of this service which will bring you up-to-date information as far as is possible about conditions in your area, the country and those countries off our shores. You should stay tuned to this frequency until further notice and we will give you information about the times of broadcasts so that you are able to preserve your batteries. It is in your own interests to turn your set off from time to time to preserve your batteries. We will bring you information when we have it. We will now broadcast region by region in order to confirm that you are tuned to the transmitter that will give you the best local information for your locality. This is the Wartime Broadcasting Service.[43]

Selected BBC staff would operate the WTBS, and they would be permitted 'controlled' time off to make the necessary domestic arrangements.[44] It would have been cruel indeed to have staff broadcasting advice on how to stockpile food and fortify your home, whilst denying them the chance to do so themselves. The BBC pledged to look after the families of staff who were on WTBS duty, or to 'assist with financing the move of immediate families to a selected area in the United Kingdom.'[45] The letter from the dispersing officer that alerted the chosen staff of their dreaded duty told them, 'You should be ready to go at 24 hours' notice. It cannot be foreseen how long you might be away, but it could be for several weeks. <u>Only your wife and any dependent members of your households should be told in confidence of these plans.</u>'[46] As with the staff designated for the Burlington bunker, they were given the option to have their salary paid to their wife; or they could draw an advance for them, from which they might take some 'pocket money'. They were warned that at their wartime destination, 'facilities for entertainment will be limited. It is, therefore, suggested that you should include some reading material and other small recreational items in your baggage.' They were advised to bring some food and to eat it first before tucking into the ration packs waiting for them at their destination. Disposable cutlery would be provided so that water need not be wasted on washing up.

The WTBS duty staff would be scattered around the country, with some being sent to Wood Norton, a stately home near Evesham in Worcestershire, which the BBC had obtained in 1939 as a potential secondary headquarters in case the corporation was forced to flee London. But most would be inside the bunkers serving as the seats of regional government, each fitted with a small studio from where the interim leaders could issue local news, advice and instructions.

Sounding the Alarm

The WTBS aimed to be operational in time to issue the dreaded four-minute warning to the nation. Of course, there was always the prospect of a bolt-from-the-blue attack, in which enemy missiles would be launched unexpectedly, meaning there might not be time to properly send the alarm down through the chain of command. In that case, the first notice of a nuclear attack might be a burst of light in the sky. But if the four-minute warning was received by the authorities, and if they managed to cascade it down through the police stations, bunkers and monitoring posts, to the various vicars and pub landlords across the country, then the BBC would join them in sounding the alarm.[47]

A red telephone on the desk of the technical operations manager at the BBC in London would ring, and the caller would say: 'This is the UKWMO[48] at United Kingdom Air Operations Centre. Falsetto. Radiate national warning immediately.' 'Falsetto' was the code word that authenticated the instruction from UKWMO. The manager would then select a cassette marked with a red dot and set it to play on all channels. The national air attack warning consisted of the distinctive warbling note of the siren, followed by a verbal message saying: 'Here is an emergency announcement. An air attack is approaching this country. Go to shelter or take cover immediately.' This would be repeated twelve times. The whole warning would last for two and a half minutes, taking up over half of the four-minute warning. After that, you were on your own.

After the bomb had fallen, survivors would be advised to tune in to WTBS every hour on the hour for transmissions; otherwise, they should switch off their devices. Having helped alert the nation to the attack, the next task of the WTBS would be to confirm that a nuclear attack had occurred, as it might not be immediately obvious to some regions. A script for this first post-apocalyptic broadcast had been prepared and recorded by the newsreader Peter Donaldson, who was known as 'the Voice of Radio 4'. He recalled being given some pieces of paper and asked to read the script. 'It felt really spooky,' he said. 'Here I was talking about the end of the world as we know it.'[49] His message was:

This is the Wartime Broadcasting Service. This country has been attacked with nuclear weapons. Communications have been severely disrupted and the number of casualties and the extent of the damage are not yet known. We shall bring you further information as soon as possible. Meanwhile, stay tuned to this wavelength, stay calm, and stay in your own homes. Remember there is nothing to be gained by trying to get away. By leaving your homes you could be exposing yourselves to greater danger. If you leave, you may find yourself without food, without water, without accommodation, and without protection. Radioactive fallout which follows a nuclear explosion is many times more dangerous if you're directly exposed to it in the open. Roofs and walls offer substantial protection. The safest place is indoors. Make sure gas and other fuel supplies are turned off, and that all fires are extinguished. If mains water is available, this can be used for firefighting. You should also refill all your containers for drinking water after the fires have been put out because the mains water supply may not be available for very long. Water must not be used for flushing lavatories. Until you are told that lavatories may be used again, other toilet arrangements must be made. Use your water only for essential drinking and cooking purposes. Water means life. Don't waste it. Make your food stocks last. Ration your supply because it may have to last for 14 days or more. If you have fresh food in the house, use this first to avoid wasting it. Food in tins will keep. If you live in an area where a fallout warning has been given stay in your fallout room until you are told it is safe to come out. When the immediate danger is past, the sirens will sound a steady note. The all-clear message will also be given on this wavelength. If you leave the fallout room to go to the lavatory or replenish food or water supplies, do not remain outside the room for a minute longer than is necessary. Do not, in any circumstances, go outside the house. Radioactive fallout can kill. You cannot see it or feel it, but it is there. If you go outside, you will bring danger to your family and you may die.

We shall repeat this broadcast in two hours' time. Stay tuned to this wavelength but switch your radios off now to save your batteries until we come on the air again. That is the end of this broadcast.

Epilogue

The Iron Curtain fell. The Soviet Union broke apart. The Cold War was over. In Berlin they partied on top of the Wall, and in Prague the streets 'literally ran with champagne', but in Britain there was no obvious celebration – no conga lines down the Mall, no kisses in Piccadilly Circus, no boats hooting on the Thames. It wasn't that type of war. Neither was there one fixed date on which to rejoice. Across Eastern Europe and the Soviet space, states declared their freedom at different times and in different styles: with the Velvet Revolution, with an agreement signed in a wintry forest, or with a dictator and his wife shot against a wall.

Much of Britain's Cold War civil defence planning had been shaped by the constant need to save money, and it was that same parsimony that meant her air raid sirens were dismantled with haste. In January 1993, the Home Office complained it would have cost £38 million to refurbish them and that the pesky contraptions would be gone by April. Vicars in their country churches and landlords in their rural pubs handed over the dusty boxes containing their handheld sirens, and the larger ones were disconnected and hauled down from roofs and poles and bell towers across the land. This was how we marked the end of the Cold War. A few were left in place to be used as flood warnings, and they are still in use today and can be heard in watery YouTube footage wailing over the wet rooftops of Hebden Bridge or Todmorden. Other sirens remain for no obvious reason – perhaps they have been forgotten about, or lie in an awkward position, or are still waiting to be ticked off some crinkled council to-do list from 1993.

These forgotten sirens are no longer powered, and the early-warning system that fed them no longer exists, so there is no chance of them whirring into life and terrifying everyone. They are just frozen

Cold War ghosts. You can find one atop a pole on a Lewisham street, poking up through the trees like a triffid, and there is another perched on a vandalised railway bridge outside Waterloo, silent and rusting and forgotten. But not by me. I seek them out. I hunt these ghosts and snap them with my camera. I track them on Google Street View. I zoom in. I scroll back. I click across the years and scrutinise them in ruddy evening glow and cold morning light. They fascinate me. They appal me. They are studded across Britain – bulbous, rusting reminders of what might have happened, and of what could happen still.

In March 2022, following the Russian invasion of Ukraine, Vladimir Putin ordered his country's nuclear forces onto high alert, and the Kyiv skyline echoed to the old wail of the air raid siren. Yet it was not an 'old' sound to the people of Kyiv. Neither is it 'old' to the population of Prague or Krakow or Stockholm, all of whom have maintained their siren networks and test them regularly. Germany conducted a nationwide test of its sirens in September 2020 on Warntag (Warning Day), the first time they had sounded since the end of the Cold War. Many European countries retained, or are rejuvenating, their siren networks, and with war raging in Europe again, and Putin's nukes on high alert, they are vindicated in those decisions.

In Britain, having stripped most of our sirens and sold them for scrap, we need an alternative warning system. Since the end of the Cold War, we have been reliant on TV and radio alerts. We now have emergency alerts on our smartphones, but the buzz and beep of a mobile cannot dredge up the same anxiety we would feel on hearing a siren. The air raid siren delivers its dreadful message instantly – as elemental as a dog's growl or a baby's cry.

With a terrifying war back on European soil, and the awful sense that the Cold War has revived, Britain's decision to dismantle its siren network seems hasty and short-sighted. A recognised, tried and tested warning system is needed. On that pleasant Lewisham street, the forgotten siren peeps through the leaves as if to say *I told you so.*

Acknowledgements

I thank my husband David Blair for freeing me from the call centre.

I will always be grateful to the late Calum Macdonald for giving me my first writing opportunity at *The Herald*. Dear Calum, you are missed.

Thanks to Mike Kenner for being a tireless source of knowledge, expertise and advice. I am also grateful to Mike for offering comments on the draft of this book, as did Sean Judge, Martyn Edwards and Phil Catling.

I must also thank my Dad, Sandy McDowall, for watching *Threads* back in 1984 whilst I was playing with my toys beside the TV, and for all our Saturday trips to libraries, bookshops, and the China Sea on Renfield Street.

I thank my agent, Will Francis of Janklow and Nesbit, and my editors at Bodley Head, Jörg Hensgen, Stuart Williams, Laura Reeves and Rowena Skelton-Wallace. I was daunted by the publishing world, but everyone I've had the fortune to meet has been generous, patient, wise and kind. I would also like to thank my copy-editor, Jane Selley, proof-reader, John Garrett and indexer, Vicki Robinson.

I also thank the following excellent people who have given me financial support via Patreon. This has provided a steady source of income to let me work and has funded much of my nuclear research, book-purchasing, archive access, and travel: Jonathan Abolins, Tom Allen, Anna Brotherton, Gareth Carthew, Tamzin Cater, Elisabeth Dellinger, Stephen Deutsch, Martyn Edwards, Scott Essery, Adam Gilmore, Eric Graves, Tom Higgins, Erica Lamont, John Layne, Amanda Lee, Marlee MacLeod, Tracey MacRobert, Mark Nelson, Chas Newkey-Burden, Richard Plaskett, Louis Pouw, Jeremy Rhodes, Simon Robinson, Andreas Rolland, Paul Jonathan Viner, Helen Walsh, Kevin Wingfield and Linda Woolnough.

Illustration & Picture Credits

Selection of *Protect and Survive Monthly* covers, published 1981 and 1982. Adam Firth and Sean Judge.

Barton Quarry, a bunker in the Edinburgh suburbs. Andrew Brooks Photography.

Hack Green, a bunker outside Nantwich in Cheshire. Hack Green Secret Nuclear Bunker and Grant Harper.

Royal Observer Corps monitoring post in Skelmorlie, North Ayrshire. Frank Alexander.

The Columba. CRSC/A. E. Bennett.

An advert from *Protect and Survive Monthly*. Adam Firth and Sean Judge.

The traffic warden from the film *Threads*. © BBC Archive.

A scene from the film *The War Game*. © BBC Archive.

Collapsible coffins. National Records of Scotland, catalogue reference HH51/277.

Protect and Survive booklet, 1980. Originally published under Crown Copyright 1980/Open Government Licence v2.0; replica photographed by Julie McDowall.

Carrier control point. Frank Alexander.

Endnotes

Abbreviations

BL: British Library
NRO: Norfolk Record Office
NRS: National Records of Scotland
TNA: The National Archives
TWL: The Wellcome Library

1 The Family That Feared Tomorrow

1 'SOS – Find These Parents', *Daily Mirror*, 9 August 1957.
2 Ibid.
3 I was first alerted to this incident by Jonathan Hogg's 2013 article 'The Family That Feared Tomorrow': British nuclear culture and individual experience in the late 1950s.
4 'It was an oil painting from hell', *Daily Mirror*, 3 June 1957.
5 Nevada Test Site Oral History Project. Interview with Raymond Harbert, 14 July 2005.
6 'Hiroshima' by John Hersey, *The New Yorker*, 23 August 1946.
7 'Trades Council urges ban on hydrogen bomb tests', *Lancashire Evening Post*, 7 June 1957.
8 'Readers' Letters', *Lancashire Evening Post*, 24 May 1957.
9 'End H-Bomb tests call by women', *Lancashire Evening Post*, 8 May 1957.
10 'Royal Navy still needs the ships', *Lancashire Evening Post*, 20 March 1957.
11 'This Unfunny Column', *Daily Mirror*, 15 February 1957.

12 See Chapter 3 for a further discussion of fallout and the Lucky Dragon incident.

13 'The Family That Feared Tomorrow', *Daily Mirror*, 16 August 1957.

14 Braithwaite, R., *Armageddon and Paranoia: The Nuclear Confrontation* (Profile, 2017), p.349.

15 'Transcript of President Reagan's Address on Downing of Korean Airliner', *The New York Times*, 6 September 1983.

16 Braithwaite, *Armageddon and Paranoia*, p.352.

17 Macintyre, B., *The Spy and The Traitor* (Penguin, 2018), p.182.

18 Kynaston, D., *Family Britain 1951–57* (Bloomsbury, 2010), p.663.

19 Ibid., p.666.

20 Ibid., p.671.

21 Advert in *Birmingham Daily Post*, 24 June 1957.

22 Advert in *Lancashire Evening Post*, 8 May 1957.

23 Advert in *Belfast Telegraph*, 27 December 1954.

2 Four-Minute Warning

1 Interview with the author.

2 *Tocsin Bang: The Cold War Story of the Royal Observer Corps*, Cyclops TV, 2002.

3 Interview with the author.

4 Interview with the author.

5 Interview with the author.

6 Interview with the author.

7 TNA, HO 393/60. 'The UKWMO and the Broadcasting of Air Raid Warnings and Other Alerts'.

8 Campbell, D., *War Plan UK* (Burnett Books, 2015), p.296.

9 *A British Guide to the End of the World*, BBC Four, 4 November 2019.

10 'When the sirens rocked a whole county', *The Guardian*, 8 July 1986.

11 'At the third stroke it will be World War Three', *Daily Mirror*, 9 February 1984.

12 'The Solzhenitsyn syndrome', *The Guardian*, 11 February 1984.

13 'Regulars ignore last orders', *The Guardian*, 29 October 1981.

14 *London Under Attack: The Report of the Greater London Area War Risk Study* (Basil Blackwell, 1986), p.29.

15 *Protect and Survive* (Central Office of Information, 1980).

16 Ibid.

17 Ibid.

18 Ibid.

19 *Advising the Householder on Protection Against Nuclear Attack* (Her Majesty's Stationery Office, 1963).

20 Interview with author.

21 Interview with author.

22 'Red for Danger', *The Guardian*, 3 November 1981.

23 Interview with author.

24 'Dad's army . . . where are you now?', *The Guardian*, 14 November 1980.

25 *Tocsin Bang*.

26 Interview with author.

27 *Tocsin Bang*.

28 Ibid.

29 Interview with author.

30 Interview with author.

31 Dalton, M. *The Royal Observer Corps Underground Monitoring Posts* (Folly Books, 2011), p.93.

32 Interview with author.

33 Interview with author.

3 Evacuation

1 Titmuss, R., *Social Welfare and Health Care in World War II: Problems of Social Policy* (HMSO, 1950), p.2450.

2 Calder, A., *The People's War* (Vintage Digital, 2012), p.36.

3 'Sanctuary Hotels', *The Times*, 10 August 1940.

4 'Sanctuary Hotels', *The Times*, 27 July 1940.

5 Advert in *The Times*, 19 April 1940. .

6 'Food surplus at luxury hotels?', *Lancashire Evening Post*, 7 July 1941.

7 Titmuss, *Social Welfare*, p.290.

8 Calder, *The People's War*, p.660.

9 Titmuss, *Social Welfare*, p.273.

10 Partington, S. V. (ed.), *Mrs Miles's Diary: The Wartime Journal of a Housewife on the Home Front* (Simon & Schuster, 2013), p.60.

11 Ibid., p.54.

12 Titmuss, *Social Welfare*, p.113.

13 Grant, M., *After the Bomb: Civil Defence and Nuclear War in Britain, 1945–68* (Palgrave Macmillan, 2010), p.62.

14 Ibid., p.63.

15 Ibid., p.64.

16 Ibid., p.109.

17 Titmuss, *Social Welfare*, p.796.

18 Ibid., p.797.

19 Ibid., p.227.

20 Bourke, J., *Fear: A Cultural History* (Virago, 2005), p.224.

21 Titmuss, *Social Welfare*, p.797.

22 Hodgson, V., *Few Eggs and No Oranges: The Diaries of Vere Hodgson, 1940–45* (Persephone Books, 1999), p.61.

23 Bourke, *Fear*, p.230.

24 A quote from the Bhagavad Gita, used by J. Robert Oppenheimer to sum up his feelings at the first nuclear test.

25 *Survival Under Atomic Attack* (Federal Civil Defense Administration, 1950).

26 Ibid.

27 Ibid.

28 Oakes, G., *The Imaginary War: Civil Defense and American Cold War Culture* (Oxford University Press, 1994), p.55.

29 Ibid., p.56.

30 Lapp, R., *Must We Hide?* (Addison Wesley, 1949), p.18.

31 Thompson, J., *Psychological Aspects of Nuclear War* (The British Psychological Society, 1985), p.13.

32 Ibid.

33 Royle, T., *Facing The Bear: Scotland and the Cold War* (Birlinn, 2019), p.71.

34 Ibid., p.67.

35 Hennessy, P., and Jinks, J., *The Silent Deep: The Royal Navy Submarine Service from 1945* (Penguin, 2016), p.200.

36 Ibid., p.211.

37 Macmillan, H., *At The End of the Day, 1961–1963* (Harper & Row, 1973), p.358.

38 Moss, N., *The Men Who Play God: The Story of the Hydrogen Bomb* (Penguin, 1970), p.19.

39 Ibid., p.39.

40 Mathematical Analyser, Numerical Integrator, and Automatic Computer.

41 Nevada Test Site Oral History Project, interview with Jay Marshall, 21 April 2005.

42 Ibid.

43 Nevada Test Site Oral History Project, interview with Robert William Mackenzie, 1 May 2005.

44 Ibid.

45 Schlosser, E., *Command and Control* (Allen Lane, 2013), p.137.

46 Ibid., p.138.

47 Kendall, B., *The Cold War: A New Oral History of Life Between East and West* (BBC Books, 2017), p.127.

48 Ibid.

49 Some of the tuna was canned at the Shimizu plant before the danger was realised. Orders were quickly issued for all cans to be destroyed, along with the rest of the tuna, and the remains buried in a deep trench.

50 *Hansard* HC Deb, vol. 526, col. 48, 5 April 1954.

51 Hennessy, P., *The Secret State: Preparing for The Worst, 1945–2010* (Penguin, 2014), p.165.

52 For comparison, the Hiroshima bomb was 15 kilotons. A kiloton is equivalent to 1,000 tons of TNT. With the hydrogen bomb we leave puny kilotons behind and move into the language of megatons. One megaton is equivalent to one million tons of TNT.

53 Hennessy, *The Secret State*, p.165.

54 TNA, CAB 134/940: the Strath Report, 'The Defence Implications of Fall-out from a Hydrogen Bomb', 8 March 1955.

55 Ibid.

56 TNA, HO 322/998, 'Planned Evacuation Options – Note by the Chairman of the Official Committee on Home Defence', 1982.

57 *Protect and Survive* (Central Office of Information, 1980), p.7.

58 TNA, HO 322/998.

59 Ibid.

60 Ibid.

61 Sandbrook, *Who Dares Wins: Britain, 1979–1982* (Allen Lane, 2019), p.390.

4 School's Out

1 'But mum, will there be a nuclear war?', *The Guardian*, 29 April 1986.
2 Ibid.
3 The Wellcome Library, SA/MED/H/1/6/2, Study Group on Psychosocial Issues in the Nuclear Age, 1988.
4 Greenwald, D. S., and Zeitlin, S. J., *No Reason To Talk About It: Families Confront The Nuclear Taboo* (Norton, 1987).
5 Oakes, *The Imaginary War.* p.63.
6 Ibid., p.64. An extract from a report on panic by Project East River. See Chapter 3 for more on the project and its attempts to emotionally manage Cold War Americans.
7 *Duck and Cover*, https://www.youtube.com/watch?v=IKqXu-5jw60.
8 Rose, K., *One Nation Underground: The Fallout Shelter in American Culture* (New York University Press, 2001), p.131.
9 Bourke, J. *Fear: A Cultural History* (Virago, 2005), p.256.
10 George, Alice, L., *Awaiting Armageddon: How Americans Faced the Cuban Missile Crisis* (University of North Carolina Press, 2003), p.146.
11 Garrison, D., *Bracing for Armageddon: Why Civil Defense Never Worked* (Oxford University Press, 2006), p.46.
12 '1,250,000 pupils are calm in drill', *The New York Times*, 29 November 1951, p.22.
13 TNA, 322/142.
14 Ibid.
15 'School sirens alert', *The Guardian*, 29 May 1983.
16 NRS, HH51/202, 'The Education Service and Nuclear Attack', Ministry of Education, Circular 3/64, 20 March 1964.
17 'Peace Study criticised by Boyson', *The Times*, 4 May 1982.
18 'Animating debate amid violent streets', *The Times*, 21 February 1984.
19 'Peace study guidelines called for in schools', *The Times*, 25 February 1985.
20 'How can we help the kids to cope?', *The Times*, 29 January 1985.
21 'Weighting the nuclear balance', *The Guardian*, 26 January 1982.
22 'Complaints on peace teaching', *The Times*, 29 January 1985.

23 Sandbrook, *Who Dares Wins*, p.392.

24 Thompson, E. P., and Smith, Dan (ed.), *Protest and Survive* (Penguin, 1980), p.36.

25 Sandbrook, *Who Dares Wins*, p.399.

26 'New wave of banners against the bomb', *The Guardian*, 26 October 1981.

27 'Teachers "slandered" by Baker', *The Guardian*, 10 February 1987.

28 'The school meals service in the cold war and emergency feeding today', by John Preston, https://preparednessthoughts.wordpress.com/2017/02/05/the-school-meals-service-in-the-cold-war-and-emergency-feeding-today/

29 NRS, HH51/73.

30 The Wellcome Library, SA/MED/H/2/3/6, 'Armageddon larder yields its sickly secrets', by Andrew Marr.

31 I am grateful to Mike Kenner for showing me this document.

32 See Chapter 6 for information on Burlington.

33 Originally the Women's Voluntary Service, they were awarded the 'Royal' title in 1966 in recognition of their invaluable work.

34 'Volunteer women ready for war', *The Guardian*, 31 March 1981.

35 'Volunteering others for the nuclear soup', *The Guardian*, 8 April 1981.

36 'Gift for the chauvinists', *The Guardian*, 3 April 1981.

37 TNA, HO 322/559.

5 Protect and Survive

1 A. Winkler, *Life Under a Cloud: American Anxiety About the Atom* (University of Illinois Press, 1999), p.117.

2 Ibid.

3 *Four Wheels To Survival* (Federal Civil Defense Administration, 1955).

4 Rose, K., *One Nation Underground: The Fallout Shelter in American Culture* (New York University Press, 2001), p.219.

5 'Food as weapon of war', *The Times*, 3 August 1942.

6 'The Modern Helen', *The Times*, 10 June 1942.

7 Nicholson V., *Millions Like Us: Women's Lives During the Second World War* (Penguin, 2012), p.178.

8 Gardiner, J., *Wartime Britain 1939–1945* (Headline, 2004), p.140.

9   Gardiner, J., *The Blitz: The British Under Attack* (Harper Press, 2011), p.103.

10 Ibid., p.102.

11 TNA, HO 322/727.

12 TNA, AN/174/2184.

13 The Royal Voluntary Service Oral History Archive.

14 Hansard HC Deb, vol. 685, col. 941, 2 December 1963.

15 Campbell, D., *War Plan UK*, p.86.

16 *Advising the Householder on Protection Against Nuclear Attack* (Her Majesty's Stationery Office, 1963), p.20.

17 Ibid., p.11.

18 Ibid., p.12.

19 Advert in *The Times*, 17 August 1939.

20 Kean, H., *The Great Cat and Dog Massacre* (University of Chicago Press, 2017), p.120.

21 Ibid.

22 TNA, HO 322/35.

23 Ibid.

24 'Vermin and Wild Animal Control' by Andrew M. Barnard, *Protect and Survive Monthly*, Issue No. 12, December 1981.

25 'Home Defence and the Farmer', 1961, *Nuclear War in Britain: Home Front Civil Defence Films 1950–1987* (Strike Force Entertainment, 2015).

26 https://www.margaretthatcher.org/document/106689.

27 'Stay at home' episode of the *Protect and Survive* films.

28 Ibid.

29 Ibid.

30 'Refuges' episode of the *Protect and Survive* films.

31 'Materials to use for your fallout room and refuge' episode of the *Protect and Survive* films.

32 *Panorama*, 'If the Bomb Drops', BBC1, 11 March 1980.

33 Ibid.

34 'Casualties' episode of the *Protect and Survive* films.

35 Hansard HL Deb, vol. 406, col. 367, 5 March 1980.

36 Hansard HC Deb, vol. 979, col. 628, 20 February 1980.

37 *Panorama*, 'If the Bomb Drops'.

38 'A Lethal Failure of Duty', *The Times*, 19 January 1980.

39 NRS, HH51/277.

40 TNA, HO 322/100.

41 BL, OP/LG-5507, 'War Plans Out In the Open: What Will People Think', South Yorkshire Fire and Civil Defence Authority, December 1988.

42 We might wonder if the venue was chosen for the mischief of its address, Shambles Street.

43 BL, OP/LG-5508, 'Disposal of Human Remains in War', South Yorkshire Fire and Civil Defence Authority, October 1988.

44 Ibid.

45 Ibid.

46 National Library of Scotland, *Civil Defence Planning Assumptions in Central Scotland* (Strathclyde Regional Planning Assumptions Study, 1989).

47 Wellcome Library, SA/MED/H/2/3/3, *You and the Bomb* (South Yorkshire County Council, 1984).

48 Ibid.

49 Wellcome Library, SA/MED/H/2/3/9, *London Nuclear Information Unit*, 26 October 1988.

50 'Disposal of Human Remains in War', South Yorkshire.

51 NRS, HH51/277.

52 Ibid.

6 Taking Shelter

1 The site had various code names in its lifetime: Chanticleer, Stockwell, Turnstile, Peripheral and Eyeglass. This book will use Burlington.

2 This was the plan until 1968, after which the Python plan was used (see Chapter 4 for more detail on the Python plan).

3 This plan was authorised in 1955.

4 Catford, N., *Burlington. The Central Government War Headquarters at Corsham* (Folly Books, 2012), p.109.

5 Hennessy, P., *Winds of Change: Britain in the Early Sixties* (Allen Lane, 2019), p.7.

6 I am grateful to Mike Kenner for showing me this document.

7 Hennessy, *Winds of Change*, p.7.

8 *Panorama*, 'If the Bomb Drops', BBC1, 11 March 1980.

9 'The Problem of Shelters', *The Times*, 22 November 1940.

10 'A Shelter Dictator Wanted', *British Medical Journal*, Vol. 2, No. 1470, 7 December 1940, pp.790–1.

11 Grant, M., *After the Bomb: Civil Defence and Nuclear War in Britain, 1945–68* (Palgrave Macmillan, 2010), p.29.

12 Ibid.

13 Rose, K., *One Nation Underground: The Fallout Shelter in American Culture* (New York University Press, 2001), p.89.

14 'Religion: Gun Thy Neighbour?', *Time*, 18 August 1961.

15 Rose, *One Nation Underground*, p.94.

16 Ibid.

17 Ibid.

18 George, Alice L., *Awaiting Armageddon: How Americans Faced the Cuban Missile Crisis* (University of North Carolina Press, 2003), p.74.

19 TNA, HO 322/872.

20 *Panorama*, 'If the Bomb Drops'.

21 *Check It Out*, Tyne Tees Television, July 1980.

22 Graff, G., *Raven Rock: The Story of the U.S. Government's Secret Plan to Save Itself – While the Rest of Us Die* (Simon & Schuster, 2017), p.259, Kindle.

23 TNA, HO 322/783.

24 TNA, WORK 14/3172.

25 Ibid.

26 TNA, HO322/872.

27 Ibid.

28 'Fanatics, radicals and extremists who are subverting our civil defence', *The Guardian*, 25 June 1981.

29 Hansard HC Deb, vol. 4, col. 595, 11 May 1981.

30 'Test case on nuclear shelters', *The Guardian*, 4 October 1983.

31 'Survival syndrome', *Central Somerset Gazette*, 22 January 1981.

32 'Two ways to fight Heseltine's social insecurity', *The Guardian*, 26 November 1984.

33 'Nuclear shelter grant refused,' *Liverpool Daily Post*, 7 June 1980.

34 'A mushrooming trade in shelters', *The Times*, 30 September 1980.

35 *Protect and Survive Monthly*, No. 7, July 1981.

36 *Protect and Survive Monthly*, No. 2, February 1981.

37 *Protect and Survive Monthly*, Vol. 2, No. 2, February 1982.

38 *Protect and Survive Monthly*, Vol. 2. No. 1, January 1982.

39 Ibid.

40 Ibid.

41 *Protect and Survive Monthly*, Vol. 10, October 1981.

42 'Fallout shelter ads under fire', *The Guardian*, 10 September 1980.

43 'Shelter from the nuclear cowboys', *The Guardian*, 9 December 1980.

44 'Plea for standards in fallout shelters', *The Observer*, 5 July 1981.

45 'Will we all go together?', *The Guardian*, 27 June 1980.

46 *Domestic Nuclear Shelters* (Central Office of Information, 1981).

47 'Red tape is raising a cloud over Home Office's authorised nuclear shelters', *The Times*, 15 January 1981.

48 'Pack up your troubles', *The Guardian*, 5 February 1981.

49 'Plea for standards in fallout shelters', *The Observer*.

50 The visible pipe would also be an indicator to any of the starving survivors that a stocked shelter lay below the surface, arguably prompting attacks as described in the young adult nuclear war novel *Brother in the Land* by Robert Swindells.

51 Hayden, Ben, *Ben's Bunker Book* (THAP Books, 1984).

52 Ibid.

53 Surrey History Centre, 4009/1, *A Guide to Communities for Survival in War*, Chapter 9, Health and Hygiene, 1980.

54 Advice from the Department of Health and Social Security, quoted in *Civil Defence: Bunkers or Bonkers?* (National and Local Government Officers Association, 1984).

7 The Doctor Won't See You Now

1 'Brilliant Opening of City's New Dance Hall', *Aberdeen Press and Journal*, 4 May 1929.

2 'The Band Played Through the Blitz', *Aberdeen Evening Express*, 28 April 1993.

3 NRS, HH51/175.

4 The Wellcome Library (Hereafter TWL), SA/MED/H/2/3/5, 'How many drugs in nuclear stockpile?', *Hospital Pharmacy*, Vol. 1, No. 1, May 1986.

5 NRO, ACC 2019/36, 'Pharmaceutical aspects of planning for post-nuclear attack'.

6 Ibid.

7 HDC (77)1: 'The preparation and organisation of The Health Service for war,' *The Medical Effects of Nuclear War* (John Wiley, 1983), p. 155.

8 NRO, 'Organisation of the Health Service in time of war', May 1981.

9 Ibid.

10 *Care of the Homeless*, RHR Production for the Home Office, 1965.

11 Macintyre, *The Spy and the Traitor*, pp.147–9.

12 NRO, 'Organisation of the NHS for war – Blood Transfusion Service', 1979.

13 NRS, HH51/186.

14 Ibid.

15 Advert in *The Guardian*, 16 March 1954.

16 Advert in *The Guardian*, 3 March 1954.

17 'Nuclear test for Hospital Reserve nurses', *Central Somerset Gazette*, 4 October 1963.

18 Easingwold now hosts the Emergency Planning College, while Taymouth Castle is being refurbished as a luxury hotel.

19 'Just in case the deterrent fails', *The Guardian*, 30 December 1987.

20 Interview with the author.

21 'How to survive a nuclear attack. Operation Hot Seat', *TV Eye*, 1981, via Thames TV YouTube Channel.

22 The British civil defence booklet *Home Defence and the Farmer* says of farm animals, 'although they might get radiation sickness, their flesh would be safe to eat. This is because the radioactive material which is retained in an animal's body goes into bones and to its internal organs rather than to flesh.'

23 'Dugout Britain or What Happens When the Bomb Drops', *The Observer*, 12 July 1981.

24 TWL, SA/MED/H/2/3/5, 'A war of ideas', *Health and Social Service Journal*, p.134.

25 Ibid.

26 'Role-playing away a nuclear attack', *The Guardian*, 18 January 1989.

27 Ibid.

28 Ibid.

29 NRS, HH51/225, 'Nursing under disaster conditions'.

30 NRS, HDC(77)1.

31 'The Preparation and Organisation of the Health Service for war', *The Medical Effects of Nuclear War* (British Medical Association, 1983), p.155.

32 Ibid.

33 NRS, HH51/175.

34 NRS, HH51/157.

35 NRS, HH51/186.

36 NRS, HH51/186.

37 NRS, HH51/225.

38 NRO, HDC (77)1.

39 Ibid.

40 Campbell, D., *War Plan UK*, p.378.

41 NRS, HH51/225.

42 Campbell, *War Plan UK*, p.384.

43 Hersey, John, 'Hiroshima', *The New Yorker*, 23 August 1946.

44 *The Medical Effects of Nuclear War* (The British Medical Association, 1983).

45 'Why the BMA chief exploded over the Home Office', *The Guardian*, 24 September 1984.

46 Ibid.

47 'Doctors in chilling despair', *The Guardian*, 4 March 1983.

48 *Nuclear War Civil Defence Planning: The Implications for Nursing* (Royal College of Nursing, 1983).

49 TWL, SA/MED/H/2/S/2, 'A Doctor's Dilemma'.

50 'Village vote for suicide', *Daily Mirror*, 23 December 1983.

51 TWL, SA/MED/H/2/S/2.

52 'When "controlling" the sick will mean shooting them', *The Guardian*, 9 October 1980.

8 Civil Defence Is Common Sense

1 *Festival of Britain in Colour 1951*, Crown Film Unit, 1951.

2 Kynaston, *Family Britain 1951–57*, p.6.

3 Festival of Britain advert, *The Times*, 19 June 1951.

4 'Some Misgivings on the East Coast', *Yorkshire Post and Leeds Intelligencer*, 17 May 1951.

5 'Boys "rescued" in County CD Demonstration', *Northampton Mercury*, 6 July 1951.

6   Hennessy, *The Secret State*, p.157.

7   '"Duty" of civil defence', *The Times*, 12 April 1954.

8   'Coventry to ignore Civil Defence exercise', *The Times*, 1 May 1954.

9   'Confusion at Coventry. Rival Voices at CD exercise', *Manchester Guardian*, 31 May 1954.

10 Ibid.

11 'Readers' views on Coventry Civil Defence Demonstration', *Coventry Evening Telegraph*, 1 June 1954.

12 'Exercise Priory Turns to Verbal War', *Coventry Evening Telegraph*, 31 May 1954.

13 Davis, T. C., *Stages of Emergency: Cold War Nuclear Civil Defense* (Duke University Press, 2007), p.51.

14 'Civil defence recruiting in Coventry', *The Times*, 5 October 1954.

15 TNA, HO 322/444.

16 The Pioneer section, who specialised in particularly taxing work like debris clearance and the shifting of corpses, was amalgamated into Rescue in 1952. Women could not join either section.

17 Grant, *After the Bomb*, p.65.

18 Manchester Central Library Archives, 'Town Clerk's Report to the Civil Defence Committee, 20 January 1955'.

19 Grant, *After the Bomb*, p.68.

20 Ibid., p.69.

21 Hennessy, P., *Having It So Good: Britain in the Fifties* (Penguin, 2007), p.158.

22 TNA, HO 303/4.

23 Extract from *Panorama*, BBC Television, transmission Monday 10 October 1960.

24 TNA, HO 303/4.

25 'Civil Defence Sunday', *Reading Mercury*, 7 June 1958.

26 Ibid.

27 Davis, *Stages of Emergency*, p.96.

28 Ibid.

29 Lowe, K., *Inferno: The Devastation of Hamburg, 1943* (Penguin, 2008), p.269.

30 Ibid., p.273.

31 The Strath Report, 1955. I am grateful to Mike Kenner for providing me with a copy.

32 *Advising the Householder on Protection Against Nuclear Attack* (Her Majesty's Stationery Office, 1963).

33 Grant, *After the Bomb*, p.130.

34 Ibid., p.188.

9 Control

1 Lee, C., *One of Your Own: The Life and Death of Myra Hindley* (Mainstream Publishing, 2017), pp.307, 308.

2 'A dungeon of the eighties', *Newcastle Journal*, 30 May 1989.

3 NRS, HO 322/1008.

4 Ibid.

5 http://wellcomecollection.org/articles/W6otoRIAACEAoXqO.

6 Campbell, D., *War Plan UK*, p. 136.

7 NRS, HH51/346.

8 'Rooftop protest at jail', *Aberdeen Press and Journal*, 5 April 1989.

9 'Chain Terror on the roof', *Aberdeen Press and Journal*, 1 October 1987.

10 'Letter tells of prison horrors', *Aberdeen Evening Express*, 4 March 1987.

11 NRS, HH51/346.

12 Ibid.

13 In Scottish civil defence terminology, it was Scottish Central Control.

14 Hill, Christopher R., *Peace and Power in Cold War Britain: Media, Movements and Democracy, c.1945–68* (Bloomsbury Academic, 2018), p.211.

15 Ibid., p.212.

16 Ibid., p.220.

17 https://www.newstatesman.com/node/198271.

18 https://www.subbrit.org.uk/features/struggle-for-survival/.

19 Gardiner, *Wartime Britain 1939–1945*, p.337.

20 NRS, HH51/282.

21 Gardiner, *Wartime Britain*, p.336.

22 NRS, HO 322/559.

23 Ibid.

24 NRS, HH51/352.

25 'Operation Elastic stretches churchmen', *The Guardian*, 6 October 1986.

26 TNA, HO 322/230.

27 Ibid.

28 Ibid.

29 Hennessy, *Winds of Change*, p.7.

30 Reagan, R., *The Reagan Diaries* (HarperCollins e-books, 2009), p.19.

31 'Religious Leaders Tell of Worry on Armageddon View Ascribed to Reagan', *The New York Times*, 21 October 1984.

32 Lewis, A., *Apocalypse Soon? Christian Responsibility and the Book of Revelation* (accessed in Scottish CND Archive, Glasgow Caledonian University).

33 National Police War Instructions England and Wales, 1977, https://archive.org/details/national-police-war-instructions-england-and-wales-1977/page/n1/mode/2up.

34 Ibid.

35 Ibid.

36 *Police Manual of Home Defence* (HMSO, 1974).

37 Ibid.

38 Ibid.

39 https://www.telegraph.co.uk/family/life/visitors-go-home-fear-loathing-uk-holiday-villages/.

40 https://www.bbc.co.uk/news/uk-wales-52222777.

41 Surrey History Centre 4009/1, *A Guide to Communities For Survival in War*, Chapter 7, Section 2, 'Local Peacekeeping'.

42 TNA, HO 322/210.

43 Ibid.

44 Jahner, H., *Aftermath: Life in the Fallout of the Third Reich 1945–1955* (W. H. Allen, 2021), p.23.

45 Ibid., p.19.

46 Lowe, *Inferno*, p.353.

47 Ibid., p.355.

48 Briefing Material for Wartime Controllers (ES3/1976), accessed in Scottish CND Archive, Glasgow Caledonian University.

49 Ackroyd, P., *London: A Biography* (Chatto & Windus, 2000), p.290.

50 Briefing Material for Wartime Controllers (ES3/1976).

51 *Panorama*, 'If the Bomb Drops', BBC1, 11 March 1980.

10 Nuclear War at the BBC

1   'Censored: *The War Game* Story', by Michael Tracey, in *Nukespeak: The Media and the Bomb*, ed. Crispin Aubrey (Comedia/MPG), p.43.

2   http://pwatkins.mnsi.net/.

3   Ferris, P., *Sir Huge: The Life of Huw Wheldon* (Michael Joseph, 1990), p.171.

4   'Churchill gagged BBC on H-Bomb', *The Guardian*, 20 August 1999.

5   'Censored: *The War Game* Story', p.47.

6   Ferris, *Sir Huge*, p.181.

7   Ibid.

8   'The BBC and the Censorship of *The War Game*', by James Chapman, *Journal of Contemporary History*, Vol. 41, No. 1, January 2006, pp.75–94.

9   Rosenthal, A., *The New Documentary in Action: A Casebook in Film Making* (University of California Press, 1971), p.155.

10 Ibid.

11 *The War Game Files*, BBC Radio 4, 6 June 2015.

12 Rosenthal, *The New Documentary*, p.155.

13 *The War Game Files*.

14 Ibid.

15 Ferris, *Sir Huge*, p.186.

16 *The War Game Files*.

17 Ferris, *Sir Huge*, p.187.

18 'The BBC and the Censorship of *The War Game*'.

19 Ibid.

20 Ibid.

21 Interview with Hugh Greene, 1982, BBC Oral History Collection, https://www.bbc.com/historyofthebbc/100-voices/coldwar/war-game.

22 'Auntie's fallout', *The Guardian*, 1 August 1985.

23 'The 20 Year Itch', *The Guardian*, 1 August 1985.

24 'BBC feared effect of nuclear film on elderly', *The Times*, 13 March 1981.

25 'Shield for raw minds', *The Guardian*, 26 September 1980.

26 'How Square Leg has caught out the strategy for nuclear survival', *The Guardian*, 27 September 1980.

27 'Mrs Whitehouse's ostrich approach to the bomb', *The Guardian*, 29 September 1980.

28 'The Censorship Game', *Sunday Mirror*, 13 February 1966.

29 TNA, HO 3222/941.

30 'A warning masterpiece', *The Observer*, 13 February 1966.

31 TNA, HO 3222/941.

32 Ibid.

33 Interview with the author.

34 Reagan, R., *The Reagan Diaries* (HarperCollins e-books, 2009), p. 199.

35 'What is left for debate?', *The Times*, 27 July 1982.

36 'Great fire over London', *The Guardian*, 27 July 1982.

37 Interview with the author.

38 'Most grim of reapers', *The Guardian*, 24 September 1984.

39 'Thread of hope behind the threat', *Financial Times*; TNA, HO 322/1134.

40 'Waiting for the big bang', *The Observer*, 30 September 1984.

41 TNA, HO 322/1134. The second programme referred to here was *On the Eighth Day*, shown alongside *Threads*, which was a detailed studio discussion about the theory of nuclear winter.

42 This didn't appease Watkins, who was still angry at the film's treatment and accused the BBC of 'hypocritical elitism'.

43 I thank Mike Kenner for sharing these BBC archives with me.

44 Ibid.

45 Ibid.

46 Ibid.

47 Assuming TV was still on air and the WTBS had not yet been initiated.

48 UK Warning and Monitoring Organisation, as discussed in Chapter 1.

49 Report by Sanchia Berg, BBC Radio 4, 2005.

Bibliography

Ackroyd, P., *London: A Biography* (Chatto & Windus, 2000)

Aubrey, C. (ed.), *Nukespeak: The Media and the Bomb* (Comedia, 1982)

Bourke, J., *Fear: A Cultural History* (Virago, 2005)

British Medical Association, *The Medical Effects of Nuclear War* (John Wiley and Sons, 1984)

Braithwaite, R., *Armageddon and Paranoia: The Nuclear Confrontation* (Profile, 2017)

Calder, A., *The People's War* (Vintage, 2012)

Campbell, D., *War Plan UK* (Burnett Books, 2015)

Catford, N., *Burlington: The Central Government War Headquarters at Corsham* (Folly Books, 2012)

Clarke, R., *London Under Attack: The Report of the Greater London War Risk Study* (Basil Blackwell, 1986)

Dalton, M., *The Royal Observer Corps Underground Monitoring Posts* (Folly Books, 2011)

Davis, T.C., *Stages of Emergency: Cold War Nuclear Civil Defense* (Duke University Press, 2007)

Ferris, P., *Sir Huge: The Life of Huw Wheldon* (Michael Joseph, 1990)

Gardiner, J., *The Blitz: The British Under Attack* (Harper Press, 2011)

Gardiner, J., *Wartime Britain, 1939–1945* (Headline, 2004)

Garrison, D., *Bracing for Armageddon: Why Civil Defense Never Worked* (Oxford University Press, 2006)

George, A.L., *Awaiting Armageddon: How Americans Faced the Cuban Missile Crisis* (University of North Carolina Press, 2003)

Graff, G., *Raven Rock: The Story of the U.S. Government's Secret Plan to Save Itself – While the Rest of Us Die* (Simon & Schuster, 2017)

Grant, M., *After the Bomb: Civil Defence and Nuclear War in Britain, 1945–68* (Palgrave Macmillan, 2010)

Greenwald, D.S. and Zeitlin, S.J., *No Reason to Talk About It: Families Confront the Nuclear Taboo* (Norton, 1987)

Hayden. B., *Ben's Bunker Book* (THAP Books, 1984)

Hennessy, P., *Having it So Good: Britain in the Fifties* (Penguin, 2007)

Hennessy, P., *The Secret State: Preparing for the Worst, 1945–2010* (Penguin, 2014)

Hennessy, P., *Winds of Change: Britain in the Early Sixties* (Allen Lane, 2019)

Hennessy, P. and Jinks, J., *The Silent Deep: The Royal Navy Submarine Service from 1945* (Penguin, 2016)

Hill, C.R., *Peace and Power in Cold War Britain: Media, Movements and Democracy, c.1945–68* (Bloomsbury Academic, 2018)

Hogdson, V., *Few Eggs and No Oranges: The Diaries of Vere Hodgson, 1940–45* (Persephone Books, 1999)

Jahner, H., *Aftermath. Life in the Fallout of the Third Reich, 1945–1955* (W.H. Allen, 2021)

Kean, H., *The Great Cat and Dog Massacre* (University of Chicago Press, 2017)

Kendall, B., *The Cold War: A New Oral History of Life Between East and West* (BBC Books, 2017)

Kynaston, D., *Family Britain 1951–57* (Bloomsbury, 2010)

Lapp, R., *Must We Hide?* (Addison Wesley, 1949)

Lee, C., *One of Your Own: The Life and Death of Myra Hindley* (Mainstream Publishing, 2017)

Lowe, K., *Inferno: The Devastation of Hamburg, 1943* (Penguin, 2008)

Macintyre, B., *The Spy and the Traitor* (Penguin, 2018)

Macmillan, H., *At the End of the Day, 1961–1963* (Harper & Row, 1973)

Moss, N., *The Men Who Play God: The Story of the Hydrogen Bomb* (Penguin, 1970)

Nicholson, V., *Millions Like Us: Women's Lives During the Second World War* (Penguin, 2012)

Oakes, G., *The Imaginary War: Civil Defense and American Cold War Culture* (Oxford University Press, 1994)

Partington, S.V., *Mrs Miles's Diary. The Wartime Journal of a Housewife on the Home Front* (Simon & Schuster, 2013)

Reagan, R., *The Reagan Diaries* (Harper Collins, 2009)

Rose, K., *One Nation Underground: The Fallout Shelter in American Culture* (New York University Press, 2001)

Rosenthal, A., *The New Documentary in Action: A Casebook in Film Making* (University of California Press, 1971)

Royle, T., *Facing the Bear: Scotland and the Cold War* (Birlinn, 2019)

Sandbrook, D., *Who Dares Wins: Britain, 1979–1982* (Allen Lane, 2019)

Schlosser, E., *Command and Control* (Allen Lane, 2013)

Thompson, E.P. and Smith, D. (ed.), *Protest and Survive* (Penguin, 1980)

Thompson, J., *Psychological Aspects of Nuclear War* (The British Psychological Society, 1985)

Titmuss, R., *Social Welfare and Health Care in World War II: Problems of Social Policy* (HMSO, 1950)

Index

The LISTOWEL & BALLYBUNION RAILWAY

compiled by
Michael Foster
and incorporating the original booklet by the late
A.T. Newham

THE OAKWOOD PRESS

© Oakwood Press 1989

First published 1967
Reprinted 1971
New enlarged edition 1989

Typeset by Gem Publishing Company, Brightwell, Wallingford, Oxfordshire

Reprinted by Alpha Print (Oxon) Ltd, Witney, Oxfordshire.

ISBN 0 85361 376 1

Mr Michael Barry with his restored length of Lartigue trackwork at Ballingowan, Co. Kerry.   *Author*

The drawings of the locomotives, coaches, wagons have been drawn and kindly supplied by Mr Adrian S. Garner and remain his copyright.

Published by
The OAKWOOD PRESS
P.O.Box 122, Headington, Oxford.

Contents

Dedication

Michael and Sheila Barry of Ballingowan, Lisselton, Co Kerry, have, on their own, searched out items, lengths of track from barns, buildings and fences. They have spent twenty years collecting many of the bits and pieces which will make up, it is hoped, the museum to be constructed.

Mr Sean Quinlan, writing in the "Kingdom" on 3rd July, 1984, said, to quote – "Michael and Sheila have put a lot of time and effort into restructuring and protecting a part of our heritage and it is time that somebody somewhere stands up and on behalf of this and future generations says 'thank you'. This paper does so now!"

And so do I – on behalf of all lovers of the Lartigue Railway System.

Michael Foster

Note

Throughout this history, the spelling "Ballybunnion" and "Lisselton" conforms to that used on current Ordnance Survey maps of the area, notwithstanding that "Ballybunion" and "Liselton" are in common use otherwise.

The derivation of the former place-name is "The Town of the Saplings", "Bally" being an Anglicization of the Irish "Baile" a town.

A typical Lartigue train formation, hauled by locomotive No. 1. The formation make-up is as follows: composite coach (one first and two third class sections), two door third class coach, three door first class coach, a guard's van with third and first class section at the front with six sand wagons at the rear.

Courtesy, Irish Record Society

Acknowledgements

I would like to record in order of meeting them in preparation of this new edition those people who have introduced me to the "Lartigue", and shared their knowledge and enthusiasm for this unique line.

Mr Joe Hilliard, of Cahirdown, Listowel, Co Kerry.

Mr Michael Barry, of Ballingowan, Lisselton, Co Kerry.

Mr Jack McCarthy of Lixnaw, Co Kerry.

Mr John Van Riemsdijk of the Science Museum, London.

Mr Don Boreham, of Princes Risborough, Bucks.

Mr Adrian Garner, of Woodham, Woking, Surrey.

Mr John O'Callaghan of London.

Mr Michael Lamb, of Severn-Lamb Ltd, Stratford upon Avon.

Mr D. Townsley, of the Hunslet Engine Company, Leeds.

Mr L.W. White, of the Avon Tyres Co, Melksham, Wiltshire.

Mr Ian Chisholm, of Chisholm Steels Ltd, Stafford.

Mr Tommie Cleary, of Ranelagh, Dublin.

Jane Kennedy of the Oakwood Press, Oxford.

Mr Christopher Lavery, of Hemel Hempstead, Herts.

Mr Michael Guerin, of Clieveragh, Listowel, Co Kerry.

Mr Les Warnett, of Wivelsfield, East Sussex.

Mr Ray Dudley, of London.

Mr Peter Levy, of "The Kerryman", Tralee, Co Kerry.

Mr Brian M. Deane, of the Irish Tourist Board, Dublin.

Mr Dennis Wilby, of Railway, Mine and Plantation Equipment Ltd, London.

And the

Merioneth Railway Society for permission to reproduce details from their publication *The Compleat Lartigue*.

A good front view of the locomotive at Listowel depot with Mr Paddy Boyle (*right*).
LRGP Collection, Courtesy David & Charles

A rare photograph of No. 3 locomotive seen at Ballybunion station.

Author's Collection

A train approaching Teampaillin Ban bridge, just outside Listowel station. Note the Thoumplebawn Burial Ground on the right which contains a memorial to the victims of the Great Famine.
Courtesy of National Library of Ireland

Chapter One
Setting the Scene

In recent years, renewed interest and activity has taken place in the field of the monorail system of railway construction, first enunciated by Robinson Palmer in 1821. Germany had evolved the Alweg system, whereon a powered car, with or without trailers operates on a concrete beam supported by pylons, super-elevated where necessary for the negotiation of curves; an example of this is to be found near Tokyo, Japan. There is also the older, and well-known, high-level Wuppertal Railway (on the Langen principle) between Elberfield and Barmen (Germany), where the cars are suspended from an overhead rail carried by compound girders, or shear legs. Part of this system is above a river, due to exigencies of space, whilst the problem of access to high level workshops and sidings has been satisfactorily resolved. A section of the line was destroyed during World War II, but was restored soon afterwards.

There had also been a proposal for a monorail link between West London and London Airport, in consequence of mounting road congestion, but in view of the much built-up state of the outer suburbs, including Hounslow, it was substituted by a standard underground rail-link, now operational.

It was therefore considered necessary to furnish some account of an early, albeit primitive, example of such a railway, built in the late eighties of last century between Listowel and Ballybunion, Co. Kerry, by the Lartigue Construction Company. The conception of a Frenchman, Charles Francois Marie-Therese Lartigue, it was claimed that such systems could be provided at much less cost than orthodox railways, and were therefore particularly suitable for districts of low population density, or where the terrain was of a difficult nature.

The company published a booklet *The Compleat Lartigue* in July 1886 on the Lartigue Elevated Single Rail Railway and this is included to establish the principles of the system.

THE LARTIGUE ELEVATED SINGLE RAIL RAILWAY
(As written in July 1836)

This system of railways, though most successfully tested and applied since the year 1883 in several parts of the Continents of Europe and Africa, has only been quite lately brought to the notice of the British public by the efforts of one of the writers of this pamphlet.

The lines constructed abroad were designed to be worked by animal power or electricity. Neither of these methods, it was felt, was suitable for lines of great length where speed is required, nor for the carrying of a mixed traffic of passengers and goods of a certain importance.

The adaptation of this system to such a traffic with the greatest possible economy has lately been the principal object of those interested in its development, and has been, it is believed, most completely and satisfactorily attained. Those interested in the introduction of this system into the British Empire were desirous of at once submitting it to a thorough examination by the highest authority in the land, and to obtain its sanction and approval as a test of its soundness and practical adaptability to the purposes for which it has been designed. With this object an application was made to the Imperial Parliament in the early part of 1886 for an Act to authorise the building of a Railway for the carrying of passengers and goods from Listowell to Ballybunion, about 10 miles in length, to be built on the Lartigue system and to be worked by locomotives.

The intelligent care with which the Imperial Parliament cherishes the development of any advance in science which promises to extend in any way the manufacturing, commercial and agricultural resources of the Empire is well known, and, fully appreciating the great advantages offered by the introduction of the Lartigue Railway, not only for the development of all the Colonial parts of the Empire, but also of many parts of the United Kingdom and Ireland, and its great importance for the development of agriculture, Parliament passed the above-mentioned Act unanimously, which received the Royal assent on the 16th April, 1886.

Since then another Bill authorising the construction of a Railway from a junction with the Great Western Railway to Lynton, in Devonshire, for the carriage of passengers and goods, to be worked by locomotives, on the Lartigue system, has received the sanction of both Houses of Parliament and is only awaiting the Royal assent. This Railway is of a length of about 30 miles.

But, in order fully to demonstrate all the advantages of this system, it was decided to construct a model line in the very centre of London, near Victoria Street, Westminster, on the site of the old Westminster Prison, and the principal object of this booklet is to give a description of this specimen Railway.

Before however commencing this description it will be well, in order to give our readers a general notion of it, to state briefly what are the main features of the Lartigue Elevated Single Line Railway, a system applicable now with equal ease and advantage to Military, Agricultural or Manufacturing Lines, which are intended to be constantly shifted, as well as to fixed or permanent lines of communication; the difference between lines intended for one or the other object being confined to certain details of arrangement.

In dealing with this new means of transport we must consider two very different features, viz: 1st. The Line itself; and 2nd, The Rolling Stock.

The Line, which, above all, is portable, when applied to military, agricultural or manufacturing pupurposes, is, when reduced to its minimum width, a line composed of one rail of the shape of a flat bar, extremely rigid when subjected to vertical pressure but easily bent horizontally. This rail is supported above the ground by A-shaped trestles or frames, made of angle or any other very stiff section of iron. The upper extremity of these trestles is bolted to the rail, and the lower extremity rests on the ground, being supported by a bed-plate or sleeper, to which the frame is firmly secured. The sleepers may be of different sizes and shapes according to circumstances, and may further be secured in their places, when required, by long pegs driven into the ground through holes drilled near the extremity of the sleepers, thus preventing the line from shifting. The trestles themselves can be strengthened either by cross braces, or by struts supporting them in the plane of the Railway, both giving additional stiffness and preventing any movement. These struts would be found particularly useful on heavy slopes.

The rail is divided into such lengths as can be easily handled, and connected by fish-plates, one half of each pair of fish-plates being secured to one end of each rail by two bolts or two rivets. Two more bolts or rivets connect the other extremity of the pair of fish-plates passing through holes made on purpose. The other end of the rail is provided with two slots on the under side, which fit, or hook on to, the open end of the pair of fish-plates.

In order to make the joint, the end of the rail is slightly raised so that the two slots come over the two bolts between the fish-plates, and, after letting it drop into its place, tightening the bolts, and the joint is secure. Two of the holes in the fish-plates are oval, to allow for expansion. As the rail is flat and laterally flexible, curves are made by hand, in the following way. The line is slightly raised, one man keeping it steady at the place where the curve is to begin, whilst another shifts the free end of the rail in the required direction; the line is then again dropped on to the ground and the curve is made. The direction of the line can be changed, if required, in the same way and with equal facility.

The shunting, to pass from one line to another, is carried out without any special apparatus, as the line, constructed in the manner already described, contains in itself all that is required for the operation. A free joint at the point of junction allows of the slotted end of the rail being raised from between the fish-plates of the one line and dropped in between those of the other, exactly as if the line was in course of construction, and the shunting is completed. Now, when the lightness of the rail is taken into consideration, it will be evident that it would be easier to carry out this operation than to describe it; and by this means the successive connection of one rail with six or eight others radiating from the first has been satisfactorily carried out.

It is manifest that as this line is above all things easily handled and taken to pieces, there is no difficulty whatever in crossing roads or highways on which there is traffic that cannot be obstructed; all that is necessary is to have a loose joint between two rails at one side of the road, and by raising one end of the rail in the manner already described it can be curved aside, leaving the roadway free.

If a river has to be crossed, some light piers can be made, if the amount of traffic warrants it, or two wire cables can be stretched across to receive the trestles of the line, or it may even be sufficient to construct the trestles of different heights so as to carry the line over horizontally. If, on the other hand, a ravine has to be crossed, the line can either be carried over it as it would over a river; or it can be taken down the side of the gorge by means of zig-zag lengths which can be connected by curves of as small a radius as ten feet.

On permanent lines, particularly if it is intended to convey passengers, it has been found necessary to arrange matters in a somewhat less rudimentary fashion. Guides to prevent the swinging of the cars and points, sidings, signals, &c., have been introduced, but everything has been done with the same regard to simplicity.

The same remark applies to the rolling stock, which is as free from complications as the line itself.

Two grooved wheels run on the rail; each carries a fixed axle, the extremities or spindles of which revolve in special grease boxes fitted in a frame, to which is secured on each side of the line, and, by a peculiar arrangement, a kind of car, of the shape and dimensions best suited to the work for which it is intended.

Owing to the position of these cars their equilibrium increases in proportion to the increase of the load, and several of them connected in any suitable manner form the train.

It is, perhaps, well to dwell here on the absolute safety, which is an important feature, of this system. The cars cannot be overturned or upset, and, on the single rail, running off the line, if possible, would not by any means be so serious an occurrence as on an ordinary Railway.

Any system of haulage can be adopted; animal power, steam power, electricity, compressed air, &c., being equally available, and having now all been experimented with on the single rail.

Finally, the arrangement of the trestles of the Lartigue Railway renders the attachment of insulators for telegraphic or telephonic wires very easy.

These, generally, are the essential and principal characteristics of Mons. Lartigue's invention, described superficially and without entering into any of the special details of construction; characteristics which have enabled that engineer to set aside all former data and to bestow on trade a new implement, capable of being applied in countless ways, as we shall be able presently to show.

The introduction of Railways has without doubt been the commencement of that continuous advance, which will in future ages be the characteristic feature of the present century.

It is through the introduction of Railways that every branch of manufacture has received a decided stimulus; the possibility of transporting goods to great distances in a short time has opened up important fields to all producers; a steady and strong competition has naturally led to constant improvement in every department.

Thus we see that every important centre is interesected in every direction by Railways. But Railways, although they most certainly and indisputably are the greatest factors of advancement, involve very serious expenses – of construction, of maintenance, and of working, which can only be borne by very rich, very populous, or very productive districts.

The efforts of engineers have for a long period been directed to the discovery of the best means of supplying small places with some practical means of locomotion, and, in order to do away with the objections above mentioned, decided advances have already been made in the introduction of narrow gauge Railways with steam or animal haulage. The cost of construction has been reduced in proportion to the smaller size of the line and of the plant, and many disadvantages have been greatly reduced; but the principle has remained the same, and though much reduced in their proportions, the works to be carried out on these Railways still are very similar to those on large Railways.

Preliminary surveys of the ground to ascertain the straight and curved parts of the line, the differences of level, the physical obstacles, the works necessary to overcome these obstacles, are some of the problems to be solved merely in the construction of the line. As to the plant it is exactly what it is in an ordinary Railway, only that it is somewhat smaller. There are the special points, the curves, which once laid out must remain unchanged, the crossings, the level crossings, the rolling stock with the same number of wheels, the same tractive power, the same system of construction, &c.

At an earlier date and in altogether special cases cables have been used instead of rails. These lines consist merely of a cable, usually made of wire, and on it run the cages used only for carrying goods.

This mode of transport, which has been used particularly for crossing deep ravines, involves a heavy first cost for construction, and can never be used for a line of any length, as the motive power is stationary and must be at least at one end and frequently at both ends. We are, moreover, personally acquainted with certain lines of this description in which, though owing to the nature of the ground and the character of the traffic, the work is carried on under the most favourable conditions to be expected within rational limits, the weight and the mean cost reach enormous figures.

Cables of a diameter of 1¾ in. to 2 in. and weighing about 20 to 30 lb. per yard, are frequently required over the whole length of a line on which the traffic does not exceed 100 to 150 tons per day of 12 hours. If to these expenses are added, the laying of the line and maintenance, the necessity one is under of running for considerable distances in a straight line and the consequent impossibility of following the inequalities of the ground, the outlay incurred on account of the necessary machinery which, being fixed at the ends of the line, is often of a very large size, even where the work to be done is comparatively insignificant, one can form some idea of the great cost of this means of transport. Nor is it possible to suppose that this system can ever be used for the conveyance of passengers, for the cables, however near together the supports may be placed, are always extremely elastic, a serious disadvantage under the circumstances, and one which can only be overcome by increasing the loading of the cars. This increase in the load requires in its turn a stronger section of cable, and consequently an augmentation of the weight and of the cost. Moreover, the cable, however well stretched it may be, falls by its own weight into curves, which produce a rise and a fall between each point of suspension, and entirely destroy the evenness of travelling.

We do not wish to find fault with these different kinds of Railway, which, indeed, having succeeded well in many special cases, have secured for themselves an important place; but we cannot pass over their defects in silence, for it is to the deliberate consideration of these defects that we owe the elevated single rail line of Mr. Lartigue, which, while applicable to the same class of work as the narrow gauge and cable lines, has not their disadvantages, and can always be employed with great advantage as regards cost, lightness, and strength, no matter how trying the circumstances may be. Indeed, the Lartigue line now erected in London, in which all the features which could be encountered in actual work have been introduced, will enlighten everyone as to the incontestible advantages of the single rail line.

The idea of building an experimental full-sized Railway in London to be worked by locomotives was only conceived in April last.

The plans and details of the proposed line were discussed and settled between Mr. Lartigue, Mr. A. Mallet, the eminent locomotive engineer and one of the writers of this pamphlet, as late as the end of April last, when the detailed studies for the construction of the first locomotive, the first passenger carriage as well as of the rails, switches, turntables, &c., to be adopted for this the very first line on the Lartigue system to be worked by locomotives were only begun. The ground in Westminster was secured on the 12th May last, and the whole construction of the line, including the delivery and erection on the ground at Westminster of all the rails, supports, turntables, points, signals, locomotives, carriages, &c., was completed on the 12th July, 1886. Considering that this line is the first actually constructed on a full working scale for passenger and goods traffic to be worked by locomotives on the Lartigue system, and that the whole conception, designing and construction of it have been carried out in barely two months time, it is probable that improvements in the details of construction will suggest themselves by practical experience, especially in the construction of the carriages and locomotives; in fact, since the construction of this line was begun such improvements have been already made, and will be applied in the construction of the carriages and locomotives which are going to be built at once for several lines in the United Kingdom and elsewhere. However, for the short time employed in completing this very novel work in Westminster, it is believed that it will bear witness to the careful and thorough study of the subject by all concerned in it.

The line at Westminster consists of the two types of single rail line, the portable line for military, agricultural or industrial purposes, and the permanent line for passengers. The latter is composed of two lines. The whole of the arrangements are indicated in Fig. 1 and Fig. 2. The line, KEHJ, is practically on the level. It will serve principally for experiments as to speed and to determine the consumption of water and fuel.

The second, KBMV, is an irregular line, with curves of as small a radius as 49 feet, and with gradients as steep as 1 in 10. There is a level piece, from Q to B^1, on which the turn-table is fixed, which, besides answering its usual purpose, allows of the level crossing of the siding to the carriage shed, g. It should be noticed that, at this point, there are curves of 32 feet radius. From B^1 to B the line rises on a gradient of $\frac{1}{66}$, on which there is between S and B a curve of 54 feet radius. The manner in which embankments may be avoided has been illustrated by increasing the height of the trestles in some parts of this line from 3 feet 3 inches to 5 feet. The rack rail, which will only be used to mount steep inclines, has, in the present instance, been laid from the point S, so as to have a certain length on the ordinary line, for the purpose of showing how the junction between the two is carried out, and how the former is treated when it has to be laid on curves.

A wooden viaduct, about 340 feet long, commences at S and ends at R; from B to t the line is straight with a gradient of 1 in 10. At t r one line crosses

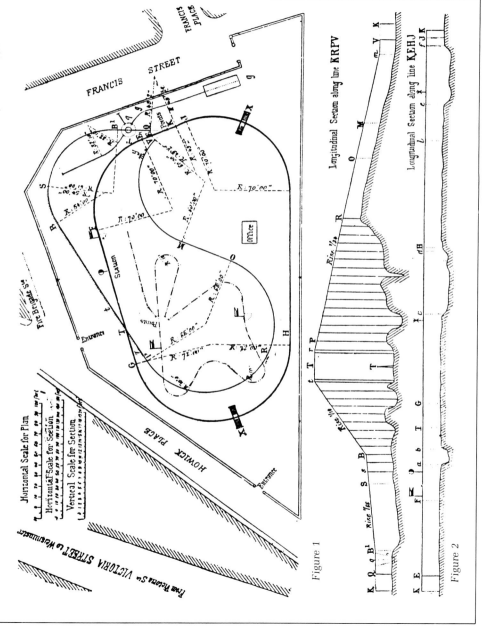

Figure 1 and Figure 2 shows the plan and sections of railway built at Tothill Fields, Victoria Street, Westminster.

Figure 1

Figure 2

over the other on the skew (obliquely), and in consequence of this obliqueness there is a bridge of a span of 33 feet; from r to m the line descends with an even inclination of 1 in 34; from r to R the viaduct continues on a curve of 65 feet radius, and from R the ordinary line goes on with its trestles 3 feet 3 inches high; from m to V the line is horizontal, and a junction is effected with the line KEHJ by means of the three-throw switch VK.

Starting from E on this line there is a level crossing at F near the Station, at T the crossing of the two lines, at X overhead crossings for foot passengers over the line, and then the line gets back to the switch.

These two lines, which are more or less of the same length, are in all about 1,540 feet long. As has been seen, every possible feature has been introduced into this experimental line, in which difficulties have been purposely exaggerated. Inclines upwards and downwards, sharp curves, junctions, switches, level crossings, everything is to be found, and the means of overcoming any obstacle may be studied on this capricious line.

The viaduct takes the place of one of those pieces of heavy work which can often not be avoided in laying out a railway, but which, on a single rail line, are reduced to what may be called their simplest form. Here the uprights of the viaduct itself serve at the same time as trestles, and the iron supports are dispensed with.

The introduction of trestles of different heights suggests a means of avoiding or, at least of reducing embankments, and of crossing any ordinary inequalities in the ground, such as ditches, ravines, brooks, &c., which are got over in the simplest manner.

The shunting depends, as we have already pointed out, on the lateral flexibility of the rail; the side guides are jointed, and there is a certain amount of play between them, so that they alter their relative positions when, by the working of the switch, the curve to the one side is changed to the curve on the other side.

The switch is formed by a piece of line 23 feet long with trestles of the usual height. The sleepers of each trestle are fitted with two runners, which move on a metal track, placed on a wooden framework. A bolt, fitted to each of the sleepers, drops automatically into a slot prepared to receive it at the spot corresponding to the three postions of the switch, and locks it during the time the train is passing. These bolts are connected together so that they can be wedged in their place when they are down, and raised by a lever placed at the end of the switch lever.

The free end of the moveable rail is fitted with locking fish-plates, whilst the extremities of the rails of the fixed lines have a tongue which fits between the fish-plates. By this arrangement the switch is perfectly secured and the train passes over the points with as much safety as over any other part of the line; indeed, it is evident that the points form true junctions with the other lines.

The switch is worked by pulling or pushing the lever after having, by means of the proper handle, withdrawn the bolts from the slots, the lever for the points being connected with the signals beyond the points, which show which of the three lines is open.

The switch, as constructed for the line at Westminster, has been made a great deal too heavy, but the time was so short that it was impossible to introduce the alterations which suggested themselves during its construction. Switches to perform the same work will hereafter be constructed on the same principle, but of a weight not exceeding at the utmost half the weight of the present switch as shown at Westminster, in such a manner that it can easily be moved by one man without any counterweight or special arrangement.

The opening of the level crossing is formed simply of one length of the line of the same dimension as the space required, which turns on a hinge fitted at one side of the road. The other extremity is fitted with runners which work on a metal track laid on a wooden framework, and the moveable rail has, at its extremity, the same fish-plate catch as the points. It is only the last trestle which is fitted with runners, the sleepers of the others being shod with wood, which slide on the framework above mentioned. When the moveable rail is open it rests only on the runners of the extreme trestle, but when it is closed these drop into hollows arranged to receive them and the rail takes its bearing on all the trestles.

The opening and shutting of this gate sets in movement a signal on either side of the level crossing which shows by its position if the line is open or closed.

The turntable is composed of a length of 13 feet of line fitted on two longitudinal beams, which are in their turn carried by an ordinary turntable. The ends of this length of line, being fitted with the above-mentioned fish-plate catch in the same manner as the points and the level crossing.

The traction on this Railway is effected by a special steam engine invented by Mons. Mallet, the well-known French Engineer, who, in this design, has given one more proof of his singular skill for this class of work.

This engine, Fig. 3, is composed of two vertical tubular boilers, AA, placed one on each side of the line and connected at one end by a large pipe, a, which both acts as a steam dome and carries the two boilers on the frame work of the machine; and at the other by a pipe of smaller diameter, which allows the water to pass from one boiler to the other.

This pipe is placed at a height at which there is always water, so that it is never empty. By this arrangement it is sufficient to feed only one boiler, which supplies the other, the pipe at the same time preventing the water in the inner boiler from rushing into the outer one, owing to centrifugal force, when the engine passes rapidly round a curve. The safety valves, whistles, &c., are fitted on the large pipe, a.

The engine is carried by two grooved wheels, FF, on a framework to which the boilers are attached by the bars, b, and the diagonal stays, d, as well as by the steam pipe, a, as already stated. The cylinders, DD, which occupy a horizontal position at the front of the engine drive the cranked axles of the wheels which are coupled, in the usual manner.

The firing is done by the engine driver, by means of hoppers fixed at the rear of the boilers, who, sitting astride of his seat, N, and protected by the roof, M, can easily throw into the hoppers, the coke which he takes out of the bucket under his seat.

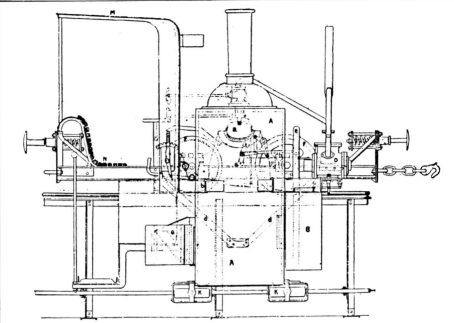

Figure 3. The vertical boiler locomotive, locally known as "The Coffee Pot", manufactured by S.A. Metalluegigue of Tubize, Belgium in 1885. It was used at the Westminster trials and during the construction of the Lartigue and capable of hauling 70 tons on the level at 5−6 mph. (See also drawings on pages 47−48)

The feed water is contained in tanks placed in front of the boiler, which are connected by a syphon which reaches to the bottom of each boiler and prevents any difference of level in the water in either tank.

Although the machine is balanced by its construction, since it is symetrically even with the plane of the line, in order to avoid its being thrown out of equilibrium by any accident or by centrifugal force when going round curves, horizontal or inclined pulleys, KK, running on longitudinal guides attached to the trestles which carry the line, as was stated above, hold the engine in a vertical position and prevent it from leaning over to either side.

Thus arranged, and in working order, this engine weighs about 2½ tons; that is, 1¼ ton on each axle. The wheels are 15 or 16 inches in diameter, and the cylinders 4½ to 5 inches, with a 7-inch stroke. The boilers, have, together, a heating surface of about 70 superficial feet. With a steam pressure of 100 lbs. to the square inch the engine will haul about 70 tons on the level, 18 tons on an incline of 1 in 100, 9 tons on an incline of 1 in 50, and 6 tons on an incline of 1 in 33, at a speed of 5 or 6 miles an hour, which, with a smaller load, can be inreased to 10 or 15 miles an hour. This engine can easily go round curves of 30 feet radius. These are the principal features of the locomotive engine which is now working on the experimental line in Victoria Street, Westminster. It is a small type only and intended for very light work; but we shall return later on to the subject of the engines to be used on the single rail line.

The carriages and waggons are of an entirely new design and are suited to do the work, if necessary, on a long length of line. All the necessary features for economy, strength, steadiness and comfort which the traveller has a right to demand from a real working Railway with a developed traffic have been introduced.

Special designs have been made for carriages to be used in hot climates, where great care has been bestowed on the arrangements for ventilation and also for converting the carriages at night into sleeping compartments, but the necessary time has been wanting for constructing one of these carriages for the line at Westminster.

The locomotive is fitted with a very powerful handbrake, which is quite sufficient to stop the train whilst the carriages are attached to the loco-motive, but to prevent accident in case of a breakage of the connections between any of the carriages Messrs. Westinghouse have fitted the train with their continuous automatic brake. The air pump and reservoir for the brake have been placed on the little additional machine to give it extra weight and steadiness.

The apparatus used is rather too large for the size of these carriages, and Messrs. Westinghouse propose to design special brakes of the same type as those they supply to large railways, but reduced to the proper dimensions for the class of engines and carriages used in this new system.

We shall confine our description of these carriages to the features of the external shell, as the rest is merely ornamental and would vary according to the class for which the carriage was intended.

The carriage then is composed at each end of a very strong horseshoe shaped wrought iron bar, placed above the rail, and which as it is prolonged downwards runs parallel with the trestles of the line till it reaches within about 1 foot 3 inches of the ground, when it turns outward and becomes horizontal. This last portion carries the flooring of the carriage, the part which is parallel with the trestles forms the back of the seats, and the horseshoe shaped upper part above the rails leaves the necessary space for the wheels and brakes and for their proper examination, &c. To this part is attached a horizontal wrought iron bar, which stretches out from the line on each side as far as the outside of the flooring of the carriage. By uniting this flooring with the horizontal bar by means of flat iron stays crossed, a stiff body of uniform shape and quite symetrical as regards the line is obtained, which forms an excellent framework, to which panels either of ornamental wood or painted and varnished sheet iron can be fitted according to circum-stances.

These carriages are also fitted with horizontal wheels, which run on the same guide rails as those of the locomotive, and which give a steadiness to the carriage which no accidental occurence can disturb.

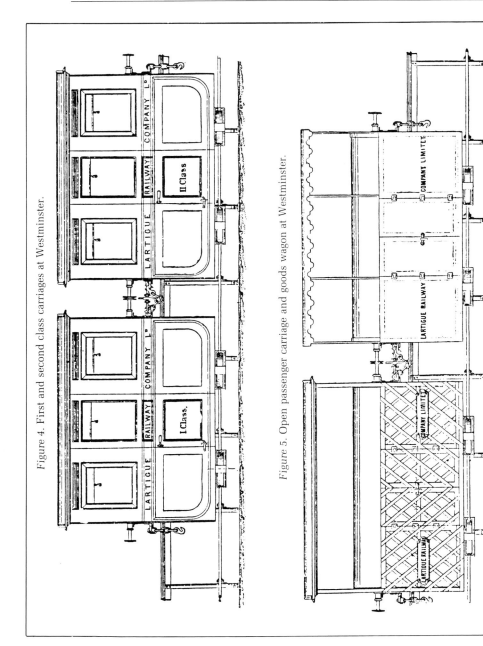

Figure 4. First and second class carriages at Westminster.

Figure 5. Open passenger carriage and goods wagon at Westminster.

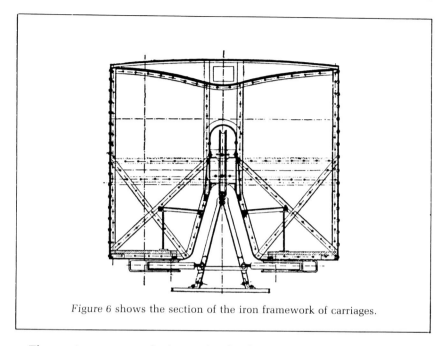

Figure 6 shows the section of the iron framework of carriages.

The carriages are attached to each other by the usual coupling hooks, and are fitted like ordinary Railway carriages with a special buffer.

We must also call attention to the carriage which, arranged in the first instance to carry goods, can, when required, be altered by a special arrangement to carry passengers. It is fitted with a shifting seat, which is fastened up when goods are to be carried, and let down if the carriage is required for passenger service. By this ingenious arrangement any special pressure on either department of the rolling stock can be met without increasing the number of carriages. This carriage is protected by a moveable awning.

The section of rail originally used has been slightly modified. In the first instance it was a plain iron bar, but now, the upper part is rounded and assumes a shape somewhat similar to that of an ordinary rail.

Although this improvement may appear to be unimportant, it has a special bearing on the line with which we are now dealing, for this arrangement, which renders the rail stiffer, produces a much smoother movement of the carriage which runs over it, a most important matter in the case of a traffic the bulk of which will be passenger traffic.

This is a general description of the single rail line now working in London, which contains the latest improvements introduced into this class of Railway. It may here be mentioned that all the parts used in the construction of the line at Westminster have been made a great deal stronger than necessary, partly from an excess of prudence, it being the first line constructed for passenger traffic with locomotives, but also because it is contemplated to use this line hereafter for larger carriages and more powerful engines, and also for conducting a series of tests and experiments of a very complete and varied nature.

Finally, that the experiments with the single rail line might be as complete as possible, a small line of the type of the agricultural or industrial lines, constructed of the simplest materials and stripped of all the improvements which one is obliged to introduce in a permanent line intended for the conveyance of passengers in the most comfortable manner possible, has been placed in the space left by one of the curves of the more stable line. The plan on which this line is marked by a dotted line (see Fig. 2) shows its sinuosities, there being curves on it of only 10 ft radius.

With these detals it will be easy to judge of the special facilities for construction, for shifting, shunting, maintenance and working, &c., possessed by the single line Railway.

It may also be interesting to state that the whole of the ironwork for the permanent line as constructed at Westminster weighs 70 tons per mile, the principal rail weighing 23 lb. per yard, and the side guide rails 11 lb. per yard, each complete trestle weighing 12½ lb. These weights can be reduced to about one-half for carriages and locomotives of the size used at Westminster. The locomotive weighs about 2 tons, the additional machine for working the rack about 11 cwt, the first and second class carriages 18 cwt each, the two open carriages – the one to be used either for goods or passengers and the other for passengers only – less than 1½ tons each. The little agricultural line, which is part of the line constructed in Tunis, weighs about 18 tons per mile complete.

The ironwork for the construction of the Railway, such as the rails, trestles, level crossings, turntables, switches, etc., have been manufactured at the works of Mons. Achille Legrand at Mons. The rails were specially rolled for this line, and the whole of the work has been done in the most complete and satisfactory manner. The locomotive and the small additional machine to work the track were constructed at the works of La Métallurgique, at Tubize in Belgium, and the carriages by the Société des Forges et Atcliers at Saint Denis, near Paris, and both have accomplished their tasks in the most complete, rapid and satisfactory manner.

The first Railway on this system was constructed in Algeria to develop the Esparto business. This precious plant, which abounds in that country, grows in thick and close tufts over vast tracts of ground. The soil which suits it best is precisely that which requires an exceedingly portable line, for it is necessary that the means of carriage should itself be moveable, as the tracts on which the crop is harvested have to be shifted every two or three months.

The carrying of the Esparto from the boundless plains on which it grows to the main lines of communication is one of the most important features of the trade, and it was natural that practical men should devote special attention to the search after the most economical means of doing this carrying work.

It was while seeking the solution of this financial problem that the Engineer, Mons. Lartigue, conceived the idea of his Railway, and it was suggested to him in a very curious manner. It was the appearance of a

Figure 7. The origin of the Lartigue system – first used in 1881 in Algeria where over 60 miles were laid to transport harvested esparto grass using mule power only.

caravan of camels on the horizon which furnished a starting point. The sight of these animals following one another in a long string and laden with thellis, a kind of wallet which hangs down on each side of them, and which he had sketched, brought to his mind's eye an elevated rail. To his mental view the legs of the camels became trestles, their humps were transformed into wheels, and the thellis took shape as a car.

The idea once conceived was rapidly matured. The first line was made of rude materials, but improvements rapidly succeeded one another, and before long there were more than 60 miles of the Lartigue single line Railway working in the Esparto trade in Algeria.

This example has just been followed, with the authorisation of the Government of the Bey of Tunis by the Anglo-French Company, to which the concession for working the Esparto fields of Tunis has been granted and which is authorised to lay about 60 miles of single line Railway. The agricultural line exhibited in Westminster is a part of the line manufactured for the Esparto Company in Tunis. For farming purposes this same type of line is adopted, but of still lighter dimensions.

The single rail line is eminently suited to those districts. As it is erected at a good height above the ground, it is never blocked or prevented from working by the heaps of sand set in motion by the Cyclone, or by the Sirocco, and its flexible rail allows of its following the curves of the natural path as it winds about amongst the tufts of Esparto, and by its means a single mule, with only one driver, can transport very considerable quantities in one day.

With regard to the results obtained with the single rail line, they can be appreciated by comparing them with those of a narrow gauge line of an improved type, the results being as follows:

If one mule, harnessed so as to walk on one side of the line of the narrow gauge Railway, of which the rails are in a clean state, can, walking at the speed of 2½ miles per hour, do 100 tons of net work in a day, he will, all the conditions being the same, do more than twice the amount of work on the single rail line. But the comparison practically gives results much more favourable to the Lartigue system, as its rail is always in a clean state, being raised several feet above the ground, whereas narrow gauge railways of the ordinary type often get their rails clogged with dirt, sand or snow.

As for the expenses of construction and working of the single rail line, in all cases where it has been possible to compare it with a narrow gauge line, and where the circumstances and the work to be done were the same, the former shows the following savings as compared with the latter:

On the purchase of the plant a saving of 30 to 35 per cent.;
On the construction (including earthwork, masonry, etc.), 60 to 70 per cent.;
On the haulage expenses, 50 per cent., at least.

The single rail system has, moreover, been applied in a singular and important manner in France at the Mines of Ria, in the Pyrénées Orientales, where iron ore had to be carried a distance of about 6¾ miles.

After having examined into the different means of transport, and particularly into the overhead tramway which, at the first glance seems so econ-

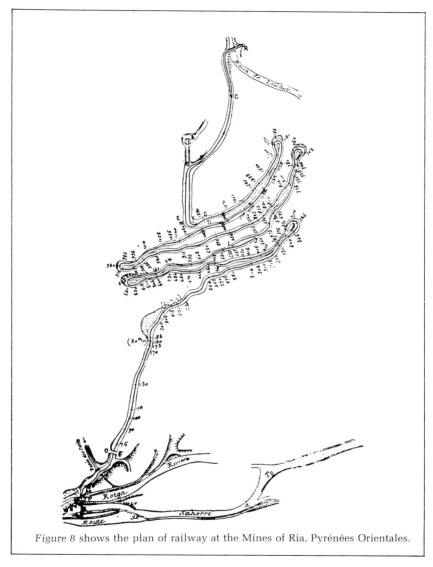

Figure 8 shows the plan of railway at the Mines of Ria, Pyrénées Orientales.

omical, but which is nevertheless unsatisfactory in its carrying out, because of the heavy expenses of maintenance, of labour, and, above all, of construction, particularly in a country abounding in tortuous ravines, it was resolved to give the single rail line a trial.

Figure 9 is an original engraving of riding the line at Ria in the Pyrénées.

In order to guard against any unforeseen obstacle to the final construction of the 6¾ miles of line, a trial was made in the first place on a length of over four-fifths of a mile, and the ground selected for the experiment was the most broken and difficult piece in the whole distance. On a slope of 45° broken by large rocks and perpendicular ravines the single rail line was made in the first instance on a slope of 30° with a cable haulage (under which circumstances the plant gave perfect satisfaction), and subsequently in zig-zags, following all the inequalities of the ground; and, as will be seen by an examination of Fig. 8, the unevenness of the ground is so great that on this piece of line there are inclines of 1 in 12 and curves of 10 feet radius.

The motive power selected for this work was electricity, which did not render any modification of the Lartigue system necessary, except that conductors were secured to the trestles at the sides, being insulated from them by common wooden brackets. In the experiments which were carried out

Figure 10 is an engraving of the electric powered exhibition line, believed to be at Rouen in France in 1884.

with the greatest care the train was made up of four ore cars weighing empty 298 lb. each, and holding about 990 lb. of ore, and of an electrical loco-motive weighing in working order 1,280 lb.

It took from 15 to 20 minutes to do the distance. The effort measured by a dynamometer was found to be 5.5 per cent. of the weight of the train drawn on a mean incline of 1 in 18. On curves of 10 feet radius the effort increased to 9 per cent. of the weight of the train and in gradients of 1 in 12 to 8.5 per cent. Such are the results obtained from the use of the single rail line over a country where all the difficulties and the most unfavourable circumstances were purposely selected.

Indeed, this experiment at the Mines of Ria gives absolute confirmation of the value of the single rail system, since it has come up to all the require-ments of work which any other known system of transport would have failed to perform. Here the bed plates or sleepers are entirely dispensed with.

The Manager of this undertaking adds in his Report that it was not necessary to entrust the management of the electric trains to any special staff, as it could be placed in the hands of the common workmen at the Mines, who, satisfied that it was impossible to go off the line ventured boldly along the edge of the tremendous precipices which there are along the line.

It is impossible to enumerate here all the cases in which the single rail line has been adopted in various countries as they are very numerous, though the patents are only of very recent date.

It has figured at all the Exhibitions, and the novelty of the idea has always attracted the attention not only of specialists but of all comers, and it has in every case received the highest awards.

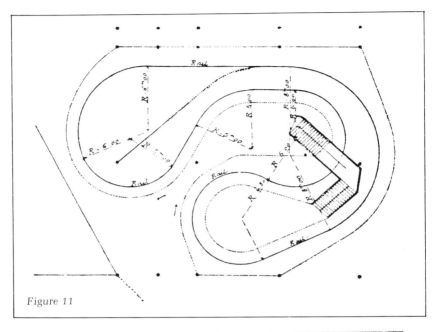

Figure 11

Figure 11 and Figure 12. Horizontal plan of railway at the Work Exhibition, Paris, from July to November, 1885, with an engraving showing the railway in action.

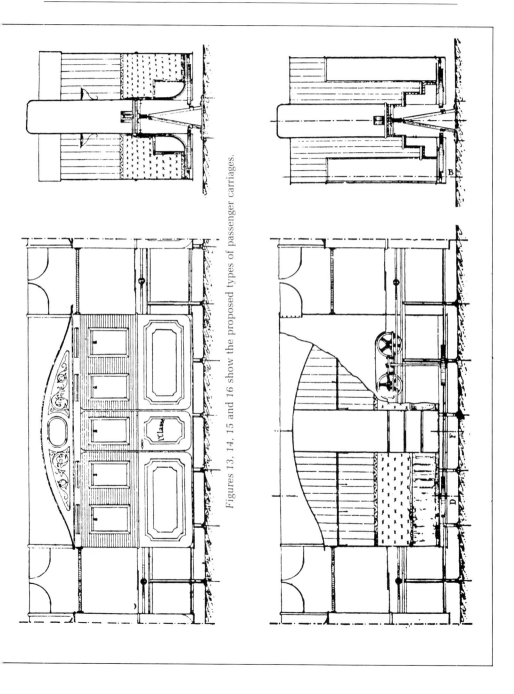

Figures 13, 14, 15 and 16 show the proposed types of passenger carriages.

In 1884 it was exhibited at the General Agricultural Exhibition in Paris, and at the Rouen Exhibition, in France, and a little line laid down in the garden enabled visitors to practically prove the simplicity of the arrangement by a journey which lasted some minutes.

It was again exhibited at the Exposition du Travail (Paris, 1885) where there was a considerable length of line in a small space. Here, again, the inventor took no trouble to avoid curves of very small radius.

In both these arrangements the motive power consisted of a Siemens' dynamo machine placed on one side of the leading car, and balanced by the Electrician who sat on the opposite side. The diameter of the driving wheels, which can be altered according to the speed to be obtained, had been arranged in this case to give a velocity of about 6 miles per hour.

At these Exhibitions various types of carriage were shown which we do not propose to describe here, as an examination of the engravings will be sufficient to understand the arrangement.

We may, however, mention a tub intended for the carriage of minerals, and so arranged as to tip out its contents, thus effecting a rapid discharge. This design of tub can be used equally well specially for earthworks.

The Lartigue Railway figured again at the Antwerp Exhibition of 1885, where it was represented by a model ¹⁄₁₀ th full size of the line which has been surveyed for the French Government, and which is intended to connect Sénégal and the Niger, and to serve the line of forts between Bafoulabé and Banmakou.

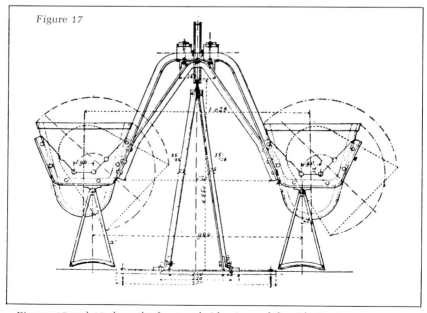

Figure 17

Figures 17 and 18 show the front and side views of the side-tipping ore wagons.

Figure 18

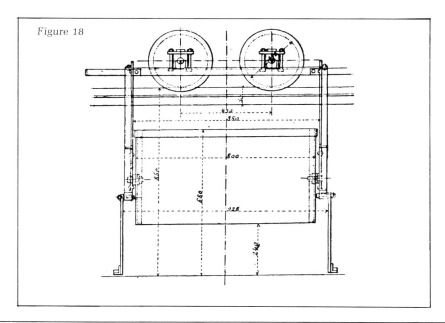

Figure 19. Behr's impression of the advantages of the Lartigue system being tight curves, light and inexpensive construction which would have been suitable for rural lines.

Figure 20 shows an engraving of a railway carriage with three soldiers seated whilst figure 21 shows a conversion for transportation of Russian wounded soldiers.

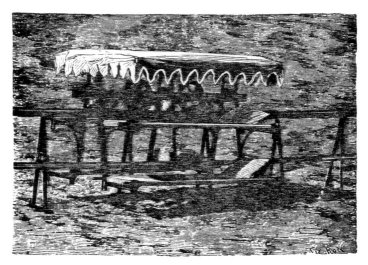

The employment of the line for this purpose is most interesting, and has been described in the Official Catalogue of the French Ministry of the Navy and of the Colonies, the model forming part of the Colonial Exhibit of the Ministry.

Amongst the experiments tried with the single rail line we must also mention some very conclusive trials made in Russia in the presence of a Committee of Engineers and Engineer Staff Officers specially appointed for the purpose.

In this case the rail was raised 3 feet 3 inches above the ground, and the line was furnished with the side guides, which we have mentioned several times already. Notwithstanding this complication, it was laid with such ease that three men could erect 6 feet 6 inches of the line in six minutes, so that it would take thirty men only eight hours to erect 1 English mile of the Railway.

An ordinary horse easily drew about 5 tons over the Lartigue line, considerable irregularities of level notwithstanding.

The end of the Report on these experiments says: "To give an idea of the important results to be obtained when it is possible to use gradients of 1 in 17, in a length of about 660 feet, a difference of level of 40 feet was obtained, and in a distance of 3,300 feet a difference of level of 200 feet was attained. It is easy to understand the advantages to be gained by the use of this system in our Asiatic possessions and on the Steppes, where it is at present necessary to use large numbers of beasts of burden for military transport. In that particular case the Lartigue Railway presents advantages which can only be described as incalculable."

Numerous experiments were also made at the Camp of the Imperial Guard at Oust-Sjord, near St. Petersburg, with the most satisfactory results. A special kind of rolling stock for transporting soldiers and wounded men was used. Cars arranged with seats carrying three men on each side of the line and protected overhead by a tent were connected, and formed a very long train drawn by a single horse.

Other cars intended to carry the wounded are arranged to make two stretchers one above the other on each side of the line, and allow of a rapid withdrawal from a field of battle, whilst providing the wounded soldiers with a secure, easy and exceedingly comfortable means of carriage.

The importance which the Russian Government attaches to these experiments can easily be understood, for this means of transport is naturally better suited than any other for crossing the great desert stretches of country far from inhabited centres and often very uneven, which abound in that huge country.

Moreover during the severe winters so common in Russia the raised rail is far less obstructed by snow than a line on the level of the ground would be, and could only be blocked by snow drifts in exceptional cases.

All these advantages have contributed to the great success achieved by the single rail line in Russia where there are already several working, the number having lately been increased by three short lines.

In considering the different lines erected which we have described in few words, it is evident that it has been possible with the single rail line to make all the alterations required by the special nature of the traffic in each case, or by the nature of the country to be traversed, without in the least degree altering the fundamental characteristics of the invention. This is a clear proof of the success which may be safely predicted for it, since it can be used anywhere, at any time, and so to speak in accordance with anyone's fancy.

In short, it is the only system of Railway in practical use which can be absolutely adapted in each case in its conjunction to the nature of the traffic to be dealt with, and thereby all waste in first outlay, as well as in maintenance and working expenses, is absolutely avoided, and it becomes possible to construct this line in many places with profit, where, otherwise, no Railway could have been built without entailing heavy loss.

We have stated above that the locomotive working on the experimental line in London was a small model only intended for light work. Mons. Mallet, whom we have already mentioned, has designed engines of a more powerful type, capable of doing as much as four or five times the work done by this little engine.

And we may henceforward say without fear of being charged with exaggeration that the Lartigue Railway can undertake transport on any scale, whether as to weight or as to distance, always supposing that owing to circumstances connected with the nature of the country or of the goods to be carried this Railway would answer the purpose better than the ordinary form of Railway.

Thus to obtain more power, the number of wheels can be increased, and the engine shown at Fig. 22 and Fig. 23 will be used. This engine has three coupled wheels, and as, in order to have them, the locomotive has to be longer, advantage is taken of this circumstance to use boilers of the ordinary locomotive type, one on each side of the line.

These boilers would each have a steam dome connected, as in the previously mentioned type, by a large tube, whilst a second tube will make a connection between the water in the two boilers.

The tanks will be fitted at B, under the cylindrical body of each boiler. The remaining details will be similar to those already described.

These engines will weigh about 4 tons, and their strength will be proportionately greater than that of the locomotive already described. They will be able to run over curves of 40 feet radius, but the groove of the middle wheel will be much wider, or will, if necessary, be done away with entirely.

These engines will draw over 100 tons on the level, 50 tons on an incline of 1 in 100, 25 tons on an incline of 1 in 50 and 18 tons on an incline of 1 in 33.

Another engine has been designed with four coupled wheels, and with horizontal boilers, like the last, but longer. An engine of this class would weigh about 5 tons, and could run over curves of the same radius as the last, owing to the following arrangement of the leading and trailing wheels.

The axles of these wheels have at their centres a spherical projection, with two studs which fit into slots in the wheels which is in two parts bolted together. This arrangement forms a ball and socket joint, and allows the

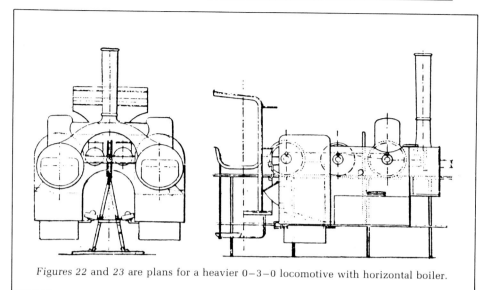

Figures 22 and 23 are plans for a heavier 0−3−0 locomotive with horizontal boiler.

wheel to play sideways on the axle while it turns, thus accommodating itself to the curve of the line, without interfering with the coupling of the axles, which remain parallel. To prevent the wheels getting out of the perpendicular they are fitted with circular check pieces, held in place by guides carried by bearings. The middle wheels will, as in the previous case, be made with very wide grooves or, perhaps, without grooves. Moreover, the ordinary sized grooves can be used and the wheels can be made to turn on a pin behind, or by allowing the central ball a little side play on a key.

Any of these arrangements of radial wheels can be fitted to the leading and trailing wheels of a locomotive with three wheels coupled, which has to work over small radius curves.

Even more powerful locomotives have been designed, but, then, the question of proper utilization becomes one of capital importance, not so much with regard to the economy of fuel as with regard to the reduction of the dimensions of the boilers.

As the single rail line will generally be used over very uneven ground, it has been considered essential in the invention of the engines to make arrangements by which the power of the locomotives can be considerably altered without interfering with economical working. For this purpose the engines will be fitted with two cylinders of different diameters, the proportion between the pistons being generally as 1 to 2.25 or 2.30. These cylinders can be worked as an ordinary engine or as a *compound* engine. To this end they will be connected by the apparatus shown in Fig. 26, the principal feature of which is a valve, m, connected with a smaller valve, n, which is connected with a piston, p. When the large valve, m, rests on its

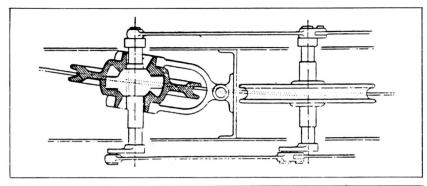

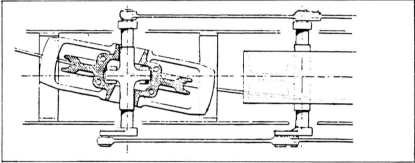

Figures 24 and 25 showing details of compensation for curved track.

Figure 26 is a section of the Compound Engine.

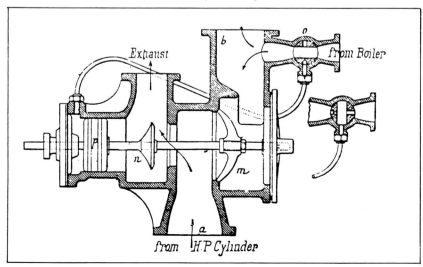

seat, as shown in the figure, the steam issuing from the small cylinder of the engine at a passes through the small valve, n, and escapes directly into the air. At the same time, by means of the cock, o, steam is supplied through the channel, b, direct from the boiler to the large cylinder – either at the same pressure as that supplied to the small cylinder or at any lesser pressure desired, and obtained by means of a self-acting reducer. In this case full power would be obtained, and a great amount of force developed for a short time; as, for example, when going up a steep incline.

If the cock, o, is closed, a small orifice is at the same time opened, which allows the steam to get behind and move the piston, p, and as the closing of the cock, o, has removed the pressure from the valve, m, it opens, the valve, n, closes, and the exhaust steam from the small cylinder at a enters the large cylinder at b. The engine is then working as a compound engine. If the cock, o, is now opened, the steam from the boiler passes through b and tends to close the valve, whilst the back of the piston, p, is no longer in communication with the steam, but with the atmosphere; the valve m therefore closes and the valve n opens and allows the exhaust steam from the small cylinder to escape. It will be seen, therefore, that the turning of the cock, o, alters the mode of working of the engine.

Now this cock, which we have shown working by hand in order to make the explanation simpler, can be connected with the speed regulator, so that the slowing of the machine, as it commenced the ascent of an incline, would start the machine working at the higher power, and the increase of speed, when the heavy strain was overcome, would automatically bring the compound working into play again. When extra power was required, the engine

Figure 27 is a plan showing the engine comprising of two bogies.

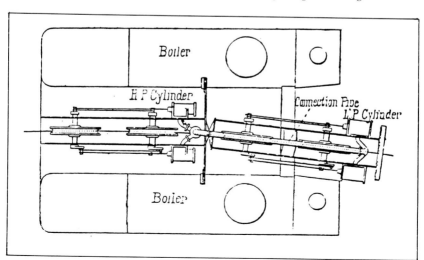

would always work at high pressure, and once the normal speed was reached the regulator would act and the engine would go on working on the compound principle.

Fig. 27 shows a front and hind bogie with two, three, and even four wheels coupled, the latter carries the boiler and the water tanks, the other is jointed to the first, which rests on it by means of sliding plates.

The wheels of the after bogie are driven by two cylinders, which are supplied with steam direct from the boilers, whilst the wheels of the front bogie are driven by cylinders of a large diameter, which receive steam from the other cylinders when the engine is working compound, but which receive it direct from the boiler when the engine is to work in usual form.

The connection between the two sets of cylinders is made by means of a valve box, similar to that which has already been described. The pipe which goes from the valve box to the large cylinders is jointed to give play in going round curves.

By this ingenious arrangement, an engine with six or eight coupled wheels could be constructed, which should run round curves of 50 feet radius and draw loads proportioned to its power.

Finally, if it is necessary to mount inclines too steep for the adherence of the engines, and in order to leave them their full power available, an auxiliary apparatus is used, such as is shown on the experimental line in London.

This apparatus consists of a small vehicle carried on two grooved wheels, which run on the rail; it is made as short as possible (about 3 feet 10 inches), and at the front of it there is a steam cylinder driving a spur wheel, which works on a rack rail placed beside the rail the whole length of the incline on which it is to be used.

A supple tube connects the cylinder with the engine, so that when the necessity arises all that has to be done is to turn the steam on in the cylinder and thus to set the apparatus to work.

This apparatus can be used in two different ways, according to circumstances. If there is only one incline on the whole of a line, the rest of which is nearly level, the extra horse is left at the foot of the incline on a siding, and it is brought by hand to the front of the train which has to be hoisted up; it is coupled up to the train, the steam pipe connection is made between the boiler and the engine and the cylinder of the apparatus, and the latter helps the engine up.

At the top of the incline the auxiliary machine is uncoupled and pushed on to a siding, from which it is taken to the foot of the incline by the next train going down.

If, on the other hand, there are several inclines at different points of the Railway system, it is better to connect the apparatus permanently with the train; it is then placed behind the engine and leaves off work as soon as there is no more rack rail to work on, and if the spur wheel continues to revolve, it revolves in space where there is no fear of coming in contact with any obstacle. If the apparatus is attached to the train in this fashion, it is well to make use of the car part of it, loading it with fuel, water, or goods, by so doing the equilibrium is increased and the apparatus is more stable.

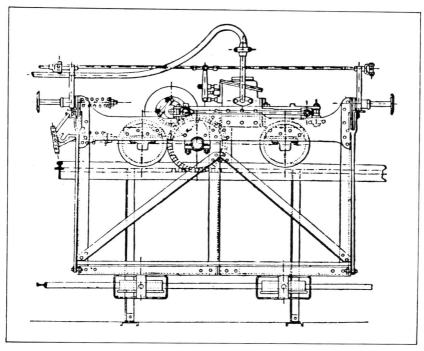

Figure 28 shows a proposed steam powered booster to work behind the locomotive on Rack Rails, for use on extreme gradients.

It is easy to ascertain the power of this machine which weighs barely 11 cwt, has an tractive power of 1,000 to 1,100 lbs., which would enable it to take a load of 4 to 4½ tons up a gradient of 1 in 10, where a locomotive of the smaller type such as the one used in Westminster could only take itself up.

This little auxiliary machine is also arranged in such a manner as to act – when going down steep inclines on which the rack rail is used – by means of its cylinder as a compressed air brake.

A general remark, which applies to all these locomotives bears on the advantage they get from the single rail principle. One of the greatest obstacles to the good working of locomotives in Railways is found in the different speeds of the wheels over curves, owing to the difference of radius of the inner and outer rail. This difficulty is finally got rid of in the Lartigue Railway which only has one rail. The same remark applies to all the rolling stock.

This short description of the different types of engines designed for use on the single rail shows that in spite of its simplicity and of the light materials of which it is made the single elevated Railway is in a postion to come up to very great requirements, we would almost say to any requirements. Out of all the different applications of the system which we have had the opportunity of seeing or of studying we have not found one in which this new kind of Railway was unable to do all that was required of it. This can be explained by the primary simplicity of the system. It is always easy to complicate things, but rarely possible to simplify them. Now this line being constructed on the plan with which we are already acquainted, we believe, in spite of the firm trust which we have in science and its advances that it is impossible to construct any line capable of the same amount of work on a more simple system.

The most competent technical men no longer have any doubt as to the future of the single rail line; it can be used everywhere.

What would be simpler than to connect the suburbs with the great centres from which they radiate by means of this Railway?

The great dockyards, which are always somewhat difficult of access from the towns whence their workmen come, would, no doubt, find in the single rail line the cheapest means of supply both of men and materials.

How many important manufactories there are which would be connected with the great Railway lines were they not stopped by the enormous outlay necessary for this work? The single rail line will enable them to attain the object in the most economical way.

Agriculture, of all works, will certainly be that to which the Lartigue line will render the greatest services, for agriculture frequently requires long stretches of line which have to be frequently shifted with few hands and with the most primitive plant.

For military purposes this line is invaluable and ought to form a part of the permanent equipment of every army, as it can be packed in a very small space and divided into light and easily handled packages. The line can be erected in any emergency in a very short time by the most unskilled workmen without any previous teaching, and will facilitate the carrying of provisions, baggage, &c., as well as the transportation of the troops and the removal of the wounded from battlefields.

Farmers in France and elsewhere are now beginning to understand the great advantage of having in stock a certain length of the Lartigue Railway for the purposes of harvesting and carrying dung. The first cost is comparatively trifling, and will in every case be less than the saving effected by being able to dispense with a number of horses and carts, and the buildings necessary for their accommodation. The Railway, when not used for the above purpose, can be converted into and used as a fence by attaching to it wires provided for that purpose, and the total cost will not exceed that of a good iron fence 4 feet high.

The putting up and taking down of the line can be effected in a few hours by a couple of men as well as shifting it from field to field. This would practically render the farmer independent of the weather as far as gathering his harvest, besides saving the expense of wages and fodder for a number of men and beasts. If the farmers are too poor and their holdings too small to enable them to own pieces of this line themselves the landlord could easily let it out to each farmer in turn, as the harvesting and dunging work would be often done fifteen to twenty times quicker than by carts and horses, or a few small farmers might club together for one set of line amongst themselves.

In the comparative experiments in agricultural working which we have been able to study, the following are the results arrived at per ton of materials transported:

By horse and cart	...	...	...	...	...	2s. 0d. to 2s. 6d.
By narrow gauge tramway	...	...	...	...	1s. 2d. to 1s. 4d.
By single rail line	...	...	...	...	...	5d.

These figures are taken from actual practice on a considerable scale.

It is clear that the single rail line will be highly appreciated in wine growing countries for collecting the grapes, seeing that the rail can be raised so as to run the tubs above the vines. This is a very great advantage, especially when the grapes have to be collected in bad weather, and owing to the wetness of the ground it is impossible to do it on men's backs.

The use of the single rail line on flooded meadows will allow of the removal of the grass as fast as it is mown, and without bringing on to the ground the carts which cut it up so badly.

In all cases where the grass cannot be dried and could, therefore, most advantageously be put into silos, the merits of the system of carriage are evident, as one of the great difficulties and drawbacks up till now in the general use of ensilage is the great weight of the wet grass, entailing a large expense in carrying; this will be entirely avoided by adopting the Lartigue system of carriage.

Oyster culture, which is carried on at the sea-side and in shallow water, will have a valued and cheap auxiliary in the single rail line.

Turning now to another aspect of the matter, it might be asked is there a question more frequently discussed now-a-days than the construction of Metropolitan lines in large towns?

We, ourselves, who, for a Metropolitan line, would seek an economical line with small plant, since very frequent trains with small loads would never keep the passenger waiting, do not see anything better to attain this object than the single rail line.

Indeed, we are satisfied that the metropolitan lines, whether constructed or projected, would derive valuable assistance from the Lartigue system, which here would play the same part as tributaries do in a river by bringing or taking passengers to or from out of the way or sparsely populated districts.

Its installation, under these circumstances, would be exceedingly simple. Light columns at short intervals connected by a girder which would be the rail, would form the line. No space taken up where space is already confined; no views broken by great and heavy constructions – for the single rail is nothing more than a plain and narrow line; no chance of accidents.

The same system as that proposed for the Metropolitan line in Paris, as shewn in Figs. 29, 30 and 31, is also proposed to be adopted for the carrying of visitors to and from the different parts of the International Exhibition to be held in Paris in 1889.

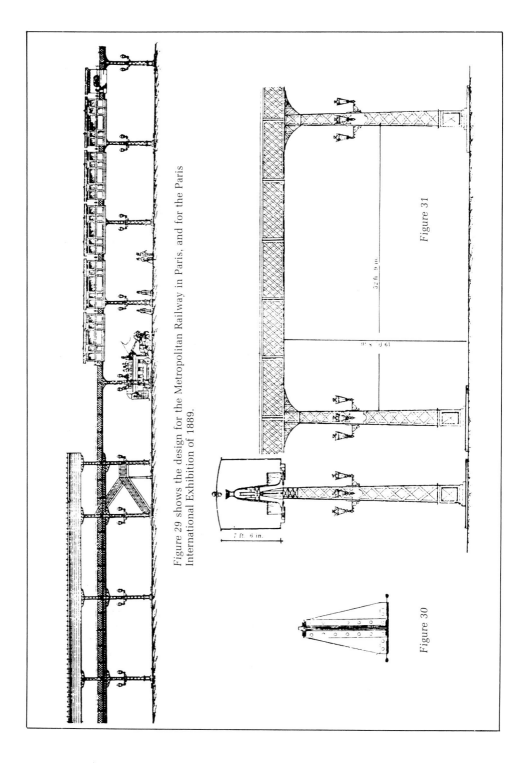

Figure 29 shows the design for the Metropolitan Railway in Paris, and for the Paris International Exhibition of 1889.

Figure 31

Figure 30

SKETCHES OF SEVERAL TYPES OF ROLLING STOCK FOR THE LARTIGUE RAILWAY.

PASSENGER CARRIAGES.

OPEN PATTERN,

Weight about 500 kilos., contains 3 persons on each side, namely, 6 for each carriage.

THE SAME,

Longer, containing 5 persons on each side, namely 10 persons ; will weigh about 1 ton.

CLOSED PATTERN,

With central covering uniting the carriages.

1st Class contains 8 people.

2nd   ,,   ,,   12   ,,

Weight about 2 tons.

PLATFORM PATTERN.

Entrance by platform, with sliding doors ; will contain 12 to 20 persons.

GOODS WAGGONS,

Covered, or Luggage Van, weight about 1 ton 13 cwt. :—Cubes 11 feet 6 inches × 5 feet 3 inches × 5 feet 9 inches = 345 cubic feet. can carry about 2½ tons of merchandise.

UNCOVERED GOODS WAGGON.

Weight about 1 ton 5 cwt. :—Cubic contents about 250 cubic feet, can carry about 2 tons of merchandise.

Sketches of several types of rolling stock for the Lartigue Railway.

For farming purposes the Lartigue Railway is supplied of a type weighing between 14 and 15 tons per mile at a cost of £220 quite ready for use, the pieces being already bolted together have simply to be carried on to the ground where they are to be used. This price includes the delivery at the principal ports and railway stations in the United Kingdom.

Trucks are also supplied with this type specially adapted to farming work. The kind of truck generally used for nearly every class of farming work is one originally designed for the transport of hay. This truck is very light and weighs empty about 170 lbs. It is fitted with a kind of basket which goes from one side of the rail to the other, covering the wheels in the centre. This truck and basket, when loaded to a height of about 6 feet from the ground, will carry about a third of a ton of hay, or it can be used for other cereals, such as wheat, barley, straw, &c., and a train of 25 of these trucks can easily be drawn by one good farm horse. This gives an average load exceeding 8 tons per horse over heavy ground such as ploughed fields. The cost of the trucks will be about £5 each. They can also be used for the carrying of wet grass for silos, dung and other materials.

Finally, the Lartigue line will be generally used in the new Colonies, towards which all great nations are tending in order to enlarge the sphere of their influence. The line will follow explorers almost step by step, and will be not the least auxiliary of a new civilization.

F.B. BEHR,   GEORGE PETIT, Civil Engineer,
Managing Director of the Lartigue   *of the Journal "Le Genie Civil," Paris.*
Railway Company Limited,
        Ass. Mem. Inst. C. E., London.
17th July, 1886.

End of The Compleat Lartigue article

Apart from the short demonstration line at Tothill Fields described in the preceding booklet, the Listowel and Ballybunnion was the only public railway of its type to be constructed in the British Isles. Before dealing with it, however, it is desirable to refer to some earlier proposals for steam tramways, and light railways, of orthodox type, in that area.

On 14th September, 1883, Father M. O'Connor, Parish Priest of Bally-bunnion, with an influential deputation of local residents, appeared before the Listowel Board of Guardians, seeking their co-operation in providing a tramway between the two places, and the following Resolution was unanimously passed: "That this meeting, having listened with much interest to Fr. O'Connor's observations, fully endorses every statement made, and pledges all co-operation in their power towards the construction of the tramway". The latter was promoted by the Munster Steam Tramways Company, Ltd., on the 3-foot gauge, with a branch from Galey Bridge (2¾ miles west of Listowel) via Ballylongford to Tarbert Pier. Opposition was soon forthcoming; on 12th October, at a meeting of ratepayers of Irraghticonnor Barony, attended by some of the tramway promoters, it was contended that the projected line would not pay and the Interest would have to be provided by the barony. The total outlay, including rolling stock, was alleged to require £130,000 which, at 5% Interest, would call for £6,500 per annum, representing a Baronial Rate of 3/9d. in the £, whilst the Ballybunnion section alone would cost £5,200 per mile, or a rate of 1/8½d. in the £. The closing Resolution stated "that the Committee formed to promote the Bally-longford, Ballybunnion and Tarbert Tramway was constituted without the ratepayers' knowledge, and therefore should not bind them and, following full consideration, they entirely oppose the scheme". Notwithstanding this opposition, the Munster Steam Tramways Company sought powers of construction through an Order-in-Council, their application appearing in the *Dublin Gazette* on 26th November, 1883. But now a competitor appeared, the Limerick and Kerry Light Railways (not to be confused with the Limerick and Kerry Ry. Company, which was worked by the Waterford and Limerick Railway) who, by notice in the same publication on 21st December, made application for a standard-gauge (5' 3") line between Listowel and Ballybunnion and, on 11th March, 1884, sought a £40,000 Guarantee from the Grand Jury; the latter, however, rejected this request a week later.

We now come to 17th July, when the Munster Tramways' project, and that of the L. and K. Light Rys., came before the Grand Jury Summer Assizes for consideration. This second scheme, terminating near the Ballybunnion Hotel (8 miles, 7 furlongs, 3 chains) was to cost £43,000, or £4,807 per mile, for which a Baronial Guarantee would produce £1,752 per annum, the Barony Valuation in 1883 having been £35,351 12s. 6d., and the promoters offered to contribute part of the Guarantee; rolling stock would comprise twenty-five wagons, and three coaches, but no mention was made about motive power. The Listowel Township Commissioners, however, did not favour this project, whilst the majority of those present were averse to that of the Munster Tramways, in view of its sizable potential impost on the ratepayers. Following an eight-hour sitting, a ballot resulted in the Munster Tramways' scheme being passed by a majority of nine votes. This company proposed three tramway sections. (1) Listowel to Ballybunnion; (2) a branch from near Ahafona, 2¼ miles east of Ballybunnion to the foreshore of the latter, this being a siding for sand traffic; (3) a branch to Tarbert. The promoters, however, withdrew their application for No. 2, and the amended scheme was accepted. (It is worth mentioning that one of the promoters informed the tribunal that the cost of transhipment of goods etc., from narrow to broad-gauge wagons at the exchange point would be nothing compared with the difference in constructional costs between his company's line and that of the Limerick and Kerry Light Railway. Moreover, a letter from the Lord Lieutenant was cited, which indicated that the 1883 Tramways Act only envisaged narrow-gauge lines, those of standard gauge being considered too expensive.)

Again, the ratepayers of Irraghticonnor Barony rose in protest, with a poster campaign, and petition for signing at the Railway Hotel, Listowel, and at Roman Catholic churches after Mass on Sundays; it was alleged the tramway would involve a Baronial Rate of 1/4d. Apparently these efforts were fruitful, the Privy Council met on 31st October and the Munster Tramways' scheme was rejected.

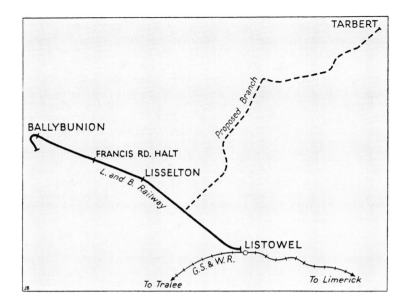

The scene now moves to London where, on 9th May, 1885, a Select Committee of the House of Commons met to investigate the Listowel and Ballybunnion Tramway Bill; this seems to have related to the project of the Limerick and Kerry Light Railways. However, it was announced the Bill had been withdrawn, due to opposition by the Waterford and Limerick Railway Company (The L. and K. Light Rys., had sought running powers over the Limerick and Kerry Railway.) But notwithstanding these setbacks, the district was destined to have railed transport, news of the above efforts having apparently come to the notice of Charles Lartigue, who approached the promoters.

On 24th November, 1885, the *Dublin Gazette* gave notice of an intended Bill in the Parliament Session of 1886 for a railway on the Lartigue system between Listowel and Ballybunnion; powers were also sought to acquire the sandhills and foreshore at Ballybunnion, then owned by George Hewson, the principal local landlord. Two "tramways" were proposed; (1) Listowel to Ballybunnion; and (2) from the latter to the adjacent foreshore, this corresponding in purpose with the No. 2 line of the Munster Tramways' scheme. No Baronial Guarantee was sought which, in the light of the company's later financial history, was unfortunate.

On 15th January, 1886, the *Kerry Sentinel*, commenting on the new venture, described it as the "Lartigue elevated single-line railway"; the latter was rather a misnomer for, as will appear later, three rails were necessary. Having remarked that it would provide rapid transport without smoke, noise, or smell, the journal added that trains could operate at frequent intervals, and negotiate curves of short radius, whilst traction by men, horses or steam, was feasible on such lines.

2nd April saw the Bill pass the Second Reading in the House of Commons, the Royal Assent being accorded on the 16th. A week later, the *Sentinel* remarked that very little land would be needed for the new railway, and that the start of construction was unlikely to be delayed beyond the mid-Autumn; the promoters hoped to have the line ready for the Summer traffic of 1887, and a contractor was then being sought.

Most of the local farmers, except two, reached agreement with the promoters regarding the acquisition of land for the railway, and hope was expressed that the others would abandon their pointless opposition to the scheme. Prior to this, on 16th April, 1886, the Listowel and Ballybunnion Railway Company had been incorporated, with a capital of £33,000 (as sanctioned by the special Parliamentary Bill). The Chairman was the Right Hon. the Earl of Devon (Chairman, Limerick and Kerry Ry). A prospectus, was published on 6th June, 1887. The Lartigue Construction Company under-took to complete the railway for the Capital authorised by Parliament; it was asserted that many farmers wished to send their children to Listowel College, and the morning and evening trains would facilitate this. Moreover, a considerable traffic in sea sand at certain periods of the year was anticipated, this commodity being much in demand by farmers for land improvement, also by builders. An agreement had been made with George Hewson, Ballybunnion, whereby as much sand as was required could be taken from the foreshore at a royalty of one penny per ton; it was therefore anticipated that the L and B Railway would be in a position to pay a favourable dividend.

Concurrently with the opening, a Building Society would be established, to provide small houses and villas at Ballybunnion, thus, in course of time, fostering a sizable residential traffic. (It may be remarked that, in those days, Ballybunnion comprised one street, with an hotel, a number of licensed houses, a Post Office and probably, a Police Station.)

Construction proceeded rapidly during the late Autumn of 1887, the engine from the Tothill Fields experimental railway being brought to Ireland to assist in the work. As the running track was normally at an elevation of 3′ 3″, both rolling stock and motive power had to be of duplex form, half of each vehicle being on either side of the running rail, pannier-fashion. The locomotive mentioned "had twin vertical boilers, the steam and water spaces being inter-connected with piping" (*Engineering*, 24th December, 1886). From the same source we learn there were "two 15 inch grooved (i.e., double-flanged) wheels, driven by two cylinders of 4½″ diameter, boiler pressure 100 lbs. per square inch, weight in working order, 2½ tons, equally divided, and speed five to six miles per hour when hauling seventy tons on the level. The engine was single-manned, the driver sitting astride the track". This machine was built at Tubize, Belgium, by S-A Tubize; the maker's plate, inscribed "L.R.C. Ltd., Mallet's Patent Locomotive No. 1" is still extant. Known on the L and B Railway as the "coffee-pots", this engine was not in regular use on passenger trains and, after languishing in Listowel engine shed until around 1900, was sold to Tim O'Connor, of Tarbert Island.

It has also been stated that some of the Tothill Fields track was brought to Ireland for re-use.

Meanwhile, on 18th November, the Listowel and Ballybunnion Company applied for a Bill to make a branch via Ballylongford to Tarbert Island, and to construct a pier and causeway at Ballybunnion, and was seeking a Baronial Guarantee for these purposes; it appears the Tarbert project was to be utilised for sand haulage, whilst the Guarantee (for part of the finance required) would be sought from County Kerry, and the Listowel Town Commissioners (Baronies of Irraghticonnor and Clanmaurice [part].) Moreover, the branch was to be so built that it could be replaced later by a light railway, if desired.

Early in the same year (1887), an order had been placed with the Hunslet Engine Company, Leeds, for three 0−3−0 tender engines, whilst the Falcon Engine and Car Company, of Loughborough, supplied thirteen passenger train vehicles. Messrs. Achille Legrand, of Mons, Belgium, were awarded a contract for twenty-one goods vehicles, which included cattle wagons, and special iron hopper tipping wagons for carrying sand. The railway and its rolling stock, including the cost of land, was built for £33,000, or just under £3,000 per mile and, with the experience so gained, it was anticipated that similar lines could be constructed for a lesser amount.

Fritz B. Behr, Managing Director of the Lartigue Construction Company, held a similar position on the Listowel and Ballybunnion Railway; Arthur Gore, an Englishman, was Resident Mechanical Engineer, and E. Cooke, General Manager; the latter had been an Inspector on the Limerick and Kerry Railway.

Early in 1888, the line was completed, after five months work, and invitations were sent to many eminent men in the engineering, and other professions, both in Britain and the Continent, to attend the official opening, which was fixed for Wednesday, 29th February. In due course, the Board of Trade inspection was made by Major-General Hutchinson, who advised the fitting of Westinghouse brakes to the stock; these modifications were expected to delay opening the railway to public service. The first complete train ran on Tuesday, 28th February, but, before this, 15,000 tons of ballast had been carried over the line during the previous six weeks.

The day of the formal opening dawned cold and dry, a special train from Killarney at 9.30 am bringing a large number of those interested in the new railway concept to Listowel, which was reached at 11 am; others travelled from Limerick, and it is said the languages of several Continental countries could be heard on the station platfrom. Shortly after 12 noon, the official L and B Rly. train, comprising eight coaches and over 100 passengers, started for Ballybunnion, which was reached in thirty-five minutes; this included a number of halts en route, where Behr pointed out the arrangements at accommodation, and other crossings. Comment was voiced regarding the considerable noise when the train was in motion, as compared with conditions on an ordinary railway, but Behr ascribed this to the newness of the vehicles; however, we shall hear more of this unpleasant feature later.

Following the arrival at Ballybunnion, and some brief sight seeing, a luncheon was held in the station waiting room. During a speech, Behr referred to Irish freight charges on materials carried to Co. Kerry as being double (£1,000) those charged to the Argentine, where his company was building a similar line. (The latter proved a failure, owing to local conditions.) In general, the visitors were markedly impressed with the new railway, in view of its low cost, and rapidity of construction. It was mentioned that, in a few days time, an application would be made to the Co. Kerry Grand Jury for a Baronial Guarantee for the proposed Tarbert branch (13 miles, 45 chains), its cost being put at £65,000, including £32,000 in loans; however, at the Grand Jury Meeting, these figures were amended to £47,000, with £25,000 Baronial Guarantee.

Beaumont gave the toast "Success to the Lartigue Construction Company", and the party returned to Listowel, running time being thirty-eight minutes, despite an engine axle overheating. Following the return of the main line special train to Killarney, a banquet was given that night in the Railway Hotel by the Lartigue Company, and during its progress, Lartigue, speaking in French, expressed pleasure at the practical demonstration of his invention. It had been indicated earlier that the site chosen was not ideal for showing the full potentialities of the new system, as the line had to be built within the deviation limits of the originally-intended steam tramway, thus requiring many accommodation, and "level" crossings.

The railway opened for public traffic on 5th March, 1888, the first train being driven by Joseph Holyoake, whose forbears came from Cornwall; this family was destined to be associated with the railway throughout its history.

It is now time to describe the track, also the motive power and rolling stock, and other installations.

A perspective drawing of "The Coffee Pot".   *Courtesy, Merioneth Railway Society*

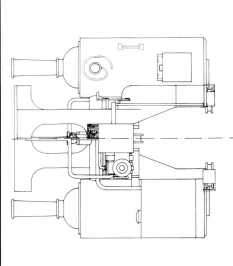

"THE COFFEE POT"

The inset shows the manufacturer's plate of "The Coffee Pot".

Lartigue Vertical 'Boilers' Locomotive

Drawing by Mr Adrian S. Garner

L. R. C. Lᴰ

MALLET'S PATENT LOCOMOTIVE

Nº 1

An official gathering at Listowel station. *Author's Collection*

A fine view of the point system at Ballybunion railway station yard.
Courtesy National Library of Ireland

Locomotive No. 3 being turned at Ballybunion station. *Author's Collection*

One of the eight Accommodation crossings on the line. These were used to gain access to the larger farms and at road crossings (*see drawing on page 57*).
LCGB, Courtesy Ken Nunn Collection

Chapter Two
The Permanent Way

The running rail, 27 lbs. per yard (33 ft lengths) was secured to the apex of a number of "A"-shaped angle-iron trestles, sited about three feet apart, also where the rails were fishplated, when they were close to the rail ends. These supports were anchored by angle brackets to steel, or timber, sleepers, the latter being used over soft ground, and at certain other places; the wooden sleepers were 6 ft long, 9 ins. wide and 3 ins. thick, those of steel being 3' 3" long and 1¾" thick. As previously mentioned, the trestles were 3' 3" high, other than where ground contours required a greater altitude. Where sideways movement might occur, holes were drilled in the sleepers, and wooden pegs driven through, thus anchoring them. The cross-bar of the "A" formation was 2' 4" below the top rail and served to brace the legs. Secured to the outer face of each trestle, at this level, were lighter horizontal rails (11 lb. per yard, 20 ft lengths), the running surfaces of which faced outwards, their object being to stabilize the rolling stock; they carried no weight, the inner sides of the engines and vehicles having nearly horizontal double-flanged wheels one foot diameter, which bore against these rails, the carrying wheels (usually four in the case of ordinary stock), running on the upper rail. The structure was designed to ensure vertical rigidity with longitudinal flexibility, so facilitating negotiation of curves. As, however, the guide rails largely restricted the tilting of rolling stock at such places, a considerable stress was imparted to the permanent way.

It will be appreciated that, with this form of track, orthodox points giving access to sidings and passing places, were out of the question. Instead, sections of rotatable curved track, similar to a turntable, were provided at each end of the stations.

Behr published a number of patents regarding the switches; in one, the running rail was bent laterally, but it is not clear what was intended to happen to the side rails in this case. He then produced a design in which two curved rails back-to-back moved through about sixty degrees radially to effect different connections. The type used on the L and B Rly. was a development of this, using only one eccentric curve, rotating through the full 360 degrees; by carefully locating the ends of the fixed trestles; remarkable things could be done. For instance, the table at the departure end of Ballybunnion (see plates) could take up the following positions: main line to platform line, main line to loop, loop to goods siding, shunting neck to platform line, goods siding to shunting neck. Thus a rake of wagons could be run out of the goods shed into the shunting neck, and then the shunting neck into the platform, and away down the main line. The layout at Listowel was somewhat more sophisticated, having two curved tables at the departure end, giving a straight run down the main from either platform, loop, or goods siding; there was also a straight run from platform to carriage siding. None of this could of course be done with a straight table. These tables had rollers running on a circular track in a pit close to the fulcrum. The ends of the curved line also carried rollers, which ran up onto ramps when they met the fixed trestles. Since these tables would never be rotated with a vehicle on them, they did not need support at the ends except where they joined the

A view of Listowel station. Note the mobile "stile" at the right, which was used to allow passengers to quickly cross over to balance the coach seating. *Real Photographs*

Ballybunion station with a loading platform seen in the right foreground.
Real Photographs

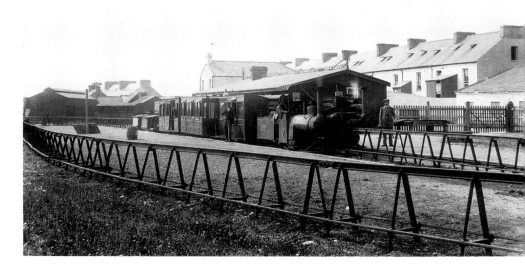

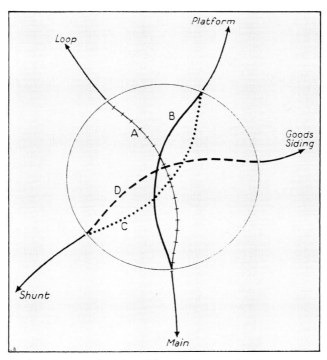

A diagrammatic drawing of the switch turntable showing the clever method of changing track. The shunting cycle using the curved turntable was as follows: *Table position A*, engine from loop to main; *B*, engine main to platform; *C*, engine platform to shunt; *D*, engine shunt to goods; *D*, engine and wagons, goods to shunt; *C*, engine and wagons, shunt to platform.

fixed track. There were however some shorter straight tables used only for turning locomotives or stock, and these had rollers at the ends running on a full circle of rail.

As regards accommodation crossings, a section of the track was hinged, being normally locked in running position, the adjacent land-owners being supplied with keys. When opened, this portion of line, as well as the field gates, was at right angles to the fixed track. The act of opening caused a small semaphore signal on a gate to rise to the vertical ("danger") position. The key could not be removed until the moveable section of track had been relocked in running postion, thus preventing carelessness in use. "Level" crossings, necessarily raised, were provided by means of a timber framework spanning the line, of sufficient height to clear the trains. Between its corner posts, a light two-piece bridge, of bascule type, was provided, and operated by

One of seventeen "Flying Gates" crossings along the line (*see details on opposite page*).   *Real Photographs*

The GSWR Listowel Station (*South end*), showing the main line platforms and goods shed (*left*), and the departure line to Ballybunion on the right (in front of the carriage shed).   *C.L. Fry*

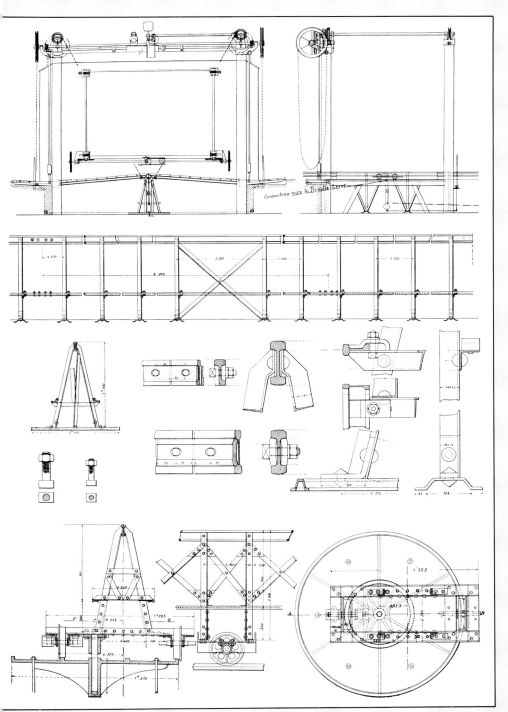

Details of the track construction (including the "Flying Gate").

Courtesy, The Engineer

Another form of transport crossing the railway on the road level "drawbridge" crossing.
Courtesy, Railway Magazine

A train departure from Ballybunion.
Courtesy the National Library of Ireland

THE LISTOWEL AND BALLYBUNION RAILWAY.

Drawing of a typical "Accommodation crossing".

Courtesy, The Engineer

chains passing over pulleys on top of the structure. When lowered, the two bridge sections rested on the running rail: simultaneously, a small signal, mounted on the gantry, rose to "danger", being operated by gear wheels and a spindle connected with the pulleys. The approach roads were of course ramped to the level of the bridge. It is not revealed, however, what method was adopted to ensure that the bascules reverted to vertical after the passage of road traffic.

A cross section of track showing the main 100 mm tall (4 inches) rail with side rails and sleeper. Almost unbelievably light construction, yet sufficient. (See *drawings on page 55*)
                                                                                          Author

Chapter Three

Locomotives, Coaches, Wagons and Stations

Locomotives numbered 1 to 3 respectively (Works Numbers, 431, 432, 433) were, as previously stated, built by the Hunslet Engine Company, Leeds. Nos. 1 and 2 left the works on 10th October, 1887, No. 3 following a week later. The livery was dark green and the makers laid down a special track at their Jack Lane Works on which to test them, prior to despatch. The company's initials, with engine number, appeared on circular brass plates fixed to the sides of the tenders,* whilst an oblong plate inscribed "Lartigue Single-rail system; Mallets' Patent" was fixed to the side sheet of the cabs. Mallet was associated with the Tubize Works, in Belgium. The three engine running wheels were coupled, the drive being to the middle axle. All wheels, including those of the rolling stock (also tender) were double-flanged, the tread width being 1½" (2" on the centre engine wheels, to allow for curves), whilst the horizontal guide wheels were 1' diameter, and 3½" tread width. There were twin horizontal boilers, one each side of the top rail, the funnels, steam domes (with Salter-pattern safety valves originally) fire-boxes, and controls, being in duplicate, whilst the main brake reservoirs were beneath the boilers; the latter were cross-braced with channel steel, fixed to lugs on the smokeboxes, and a steam pipe connected both domes. The cab and tender were also divided, the latter running on two coupled wheels, and having a pair of small cylinders; these were to augment the engine power on gradients, and could be brought into operation by a wheel on the tender, which operated friction clutches. It was found, however, in practice, that the boilers were unable to supply sufficient steam for all four cylinders, those on the tender becoming disused, and it is believed, later removed, heavy trains being thenceforth double-headed. The driver occupied the near-side of the cab, having both to fire and drive, his fireman performing the usual duties on the off-side. A large headlight was mounted between the funnels, with its beam focused on the top rail.

General dimensions were as follows:

ENGINES: Cylinders, 7" x 12" diameter. Coupled wheels, 2' diameter. Wheelbase, 8' 10". Boiler pressure, 150 lb. p.s.i.; heating surface, 140 sq.ft; grate area, 5 sq.ft (both combined dimensions). Tractive effort (at 85% boiler pressure) 3112 lb. Coal consumption, 15 to 18 lb. per mile. Overall length of engine, 11' 9⅝". Weight in working order, 6½ tons.

TENDERS: Cylinders, 5" x 7" diameter. Coupled wheels, 2' diameter. Tanks, 200 gals. (i.e., 100 x 100) Coal, 8 cwt. Tractive effort, 926 lb. Tender wheelbase, 4' 3". Weight in working order, 3 tons. Combined length of engine and tender over buffers, 23' 7¾" (Space between engine front sheet and tender, 8').

Coaches: Two 2-wheeled bogies, and four horizontal wheels. Running wheels tread, 1½". Guide wheels 3½" wide, to allow for vertical movement of springs. 16' 10" long by 8' 6" wide (3' 5" x 1' 8" x 3' 5") 1st, and 3rd class, and composites. The two halves of each coach were joined with wrought-iron ribs which, forming a horseshoe above the top rail, passed down the

---

* Later on the cab sheets; patent plates were moved to the tender.

LOCOMOTIVE ENGINE, LARTIGUE SYSTEM, LISTOWEL AND BALLYBUNION RAILWAY.

MESSRS. THE HUNSLET ENGINE COMPANY, LEEDS, ENGINEERS.

inner sides, bending outwards to conform with the shape of the trestles, and ending horizontally as supports for the coach floors. The end bulkheads were cross-braced with angle-iron stiffeners. The coach roofs canted in-wards, but guards' vans had curved full-width roofs, with a "birdcage" lookout akin to South Eastern and Chatham Railway practice. The seating, cushioned for 1st class, wood slats for 3rds, accommodated twenty-four passengers (twenty in firsts) and backed against the running rail, thus giving passengers a good view of the landscape. Window blinds were not fitted, but the late H. Fayle mentions that "on sunny days a primitive arrangement of calico sheets was suspended from the window frames". Resulting from the amount of iron and steel in the permanent way, and the running wheels being approximately level with passengers' heads, the noise in transit was markedly noticeable. As loading had to be equalised, the vans had stairways fixed outside an end bulkhead; a variant was a staircase on wheels, mar-shalled between coaches, and known as a "crossover". The livery was brown, lined out in yellow and black, the coach serial numbers, for some unknown reason having the prefix "A".

Wagons also were duplex, generally on two running wheels (timber trucks had a pair of two-wheeled bogies), also the usual horizontal guide wheels; their capacity was very limited, cattle vehicles holding only two beasts per side; but by inserting a temporary floor, double this number of sheep and pigs could be carried. The covered wagons (four tons capacity) had internal communication between each side. Sand wagons carried five tons; it is said 200 tons per day of this mineral were carried over long periods, the rate being originally 1/6d. per ton. All the stock was fitted with combined buffers and couplers.

Official returns in 1890 showed that there were eight coaches, eight other vehicles used in passenger trains, twenty-eight wagons and two other vehicles.

Stations were constructed largely of corrugated iron, with iron roofs, having the usual offices and very low platforms. Ballybunnion was the largest installation, having in addition a goods store, engine shed, and sidings, also the lengthy spur to the foreshore for the sand traffic. At Listowel, there was a small repair shop, engine, and goods sheds, and a high-level siding for tipping sand into standard-gauge wagons. Lisselton, 4½ miles west of Listowel, had a siding and passing place, also an island platform, the small station structure abutting on the main road. Tickets were collected here. Many years later, Francis Road Halt was opened to the east of Ballybunnion. It is said there were also two other points where trains would stop by signal, but Fayle makes no reference to this.

An official works photograph of locomotive No. 1. *Courtesy, Hunslet Engine Co. Ltd.*

A further rear-end view of locomotive No. 1.   Courtesy, Hunslet Engine Co. Ltd.

The Gloucester Wagon Company undertook a survey of the whole line in 1897, prior to the construction of the Lightening Express for the Brussels Exhibition and these two views were included.   *Courtesy, Gloucester County Council Archives*

HE HUNSLET ENGINE CO. LTD *Engineers* LEEDS ENGLAND

0-3-0 TYPE

SINGLE RAIL TENDER ENGINE

Gauge of Railway	... ...	Single Rail
Size of Cylinders ...	... ...	7 in. dia. × 12 in. stroke
Dia. of Coupled Wheels ...	... ...	2 ft. 0 in.
,, Tender Wheels ...	... ...	2 ,, 0 ,,
Rigid Wheelbase (Engine)	... ...	5 ,, 8 ,,
Total Wheelbase (Engine)	... ...	5 ,, 8 ,,
,, ,, (Engine and Tender)	... ...	15 ,, 1¼ ,,
Height from Rail to Top of Chimney (Elevated Rail)	... ...	4 ,, 5½ ,,
Extreme Width ...	... ...	8 ,, 0 ,,
Heating Surface—Small Tubes ...	... ... 114 sq. ft. } Total for	
,, ,, Firebox	... ... 29 ,, } Twin Boilers	
Total	... ... 143 ,, ...	143 sq. ft.
Grate Area (Twin Fireboxes) ...	... ...	5 ,,
Working Pressure	... ...	150 lbs. per sq. in.
Tank Capacity ...	... ...	200 gallons
Fuel Space (Coal)	... ...	8 cwts.
Weight in Working Order (Engine)	... ...	(about) 6 tons 0 cwts.
,, ,, ,, (Tender)	... ...	(,,) 4 ,, 0 ,,
Total Weight of Engine and Tender in Working Order	... ...	(,,) 10 ,, 0 ,,
,, ,, on Coupled Wheels	... ...	(,,) 6 ,, 0 ,,
Tractive Effort at 75 per cent. of Boiler Pressure ...	... ...	2751 lbs.
Ratio Adhesive Weight ÷ Tractive Effort	... ...	4·9
Minimum Radius of Curve Engine will traverse with ease	... ...	100 ft.
Load Engine will haul on Level	... ...	140 tons
,, ,, ,, up Incline of 1 in 100	... ...	70 ,,
,, ,, ,, ,, ,, 1 in 50	... ...	40 ,,

Copy of Hunslet's official specification sheet.

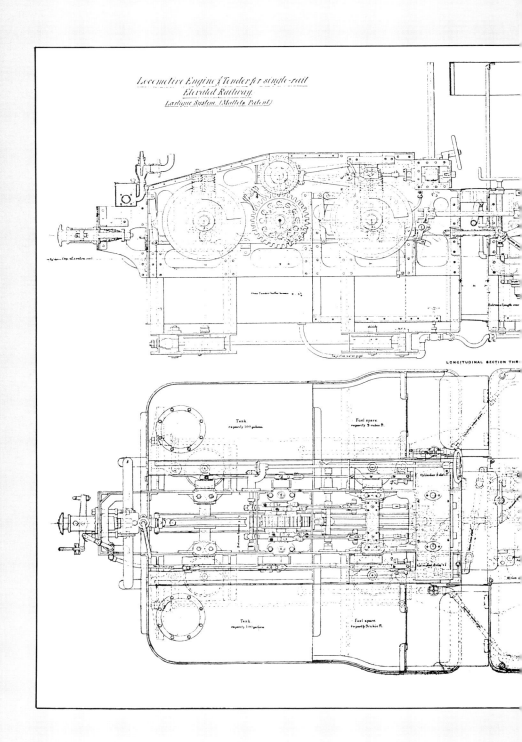

Locomotive Engine & Tender for single-rail
Elevated Railway.
Larligne System. (Mallet's Patent)

LONGITUDINAL SECTION THR

Tank
capacity 100 gallons.

Fuel space.
capacity 3 cubic ft.

Tank
capacity 100 gallons.

Fuel space.
capacity 3 cubic ft.

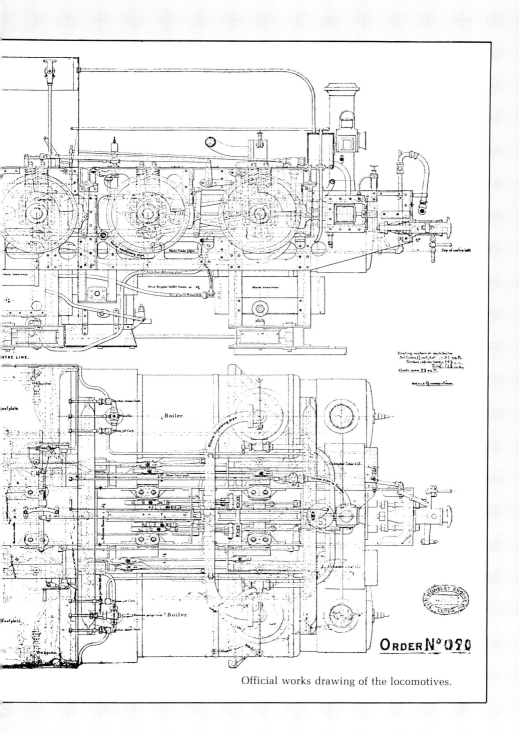

ORDER N° 090

Official works drawing of the locomotives.

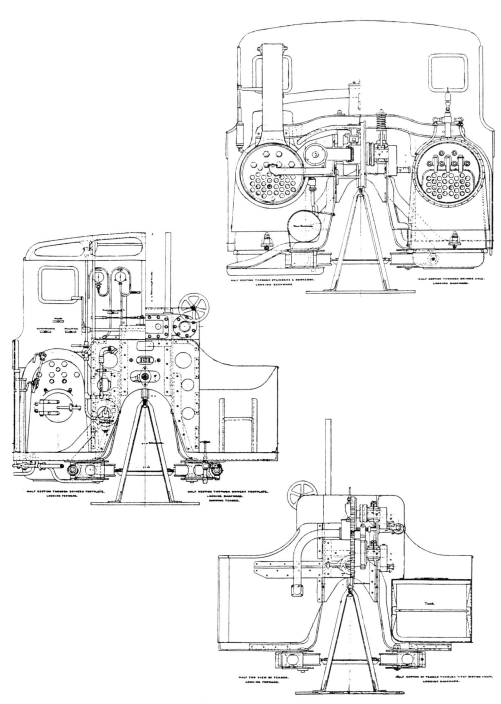

General assembly of the Lartigue locomotives in sections.

Driver Paddy Callaghan on the locomotive and John M. Reidy on the platform.
Courtesy, Irish Record Society

Passengers on the steps, by means of which they pass from one side of the line to the other.
Courtesy, Railway Magazine

A fine engraving of two coaches.   *Courtesy, The Engineer 1888*

The 4 ton open goods wagon (*note side loading ramp*).

Sand wagons; carrying 2½ tons (each side), i.e. total 5 tons capacity per wagon.

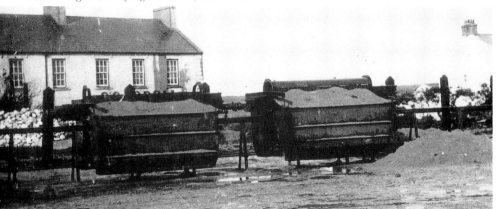

The brake third composite van, with steps on the rear to cross over the line (see drawing opposite).

(*These three photographs courtesy Gloucester County Council Archives*)

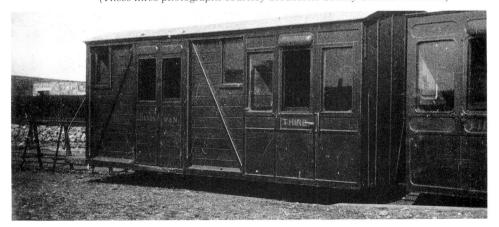

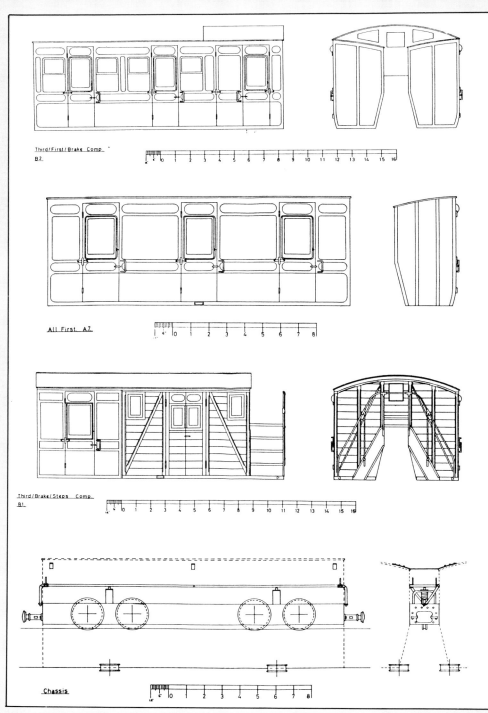

Third/First/Brake Comp.
B2

All First A7

Third/Brake/Steps Comp.
B1

Chassis

Scale drawings of coaches, brake vans and chassis units. *Drawn by Adrian S. Garner*

A train about to depart from Ballybunion station on a wet day with guard, Paddy Boyle poised on the coach steps.   *Courtesy, Daily Mirror*

Mr Patrick McCarthy (General Manager) in the bowler hat on the steps of the guards van at Ballybunion.   *Courtesy of the National Library of Ireland*

An unusual view of a sand wagon.   *Courtesy, Gloucester County Archives*

A train arriving at Ballybunion station.   *Author's Collection*

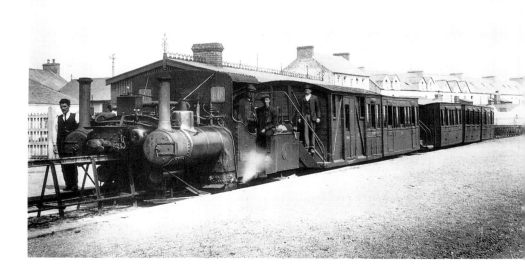

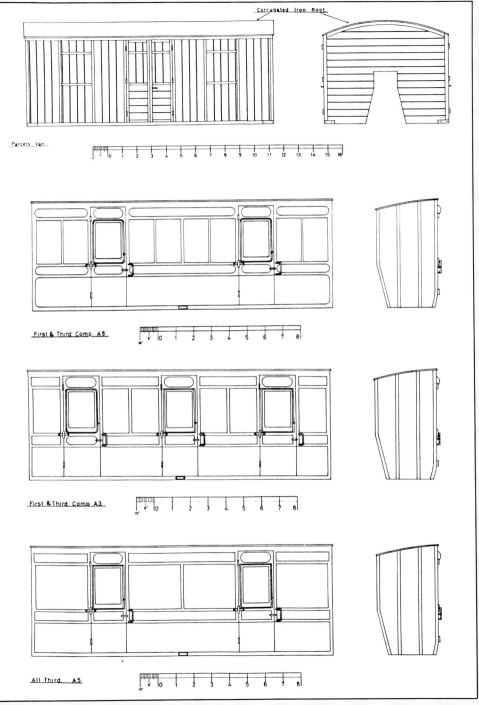

Corrugated Iron Roof

Parcels Van

First & Third Comp. A8

First & Third Comp. A3

All Third. A5.

More scale drawings of coaching and freight stock.   *Drawn by Adrian S. Garner*

The Listowel and Ballybunion Railway
will be opened for Traffic, on Monday,
5th MARCH. inst. All trains are 1st & 3rd Class.

TIME AND FARE
TABLES
ARE AS UNDER UNTIL FURTHER NOTICE.

Miles from Listowel.	DOWN TRAINS. Stations.	WEEK DAYS.								SUNDAY'S.	
		(1) 1st & 3rd Class a.m. a.m.		(2) Goods. a.m a.m		(3) 1st & 3rd Class p.m. a.m.		(4) 1st & 3rd Class p.m p.m		(1) 1st & 3rd Class a.m a.m	
		Arr.	Dep.	Arr.	Dep.	Arr.	Dep.	Arr.	Dep.	Arr.	Dep.
..	Listowel. -	..	7.0	..	9.0	..	11.50	..	2.30	..	11.0
4½	Liselton. -	7.24	7.27	9.44	9.47	12.14	12 17	3.54	3.57	11.24	11.27
9½	Ballybunion	7.50	..	10.10	..	12.40	..	4.20	..	11.50	..

Miles from Ballybunion	UP TRAINS. Stations	WEEK DAYS.								SUNDAY'S.	
		1st & 3rd Class a.m a.m		Sand & Goods a.m a.m		1st & 3rd Class p.m p.m		1st & 3rd Class p.m p.m		1st & 3rd Class p.m p.m	
		Arr.	Dep.	Arr.	Dep.	Arr.	Dep.	Arr.	Dep.	Arr.	Dep.
..	Ballybunion	..	8.10	..	10.30	..	1.0	..	5.20	..	5.20
4½	Liselton -	8.33	8.36	10.53	10.56	1.23	1.26	5.43	5.48	5.43	5.46
9½	Listowel .	9.0	..	11.20	..	1.50	-	6.10	-	6.10	..

PASSENGER FARES FROM

TO	LISTOWEL.				LISELTON.				BALLYBUNION			
	Single		Return		Single		Return		Single		Return	
	1st Class	3rd Class	1st Class	3rd Class	1st Class	3rd Class	1st Class	3rd Class	1st Class	3rd Class	1st Class	3rd Class
Listowel.					0 10	0 5	1 3	0 8	0 10	0 5	1 3	0 8
Liselton,	0 10	0 5	1 3	0 8					0 10	0 5	1 3	0 8
Ballybunion	0 10	0 5	1 3	0 8	0 10	0 5	1 3	0 8				

E. COOKE, General Manager.

Listowel 2nd March 1888.

Copy of the original timetable for the L and B Railway. *Courtesy, M. Barry's Collection*

Chapter Four

Operation of the Line

The line was worked on the electric staff system. Apart from the semaphores installed at accommodation and level crossings, coloured bulls eye lamps, backed with large white discs on pivots operated by the usual rodding, were in use. The rods appear to have been keyed to the base of the "points" pivots.

The summer train service at first comprised four each way on weekdays, and two on Sundays, apart from "extras", the frequency being much curtailed in Winter. Two weekday workings (one each way) were "mixed", and only carried 3rd class passengers; their running time was 55 to 60 minutes, compared with 45 to 50 minutes for purely passenger trains.

The top speed was 20 mph, with an average of 15, although 27 mph had been attained on trial runs. Even at this sedate pace, Fayle mentions "there was an uneasy pitching motion, due to the light construction of the rolling stock."

Although a good deal of the line was relatively level, there were, however, grades up to 1-in-45, one occurring east of Ballybunnion. At this point, occasions arose when heavily-laden trains overtaxed the power of two engines, whereupon a number of passengers would alight and walk the remaining distance!

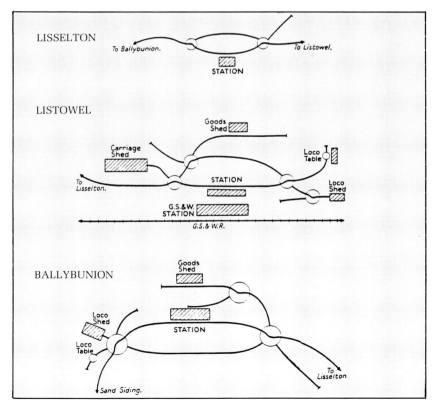

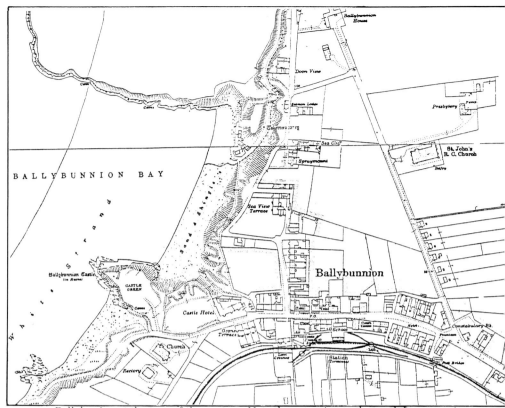

Ballybunion at the turn of the century. Note the extension to the sand dunes coming down to the left. Listowel line runs to the right. *Courtesy, Ordnance Survey*

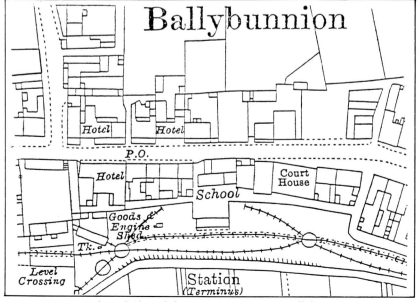

Enlarged plan of the station terminus at Ballybunion.

BALLYBUNION RAILWAY. Co·KERRY. 9852·W.L.

Ballybunion station. Note open goods wagon behind the employees seen on the left, and the simple, but effective switch turntable at the lower right. *Real Photographs*

Listowel station during construction. Note the "Coffee Pot" locomotive at the left, and one of the Hunslet locomotives on the right. Probably photographed in January 1888.

Listowel station with the mainline station buildings on the right.
Courtesy, National Library of Ireland

Ballybunion station note the bar signal protecting the switch turntable.
Courtesy, National Library of Ireland

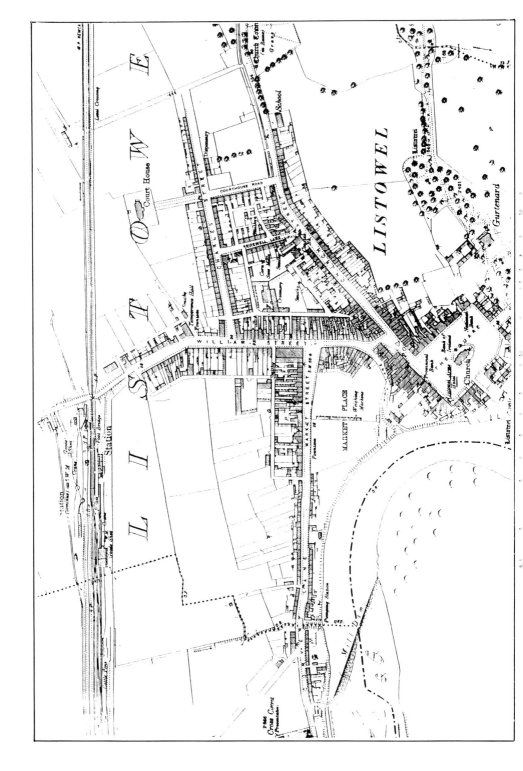

Lisselton-Lartigue Monorail Station, Co. Kerry.

A fine elevated view of Lisselton station showing clearly the track layout and switch protecting signal.

Courtesy, National Library of Ireland

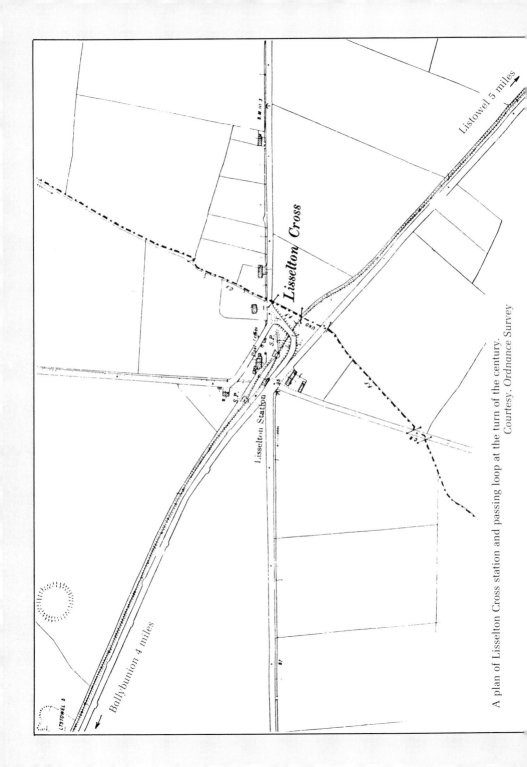

A plan of Lisselton Cross station and passing loop at the turn of the century.
Courtesy, Ordnance Survey

Chapter Five

1888–1924

To continue the general history of the line: On 8 March, 1888, the County Kerry Grand Jury considered the Tarbert branch proposal. Having questioned several merchants as to its likely utility and effect in reducing freight charges on goods brought into the district, the Baronial Guarantee was sanctioned by 12 votes to 8, subject to some reservations. (It is possible the Ballybunnion Pier project was abandoned.) This decision led to a hastily-convened meeting of local ratepayers, to oppose it. The principal speaker, George R. Browne, regarded the level crossing arrangements on the L and B Railway unfavourably, from the practical aspect, and refused to accept that the Lartigue principle was suitable for the county. A further opposition meeting was held in private at the end of April, the Waterford and Limerick Railway adding their objections, and the Tarbert scheme was defeated by 13 votes to 4 (vide Waterford and Limerick Railway Minutes).

In June, 1889, it was revealed that numerous complaints had arisen concerning the noise of travel on the "Lartigue" (as the railway was popularly known) but following improvements effected by Arthur Gore, conditions had been much improved.

Early in October, a serious mishap occurred to a train at Galey Bridge, due to someone having removed some trestle bolts, causing the track to collapse suddenly, and five coaches were upset. Fortunately, no one was injured, which is surprising, and traffic was soon resumed following repairs.

This was by no means the first instance of sabotage, several earlier attempts to upset trains by putting sleepers on the line having occurred, and on one occasion a train running at 20 mph had collided with such an obstruction. No derailment ensued, but the track was twisted.

Meanwhile, expectations of a prosperous future for the railway had not materialised; the promoter had anticipated a gross yearly income of £3,000 (£1,500 net), whereas the winter takings did not meet working expenses, the line being too remote from heavily-populated areas. On 1st October, 1890, Patrick McCarthy, formerly Chief Clerk to the General Manager (and late of the Waterford and Limerick Railway) became manager, and was destined to hold this postion for twenty-seven years, until ill-health compelled his resignation in 1917. Thanks to his energy and enterprise, the railway showed a better financial picture from the turn of the century until the First World War, notwithstanding having gone into Chancery in 1897, when McCarthy was appointed Receiver in addition to his managerial duties.

The Timetable for July, 1890 shows there were then but three trains each way on weekdays, and one on Sundays (10.30 am "Down" and 6 pm "Up".) On 11th February, 1891, a Kerry Sentinel correspondent reported that a government engineer was taking levels for a proposed light railway from Listowel to Tarbert, via Ballylongford, this being the result of strong representations having been made to the "Balfour" Government by a number of influential persons. It was considered that, apart from local support, much would be derived from tourist traffic, and the scheme would afford employment for "the poor peasantry".

MR. P. McCARTHY,
General Manager and Receiver, Listowel and Ballybunion Railway.
(Lartigue Single Rail System.) **1890—1917.**

A NNUAL visitors to that most popular of Southern Irish summer resorts, Ballybunion, will learn with regret that Mr. P. McCarthy, Manager of the Listowel and Ballybunion Railway, has found it necessary to retire owing to ill-health. Mr. McCarthy has been manager for over twenty-seven years. Those who can recollect the beginning of the enterprise can well remember its hard struggle for existence, and its many reverses. However, under Mr. McCarthy it was able to survive its difficulties until eventually it became established on a firm basis, and now the line occupies a foremost position among the light railways of Ireland. Mr. McCarthy realised that success depended entirely upon the progress of Ballybunion and accordingly he devoted all his efforts towards this objective, with the result that it is now one of the most popular seaside resorts in Ireland. It is to be regretted that his efforts have proved too much of a strain on Mr. McCarthy's health, and his many friends sincerely hope that his well-earned rest will soon restore him to his former vigour. Mr. McCarthy received his railway training on the Waterford, Limerick and Western Railway. He entered the service of the Listowel and Ballybunion Railway in 1888 and occupied the dual position of stationmaster at Listowel and accountant to the railway until appointed General Manager in October, 1890.

Extract from the Railway Magazine December, 1917. Mr Pat McCarthy was born in Lixnaw, Co. Kerry in April 1862.

In June, a French Government Commission inspected the "Lartigue" railway, with a view to possibly adopting its principles for some French colonial lines. The visitors were accompanied by F.B. Behr, James Barton (Board of Works engineer) and Duff Bunce, Chairman of the Delhi, Umballa, and Kalka Railway, India, which also contemplated using the system for a very difficult line. (The system was also considered for the Lambourn Valley Railway in England.).

Early in August, Ballybunnion had a galaxy of functions. Following sports on the beach, a fireworks display was given in the evening for the benefit of tourists and the townsfolk. A special train, put on at short notice, left Listowel soon after 8 pm; such was the demand for seats that extra coaches had to be attached. The pyrotechnics were followed by a ball, a further "special" leaving Listowel at 11 pm and probably returning in the early hours of the next morning.

At the end of November, 1892, the 6 pm "Up" Mail from Ballybunnion had an engine failure, due to a boiler tube bursting. Fortunately, the crew were uninjured, but in consequence of the rapid loss of steam, the train barely reached Lisselton, where it was stranded overnight. The few passengers had perforce to walk the last 4½ miles to Listowel, no alternative conveyance being available. The guard brought eight sacks of mail to Listowel, and the company had to hire special transport owing to the resultant delay. A relief engine sent out the next morning, met with a similar fate on its return journey, at Galey Bridge; these mishaps would seem to indicate some lack of proper maintenance.

In July, 1896, four "Down" trains (with an extra on Saturdays) and five "Up" constituted the weekday service, six double journeys being worked on Sundays; the current fares were: 1st class, Single, 1s. 4d. Return, 2s. 3rd class, Single, 10d. Return 1s. 3d., rather dear for a 9¼ miles single journey in those days.

F.B. Behr, a great believer in the monorail principle, had meanwhile built a purely experimental line three miles long, with 1,000 ft. radius curves, at Tervueren, near Brussels, on which an electrically-powered car 59 ft long attained a good speed during trials. Mounted on a pair of four-wheeled bogies, there were also sixteen guide wheels. This was followed, in 1899, by the promotion of a Bill in the British Parliament for a high-speed line on similar principles, between Manchester and Liverpool. The cost was estimated at £1,400,000, and a 10% dividend anticipated; the thirty miles between both cities would be covered in eighteen minutes, using electricity for motive power. The floor of the car was to be above the running rail, other than at the ends, where the running wheels would be housed. However, the Bill did not succeed.

During the first decade of the present century, numerous attempts were made to obtain a free grant from the British Government to build the Tarbert line, rural, and county councils (and local meetings) passing Resolutions in favour, and copies being sent to several Government bodies. However, it was never built, which maybe was as well because with the advent of motor transport in Ireland, it would probably have been closed long since as uneconomic, such having occurred in the case of the former Limerick and

Kerry Railway passenger services. In 1901, the Waterford, Limerick and Western Railway (late Waterford and Limerick) and its satellite, the Limerick and Kerry, was absorbed by the Great Southern and Western Railway, which thus gained control of the principal railways in those counties.

As the years passed by, the Listowel and Ballybunnion Railway became quite an institution, being regarded by the local people and its employees with affection; several generations of local families were members of the staff. A two-reel silent film of the railway, made by a travelling unit headed by Messrs. Charles and Leslie, who opened the first cinema in Listowel, had its premier in the local Gymnasium Hall, when the audience went almost wild with excitement at seeing themselves and their friends on the screen. Such was the din that a pianist and violinist providing the incidental music had to abandon the struggle, and join the spectators! The film ran to "full houses" and later found its way to America.*

On 10th July, 1906 the Lartigue Construction Company, which had been voluntarily wound up on 30th July, 1890, and reconstituted on 15th August of that year, was finally dissolved, so terminating this method of railway construction.

During the evening of 8th October, 1907, a serious outrage occurred on the L and B Railway due to the malicious insertion of some G.S. & W. Ry. sleepers in the trestles supporting the permanent way; but for fortunate circumstances, this could have caused a major disaster. The incident took place at the time of Listowel Races, when a number of special trains were running, two of which had previously brought 510 spectators back to Ballybunnion. The second train, comprising nine coaches and a "crossover", drawn by Nos. 1 and 3 engines, was returning empty to Listowel when, about 380 yards from the eastern terminus, it collided violently with the obstruction. McCarthy, who was in the leading coach (a composite) was thrown across it with, as he later testified, "such force as he would remember for some time". The leading engine (No. 3) had broken through the sleepers. The coach McCarthy had been in was almost useless, several others being damaged, and one telescoped, whilst most of the train was derailed. Ten trestles were broken, fifty-nine yards damaged, and sixty-six feet of rail badly twisted, causing a complete interruption of train services.

In due course, McCarthy filed a claim for £1,300 compensation against the Urban and County authorities, in respect of damage to the track, engines and rolling stock, the case coming up at the Listowel Quarter Sessions on 6th November. The Manager deposed that the railway was nearly twenty years in existence, and during that period had cost the ratepayers nothing, being self-supporting; in fact, it has saved them almost £300 annually on public road maintenance in its immediate vicinity. Since his appointment as manager in 1890, no serious accident had occurred, and not a penny in compensation had to be paid out for injury to life or property, nor for loss or damage to goods in transit – a truly remarkable record. The recent Season had been particularly busy, 33,000 passengers having been carried between

---

* Mr C.L. Fry (Dublin) now possesses this film.

Mr Joe Holyoake (leaning on the rail) watches Bill O'Reilly run his locomotive over a switch at Ballybunion station. Bill was originally a fireman and stands on the fireman's side of the locomotive.

Courtesy the National Library of Ireland

1st July and 8th October, and receipts were £100 in excess of those for the same period in 1906. The train, which was running at 10 mph prior to the collision, would have formed a 7.30 pm. Special to Ballybunnion, for which 200 passengers were expected. In conclusion, he assessed the damage to permanent way and rolling stock at £1,097 9s. 10d.

In the course of lengthy cross-examination, McCarthy denied that the woodwork of the coaches was rotten, or that engines were past their work, and refuted suggestions that the concern was bankrupt, but admitted it was in Chancery. A Mr Gadd, of the G.S. & W. Ry. Works, Limerick, gave evidence respecting the "life" of an engine; taking a daily mileage of 150, he assessed its working period, with renewals, at twenty-five years, whereas the L and B engines with a daily average of about forty miles, would last far longer.

The judge gave a decree for £850.

And now for a brief look at the financial Returns between 1902 and 1908, as furnished by the Stock Exchange Year Book of 1910:

1902	Working Profit	–	£117		1906	Working Loss	–	£58
1903	Working Loss	–	£318		1907	Working Loss	–	£127
1904	Working Profit	–	£243		1908	Working Loss	–	£66
1905	Working Profit	–	£156					

Francis Road Halt, which had appeared in the timetables from January inclusive, albeit with no trains calling opened to traffic in April 1912. This "flag" stop was in the Ahafona locality, 2¼ miles east of Ballybunnion, and was subsequently served on weekdays and Sundays.

During the years from 1912 to 1916 inclusive, the railway managed to "keep its head above water" financially, but without providing for payment of interest arrears to the debenture holders, who held the entire capital. As the following working profits tables show 1913 was the peak year thus following the pattern of several other small Irish lines: 1912 – £254; 1913 – £875; 1914 – £38; 1915 – £233. In 1916 there was a loss of £1, but a carry forward of £732.

Near the end of 1916, the British Government assumed control for the War period (and two years thereafter) of all the Irish railways, similar action having been taken previously in Britain. This resulted in the banning of trains run at excursion fares.

In July, 1919, the train service was generally very similar to that of pre-War years. By 18th August, and for a number of weeks previously, the "Lartigue" railway was exceptionally busy, no less than three trains running each way on Sundays; in fact, the recent Sunday had witnessed record traffic from Listowel, despite the lack of connecting services from Limerick and Tralee. The entire staff, from the manager to the youngest employee, were most assiduous in ensuring the welfare and comfort of their patrons; at such periods, when passenger traffic exceeded the capacity of the coaching stock, a number of wagons, with temporary seating would be pressed into service, and it was on these occasions, when nearing Ballybunnion, that a number of the "overflow" passengers would alight, thus easing the burden on the motive power!

A train at Ballybunion station (*note sand wagons at the rear*).
LCGB, Collection Ken Nunn

The Listowel locomotive depot and repair shops, with Paddy Boyle by the side of the locomotive.
LCGB, Collection Ken Nunn

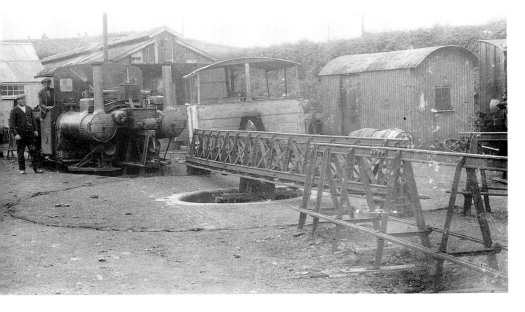

The *Kerryman* of 24th July revealed that Ballybunnion had been selected as the venue for testing the Johnson monorail principle which, according to its inventor, would revolutionize rail travel. The journal added that the "Lartigue" system had not resulted in providing rapid transport. Preliminary trials of the new principle had given entire satisfaction, and its inventor claimed that his type of locomotive would develop speeds of 105 to 150 mph. However, nothing more was heard of this.

A startling incident took place towards the end of September, 1920, when the 4.48 pm train from Ballybunnion was held up by masked men, who abstracted the mailbags, and decamped. At this period, and during the ensuing two years, the country was in a very disturbed state, and the outrage may have had some connection with the warlike activities. This was followed by a report in the *Kerry People* of 9th July, 1921, of the closing, for an indefinite period, of the L and B Ry. by order of the British military authorities. It was surmised that this arose through recent seizures of mails and despatches from trains by raiders; however, the order was in keeping with the general policy of the time, the Tralee and Dingle Railway having been closed since 20th April.

Fortunately, the closure was of brief duration, as on Wednesday of the ensuing week, General Army Headquarters, Dublin, lifted the embargo on the various lines, and an advertisement in the above journal announced the resumption of traffic from the 14th inst., with the additional attraction of two cheap trips to Ballybunnion on the forthcoming Sunday.

On 15th August, 1921, the (British) Government control of Irish railways terminated, and the minor companies were faced with the problem of carrying on, and making ends meet, in consequence of the greatly increased wages and fares imposed during the period of control, also the enhanced costs of operation.

Although the Irish Railways (Settlement of Claims) Act, 1921, provided for compensation to the various lines (based on trading profits for the year 1913), the total sum allotted was but £500,000 of which the L and B Company's share amounted to £3,675, and many lines had large arrears in maintenance to make good. During the years 1917 to 1920 inclusive, the Working Profit on the "Lartigue" line had ranged from £649 to £400 (although this was at the expense of the debenture interest, which was neither regularly nor fully met), but in 1921, there was a deficit of £236, which by the following year had jumped to £1,446. On 31st December, 1922, the debenture interest due was £9,432, and a working deficit of £715 was carried forward.

The Civil War, which was in progress during the above year resulted in considerable damage to the company's rolling stock and installations, trains being derailed, and several coaches almost entirely destroyed. At Ballybunnion, the station house was blown up, and No. 1 engine run off the end of the fixed track by opening an accommodation crossing. Due to the parlous financial position, a number of coaches were never repaired.

At a meeting of Listowel Urban District Council early in June, 1922, complaints were voiced about the L and B Rly. train service. The Manager replied that he regarded it as excellent, and giving much public satisfaction,

The Lartigue never really recovered from the damage caused by the Civil War in 1922/3 as shown vividly in this photograph with the remains of coach No. 1 after the Francis Road accident on the 26th January 1923.   *C.L. Fry*

Locomotive No. 1 apparently run-off an occupation crossing on 17th January 1923.   *C.L. Fry*

Looking towards Listowel station from Teampaillin Ban bridge (*opposite view from*

and no improvements were justified; the matter was subsequently dropped. Meanwhile, a Commission was investigating the position of the Baronially-Guaranteed railways in the newly-constituted Irish Free State; this prompted the *Kerry People* to enquire "will any relief be given by the Commission? Kerry has suffered more than any other county from the burden of railway guarantees".

Although the Lartigue railway did not come under the above category, its Manager and Receiver, also the County Kerry Accountant, gave evidence before the Commission, the first-named indicating that his company was only continuing to operate at the request of the Provisional Government. Their main source of revenue was derived from tourists, but this had fallen off (little wonder, in view of the current state of the country!).

With the return of settled conditions, Ballybunnion Station was rebuilt, and the line and its stock put in order. In August, 1923, the weekday service comprised three trains each way, with the usual extra working on Saturdays. The 7.15 pm (S.O.) from Ballybunnion ran non-stop to Listowel; otherwise trains in both directions served Lisselton and Francis Road Halt. On Sundays, there was one regular train each way, viz: 2.30 pm ex-Listowel, and 8.30 pm ex-Ballybunnion, calling at both of the above intermediate places.

The Irish Government had decided to merge the numerous railways, large and small (other than cross-Border lines) into a single cohesive unit, which became the Great Southern Railways, and no little dismay, and indignation, arose when it became known that the Lartigue line would not be included. It seems likely that the major railway company, and the Government, realised that its inclusion would be largely uneconomic, that both engines and rolling stock would require replacement, or heavy repairs, and that its continuance in operation would only perpetuate an anachronistic, albeit novel, form of rail transport. Another determining factor may have been the nature of the line and its stock, which precluded the employment of surplus vehicles from other small systems, whilst the rising incidence of motor transport would hasten its demise. (It is worth mentioning that by the end of 1922 livestock traffic was virtually nil, only thirty-five cattle, two calves and four pigs having been carried during the year; in 1923, sixteen cattle, one calf and four pigs were conveyed.)

Nevertheless, strong local efforts were made to have the line included in the merger. At a specially-convened meeting of the Ballybunnion Improvements Committee at the end of January, 1924, the following Resolution was passed:

Whilst welcoming the proposed Government scheme for the unification of railways the above body, representing all interests, views with alarm an announcement that the L and B Railway is not to be included in the scheme, and calls upon the Government and T.D's (i.e., M.P's) for County Kerry to safeguard the interests of this popular resort.

The importance of the railway is shown by a Return of Tourist Traffic in normal times, viz: over 70,000 (1913), over 68,000 (1914/1915) or, over three years, 207,000 odd. The maintenance of an improved railway system is indispensable to the farmers, shopkeepers, and fishermen of surrounding districts, and more im-

Out in the country, a two coach train and three wagons with locomotive No. 1 and a full head of steam. *LCGB, Ken Nunn Collection*

Taking on water and getting ready for duty. *LCGB, Ken Nunn Collection*

portant is the great advantage of this railway's close connection with the G.S. and W. Ry. at Listowel, to farmers and contractors who for as far as forty miles inland, have been supplied with (sea) sand from Ballybunnion to an extent of over 150,000 tons at very cheap rates.

This meeting desires to impress on the Government the national importance and necessity of maintaining and improving the existing railway service between Listowel and Ballybunnion, and expects the benefits proposed by unification will be extended to this district, and thus promote the development of Ballybunnion, where ten houses have recently been erected, and sites acquired for twenty others, to provide accommodation for the increasing number of visitors.

(Signed Canon M. Fuller, P.P., V.G. (Chairman) Joseph Costelloe, M.D. William O'Sullivan (Hon. Treasurer), W. O'Carroll (Hon Secretary).

This was followed by a deputation travelling to Dublin at the beginning of March, to see the Minister; however, time proved their efforts to have been unavailing.

On Sunday, 10th August, 1924, a large excursion was run from Limerick to Ballybunnion, carrying no less than 860 passengers. As these numbers were far beyond the capacity of the L and B Rly Co's depleted rolling stock, it was decided to make two journeys, 460 travelling by the first train. Unfortunately, this broke down when half-way to its destination, its occupants being obliged to walk the remaining distance! Meanwhile, the rest of the party awaiting the return of the train to Listowel, did not see it again until 9 pm!

Two months later, the end came. On 7th October, 1924, an application was made in the High Courts, for an Order to permit closure of the railway from the 14th inst. Having referred to the unsuccessful efforts to get the line included in the general railways merger, it was stated that the Manager and Receiver had no funds left to keep the line in operation, due to working losses (now £30 per week). The Order was accordingly made, and on 14th October, the final train was driven by Michael Holyoake, whose grandfather had been in charge of the first train, and with its arrival, the Listowel and Ballybunnion Railway, following a life of thirty-six years passed out of existence.

Several months later, the well-known firm of Thos. W. Ward Ltd., of Sheffield, dismantled the former railway and its stock using one of the locomotives, sand-wagons, and goods wagons.

Near the end of October, 1960, a unique ceremony took place in the new National School, Listowel, when J.A. Fennell, radio engineer, donated a large cast bell, which had originally been used at Ballybunnion Station to give warning of the imminent departure of trains during peak periods. Canon O'Sullivan, Parish Priest, and manager of the school, who presided, accepted the memento on behalf of the pupils and parish. Others present included Bryan McMahon (well known author), Frank Sheehy, Revd Father Dillon, Mrs Fennell, M. Walshe (late stationmaster, Lisselton) Patrick McCarthy (son of an earlier manager of the railway), Mrs T.C. Moore, and several relatives of deceased employees. McMahon, recounting the history of the line, added that although it was "the queerest railway in the world", the people loved every wheel of it, and it became part of their heritage. Continuing (in Irish), he quoted an example of how "human" both the line

Turning an engine at Ballybunion station.   *C.L. Fry*

Ballybunion locomotive No. 1 being prepared for duty with manager (McCarthy) in foreground.   *Courtesy, National Library of Ireland*

and its staff were, mentioning an occasion when Driver Jack Reidy held up the train because a young boy had lost his new red hat!

Canon O'Sullivan remarked that, for most of those present, the "Lartigue" was but a legend, yet to others who, like himself, had been privileged to know it, it evoked a happy memory. "As young lads", he continued, "we went to Ballybunnion from many parts of County Kerry. Having cycled to Listowel, we would leave our machines there, and continue by train; we would not be "doing" Ballybunnion properly unless we arrived by the "Lartigue". "When the bell rang in the evenings at the latter station, the crowds would rush to their seats, the townsfolk waving 'good-bye' as if we were going to Hong Kong, or other distant places. What a tourist attraction it would be today"! he added, "but, alas! only this bell is left." Expressing thanks, on behalf of the pupils and parish, to Fennell for his gift, despite the latter having received several offers for it from outside sources, Canon O'Sullivan added that it would perpetuate the memory of the railway for many years to come.

A pupil, Philip O'Connell (nephew of Patrick Maloney, New York, who had been a guard on the line for many years) then rendered the "Song of the Lartigue" (see Appendix "A").

Several anecdotes have been current, mostly concerned with the need to equalise loads in the wagons. One concerns the Ballybunnion lady who purchased a piano in the days before large motor vans were available. When the instrument arrived at Listowel, the above problem arose; however, this was overcome by placing two calves in the other part of the wagon, animals and piano then travelling safely to Ballybunnion.

Joseph Biggar, M.P., Belfast, when "spinning out" a speech in the British Parliament, is reputed to have given a humerous dissertation to the members on the above factor. The story goes that a farmer, who had bought a cow at Listowel Fair, had to borrow another to enable his beast to be carried by rail to Ballybunnion. On arrival, another cow was needed, to facilitate the return of the first one borrowed. This proceedure continued for a time, cattle shuttling to and fro, until the farmer had lost one cow, and paid the price of his own beast in freight charges in his efforts to avail of the railway livestock service! The story was probably apocryphal, and exaggerated!

And what of the future of the monorail? As already indicated, considerable improvements have been effected as regards both track construction, and the form of motive power employed. Where space limitations exist, and a railway is only required to provide shuttle services between two or three points in line, including, if necessary, Up and Down roads with turning loops at each end, but devoid of sidings, branches, or crossovers, there may be some justification for adopting the monorail principle. But where such factors do not apply, and yet the monorail is selected in lieu of building an orthodox railway, this amounts to undertaking what would otherwise be a straight-forward task in the most difficult way.

A switching turntable in action at Ballybunion. *Courtesy, Railway Magazine*

A Listowel and Ballybunion Railway "Free Pass" ticket issued to Mr H. Hunt in 1923.
Courtesy, Dr Patterson

Listowel and Ballybunion Railway

No. ———

FIRST CLASS—FREE PASS

Available during Year

(Unless previously cancelled or withdrawn)

ISSUED TO

H. HUNT, Esq.
Station to Station.

CONDITIONS.

This Pass is issued upon the understanding, and the use of it shall be taken as conclusive evidence of an agreement with the Company, that the latter are relieved from all liability in respect of any delay or injury to the person or property of the party using it.

It is to be exhibited when required, and the holder of it is subject to the Bye-laws and other regulations of the Company.

General Manager.

Acknowledgements to First Edition

I would acknowledge my indebtedness to the Public Record Office, London, for facilities to inspect a file relating to Charles Lartigue, and the Construction Company bearing his name; also, and especially, to the Assistant-Director, Ordnance Survey Office, Phoenix Park, Dublin, for according permission to reproduce details of track layouts from the 25″ O.S. maps. To Coras Iompair Eireann, for access to the Minute Books of the Waterford and Limerick Railway, and to Mr T. Cott, Dunlaoghaire, for loan of the L and B Rly Balance Sheets. To Mr C.L. Fry, Dublin, for loan of photographs, and other assistance, and Mrs and Miss Holyoake, for other information, also to the Hunslet Engine Co. Leeds, for other data, and the Librarian, Birmingham Reference Library. Also, to my good friends, the officers and staff of the National Library of Ireland (Dublin) who, in addition to producing many volumes of the Kerry newspapers for perusal, also supplied photographs (from the Lawrence Collection) and photostats to order. Other sources of information were:

The late H. Fayle's *Narrow-gauge Railways of Ireland*.
J.C. Conroy, *History of Irish Railways*.
Irish Railway Record Society, Journal No. 16 Vol. 4.
Cuisle na Tire. Article by M. Kelly.
The Kerryman. Two articles (January 1954) by Walter McGrath (Cork) and Tony Welsh.
Railway Magazine. Two issues in 1900 and 1910. Articles on L. and B. Ry. (Goodman) and data on the Wuppertal Ry. (Germany).
The Engineer, and *Engineering* Volumes for 1886.

A.T. Newham
1967

A photograph of Thos. Ward's Demolition train.   R.W. *Kidner*

Song of the Lartigue,

by a local bard. (From *The Kerryman* 20.1.54).

VERSES

Of railways let anyone speak,
Of the Grand Trunk or Western Union,
Sure there isn't one like the Lartigue,
That runs into famed Ballybunion.

It's built on a plan of its own,
And they say 'twas invented in France, Sir,
But however the truth isn't known,
Which leaves us to make out the answer

Oh, 'tis nice to jump into a car,
When Jack Reidy is driving the train, Sir,
But be careful you stop where you are,
And maybe you won't fall out against her.

Then Paddy Boyle comes on the way,
For a taste of a chat with the neighbours,
And if you ask him how long she will stay,
"Till the old engine's done cutting queer capers".

The old train's held together with rope,
And the tackling they say won't endure, Sir,
Sure they balance the people with soap
And sometimes with bags of manure, Sir.

If you travelled it once in your life,
Though for six months before you were seedy,
And come back the next year with your wife,
You'll be welcomed again by Con Reidy.

CHORUS
(After each verse).

There's only one wheel on the line,
And the track like the story is single,
Sure there isn't a railway so fine,
Not excepting the Tralee and Dingle.

Appendix Two
Tickets
(From Notes by Charles R. Gordon Stuart)

1st class, Single: Ballybunnion to Listowel, and reverse direction. – White.
Lisselton to Ballybunnion, and reverse direction. – White, with red stripe.

Return: White, and yellow inward half, with red stripe.

3rd class, Single: a different colour scheme for each issuing station, thus:
Listowel to Francis Road: – Yellow
Ballybunnion to Listowel: – Green
Lisselton to Listowel: – Buff
Lisselton to Ballybunnion: – Buff, with horizontal Red stripes.
Ballybunnion to Lisselton: – Green, with three vertical stripes.

3rd class, Returns: These, in most cases followed the above scheme, but where background colours would have made Red overprints indistinguishable, two vertical White stripes were employed, on each ticket half; otherwise, Red stripes prevailed. Ordinary Returns from Listowel to Ballybunnion had Blue outward portions, and Red inward halves.

EXCURSION, AND CHEAP FARES: Diagonal Red stripes on inward halves.
Inward portion of a Return Excursion Listowel/Ballybunnion/Listowel was Green, with Red diagonal stripe.

SATURDAY TO MONDAY
Return (ex-Listowel): Pink, with Red diagonal stripe.

MARKET TICKETS: Apparently a different colour scheme was used for these.

DOG TICKETS: Red and Yellow.

CYCLE TICKETS: Pink and Buff.

Block numerals on earlier printings, open ditto from about 1914. Fares not shown on earliest issues. "Lisselton" originally spelt thus, but from about 1900 "Liselton".

Appendix Three
Level Crossings and Overbridges

LEVEL CROSSINGS: There were eleven of these, nine on the Main Line between Listowel and Ballybunnion, and two in the latter area. The 11th was on the spur to the foreshore (for sand traffic) at its outer end.

OVERBRIDGES: Two, one at the S.W. end of Listowel Station, the other at Ahafona.

Appendix Four

The Future – A Rebuild!
A Feasibilty Report by Michael O. Foster

Listowel & Ballybunnion Railway, Co. Kerry, Ireland 1988

The best example of how the restoration – in our case – total rebuilding – of an interesting steam railway can increase the fortunes, security and quality of life of the local people is to look at the Great Little Trains of Wales, across the water.

These wonderful little railways give hours of delight to the whole family, give them something to do while they visit a hitherto quiet corner of the country. The benefit in this influx of tourism on local people can be in supplying their needs in accommodation, food, souvenirs, local craftwork, etc., in fact, *work.*

"The Lartigue", as the Listowel and Ballybunnion Railway was called, is unique. Unique not only as the only successful steam working monorail ever built anywhere in the world but it is Ireland's own. North Kerry is as North Wales used to be; a quiet area with few jobs for its young people thus forcing them to leave the area.

By the reconstruction* of the "Lartigue" – which has to be in total, from Listowel to Ballybunnion – a catalyst is created which will bring a very real turnround and *improvement* to local people. I can see it will become one of the greatest tourist attractions in all Ireland. The C.I.E. main line, dormant these twenty years from Tralee to Listowel and on to Limerick Junction could be retained, made whole again. By happy coincidence, the Tralee–Fenit branch of seven miles is the first line to be restored by the Great Southern Preservation Society. Tralee to Listowel is just waiting for similar treatment. A short walk of one hundred yards to the Lartigue centre at Listowel . . .!

You can see the potential, the fun, the work experience, the varied needs of the visitors, the secure jobs such a project will create.

All very well, you say, but how does one do it? A mansion, just like a hovel, is built of bricks. The mansion simply needs more bricks. I hope to show you in the forthcoming paragraphs how I have attempted to solve the technical aspect required. As my many Irish friends would say: "wait till I tell you now . . .!"

The Route

Much land originally used by the Lartigue is available, but some has been built on. No one can steam roller the project through, causing noise, nuisance and general inconvenience to local people. The aim must be to cause as little inconvenience as possible – to go round, behind, far away from peoples' homes. We want them to love the "Lartigue" not curse it. This will need tact, logical alternatives. When driving on a road, when one comes to a round-about, you do not have to crash right over the top of it, but slow down, see if the road is clear, then gently go round it. Problems and obstacles in life should be so treated too if you want to take the bumps out of it.

---

* John Fisher (a fitter on the line) in 1924, wrote a letter to the papers, suggesting that a section of the line (*about two miles long*) complete with a turn-table, drawbridge and a locomotive with a few carriages, should be sent as the Irish exhibit at the International Exhibition at Wembley and then put in a museum.

Listowel mainline station, as it was in June 1988. It is hoped it will be the head-quarters for the proposed reconstruction of the Lartigue.   *Author*

Teampaillin Ban Bridge, just west of Listowel from which the photographs on pages 6 and 94 were taken. This was reported to be the first structure in Kerry to use re-inforced concrete. Seen here restored for the Centenary in June 1988 by the Listowel U.D.C.   *Author*

The track

The original top running rail is double headed, being 100 mm tall with a 35 mm wide railhead. By happy coincidence I have worked alongside Railway, Mine and Plantation Limited, a wonderful company who have supplied such equipment for over a hundred years all over the world. Their engineers have told me *no such similar rail exists*. This is important, as it not only does not exist, but the steel mills they contacted for me could not roll it for anything like a viable cost.

Now, C.I.E. main line rail is only 135 mm tall, with a head section of 70 mm width. This latter dimension is important as we will see later. Not only that, but if the lines and sidings are lifted, as planned sadly from Listowel to Limerick Junction – one has a ready source of rail, on the doorstep. It could be purchased, transported, drilled and laid, just like bricks, end on end till the line is complete. Of course this is a monorail, so less than five linear miles of C.I.E. line would be needed from the thirty miles odd from Listowel to Limerick Junction.

To fly to Shannon Airport – visit Bunratty Castle, the lovely town of Limerick – and travel gently by preserved railway to Listowel, the Lartigue – and on to Tralee makes a wonderful excursion trip. It needs a tourist plan and programme of long term vision, to see the logic of it. Sadly, in politics, the time span is usually too short to grasp the potential and see it through. Lifting the line breaks the circle, makes it much more difficult for the visitor to get to his destination. So one follows the mistakes of one's predecessors, by choosing the cheapest option. Use buses, over-crowd the roads, enlarge the roads, etc., etc., when all along there is a perfectly usable, neglected railway line, meshed into the landscape waiting to be restored. The tragedy of injury and death on our roads is too high as it is. By far the cheapest option is to re-open the rail route.

So, by using the C.I.E. rail as the running rail, identical 45 mm x 45 mm x 4 mm angle iron legs can be made, fixed to sleepers. C.I.E. sleepers cut in half, will perfectly fit the bill. So, instead of giving money to the project – buy a sleeper. Wouldn't it be fun to number each sleeper so that one can walk the line, pointing out to friends and family alike – "Look, we purchased that one, and that one" etc.

Think of the training skills gained from drilling, welding, bolting, assembling panel length by panel length of track slowly, as time and funds permit, extending the line to completion. It took the original contractors only five months, according to some records.

The Locomotives

The natural, logical choice, would be identical replacements for the original three locomotives. This area will be keenly discussed and fought over. That they be identical in appearance externally is beyond doubt. That they puff and smell of steam and hot oil is also beyond doubt. That they be powered by coal, wood or turf is out, I feel, so the choice is between an oil fired steam design or diesel hydraulic.

Modern construction techniques, and reliability of oil fired steam units have a large appeal, but running a tourist railway demands schedules.

Severn Lamb Ltd, of Stratford-upon-Avon, supply the majority of narrow gauge tourist railway locomotives and rolling stock. Their experience is worth noting in their letter to me of 25th October, 1984.

> As I said during our meeting last week, I am not convinced that steam is immediately necessary for the tourist trade the railway will indoubtably generate. The vast majority of public commercial lines with which we are involved have concluded that, high days and holidays excluded, steam can be a definite liability to the financial success of their venture, with high capital and operational costs, and the fact that instant availability is a must, which steam does not cater for.
>
> It seems to us that what is important is that the railway be built to the Lartigue system and that overall dimensions and cosmetics should be in line with the original. Although the purists will demand steam and pooh-pooh any form of lateral thinking on the subject, they do not pay the bills, and we suggest that an I.C./hydraulic system be considered for motive power, built into the original envelope.
>
> With the use of commercially available and proven components (bearings, braking system, controls etc.), and the fitting of rubber tyred wheels, so reducing the gross weight for a similar tractive effort, capital costs can be substantially reduced. One would then look to the day when a steam locomotive can be sensibly designed with the benefit of operational experience and actual traffic figures, and be paid for out of revenue.
>
> We would envisage a price of in the region of £60,000 for such a locomotive, a final price to be dependant on a clear definition of duties, speeds etc..
>
> Having stated our apprehension at building this type of steam locomotive, the small loco* on the front cover of the Merioneth pamphlet intrigues us and we would have little hesitation in offering to construct a working replica in steam. It is so much more manageable than its larger counterpart, and, to our mind, a more interesting locomotive.

I have been in contact with the original builders, the Hunslet Engine Company of Leeds, England. They still, and all credit to them, have all their records and drawings of these three Lartigue locomotives they built over one hundred years ago. They too would like to be involved. Their letter to me of 18th April, 1984 states:

> We are anxious to be of as much help as possible and to see the scheme come to fruition. This must be on a commercial basis whereby we are given a fair chance of some tangible return and workload.

Their estimate of a replica locomotive would be £125,000.

The fact remains, the locomotives, beautiful in their shining green paint, can be built. The technology exists. The finance can be obtained, by appeals, subscriptions from not only North Kerry people, but from all Ireland, from all expatriate Irish, especially in America and Australia and from steam enthusiasts worldwide.

Make no mistake – this unique, Ireland's own, Lartigue line will be a Mecca for railway enthusiasts the world over.

One interesting feature was raised by Mr John van Reimsdijk, since retired Keeper of Engineering at the Science Museum, London, who writes:

> The idea of reconstructing a part of this line appeals to me quite a lot because it is in fact very portable and one could arrange for the track elements to allow adjust-

---

* Reference is to the "Coffee Pot" locomotive.

Original employees and passengers of the Lartigue seen here in 1982 on Michael Barry's reconstructed railway.

From left to right:
Mr Patrick Burns – a passenger on the original line
Mr Martin Deanighan – a passenger on the original line
Mrs Brigitte Barry – a passenger on the original line and Michael Barry's mother
Mrs Mary Moore – a passenger on the original line
Mr Henry Sullivan – A linesman on the Lartigue
Mr Patrick Roche – worked on the Lartigue and travelled on the last train in
          October 1924.   *Photograph Courtesy Michael Barry*
                                                                              Author

---

LISTOWEL AND BALLYBUNION RAILWAY.

Parcels for the undermentioned Stations on the Listowel and Ballybunion Railway must be booked to **Listowel (G.S. & W. Railway).**

| Ballybunion. | | Liselton. |

The charges from Listowel to destination are as follows :—

Weight not exceeding	4 lbs.	8 lbs.	24 lbs.	40 lbs.	56 lbs.	84 lbs.	112 lbs.
	3d.	4d.	6d.	7d.	8d.	9d.	1s.

Perambulators and Bicycles, as passenger's luggage, **6d.** ; as parcels, **1s.** Dogs, at owner's risk, single journey, **3d.**

ments for minor ground irregularities and to have adequate footing area to spread their load on the surface. The weights involved are quite modest. The locomotive with two small boilers presents a less formidable problem of construction than with something more orthodox. Yes, it could all be great fun and with your energy and enthusiasm behind it it should get somewhere. The question of portability is not trivial. There is now some major railway festival or centenary somewhere in the world, every year. The Science Museum's working Rocket replica is constantly on the move but there is clearly room for more things of this kind. There are sufficient annual events to make sure that there is scope for variety in the working, joy-riding, exhibits.

One could construct a loading bay, whereby a locomotive could drive straight onto a piece of track fixed to the bottom of a 20 ft container – and be driven away to whatever exhibition, location demanded. Just imagine the pulling appeal of such as a promotion for Irish exports world wide.

The locomotive was originally 7.8 metres (25′ 8″) long, buffer tip to buffer tip. By hinging the buffers and their stocks upwards will bring us within a couple of feet of the maximum 5.9 metres (19′ 4″) effective length of a container. One container taking the loco, two more carrying two coaches each. One can quickly see the ease of transportation and potential.

My own thoughts are that we would need six locomotives in all. I would name them after a wonderful Irish family – the Harney's of Tynagh, Nr Loughrea, Co. Galway, who amongst others taught me to love Ireland as much as my own country.

Locomotive No. 1   –   Máire
          No. 2   –   Breda
          No. 3   –   Rosalie

          No. 4   –   Molly
          No. 5   –   Michael

          No. 6   –   Ignus

Locomotives 1, 2 and 3 are named after the daughters of the house, and would be possible Diesel hydraulic with steam generation capacity.

Locomotives 4 and 5 after mother and son of the house, as well as Molly's brother and me! Well, why not? These would be oil fired steam locomotives.

Locomotive No. 6 would be the younger son Ignus. What better name for the twin vertical boilered original locomotive, that was used in the construction of the original line.

The idea of diesel hydraulic powered, steam generating look alike locomotives is not new. For over fifty years the famous North Bay Miniature Railway at Scarborough has been hauling hundreds of thousands of visitors. An excellent Jubilee brochure was published in 1981 which delved deep into their records. They state:

Compelling reasons for the preference for Diesel traction were set out by Hudswell Clarke. Chief amongst them was the low operating cost. Running 8 hours a day a Diesel engine would use only 6 gallons of fuel, which then cost 4d. (less than 2p) per gallon. A week later came a hurried postscript that a 30 hp Diesel engine ran for 67 hours per week on 3 gallons per day. Hudswell Clarke suggested that the locomotive they could produce for Scarborough would need only 1½ gallons. The Vickers-Coates converter which they would fit would eliminate the need for gear changing and ensure a smooth pull-away. Controls would be by a throttle and a forward/reverse lever. Steam locomotives eventually need boiler repairs, and there are washing out problems with small boilers: their locomotive would have no boiler. Besides, steam operation demands that steam should be raised well before the start of the running, adding to the expense of staffing. It was also pointed out that no coal, and practically no water would have to be brought to site. Transmission by the converter, which would have a torque multiplication of 3½ : 1, and shaft drive to a final reduction gear box mounted on the leading coupled axle would make this the first locomotive in the world to use this form of transmission, and the Diesel engine would be cooled by water carried in the tender.

Although these considerations tipped the balance in favour of diesel traction, one thing is certain – from the beginning the plans for the railway included a locomotive modelled on the Gresley "Pacific" class. This is hardly surprising. Scarborough, with its railway links stretching back to the days of George Hudson, "The Railway King", was deep in LNER territory, and that best-loved steam locomotive of all times, 4472 "Flying Scotsman", had quite recently captured the public's imagination by its non-stop run from King's Cross to Edinburgh Waverley on 1st May, 1928. It had become the epitome of locomotive engineering at its most powerful and most graceful. It seemed fitting then that Scarborough's miniature locomotive should be a replica of Mr (later Sir) Nigel Gresley's 4–6–2 masterpiece. Purists argued then, as they do today, against a sham steam locomotive, and a former chief official comented some years later: "So far as the use of diesel motive power is concerned, you lose a great deal of goodwill among the children. My youngster sniffs at the whole thing, and started doing so when he was about seven years old – regards it as a cheap money-making dodge powered by a motor car engine!" Whilst one professional railway executive firmly avowed that he cared not if a donkey pulled the train, provided it maintained the advertised service!

Whilst the workforce in Scarborough were tidying up, draughts-men and engineers in Leeds were hard at work producing the locomotive. Mr R.N. Redman in *The Railway Foundry, Leeds* recalls the specification*:

Fuel – 5 gal, capacity tank (inside the firebox space).
Brakes – Westinghouse air brakes and hand-brake.
Wheels – Driving 2 ft 4 in. diameter, bogie and tender 1 ft 2 in., coupled wheelbase 5 ft 1½ in.
Overall length over buffers, engine and tender – 26 ft 1 in.
Maximum width – 4 ft
Maximum height – 5 ft 5 in.
Weight in full working order of engine and tender – 10 tons 5 cwt.
Speed range – 0–22 miles per hour.'

Mr Redman also describes an attempt to placate the lovers of steam.

The only complaint about the engines was that they lacked "puff" in not having sufficient exhaust out of the chimney when working, for the children.
Experiments were carried out at Scarborough to improve the effect by injecting a small quantity of water into the exhaust manifold which, of course, immediately

---

* Note how closely the specification matches the original Lartigue locomotives.

turned to steam in the exhaust heat and created a rather nice plume – unfortunately the practice had to stop as the exhaust turned out to be the perfect paint remover.

The Wheels

A drawback to the original line, we are told, by old passengers was the noise. Within two feet of their heads, the other side of the carriage wall, a steel rimmed wheel ran on a steel track.

My proposal is for rubber tyres, which I investigated in depth; I discovered that a 60 cm, 24 inch diameter solid rubber wheel, rotating at 420 rpm would give 30 mph.

This would be an absolute maximum speed as one does not want such an "experience" to be over too quickly, and the 9¼ miles to Ballybunnion should be at least a trip of half an hour's duration.

The Avon Tyre Company responded in the most helpful way to my request for help:

> I am sorry for the delay in replying but I felt it essential that a rig test should be carried out on a similar size tyre to confirm my recommendation. The tyre size proposed is the 24″ x 3½″ x 20″ and a drawing is enclosed. The recommended load for this tyre is a maximum of 680 Kg @ 20 mph, and based on our telephone conversation, this should meet your requirements for the vertical wheels (4 tyres @ 680 Kg = 2.7 tonnes), and the four guide wheels. The rig test was carried out on a 21¼ x 4 x 16 tyre at an equivalent load rating of 725 Kg at 20 mph and 625 Kg at 30 mph. The tyre temperatures generated at 20 mph were satisfactory, but at 30 mph the temperatures were far too high. Therefore I do not recommend that tyres are run above 20 mph until you have been able to carry out extensive field service trials. My best guess is that at 30 mph the load rating would have to be reduced to approx. 430 Kg per tyre.

We mentioned the rail earlier. The rail head has a 70 mm width, the standard rubber tyre 24 inch diameter has a tread width of 69 mm! Allow for a double nylon or rubber flange and noise is eliminated, solid rubber means maintenance-free running.

I plan for two wheels on a central pivot per axle – and two axles i.e. four wheels per coach. I cannot see a carriage weighing more than 1000 Kg unloaded, and 2500 Kg (2.5 tonnes) loaded with 10–15 passengers and their bags, etc. There will be no steel wheels to make noise or requiring machining to profile, no flat tyres from pneumatic wheels – just solid rubber. Shock absorbers on the central axle and air/disc brakes complete the safety aspect.

The Coaches and Wagons

A wide variety of enclosed, open, verandah and bar cars – all *on a standard chassis design* could be built. The original line had them built by the Falcon works in Loughborough. Research has shown this to be the Falcon Railway Plant Works of Henry Hughes & Co. – now the Falcon Works of Brush Electrical Machines. As so often happens drawings etc., of current products do not become old enough to be archive material, before the space they occupy is needed and they are cleared out.

The traction engineering manager of Brush Electrical Machines Ltd wrote to me on 10th September, 1984 saying just that.

I am sorry to have to tell you that so far as I have had no success in tracking down any GA drawings for the coaches of the Listowel and Ballybunnion Railway, and very much doubt whether any exist. Certainly the Company has retained none in its archives: they would have been destroyed some years ago during a periodic clear-out of old drawings. The only possible source would be any copies kept privately by an enthusiast, but I have not managed to locate any.

I would anticipate needing three full sets or trains, say of six coaches each. Allowing for a spare set it seems logical to have 26 coaches, each named after a county in Ireland, again reflecting Ireland's own: each county sponsoring its own coach.

Ten goods/freight wagons, on an identical chassis would be needed for maintenance, display, extra passenger carrying and even freight.

The Museum, Shop, Cafe and Facilities

The museum, housing artifacts that have survived, a shop selling good souvenirs, not only of the Lartigue, but of All Ireland. The quality of food, glassware, knitted items, etc. being a constant source of pleasure and delight to me, a regular traveller to and lover of Ireland and the Irish.

Good, large, spotless rooms for a mother to clean and cope with her young family. I have usually found the places with the finest "facilities" prove to be the most popular. A family will visit again and again such a place.

So, such a project can be undertaken and guided to a financially successful and rewarding future to the benefit of the people of North Kerry. The Lartigue, just like Sleeping Beauty after one hundred years awaits the Kiss of Life.

. . . IT CAN BE DONE, IT COULD BE DONE, IT SHOULD BE DONE . . .

For further details of how you can help,
write with a stamped addressed envelope
or international reply coupon to:

The Secretary
The Lartigue Centenary Committee
Clieveragh
Listowel
Co. Kerry
Ireland

THE BEOTHUK

Ingeborg Marshall

BREAKWATER BOOKS LTD.
JESPERSON PUBLISHING • BREAKWATER DISTRIBUTORS
www.breakwaterbooks.com

National Library of Canada Cataloguing in Publication Data

Marshall, Ingeborg, 1929-
    The Beothuk

Includes bibliographical references.
ISBN: 0-9680803-3-2
ISBN 13: 978-1-55081-258-9

1. Beothuk Indians.   2. Beothuk Indians-History
I. Newfoundland Historical Society.   II. Title

E99.B4M358 2001   971.8'004979   C2001-902128-3

© Ingeborg Marshall   Editor: J.K. Hiller

Originally printed in Canada in 2001 by The Newfoundland Historical Society with financial assistance of the Beothuk Institute.

Reprinted in 2009 by Breakwater Books Ltd.

ACKNOWLEDGEMENTS

Breakwater Books Ltd. gratefully acknowledges permission from McGill-Queen's University Press to use material from *A History and Ethnography of the Beothuk*, by Ingeborg Marshall, published 1996, reprinted 1997, 1999.

The author gratefully acknowledges the helpful suggestions from readers of the manuscript: James K. Hiller, Alan Macpherson, William Marshall, Priscilla Renouf, Shannon Ryan, Hope Squires, and additional editorial work by Garfield Fizzard and Anne Hart.

On the cover is shown *"The Spirit of the Beothuk," a bronze sculpture, created by Newfoundland artist Gerald Squires, commissioned by the Beothuk Institute.*
Photograph by Ingeborg Marshall, reproduced with permission of Gerald Squires.

CONTENTS

CONTENTS (CONT'D)

Maps and Illustrations

1

INTRODUCTION

The extinction of the Beothuk—at once the most distressing aspect of their history and the most complex—has often been the focus of interest in this aboriginal population. But there is more to know about the Beothuk than their tragic fate. The Beothuk were a proud and independent people who had successfully adapted to their environment and who flourished until incursions by other populations deprived them of much of their resource base. The purpose of this booklet is to present a more complete picture.

The monograph starts with an overview of the Beothuk's position in Newfoundland prehistory, followed by an outline of their distribution and population size at the time of first contact with Europeans, of their social organization, subsistence strategies and burial practices. With this information as a basis, attention is focussed on their history. Due to the nature of the available documentation, it largely centres on the development of relations between Beothuk and those Europeans who came to fish or settle in Newfoundland and on the impact of other native groups. Additional cultural information on such matters as the Beothuk's appearance and clothing, their houses and means of transportation, their language and beliefs are described in the context of reports written by contemporary observers. The intent of presenting cultural data in this sequence is to indicate how little the people in fishing communities as well as in government knew about the traditions of their native neighbours or subjects. This lack of understanding promoted misperceptions and disregard for the Beothuk and exacerbated growing suspicion and hostile attitudes. The deterioration of relations as well as other factors that contributed to the eventual demise of the Beothuk are discussed as they emerge from the records.[1]

2

PREHISTORY

Where did the Beothuk came from and how long had they lived in Newfoundland? The short answer is that the ancestors of the Beothuk, known as (prehistoric) Recent Indians, came across from Labrador about 2000 years ago. But the Recent Indians were not the first people to live in Newfoundland. The earliest native group to arrive on the island, around 5500 years ago (3500 BC) were the Maritime Archaic Indians who had already hunted and fished in Labrador for several millennia.[2] They gradually spread across much of the island, predominantly along its coast, where they made use of marine resources primarily, although they would also have hunted in the interior. Among the many Maritime Archaic Indian sites that have been excavated are those at Port au Choix on the west coast of the Northern Peninsula and at The Beaches and Cape Freels in Bonavista Bay.[3] The story of the Maritime Archaic Indians in Newfoundland ends about 3000 years ago (1000 BC). They either died out, or remnants of the group returned to Labrador. Some archaeologists favour a third possibility, namely that small groups may have survived in the interior of Newfoundland, though signs of their presence after 1000 BC have not (yet) been found (Fig.1). Since some Maritime Archaic Indian practices, such as the use of red ochre and pendant-like carvings have also been noted from the Beothuk, a link between these two populations is considered possible.

A century or two after Maritime Archaic Indian occupancy, Early Palaeo-Eskimos came across from Labrador (ca. 850 BC). They spread across the North American Arctic from west to east before moving down the Labrador coast and to Newfoundland. Being primarily sea-mammal hunters, they lived close to the coast for much of the year. Their small and finely chipped points, knives and blades can easily be distinguished from the large axes, adzes, and gouges of their Indian predecessors.[4] After about

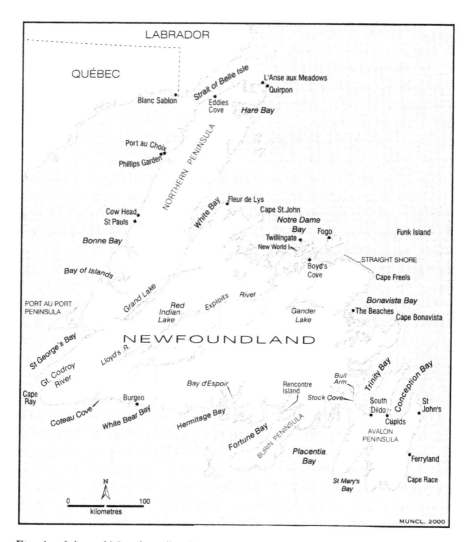

Fig. 1   *Map of Newfoundland.*

850 years this native group disappeared from Newfoundland and was replaced around the beginning of the Christian Era (ca. AD 1) by Late Palaeo-Eskimo groups (also known as Dorset) from Labrador. Like their predecessors, they focussed on coastal resources, particularly seal. In addition to producing finely chipped tools, Late Palaeo-Eskimo groups introduced the use of soap stone bowls and oil-burning lamps. Some of these

bowls were quarried at Fleur de Lys where half-finished pots can still be seen on a soapstone outcrop. They also carved small, stylized bone and ivory images, often representing animal forms. Stylized carvings were also recorded from the (historic) Beothuk but whether they could have been influenced by the carvings of the Late Palaeo-Eskimos remains an unresolved question. Judging by the many Late Palaeo-Eskimo sites in Newfoundland—among them those at Phillip's Garden at Port au Choix and Stock Cove in Trinity Bay—this population appears to have been numerous, particularly between AD 200 and AD 500. After this date their numbers declined, though small groups persisted until about 1150 years ago (AD 850).

This brings us to the (prehistoric) Recent Indian population, which arrived from Labrador about 2050 years ago (50 BC), shortly before the Late Palaeo-Eskimos or Dorset. Archaeologists use the name Recent Indians to distinguish them from the earlier Maritime Archaic Indians, and from the later Beothuk who lived in Newfoundland during the period for which we have written records—hence the "historic" Beothuk. Stone tools from different Recent Indian sites show notable differences in manufacturing technique and shape, which has prompted archaeologists to identify three Recent Indians populations or subgroups.[5] The earliest was the "Cow Head" group (ca 50 BC to AD 850), named after the community of Cow Head on the Northern Peninsula where it was first identified.[6] Many Cow Head tools are roughly made but some finds at Port Au Choix include well-fashioned projectile points as well as shards of decorated pottery. The connection between Cow Head people and both the earlier and later Indian groups in Newfoundland, and with Indian groups from the mainland, remains uncertain.[7]

A second Recent Indian occupation were "The Beaches" people named after The Beaches in Bonavista Bay.[8] They were originally thought to have lived in Newfoundland after AD 400 but we now have carbon dates as early as AD 50. These people largely inhabited the inner reaches of bays, suggesting that they used a wide range of marine as well as inland resources. Some of their tools are similar in style to tools found at few archaeological sites in Labrador from the same period. This similarity suggests occasional direct or indirect contact between The Beaches and Labrador Indian populations, perhaps through trade links or social networks.[9]

The descendents of The Beaches people are known as the "Little

Passage" Indians (ca AD 850 to AD 1500). Their distinctive tools were first identified in a passage leading from Hermitage Bay to bay d'Espoir.[10] Their remains have since been discovered in all major bays of the island—usually in the inner reaches—as well as on the banks of rivers and lakes, particularly the Exploits River and Red Indian Lake. Little Passage people used a wide variety of marine foods; they were also caribou hunters, trapped fur bearers, and utilized other inland resources. Although their tools were similar to those of The Beaches people, their projectile points became smaller over time. This reduction in size has also been observed in the projectiles from contemporary Point Revenge people in Labrador, suggesting that Labrador Indians were not only in contact with the Newfoundland Beaches population but continued interchange with the Little Passage people.[11]

In conclusion, archaeologists think that social and economic links between The Beaches and Little Passage Indians existed and that the Little Passage people were the direct ancestors of the Beothuk, the Beothuk representing the historic phase of this population. The most convincing evidence for this relationship comes from the Boyd's Cove archaeological site in Notre Dame Bay where layers of Little Passage and historic Beothuk deposits have been found in close succession, sometimes mixed. Both groups also used similar arrow heads, knives and scrapers.[12] Archaeologists also propose a sustained close contact between Newfoundland and Labrador Indians into the historic period. Thus, the Labrador Innu and the Beothuk may not only have shared cultural features but may also have been genetically related.

Prehistoric native populations in Newfoundland

5500 yrs. ago (3500 BC)	Arrival, Maritime Archaic Indians
3000 yrs. ago (1000 BC)	Last traces, Maritime Archaic Indians
2850 yrs. ago (850 BC)	Arrival, Early Palaeo-Eskimos
1900 yrs. ago (AD 100)	Last traces, Early Palaeo-Eskimos
2000 yrs. ago (AD 1)	Arrival, Late Palaeo-Eskimos
1150 yrs. ago (AD 850)	Last traces, Late Palaeo-Eskimos
2050 yrs. ago (50 BC)	Arrival, Recent Indians:
2050-1150 yrs. ago (50 BC-AD 850)	Cow Head phase
1950-1050 yrs. ago (AD 50-AD 950)	The Beaches phase
1150-500 yrs. ago (AD 850-AD 1500)	Little Passage phase
500-170 yrs. ago (AD 1500-AD 1830)	Beothuk phase

3

Distribution, Population Size and Social Organization

Before Europeans came to Newfoundland, the Beothuk and their fore-bears were widely dispersed over the island.[13] Beothuk and/or Little Passage remains have been found in several places on the south coast, including Coteau Cove, Bay D'Espoir and Placentia Bay, and on the Avalon Peninsula at the former English colony of Ferryland; also at South Dildo, Dildo Pond and Bull Arm in Trinity Bay. Following their prehistoric ancestors, Beothuk camped on the large shingle bar at The Beaches in Bonavista Bay and visited the nearby quarry at Bloody Bay to gather raw material for tool manufacture. The long, sandy beaches at Cape Freels on the northern headland of Bonavista Bay, close to the migration route of the harp seal herds (an important staple food), were another favoured camp site. An additional advantage of this location was its proximity to Funk Island with its large breeding colonies of seabirds. These beaches had also been resorted to by other prehistoric native populations.

The bays, coves and islands of greater Notre Dame Bay were home to Beothuk from prehistoric times. Stories of encounters with them are still told by local inhabitants of this district and many Beothuk burial sites have been found here. The best known Beothuk site in this area is the long-term habitation camp at Boyd's Cove, now a Provincial Historic Site with an attractive interpretation centre (Fig.2). In fall and winter the Beothuk moved inland, hunting and trapping along waterways, such as the Exploits River and Red Indian Lake. In the late 1700s this area became the heartland of Beothuk occupancy and their last refuge. On

Fig. 2   The Boyd's Cove Beothuk camp site on the plateau to the right, Indian
Brook in the centre.

(Photograph by Ingeborg Marshall)

Newfoundland's north and west coasts Little Passage remains have been
identified at Eddies Cove, Port au Choix, St. Pauls Bay and the Port au
Port Peninsula; early reports mention Beothuk camps in Hare Bay, Bonne
Bay and St. George's Bay.

Speculations about the size of the Beothuk population aboriginally,
that is at the time Europeans came to Newfoundland to fish and settle,
vary considerably. Some writers have claimed that there would have been
20,000 to 50,000 Beothuk but these figures are unsubstantiated and
entirely unrealistic.[14] Taking into account the number and size of known
Beothuk/Little Passage sites, their life style and 18th century estimates it
is reasonable to postulate an aboriginal population of about 500 to 700.[15]
This number coincides with population densities calculated for other
native hunter-fisher-gatherers in sub-arctic northeastern America.[16]

Like other northeastern peoples, the Beothuk lived in independent
bands of about 30 to 55 people.[17] These were the important social and

political units, while tribal affiliation was based on language and other cultural features. Perhaps the Beothuk's most significant cultural tradition was the annual ochring ceremony at which all members of the tribe received an application of red ochre on the face and body. This was a mark of tribal identity; for infants, born during the previous year, the first coating was a sign of their initiation into the tribe.[18] To be told to remove the ochre was considered a form of punishment. The ochring ceremony, celebrated in spring, lasted for about 10 days and was accompanied by dancing, feasting and dice games. The Beothuk also painted their belongings with ochre and covered the bones and grave goods of their dead with it, suggesting that it had an additional religious significance. Although the use of ochre has been recorded from Maritime Archaic Indian burials and from native groups on the Atlantic seaboard, such as the Mi'kmaq, its extensive application by the Beothuk in the 1700s and 1800s appears to have been unique.[19]

Leadership in hunter-fisher-gatherer bands was usually provided by an experienced male who was respected for his wisdom, charity and other outstanding qualities. The Beothuk most likely followed this tradition. Privileges enjoyed by their leaders or "chiefs" included status symbols such as staves, larger houses, burial huts and lavish grave goods. The term "chiefs" is set in quotation marks because it tends to be associated with a more formal power position than might have been the norm for Beothuk leaders. At least in the early 1800s, their power was informal rather than authoritarian, and important decisions were probably made by a council.[20] It is assumed that the Beothuk also had shamans, who can be described as an "interface" between the people and the powers that controlled the environment. Shamans practised rituals and ceremonies to keep relationships with these powers harmonious and to ensure success in hunting. They were also called on to perform curing rituals for the sick and for other services.

Given the extent of the Beothuk territory and the geographic separation of the bands, it is easy to see that each would have been self-sufficient. In fact, bands do not seem to have cooperated with one another when facing hostilities from intruders. This practice of non-alliance had changed by the early 1800s when groups from what might have been different Beothuk bands came together to support each other in their struggle for survival.[21]

4
HUNTING, FISHING AND GATHERING

The Beothuk were hunters, fishers and food-gatherers who relied most
heavily on caribou, salmon and seals, all of which migrate seasonally
and could only be harvested in specific locations at certain times of the
year. Hence the Beothuk moved from place to place in accordance with
the habits and habitats of these species. To supplement these staple foods
they also exploited a great variety of other marine and terrestrial resources
including small fur bearers, fish and sea mammals, lobster and crab, shellfish such as oysters, mussels, clams and scallops, birds and eggs, roots and
berries.

Although the Beothuk are often pictured as engaged in hunting in the
woods, they actually spent the best part of the year on the coast. Between
late December and May, hunting parties went out to headlands to catch
harp seals on the edge of the ice or on ice floes. Fresh seal meat and oil
would have been a welcome addition to diminishing food reserves, and
much appreciated after months of living mainly on caribou meat. Seals
were hunted with harpoons, called *a-a-duth*, or "spear for killing seals"
(Fig.3). These harpoons consisted of a staff with a detachable head that
was tied to a long line. The hunter would lodge the harpoon head in the
body of the seal and then disengage the shaft. A tug on the line caused
the harpoon head to swivel and become firmly imbedded in the animal,
preventing it from escaping. When the seal was exhausted from struggling
to get away, it was hauled in.

Once the rivers were free from ice the families came to the sea shore,
around April or May. Here, they collected clams and mussels, caught

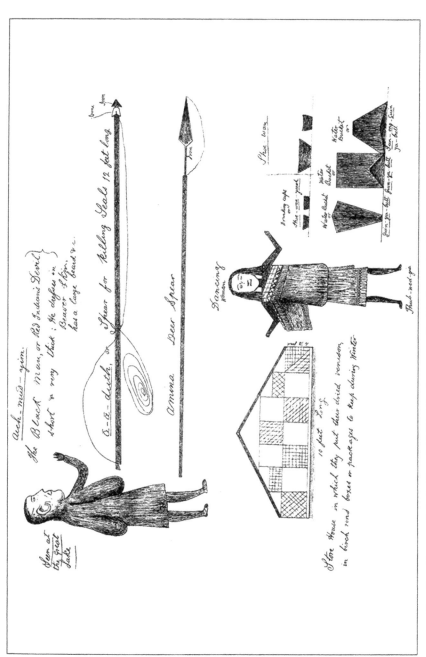

Fig. 3   Shanawdithit's Sketch VIII. Black man or Red Indian's devil, dancing woman, sealing spear, deer (caribou) spear, store house, drinking cups, water buckets.

winter flounder, smelt, herring, eels and later capelin, some cod and other marine species. They also shot overwintering sea birds, such as murres and sea ducks, and caught harbour seals which come ashore to whelp. When migrating sea birds returned to their breeding colonies, in May and June, the Beothuk collected their eggs. They boiled and then dried the eggs in the sun and stored them in powder form or as cakes. They also stuffed eggs into guts, together with seals' fat, livers, and other ingredients, to make a kind of sausage or pudding to be preserved for times of scarcity. An 18th century observer noted: "During the egg season they [Beothuk] are supposed to feed luxuriously and by no means want after the young have taken to wing, for in archery they have an unerring hand that amply supplies their wants."[22] To knock down small birds they used blunt arrows on which the leading end was a knob of wood.[23]

A little later in the year, porpoises and whales came inshore which were greatly prized by the Beothuk who considered it "the greatest good luck to kill one."[24] Whether the Beothuk pursued whales in their canoes, as did the Penobscot in New England, or only took beached whales has not been recorded.[25] They may have driven pods of porpoises or small whales into the shallows of a bay where they could kill them with clubs and axes.

An important event in the cycle of food gathering was the annual salmon run, in July, when Atlantic salmon entered many of Newfoundland's rivers to spawn upstream. This was a time when families assembled at the rivers to harvest large quantities of this readily available fish. The Beothuk not only depended on salmon for immediate consumption but also dried or smoked it to store as a reserve when other food was wanting. To catch salmon they may have built stone weirs or enclosures in rivers or may have speared them from their canoes at night, attracting the salmon with flaming torches.

After the salmon run, the Beothuk moved along the coast in smaller groups, fishing, hunting and collecting lobster, crab and shellfish as they went. At the end of summer they picked berries and gathered edible roots; the onset of fall marked the beginning of the hunting and trapping season. Caribou and beaver were much sought after for their meat as well as their skins; fox, marten, otter and other fur-bearers were also trapped to provide pelts for the manufacture of clothing. During the winter months the Beothuk fished through lake ice and procured birds, particularly ptarmigan. These birds congregate in large numbers and as they do not easily take flight in cold weather, they can sometimes be knocked off the branches on which they roost.[26]

Some Beothuk bands hunted and trapped near their coastal camps, remaining there until winter storms forced them into sheltered areas inland. They may then have divided into smaller groups. In contrast, the bands which specialized in hunting caribou left the coast by mid-September to prepare for the caribou drive along rivers and lakes. Fence works had to be constructed or repaired and storage facilities put in order. After a summer of grazing on open ground, the caribou migrate in fall in herds of more than a thousand head to sheltered feeding places. At this time of year, the caribou are fat and their fur is at its best for winter clothes. Before the construction of the Newfoundland railway, the main migration route led from the Northern Peninsula across Sandy and Birchy lakes, the Exploits River and the northern end of Red Indian Lake, and from there further south. Caribou stubbornly follow lead animals. By obstructing their route with fence works, the Beothuk would funnel the lead animals—and the herd that followed them—into enclosures, or towards fence barriers along river banks or lake crossings. These barriers had narrow openings where hunters were stationed to shoot at the animals as they passed through.[27] Other hunters took to their canoes and pursued the caribou while they were swimming across a river or lake. By these methods the Beothuk secured large numbers of animals for winter provisions.

They hunted caribou with bows and arrows, which were their most versatile hunting tools. The bows measured about 1.7 metres and were cut obliquely on the inside "for the true delivery of the arrow." The arrows were close to a metre long and fletched with two strips of feathers. The bone or stone points (arrow heads) were later replaced by two-edged iron points, often made from iron nails collected from European premises.[28] In the 1800s, if not earlier, the Beothuk also used three metre long spears with long, slender iron points for the killing of caribou; they called these spears *amina* (see Fig.3).[29]

After the hunt the Beothuk cut the meat from the caribou into strips and dried it. In this form the meat was easy to carry and could be reconstituted through boiling. Other methods of preservation were less labour

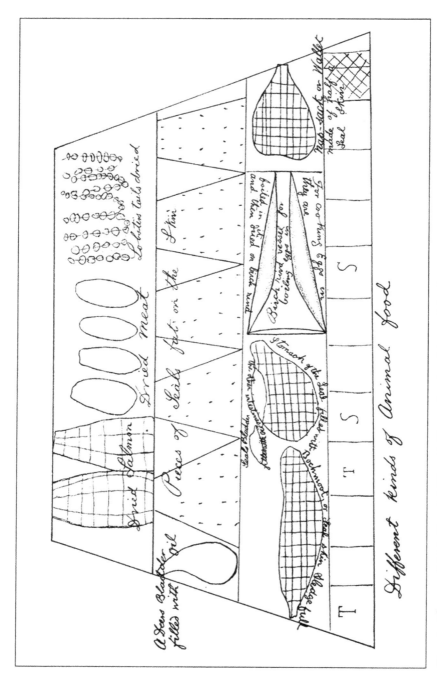

Fig. 4 Shanawdithit's Sketch VII. Different kinds of Animal food.

intensive. Very fat venison was removed from the bone and stowed in large chunks in birch or spruce bark boxes, lean venison was left in quarters and stored in bulk. Once the frost set in, the meat would freeze solid and remain unspoiled for weeks or months.[30] The Beothuk rendered caribou fat into clear grease, and seal blubber into oil which they kept in seal bladders or stomachs (Fig.4). A unique feature, not recorded for other northeastern native groups, was the Beothuk's construction of substantial store houses in which they stockpiled their food (see Fig.3). Cooking was done over an open fire, lit by striking together pieces of iron pyrites and catching the sparks with dry moss or down.[31] Meat was roasted on sticks or spits. Liquids were boiled in large bark vessels "sewn and fashioned like leather buckets" (see Fig.3), into which the Beothuk placed a succession of heated rocks.[32] This method is cumbersome, and the Beothuk were keen to obtain European iron kettles and cooking pots.

5
BURIAL PRACTICES

The Beothuk took great care in the disposal of their dead. In the early 1800s, residents in Notre Dame Bay said that the Beothuk would bring their dead from a distance to the sea shore to bury them there. This claim is supported by the fact that all 24 Beothuk burials that have been verified—other than a 19th century cemetery at Red Indian Lake—were located in remote places close to the coast or on uninhabited islands.[33] Other native people in the Atlantic region who adhered to the same practice did so because they were afraid of the ghosts of the dead.[34] It is possi-

Fig. 5   *Burial cave at The Launch, Long Island, Green Bay.*

(Photograph provided by Gerald Penney)

ble that the Beothuk's preference for coastal burial was based on similar fears.

The most common burial method used by the Beothuk was to wrap the body in birch bark and place it on or below the surface of the earth, often in a cave or a rock shelter (Fig.5). As a rule, the spot was covered with a pile of rocks. Another method was to lay the wrapped-up body on a scaffold that was constructed from four poles from which a crib was suspended. This could have been a temporary repository used to preserve the remains for later burial on the coast. A body could also be wrapped with the knees folded onto the chest and placed into a burial box. The most conspicuous burial structure, recorded in 1827 from a cemetery at Red Indian Lake, was a small hut. It measured 2.5 by 3 metres, was about 1.5 metres high in the centre and well secured against the elements. This hut, in which the Beothuk captive Demasduit and her husband "chief" Nonosabasut had been laid to rest, also contained the bodies of children as well as a great variety of grave goods; among the latter were small

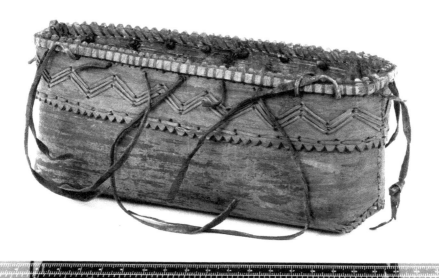

Fig. 6   *Birchbark container collected by W.E. Cormack from Nonosabasut's burial hut in 1827.*

wooden images of a man, woman and child, replicas of canoes and boats, an iron axe, a bow and quiver with arrows, two fire-stones (radiated iron pyrites), utensils made of birch bark (Fig.6) and other items. Many—or possibly all—Beothuk burials included such offerings.[35] A particularly large array of grave furnishings was found with the mummified body of a four- or five-year-old child, discovered in the 1880s on Big Island, in Pilley's Tickle. The body was clothed in skin pants and moccasins and encased in a fringed skin cover to which 32 carved bone pendants and several birds feet had been fastened. Arranged around the body were a small male figurine, miniature bows and arrows, three small birch bark canoe replicas and paddles, three pairs of moccasins, packages of red ochre and some dried or smoked salmon (Fig.7).[36] The lavish offerings in this

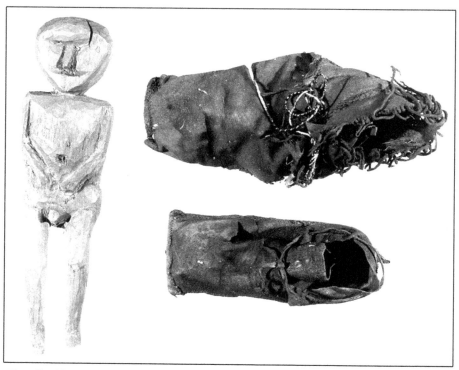

Fig. 7   *Two moccasins and wooden figurine from child's burial on Big Island, Pilley's Tickle.*

(Collection of The Rooms Provincial Museum)

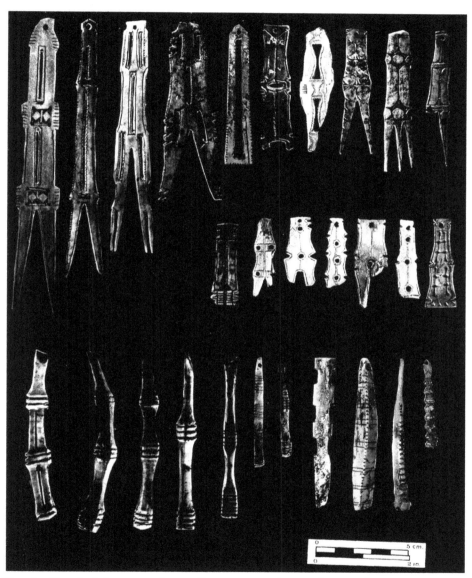

Fig. 8   Beothuk bone pendants. Rows one and two: diverse shapes, row three: five skeletal finger- or claw-shaped pieces.

(Private collection and collections of The Rooms Provincial Museum
and the Canadian Museum of Civilization, reproduced by permission
of the Canadian Museum of Civilization.)

23

interment and in the burial hut at Red Indian Lake suggest that the persons who were interred there had enjoyed special status or, in the case of the child, might have been related to a person of high status.

The function of the items placed into the graves related to the belief of the Beothuk and other North American native people in a life after physical death, which would be spent in the "country of the good spirit." The journey to this country was long and the spirits of the dead required certain objects to assist them on the way.[37] These could include clothing, weapons, tools, canoe replicas, bark containers, ochre and food as well as tokens of guardian spirits for protection against evil powers. Bird skulls and feet, animal teeth, and pendant-like bone carvings may have served this last purpose. The carvings are flat and decorated on both faces with geometrical patterns; rubbed with ochre, the markings stand out prominently against the light polished surface of the bone. Although the pieces conform to a certain overall design, each one is unique. Several carvings appear to be stylized representations of skeletal fingers or claws (Fig.8, bottom row, the first five carvings), and others could represent mammalian figures or birds' feet, but the meaning of most of these carvings cannot be decoded. The pieces may have been worn as amulets signifying an intimate relationship between these individuals and particular species of game animals; or, where bundles of carvings were buried without human remains, they may have represented a communal veneration of (animal) spirits.

The foregoing information gives a general idea of the extent to which the Beothuk were present on the island of Newfoundland and of their way of life at the time of first contact with Europeans. Attention is now focussed on the history of relations with newcomers, for the most part based on English records. As the Beothuk lived in relative isolation and refrained from interacting with the English or other Europeans, little information has been collected from them directly—other than what was obtained from captives—and their voice is nearly absent from the records. This imbalance in the documentation of historic events cannot be compensated for and remains a limiting factor of the story.

6

RELATIONS BETWEEN
BEOTHUK AND NEWCOMERS
IN THE 1500S AND 1600S

When John Cabot landed on the Newfoundland coast in 1497, he did not meet native people although he found signs of human habitation: snares, a needle for making nets and felled trees.[38] Other explorers and fishing crews followed, but accounts of meetings with native people in those early days are very sparse, and in most recorded cases it has not been possible to establish whether these encounters took place in Newfoundland or elsewhere on the Atlantic seaboard. Descriptions of native people that were captured in this general area and taken to England or Spain, for example by Gaspar de Corte Real (1501), and by John Cabot's son, Sebastian (1508-9), only give an idea of the appearance and way of life of native people in northeastern North America.[39] They do not specifically identify Beothuk.

With an increasing number of European ships coming to Newfoundland to fish, the Beothuk became ever more reticent towards strangers. They might have experienced aggressive behaviour from fishing crews and it is possible that some Beothuk were carried away. Whatever the reason, by the mid-1500s they generally avoided strangers and were reputed to be "intractable" and uncooperative. An account by men from the Bristol ship *Grace* confirms this.[40] In 1594, when the *Grace* anchored in St. George's Bay, the crew found several dwellings made of "firre trees" and bark, whose occupants had fled. Judging by the footprints in the sand, the crew estimated their number at about 40 to 50. During the ten days in which they fished in the vicinity they never set eyes on the native inhabitants, who clearly avoided them. The *Grace* moved on to a sheltered harbour on the Burin Peninsula, in Placentia Bay, where native people cut the ropes of three of their boats. Although the crew were able to retrieve two of them, the captain chose to depart for fear of "a shrewder turne of the Savages."

Despite this and other misadventures, a friendly interchange between Beothuk and English colonists occurred in Trinity Bay in 1612. The English party was headed by John Guy, governor of the colony at Cupids, Conception Bay, who had come to Newfoundland with 39 men two years earlier.[41] Learning that native people lived in Trinity Bay, he decided to investigate, and set off with 18 men in two boats. At Dildo South, the party found a deserted Beothuk camp and, following a path inland, came to three mamateeks (the Beothuk term for dwellings) at Dildo Pond in what is now the community of Blaketown.[42] The occupants had fled. Sailing farther up the coast Guy and his men noted more mamateeks at the bottom of Bull Arm (near Sunnyside) and hoisted a white flag to signal peaceful intentions. Presently, two canoes, occupied by eight Beothuk, approached and beckoned for some of the colonists to come ashore. The welcome ritual included an oration and the shaking of a white wolf skin as well as an exchange of gifts: the Beothuk presented their guests with a chain of periwinkle shells, a feather and an arrow without head, and the colonists brought a linen cap and a towel. This was followed by prolonged dancing, leaping and singing, in which the colonists participated. They then shared a meal. Guy contributed bread, butter, raisins, aquavit and beer; the Beothuk brought smoke-dried caribou meat and a root. They were amicable and friendly; when one of them produced a strange sound by blowing into the aquavit bottle they all burst into laughter. After the meal the Beothuk exchanged their white wolf skin for the white flag of the colonists and motioned for them to leave. On the following day, Guy's party discovered a display of furs on poles further down the coast. Assuming that this was an offer for "silent barter", a form of exchange in which the trade partners are not present, they left a hatchet, a knife, four needles, scissors and other goods for the furs they took, and then sailed homeward.

John Guy described the Beothuk as men with a bold and upright posture, broad breasted, and of medium height. Their hair was long, some of it plaited and decorated with feathers at the back of the head. Their face, body and apparel were painted with ochre. They wore short gowns made from fur, with the furry side turned inwards. The gowns had sleeves and were fitted with collars of beaver skin. The outfit of one of the Beothuk who "seemed to have some com[m]and over the reste" included shoes made from caribou and seal skin as well as mittens. Other sources tell us that the Beothuk wore loincloths, pantlike leggings that came up to the waist, and knee-high legskin boots or moccasins. On occasion, the Beothuk were seen with hats.[43] Guy was much intrigued by the shape of the Beothuk's canoe which, to him, looked like a "new moon" in side profile. It had a rounded bottom and elevated stem and stern sections and at the centre (beam) the sides rose sharply to a point. One hundred and fifty years later Lieut. John Cartwright confirmed these observations.

Both John Guy and the colonist Henry Crout, who had taken part in the expedition, thought that the Beothuk were personable, trustworthy and bold, but distrustful of the English and given to revenge.[44] Other observers considered them to be gentle, ingenious and harmless.[45] Crout, who hoped for a profitable trade, believed it would be worthwhile to have a few Beothuk stay with the English and to leave Englishmen in their place. He knew a man who had lived with the Beothuk for five years and could speak their language (perhaps a Frenchman?)—presumably this made him a suitable candidate. But nothing came of the exchange and Guy's plan to meet with the Beothuk in the following year misfired. When a group of them assembled on the beach a fishing vessel passed. Feeling threatened by the crowd the crew "let fly their shott." The Beothuk fled. From that day on, as a result of this and probably of other similar incidents, they were said to be responsible for much "mischief", which usually took the form of taking or destroying fishermen's gear.[46] They also became more elusive. Contact with the white newcomers may not have been entirely severed, but the delicate balance of mutual tolerance was soon destroyed.

7

Relations Between Beothuk and Mi'kmaq, Labrador Montagnais (Innu) and Inuit

Not only European fishing crews and colonists made inroads into the Beothuk's traditional resource centres on the coast. The Beothuk also experienced encroachment and eventual hostility from native neighbours. Mi'kmaq are likely to have come to the south coast of Newfoundland to hunt and fish from the 1500s onwards. They crossed the 100 kilometre wide Cabot Strait from Cape Breton Island to Cape Ray in their bark canoes, a feat that is still greatly admired.[47] Since Beothuk also hunted and fished on the south coast both groups may initially have shared the region's resources.[48] Once Mi'kmaw families came in larger numbers and the French established a fort at Plaisance (Placentia), in the 1660s, the Beothuk appear to have withdrawn. Relations between the two native groups may have remained unproblematic until the early 1700s when Mi'kmaw groups, deprived of their hunting grounds in Nova Scotia and Cape Breton Island, settled in St. George's Bay.

Mi'kmaw tradition has it that they coexisted peacefully with the Beothuk in St. George's Bay until disagreements caused enmity.[49] Two traditions recorded in the 1820s claim that the enmity was caused by Mi'kmaq taking Beothuk scalps; in 1914 a Mi'kmaw informant told the anthropologist F. G. Speck that Mi'kmaq killed a Beothuk boy. All three traditions agree that there was eventually a confrontation in which the Mi'kmaq emerged as the victors and the Beothuk were dislodged. It may be significant that the Beothuk, who were formerly considered invincible, were armed with bows and arrows while Mi'kmaq had guns.[50] In 1839, the Mi'kmaq Sulleon told the geological surveyor J. B. Jukes that about 30 years after the Beothuk's defeat in St. George's Bay, another confrontation at the northern end of Grand Lake led to the displacement of the Beothuk from that region.[51] Thus, by the mid-1700s Mi'kmaq occupied Newfoundland's south and west coasts and hunted and trapped inland from there, while the Beothuk became largely confined to the coast of Notre Dame Bay, the watershed area of the Exploits and Gander rivers, and Red Indian Lake.

Shanawdithit, the last known Beothuk, later corroborated the main points of the Mi'kmaw traditions, and in 1827 told Bishop John Inglis that "the Micmac who had been visitors here [in Newfoundland] for centuries were formerly on friendly terms but their enmity has been implacable . . . for about 150 years."[52] If Bishop Inglis understood Shanawdithit's manner of reckoning time correctly, friction between the two groups may actually have begun before 1700. Representatives of the Conne River Band today assert that the Mi'kmaq never used weapons against the Beothuk but helped them and protected them from the English.[53]

A legend embedded in Newfoundland folklore, dubbed the "Mi'kmaw Mercenary Myth," states that the French brought the Mi'kmaq to Newfoundland to kill Beothuk, and offered them a cash reward for every Beothuk head or scalp.[54] This is completely untrue. Mi'kmaw hunters and their families came to Newfoundland of their own accord. Although they were allied with the French at that time, there is no evidence that the French ever encouraged them to kill Beothuk.[55]

There seems to have been little friction between Beothuk and Labrador Montagnais (Innu), even though Innu may have hunted and trapped in northwestern Newfoundland since the 1600s or earlier.[56] However, in the early 1700s, when the French in Labrador encouraged large numbers of Innu hunters to go trapping in Newfoundland, and to make contact with the Beothuk, the Beothuk are said to have avoided them.[57] The Innu may have become suspect because of their association with the French, and also with the Mi'kmaq, with whom they intermarried.[58] The Beothuk would not have been so elusive had the Innu been trusted as friends, and the Innu would not have tried to meet with them had there been a history of warfare. Towards the end of the 1700s, Innu hunters who had taken Mi'kmaw spouses may have come to identify with Mi'kmaw interests, but this affiliation did not lead to hostilities between them and the Beothuk.

Inuit from Labrador are unlikely to have had a major impact on the Beothuk. Frequenting the Strait of Belle Isle from the late 1500s onward, the Inuit exploited resources on the Northern Peninsula, where they came into conflict with French fishermen.[59] Forays into Notre Dame Bay led to tension and occasional fighting with Beothuk. In 1701, Commander Graydon reported "great hatred" between the "Canada Indians" (Inuit) and the Newfoundland Indians (Beothuk).[60] This animosity was later confirmed by Lieut. John Cartwright who recorded, in 1768, that "former-ly" clashes had occurred. The "Esquimaux" (Inuit) had kept "to their own element, the water" where their missiles for killing whales had proven to be superior to the weapons of the Beothuk and as a result had usually kept the upper hand.[61] Yet, despite hostilities by some Inuit groups others may have traded with Beothuk, as is alluded to in a report by Pierre Francois-Xavier Charlevoix.[62] By the mid-1700s Inuit no longer came far enough to the south to encounter Beothuk, and interactions would have ceased.

8

COMPETITION FOR RESOURCES
WITH FISHERMEN/SETTLERS

During the first half of the 1700s the Beothuk lost access to the south and west coasts due to the Mi'kmaw presence, and were forced to share resources on the Northern Peninsula with the Innu. In addition, the continued expansion of the British settler population from the Avalon Peninsula into Trinity and Bonavista bays deprived them of much of their resource base in this area. Thus, their hunting and fishing activities were much curtailed, and their competition with fishermen/settlers for food created tension and hostilities between the two groups.

In the 1720s, when George Skeffington erected salmon posts on rivers north of Cape Bonavista, the Beothuk broke down the salmon weirs and killed several of Skeffington's men. This is the first recorded instance of the Beothuk resorting to violence. Skeffington responded by sending a force of 30 men to protect his posts.[63] Being armed with guns they may well have driven the Beothuk away. Over the following decades, settlers set up salmon stations in every sizeable bay and inlet, particularly on the Exploits River, which became widely known for its productive salmon runs. By 1735 the annual harvest of salmon in Newfoundland amounted to 145,000 kilograms and by the end of the century catches reached an average of 550,000 kilograms per year.[64] As a result the Beothuk were increasingly excluded from most of the salmon rivers in greater Notre Dame Bay. This posed a serious threat to their survival, since salmon was one of their major staple foods. In 1768, Lieut. John Cartwright noted that the Beothuk "used formerly to kill considerable quantities of salmon in the rivers and small streams; but the English have now only left them in possession of Charles's and another brook." A short time later settlers also took salmon from Charles's Brook which would have reduced the Beothuk harvest even further.[65]

Settlers also competed for sea birds, particularly at Funk Island, where great auks nested in prodigious numbers. On their way to the island, settlers would attack Beothuk in their canoes to frighten them away. To escape injury the Beothuk often canoed to sea in "the thickest fog," a feat greatly admired by settlers but hazardous for the canoeists.[66] The bird catchers not only collected birds and eggs for food but killed large numbers of the flightless great auk for their feathers.[67] In the 1770s George Cartwright stated that "the bird islands are so continuously robbed [by the settlers] that the poor Indians must now find it much more difficult than before to produce provisions for the summer and this difficulty will annually become greater."[68] Cartwright's words were prophetic. At the end of the century the great auk had become extinct and the Beothuk had lost an important food resource.[69]

In addition to problems with procuring salmon, birds and eggs, the Beothuk experienced frustrations in their efforts to catch harp seals. Settlers used seal skins and meat, but were mainly interested in the fat to produce oil—a business venture that resulted in a growing exploitation of this resource.[70] Though there were plenty of harp seals, sealers routinely set their nets in the best places and the Beothuk may have come to rely more heavily on harbour seals, which can be caught from shore. A high percentage of the seal bones in several Beothuk middens came from harbour seal. However, the relatively small size of the harbour seal population made it vulnerable to over-exploitation, and the species may have become depleted.[71]

The Beothuk also faced competition for fur-bearing animals. By the 1720s the number of trappers—locally known as furriers—had greatly increased, as men who had come out to work in the fishery chose to stay behind for the winter.[72] To set up trap lines, they penetrated deeply into Beothuk country. This trespass led to altercations in which furriers killed several Beothuk—the first killings of Beothuk on record. In turn, the Beothuk killed several furriers.[73] Although the value of furring never rivalled that of the salmon fishery, it nevertheless became an established business. In the 1770s, George Cartwright commented: "I fear that the

[Beothuk] race will be totally extinct in a few years, for the fishing trade is continually increasing . . . the bird islands are . . . continually robbed . . . our furriers are considerably increased in number . . . and venture further into the country than formerly, by which the breed of beavers is greatly diminished".[74] Moreover, together with Mi'kmaw and Innu trappers, the furriers not only reduced the beaver population but the stock of all fur-bearing animals.

Whether the furriers' hunting of caribou—often for consumption rather than for hides—unsettled the herds and adversely affected the Beothuk's caribou drive, is not known.[75] It is possible however, that hunters' practices and the use of guns had an impact on the herds' migration pattern. In 1768, Lieut. John Cartwright recorded caribou fences on the Exploits River below Badger; by the early 1800s fences were seen only on the upper course of the river and at Red Indian Lake.[76] This suggests that the herds came to favour crossings closer to Red Indian Lake, forcing the Beothuk to build new fences upstream.

Fishermen/settlers trapped because the Beothuk refused to trade in furs, unlike other northeastern native groups. Encounters between Beothuk and Europeans cannot have been much different from those of mainland tribes, and there must have been other reasons why the Beothuk were unwilling to trade. One clue may be that they were able to obtain iron goods and other useful materials by scavenging seasonally vacated fishing premises, so that their need to trade was considerably reduced.[77] Another factor might have been the Beothuk's strong adherence to traditional values and practices, combined with an early rejection of Europeans. While other northeastern native groups came to emulate European customs, the Beothuk largely continued with their traditions, such as the application of red ochre on the face and body and the use of bows, arrows and spears instead of guns. Although they clearly appreciated metal tools, canvas, rope and nets, they incorporated these materials into their technology and did not, to any great extent, use them to replace their own methods. The Beothuk probably also realized that trade with Europeans posed a threat to their culture, and would have made them vulnerable to European influence and pressures. Similar considerations may have led the Beothuk to reject guns. When firearms came into their possession they destroyed them, together with the ammunition.[78]

9

LIEUTENANT JOHN
CARTWRIGHT'S EXPEDITION
INTO BEOTHUK COUNTRY

By the 1730s, the Beothuk were seldom seen, but fishermen and settlers in Notre Dame Bay felt threatened by their presence, "lurking" in the woods. When hunters from Fogo chanced upon a Beothuk mamateek in 1758, they killed a woman and a child and carried away a young boy, known as Tom June.[79] A few years later, the Beothuk revenged this and possibly other assaults by attacking shipmaster Scott and his fishing crew, who had built a fortified residence in the Exploits River estuary. Scott had approached a group of Beothuk unarmed, when they suddenly uttered a "war-whoop," stabbed him, and killed four of his companions with arrows. The rest of the party fled. An attempt by five settlers to establish themselves in Halls Bay also ended in tragedy, when "they were all killed by the Indians."[80]

The settlers retaliated, and accounts of cruel treatment of Beothuk came to the attention of Governor Hugh Palliser (1764 -1768). Anxious to improve relations with the Beothuk, Palliser commissioned Lieut. John Cartwright, in 1768, to lead an expedition into the interior to contact the Beothuk and explore the country.[81] Accompanied by ten seamen, a chaplain and his brother George, John Cartwright sailed to the Exploits River where he hired a local furrier as guide. He also consulted the Beothuk captive Tom June, who told him about a Beothuk village by a large lake. At the end of August the party rowed up the Exploits River as far as Jumpers Brook, and from there proceeded on foot. Trekking upriver, they soon discovered many mamateeks and extensive fences. But the dwellings were deserted; presumably the Beothuk were still on the coast. Despite persistent rain and diminished provisions Cartwright and his men pushed on to Red Indian Lake where they found the Beothuk village June had talked about. By June's account it had been the residence of a great part of his tribe, but it was now in an advanced stage of decay. After examining the houses, Cartwright's party retraced their steps as fast as their tattered footwear and the rainy weather allowed, and arrived back at their boat ten days after they had started.

Although John Cartwright failed to meet Beothuk—a second attempt in the summer of 1769 along the coast ended in shipwreck—his report contains valuable information on their numbers and means of subsistence, their campsites, dwellings, canoes and other artifacts. No first-hand information of this nature had been recorded since John Guy described his meeting with Beothuk in 1612. Cartwright also remarked on the settlers' behaviour towards the Beothuk and outlined the geographical features of the region on three maps.[82]

In Cartwright's opinion, the local inhabitants made no attempt to accommodate the aboriginal population and were guilty of many cruelties and murders. While amicable relations had previously existed, it was not the conduct of the Beothuk that had caused a rupture in relations. Their eventual hostility was "founded on their part upon a just, and . . . noble resentment of wrongs. On the part of the English fishers . . . the wantonness of their cruelties . . . has frequently been almost incredible." Local inhabitants thought that no more than 200 to 300 Beothuk were still alive, now coming to the coast only between Cape St. John and Cape Freels (Fig.9). Since he had found close to 90 mamateeks, Cartwright thought that the population was nearer 400 or 500. He suggested that up to two-thirds assembled during the fall for the caribou hunt at the Exploits River, where they remained for the winter, while the other 200 or so lived in more remote places in the interior, relying on beaver rather than caribou for their subsistence.

According to Cartwright's report, the Beothuk constructed their cone-shaped dwellings from straight poles, set in a circle, and tied together at the top. This framework was covered with sheets of birch bark laid on the poles like tiles. To keep the bark cover in place, more poles were leaned against the outside. An opening at the top allowed the smoke from

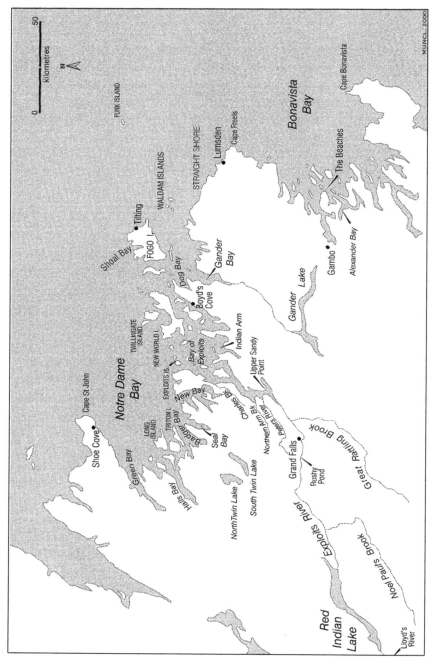

Fig. 9 *Map of Northeastern Newfoundland, the centre of Beothuk activities from the mid-18th century onwards.*

a fire to escape (Fig.10). Oblong hollows in the ground, arranged around a central fire place and lined with the tender branches of fir or pine, served as sleeping places. Such hollows are unique to the Beothuk. Cartwright also saw two rectangular dwellings. Three of the walls consisted of an outer and inner wooden frame; hair adhering to the studs indicated that when in use the space was filled with caribou skins for insulation. The fourth wall was constructed of squared tree trunks placed horizontally, with moss wedged into the seams. The structures were topped by low pyramid-shaped roofs, held together inside by a hoop that was tied to the rafters.

Cartwright was much impressed by the extensive fence works along the banks of the Exploits River, which the Beothuk used in their caribou drive. The trees were felled without the trunks being chopped completely through, each freshly cut tree falling on the previous one. The weak parts of the fence were reinforced with branches, tops of trees, and occasionally by large stakes or bindings. Two to three metres high, the fences would have been impenetrable. On the north bank there were leads extending into the forest, funnelling the animals towards narrow exits by the water. Where there were not enough trees, the Beothuk substituted "sewels"— slender two-metre-long sticks stuck into the ground at an angle, with bark tassels (see foreground Fig.10) which moved with every breath of wind, frightening the caribou, and thus acting as a fence.[83] Cartwright estimated the length of the fences on both banks of the Exploits River, between Bishop's Falls and Badger, to be about 15 kilometres.

Of particular interest to Cartwright was a 4.27 metre bark canoe, large enough for two or three people. The canoe was curved upwards at both ends, looking like a half-moon in side profile, and was V-shaped in cross-section (Figs. 10 & 11). The sides rose to a point half-way between the stem and stern, as described earlier by John Guy. Cartwright correctly believed this shape to be unique for North American bark canoes. The shell of the canoe was made from good quality birch bark sheets, neatly sewn together with split spruce roots. The inner frame consisted of a pole, or keelson, placed lengthwise along the centre. The bark cover was sharply folded upwards on either side of it, so that the canoe had "no [flat] bottom at all." The bark hull was protected inside with flat boards, held in place by ribs. Cross pieces, or thwarts, kept the sides apart and helped to maintain the canoe's shape. The upper edge was strengthened by slender

Ingeborg Marshall

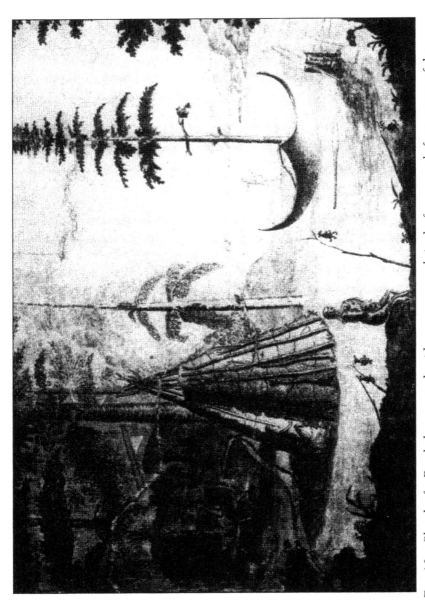

Fig. 10 *Sketch of a Beothuk mamateek with a canoe, sewels in the fore ground, from a map of the Exploits River by Lieut. John Cartwright, 1768.*

poles that served as gunwales. Seams were covered with a mixture of resin, oil and ochre. Having a "pointed" rather than a flat bottom (in cross-section), the canoe required ballast to make it float upright (Fig.11). For this purpose the Beothuk used rocks, which they covered with moss to kneel on. They propelled the craft with paddles. In fine weather they sometimes set a sail on a very slight mast, but Cartwright thought that the delicate and unsteady vessel he saw was not suited for this practice.

The extraordinary draft of this canoe combined with a strong curvature at the ends (known as rocker) made it easy to manoeuvre and prevented it from being blown off course. It was certainly seaworthy. A modified design, demonstrated by a replica made by Shanawdithit in the 1820s, had a straight bottom that turned at an angle rather than a curvature into the end sections. This canoe type had less draft and would have been better suited for shallow inland waterways (Fig.12).[84] (In replicas found in burials, the sides curved upward but did not come to a point in the centre).

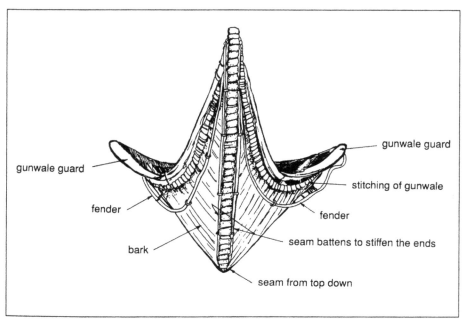

Fig. 11   *Drawing of end profile of canoe replica made by Shanawdithit, showing structural parts.*

(Provided by Cliff George, reproduced by permission of the Canadian Museum of Civilization)

Fig. 12 *Canoe replica made by Shanawdithit for Capt. W.H. Jones of HMS Orestes in 1826-27 while she was living with the Peytons on Exploits Island.*

(© National Maritime Museum, Greenwich, London)

John Cartwright's expedition along the Exploits River and his subsequent search in Notre Dame Bay was a promising initiative. It was tragic that he failed to make contact with the Beothuk, since he was sympathetic to their plight, acutely aware of the delicate nature of his mission, and anxious to succeed. Cartwright was also fully supported by the Governor. Circumstances were never as favourable again. Later attempts to conciliate the Beothuk had no real chance of success, because the Beothuk became opposed to any form of interaction and, at least in the 1800s, taught their children "to cherish animosity and revenge against all other people."[85]

10

HOSTILITIES BETWEEN
FISHERMEN/SETTLERS,
FURRIERS AND THE BEOTHUK

In the second half of the 18th century, after a long lull in encounters, the Beothuk started to make their presence forcefully known by taking sails, fleets of nets, hatchets and other equipment.[86] Occasionally they ambushed fishermen at work and sometimes wounded or killed a man. Presumably, these actions were caused by the Beothuk's need to take revenge for wrongs they suffered. For example, in 1780, they shot a youngster while dipping salmon at a pond. Nine years later, salmon catcher Thomas Rowsell lost his life to Indian arrows.[87] The ambush of nine men who had gone to fetch rock ballast at Shoal Bay, south of Fogo Harbour, was long remembered in the northern district. To test whether the men had brought guns, the Beothuk had placed a decoy pigeon in the entrance of the bay. When no shot was fired, the Beothuk correctly assumed that they had come without firearms and showered the men with arrows, wounding five of them.[88] Reputedly, the Beothuk could "arrange five or six arrows at a time between the fingers and shoot them off, one after the other, with great rapidity and unerring aim."[89] On another occasion, the Beothuk were said to have concealed themselves under the fishing stages at Herring Neck and to have cut up the sails of a fishing boat and all the fishing lines, besides doing other mischief. Though detected, they made their escape.[90] The Beothuk cut loose fishing boats from their moorings, and there were other complaints. However, they did not take every opportunity to harm settlers or fishermen, and sometimes spared lives they could easily have taken.[91]

An example of the Beothuk's occasional generosity is the story of four Breton sailors who were shipwrecked near Shoe Cove, south of Cape St. John, in 1787.[92] Wandering along the shore they met a group of Beothuk who took them to their camp, which turned out to be a large, half-open dwelling with a huge fire in the open space. The sailors were afraid that they would be killed because the Beothuk were reputed to be dangerous. But instead they were fed and invited to stay. A young woman took a fancy to one of the sailors and seduced him. This seems to have started a romance with the sailor deciding to stay and live a hunting life. To the girl's sorrow he later changed his mind and joined his comrades when a French ship came to rescue them. The Beothuk did not interfere with their departure.

Fishermen/settlers were indignant when the Beothuk took gear or otherwise caused damage. Some of them retaliated by pursuing and killing Beothuk, "thinking it no Crime to take away [their] Life or Property."[93] There are many accounts of brutal acts perpetrated against the Beothuk. In 1779, one Wells was said to have shot at the occupants of a canoe from his boat and, after landing, to have searched for those too badly wounded to escape into the woods. He shot at them again and then took their canoe and its contents, leaving the survivors stranded. According to another story John Moore, from Trinity, came across a Beothuk woman who begged for mercy by exposing her breasts; he shot her dead and wounded her child.[94] However, some of the tales that circulated in the northern district are clearly distortions or gross exaggerations of facts, or amalgamations several different incidents. An example is the claim that 400 Beothuk were killed on a headland near Hants Harbour, Trinity Bay. Considering the size and distribution of the Beothuk population, this is an impossibility. Claims by individuals to have shot 60 or even "ninety-nine Indians" single-handedly (and wanting to make it 100) must also be rejected as boastful fabrications, tales embellished in the telling.[95]

The majority of those who came into conflict with the Beothuk were men who worked in the fishery during the summer and/or trapped in winter. They often made a scarce living, and the loss of equipment or boats would have caused them real hardship. Considering that under English law punishments for property offenses were severe—the stocks, flogging, and imprisonment being common sentences—it is not surprising that those who suffered losses were outraged. But not all of them sought revenge and, to their credit, most people in the northern bays appear to have behaved in a reasonable manner.[96] It is all the more regrettable, then, that John Peyton Sr., owner of salmon stations on the Exploits River and a respected member of the community, had no compunction about persecuting the Beothuk.[97] Instead of using his influence to discourage violence against the Beothuk, he encouraged mistreatment, and took part in at least one murderous raid.

This took place in the winter of 1781 when Peyton Sr., his partner, Harry Miller, and their headman, Thomas Taylor, travelled up the Exploits River in pursuit of Beothuk.[98] After three days of walking they spotted several mamateeks at the edge of the forest and immediately discharged their guns. They then pursued the Beothuk, who ran out screaming and terrified, many of them wounded. On entering one of the mamateeks Peyton faced a wounded man who defended himself with the remains of a trap; Peyton wrested it from him and killed him with it. After hurriedly packing up as many caribou skins as they could drag away, the men marched home. They had intended to take a young Beothuk girl with them, but decided against it because they did not want the responsibility of looking after her. Nine years later, Harry Miller sent eight of his men on another expedition with similar results. The men did not admit to having fired at the Beothuk even though they had originally intended to "kill everyone . . . both Big & small" in revenge for the killing of Thomas Rowsell and for "stealing from us as they do."[99]

For the most part, people in authority ignored what was going on and failed to live up to their moral obligations. Owners of salmon stations, like John Skeffington and John Peyton Sr., actively encouraged their men to persecute the Beothuk. Merchants with interests in the northern district who could have lodged protests with the governor, were said to have been too self-serving to care. There was no resident magistrate in the area between Cape Freels and Cape St. John where the conflicts occurred, and magistrates in adjacent districts were either not able or not willing to deal with wrongdoing beyond their own boundaries.[100] Naval officers who patrolled the coast usually turned a blind eye to the problems, as did the majority of the Newfoundland governors, presumably because they did not want to admit that persecutions were going on under their jurisdiction.

Officials in Britain did nothing about the problems either, not wanting to become involved in unpopular measures which might affect the profitability of the fishery. All this reflects self-interest, prejudice, lack of understanding and total disregard for the rights and needs of the Beothuk.

Why did the Beothuk persist in taking and destroying equipment if the retaliation was so severe? The reduction in their territory, and the consequent need for more efficient hunting tools and strategies might have forced them to take nails, traps and other such items. Iron points and spear heads, which they manufactured from these articles, and axes for the construction of new caribou fences, may have become essential implements. Since the Beothuk did not trade they had to obtain these tools by stealth. The destruction of gear and boats, which was of no material benefit to them, was probably an outlet for mounting anger over injustices. Such deeds may also have provided an opportunity to show bravery and could have played an important role in their cultural survival, when celebrated in songs and legends. For example, some of their songs were about "stealing man's boat," "Whiteman's houses, stages, guns," "Whiteman's jacket," "Whiteman's head."[101] The Beothuk must have known they were taking risks, and might have considered their defiance worth the price they paid for it.

11
PLANS TO CONCILIATE THE BEOTHUK

From 1769 onwards, Newfoundland governors issued proclamations ordering residents and others to live in peace with the Beothuk, and requesting magistrates to bring wrongdoers to justice. This measure was ineffective, but when alternatives were proposed to colonial administrators in London, they were either ignored or rejected.

The first to approach the British government, in 1784, was George Cartwright, owner of sealing and fishing stations on the Labrador coast. In a submission entitled "The Case of the Wild or Red Indians of Newfoundland," he advocated the establishment of an Indian reserve between "Gander Bay Point" (possibly Dog Bay Point) and Cape St. John.[102] It was to be out of bounds for settlers and fishermen for most of the year, though they would be allowed to go there in the fall to cut hay, collect wood and gather berries. The area would be patrolled by a naval vessel, and a Superintendent of Indian Affairs would be commissioned to contact the Beothuk. Cartwright considered himself a suitable candidate for this position since he had already succeeded in befriending groups of hostile Inuit in Labrador. The government was not interested.

Two years later, in 1786, able seaman George Christopher Pulling suggested that a naval vessel should be sent to the Bay of Exploits, and offered to head a mission from there into Beothuk country. To have the necessary authority to keep salmon catchers and furriers in check, he asked to be made a surrogate magistrate for the northern district.[103] Pulling's plan was not accepted. However, in 1792, by then a naval lieutenant, he was granted leave of absence to gather information about relations with the Beothuk. Starting out with a boats master in Trinity, Pulling questioned owners of fishing stations, their servants, fishermen/settlers, furriers and salmon catchers and recorded eyewitness accounts of hostile encounters, as well as observations about Beothuk practices. In his lengthy report, Pulling reiterated his plan to send a peace mission to the Beothuk. He probably sent this document directly to Sir Charles Jenkinson, later first Earl of Liverpool, who was to chair the Parliamentary Enquiry into the State of Trade to Newfoundland, to be held in March, April and June 1793.[104] On his homeward journey as captain of the merchant ship *Trinity*, Pulling was captured by the French and held in Marseilles until the fall of 1793. He therefore missed the enquiry. Immediately after his return to Britain he offered to head the peace mission to the Beothuk which he had "so much at heart."[105] But no such mission was authorized, and Pulling was sent to the West Indies.

Another advocate of fair treatment for the Beothuk was John Reeves, law adviser to the Board of Trade. His 1792 report on the judicial system in Newfoundland included the following statement about the "Wild Indians" whom he considered

> more peculiarly our own people than any other of the Savage Tribes;...[who] are entitled to the Protection of the King's Government, and to the benefit of good neighbourhood from His Subjects; but they enjoy neither. They are deprived of the free use of the Shores and the Rivers, which deprivation should entitle them to some compensation from us; but they receive none; instead of being traded with they are plundered, instead of being taught, they are pursued with Outrage and with Murder.[106]

During the Parliamentary Enquiry in June 1793, Reeves eloquently pleaded for a change in policy towards Newfoundland's aboriginal people, and promoted Pulling's idea of a peace mission.[107] But despite convincing arguments, the committee was not willing to consider his proposals.

Other officials who advocated new measures to protect and befriend the Beothuk were Governor William Waldegrave (1797-1799) and Magistrate John Bland at Bonavista. Bland favoured the idea of sending a party of soldiers from the garrison, guided by northern inhabitants, to seek out the Beothuk in their winter settlements in the interior. The object was to convince them of their peaceful intention and to "obtain posses-sion" of a few Beothuk.[108] "Kind treatment, presents, and a friendly dis-mission" would open the way to further communication—an unfortunate idea that was to doom future attempts at making peace with the Beothuk. But neither this plan nor Waldegrave's suggestion to employ a naval vessel on a peace mission, and to reserve part of the coast and the interior for the exclusive use of the native population, were approved, and nothing was done to improve the situation.[109]

By the early 1800s, the ill treatment of Beothuk had become widely known, and there was pressure on Newfoundland governors to address the problem more vigorously. Since the authorities in Britain were consistent-ly opposed to peace missions, plans now focussed on capturing Beothuk to use as mediators. Previous opportunities for mediation had been ignored. For example, Tom June, who was captured in 1758 and later employed in the fishery in Fogo (he was questioned by Cartwright in 1768), had made frequent visits to his parents in "the heart of the country." Indeed, it was said that one winter his parents and siblings pitched their tent near Gambo and that his employer spent a day with them.[110] The Beothuk John August, taken by furriers in 1768, worked in the fishery in Catalina and Trinity. He left the community for two or three weeks every year and it was believed that he visited his family in the interior during these peri-ods. At the time, it did not occur to anyone to make contact with the tribe through these captives or to record information about Beothuk prac-tices and traditions. An exception was Pulling's effort to collect a word list from the Beothuk girl Oubee in 1791. Captured earlier that year she had been taken into the home of a Mr. Stone in Trinity. Two years later Oubee moved with the Stone family to England, where she died in or before 1795.[111]

Governors may have been anxious to create better relations with the Beothuk, but their efforts were singularly naive and unrealistic. Thus, Governor Charles Morice Pole (1800-1801), offered a cash reward to any-one who captured a Beothuk alive, even though an aggressive act of this nature was unlikely to bring about trust.[112] Within a couple of years this offer caused William Cull of Fogo to seize a Beothuk woman as she was paddling her canoe to collect birds' eggs from an island. He brought her to St. John's and was awarded the sum of 50 pounds sterling. The woman, whose name has not been recorded, was said to have been gentle, generally cheerful, and particularly fond of young children. She was introduced to a large assembly of the principal merchants and ladies of St. John's "who vied with each other in cultivating her good graces . . . presents poured in upon her from all quarters and she seemed to be tolerably contented with her situation."[113] Pole's successor, Governor James Gambier, had her supplied with a variety of articles and requested Cull to take her back. It did not occur to him to consult with the woman about the possibilities of bringing about a reconciliation with the Beothuk, or to find out anything else about her people. Moreover, Cull had great difficulty finding men who would accompany him, because people in the northern district were afraid of the Beothuk, and he had to keep the woman in his house for close to a year. Cull eventually brought her up the Exploits River, but as he did not dare to approach a Beothuk settlement, he left the woman to find her way on her own. Sometime later she visited a fishing village alone and it was believed that she never rejoined her people.[114]

In 1807, Governor John Holloway, who opposed any interference with the Beothuk, had the idea of leaving a picture in the woods, portraying Beothuk and whites exchanging furs for European goods. This plan actually found favour with administrators in Britain. A painting was commissioned and, for two consecutive summers, it was deposited, together with presents, in the Bay of Exploits. The picture did not attract any Beothuk, as Holloway had hoped, and the scheme was discontinued.[115]

12

MEETING OF
LIEUTENANT DAVID BUCHAN
AND BEOTHUK AT
RED INDIAN LAKE

Sir John Thomas Duckworth, who became Governor of Newfoundland in 1810, was well aware of the prevailing animosity towards the Beothuk. He issued proclamations ordering all persons who resided in or resorted to Newfoundland, including native people, to "live in kindness" with the Beothuk. He also offered a reward of 100 pounds sterling to anyone who could establish friendly relations with them. To make contact with the Beothuk Duckworth sent Lieut. David Buchan, commander of HMS *Adonis*, into the interior. With 24 men from the ship's crew, and three local furriers as guides, Buchan set off on his epic journey on 13 January 1811.[116] Dragging 12 sledges with equipment and provisions, the party travelled up the Exploits River, covering a distance of about 12 kilometres per day. Biting winds, drifting snow, sleet and rain made progress difficult. Reaching the upper part of the river, Buchan made camp and continued with half the party to a Beothuk settlement at Red Indian Lake. Early the next morning the men entered the three mamateeks, surprising the Beothuk in their sleep. Though initially shocked, the Beothuk soon rallied and kindled a fire to roast venison steaks for their unwelcome guests. They also exchanged small presents and, according to Buchan, "everything promised utmost cordiality." But Buchan erred when he believed that the Beothuk's amicable behaviour was a sign of their confidence and trust. After more than three hours of friendly inter-changes, he set off with his men to fetch the presents they had left at their last camp. Two of his marines asked to stay behind to repair their snow-shoes. Four Beothuk offered to accompany Buchan, but three of them turned back halfway.

When Buchan's party returned to the Beothuk camp next day, they found it deserted and in disarray. The men nevertheless distributed blan-kets, shirts, tin pots and other useful articles, until they discovered the bodies of the two marines pierced by arrows, their heads cut off and car-ried away. At the sight of the bodies, the Beothuk man who had remained with them ran away. Although some of his men wanted revenge, Buchan decided to join the rest of the party down river and to return to the schooner as quickly as possible. Despite their fatigue, the men reached HMS *Adonis* in four days.

Seventeen years later, the captive Shanawdithit, who was present at the time, recalled Buchan's unexpected arrival at the Beothuk camp at Red Indian Lake.[117] Soon after he had left to fetch the presents, her peo-ple had become fearful, believing that he would return with a larger force to carry them off to the coast. The "chief" therefore called together a council and suggested breaking camp. To ensure concealment, he wanted to kill the two marines. The council first refused, but after lengthy argu-ments agreed. The hostages were taken outside and shot in the back with arrows. Shanawdithit's mother severed the heads from the bodies. During the retreat they raised the alarm with two smaller groups of Beothuk, who joined them in an unfrequented part of the forest. They impaled one of the heads on a pole and celebrated their victory by singing and dancing around it. Shanawdithit illustrated her story in a sketch (Fig.13). It should be noted that the custom of taking head trophies had once been practised by many North American Indian tribes, but the Beothuk alone retained it until the early 1800s.

In early March, Buchan set out again. However, when he found a large store house cleared out and its skin cover pierced with arrows, he concluded that the Beothuk were prepared to resist. He abandoned any further pursuit. Buchan later attempted to meet Beothuk on the coast dur-ing the summer months, but all efforts were unsuccessful.[118] His unrivalled perseverance, matched by Governor Duckworth's continued encourage-ment and support, might eventually have led to some communication.

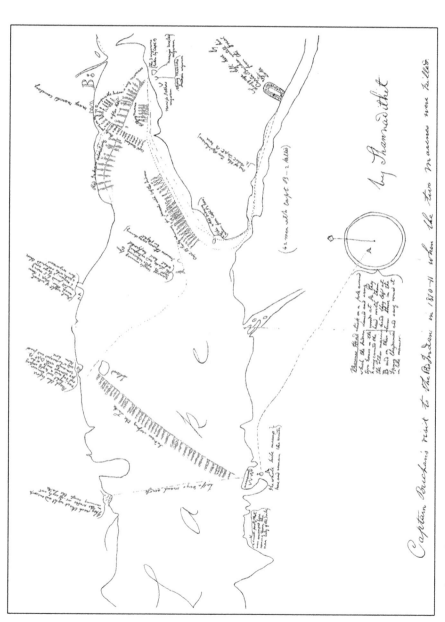

Fig. 13 *Shanawdithit's Sketch 1. Captain Buchan's visit to the Red Indians in 1810-11 when the two Marines were killed.*

But with the start of the 1812-1814 war, further searches had to be abandoned, since no naval vessel could be spared.

Buchan's diary of his winter expedition contains a considerable amount of information on Beothuk practices and their way of life.[119] He confirmed the Beothuk's use of ochre as body paint and noted that their hair was black, coarse and worn straight by both sexes. Their major garment was a coat made from caribou skins trimmed with beaver, otter or marten fur. It was thrown over the shoulders, belted, and came down to the knees. Coats could have fringes around the edges (Fig.14) and often had a collar, wide enough to serve as a hood. Women's coats had a hood large enough to carry a baby. Sleeves were a separate item (they were probably tied together across the back and chest underneath the coat). According to contemporary accounts, the Beothuk never used blankets or other European material to make clothing.

Buchan's description of Beothuk winter mamateeks is particularly interesting. In contrast to the conical and rectangular structures described by Cartwright, Buchan saw octagonal dwellings about seven metres in diameter, with walls made from tree trunks flattened (or squared) at the sides, and driven vertically into the earth close together. Poles, set on top of the walls, formed a conical roof which had an opening at the top to allow smoke to escape and light to enter. Lattice work divided the interior

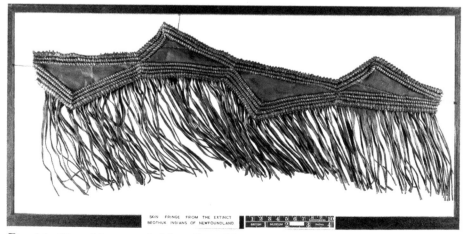

Fig. 14 *Coat fringe, probably collected by W.E. Cormack from Nonosabasut's burial hut in 1827.*

(By permission of the British Museum, London, Registr. No. 2583) into eight recesses for the storage of caribou skins. Hollows in the ground arranged around a central fireplace served as sleeping places, in which the Beothuk lay down with their feet towards the fire and their heads raised. W. E. Cormack, who examined Beothuk dwellings in 1827, thought that the hollows were so deep and short that the Beothuk would have slept in a sitting position.[120] On the outside the dwellings were banked with earth, which made them warm even when little fuel was used. By Buchan's account "the whole was finished in a manner far superior to what might have been expected." According to another eyewitness (E.S., probably a member of the Slade family), who saw a Beothuk camp in 1819, the crevices between the trunks were filled with moss. "Arms . . . implements of war and of the chase" hung on the walls. Quantities of dried food, such as venison and salmon, were stored on beams placed across the top of the walls. The roof consisted of a triple layer of birch bark with about 15 cm of moss packed between the first and second layers. The entrance was covered with skins. These observations give a fairly detailed picture of Beothuk winter mamateeks, but archaeologists have yet to find remains of houses with walls constructed in this way.

In the years following Buchan's expeditions, little was done to conciliate the Beothuk, and violence continued. John Peyton Sr. killed a Beothuk woman at Rushy Pond and a group of men from Twillingate shot several Beothuk on a small island up the bay.[121] In the summer of 1818, Shanawdithit's mother and sister and a young child were killed on their way to an island to collect eggs and birds.[122] Furriers continued to erect tilts on lakes, rivers and brooks inland from Notre Dame Bay and steadily encroached on Beothuk hunting and trapping grounds.[123]

13

DEMASDUIT

The story of Demasduit, or Mary March as she was known among the settlers, is one of the best-authenticated histories of a Beothuk captive. We have several eyewitness accounts of her capture as well as descriptions of her during her stay among Europeans. Her capture was preceded by an increase of pilfering and damage to equipment. The Beothuk coup of cutting adrift John Peyton Jr.'s boat from his wharf at Lower Sandy Point in the fall of 1818 was the last straw. The boat was later found in a small creek on the other side of the bay, completely rifled; all gear of a portable nature had been carried off, though the cargo was not damaged. The guns, battered and broken, had been thrown into a brook.[124] Shanawdithit later recounted that a group had watched Peyton's establishment for days. When Peyton inspected the wharf for the last time before going to sleep, they were already hidden in a canoe beneath it, but kept so perfectly motionless that he was not aware of their presence.[125] Peyton was so annoyed that he went to St. John's to complain to Governor Sir Charles Hamilton. He asked for permission to track down the Beothuk, recover what they had taken and let them know that he was interested in trading. Hamilton readily agreed to this venture and suggested that Peyton secure a captive.

Encouraged by this interview, John Peyton Jr. and his father, accompanied by eight furriers, all heavily armed, set out on an expedition inland in the spring of 1819.[126] They trekked up the Exploits River and on March 5 reached a Beothuk camp at Red Indian Lake. Its occupants immediately fled, except for Demasduit who had recently given birth to a baby, and could not get away. Peyton Jr. took her captive. When her husband, "chief" Nonosabasut, saw this, he advanced towards the party with a spruce branch and made a long oration; he then shook hands with Peyton and his men and indicated that he wanted to take back his wife. Peyton resisted and in the ensuing struggle Nonosabasut was stabbed in the back. "Blood . . . flowed from his mouth and nose; his eyes flashing fire" and he uttered "a yell that made the woods echo." Several men fired and the Indian fell. Demasduit seemed to be in a daze, but when she was forced to leave her husband's body, she "vented her sorrow in heartbreaking lamentations." Peyton fired several shots to frighten the Beothuk away and, in doing so, killed Nonosabasut's brother.

The loss of Nonosabasut and his family—Demasduit's baby died within two days of her abduction—left the Beothuk without their leader and reduced their number to 27. If John Peyton Jr. had let Demasduit go, the encounter might have helped reduce existing tensions. Instead, Peyton seems to have been more concerned with collecting the cash reward for the captive than with demonstrating his good will towards the Beothuk. When Governor Hamilton heard about the killing of Nonosabasut, he ordered the case to be brought before the Supreme Court. However, the jury thought that Peyton's party had not intended to use violence, and that they were "fully justified under all the circumstances in acting as they did." The Indian "came to his death in consequence . . . of his . . . obstinacy in not desisting when repeatedly menaced."[127]

Demasduit, named Mary March by the settlers after the month in which she was captured, was placed under the care of the Rev. John Leigh in Twillingate. She was about 23 years old and described as gentle and interesting. She learned without much difficulty the English words she was taught, and with her help Leigh made a list of more than 200 Beothuk terms. Although Demasduit became tolerably reconciled to her situation, she seemed to "drag a lengthened chain" and "all her hopes and acts appeared to have a reference to her return."[128] In May, after the ice had broken up, Leigh took her for a short visit to St. John's. Lady Hamilton, wife of the governor, took this opportunity to paint a miniature portrait of Demasduit in watercolour. This is the only fully authenticated picture of a Beothuk in existence (Fig.15).[129]

With her modesty and intelligence, Demasduit quickly won the hearts of citizens in St. John's and caused them to revise their ideas about the "savage" Beothuk. It was hoped that once she was returned to her people, her account would convince them that the English honestly wished for

Fig. 15 *Miniature portrait of Demasduit in watercolour, painted by Lady Hamilton in 1819.*

good relations.[130] Improbable as this may seem, people believed that friendliness towards a single captive—after having killed her husband and his brother and having caused the death of her newborn—could have induced the Beothuk to trust them. But Governor Hamilton seems not to have had any doubts and sent Captain Glascock to convey Demasduit to a Beothuk settlement on the coast. He failed, and Hamilton assigned the task to Capt. David Buchan, now commander of HMS *Grasshopper*. Buchan decided on another winter expedition and, in November 1819, moored his vessel at Ship's Cove (now Botwood) in the Exploits River estuary.[131] Demasduit was suffering from a consumptive illness and her health was poor. She was in no state to travel on foot and Buchan decided to go without her. Demasduit would not hear of it. She gave Buchan to understand that she only wanted to collect her child (being unaware of the infant's death) and then return with him. But this was not to be. On 8 January 1820 Demasduit suddenly died. Her gentle manner and patience under suffering had endeared her to those around her, and her death caused much sorrow.

Buchan decided to take Demasduit's remains back to the place where she had been taken, and to make another attempt to contact the Beothuk. With a party of 49 armed men, including John Peyton Jr., he travelled up the Exploits River to Red Indian Lake. After a difficult journey, a reduced party eventually reached the former Beothuk camp. One of the mamateeks had been turned into a burial hut for Nonosabasut, and Buchan had Demasduit's coffin suspended in a tent beside it. Shanawdithit later described how her people had examined the coffin after Buchan left and, in the spring, had placed it beside her husband's remains in the burial hut.

Several of Buchan's men searched along the western shore of Red Indian Lake, as far south as Lloyd's River, and discovered old traces but no Beothuk. Others explored the chain of lakes connecting the Exploits River with Badger Bay where they found snowshoe and sledge tracks, none of them very recent. Leaving presents here and there along the way, the party arrived back at HMS *Grasshopper* 40 days after they had set out. Buchan subsequently sent small parties with boats to search along the shores of several lakes. But all efforts were in vain.[132] Discouraged, Governor Hamilton decided that it would be unwise to undertake anything further.[133] In fact, after 1820 Newfoundland governors no longer sponsored attempts to contact the Beothuk.

14

RELATIONS BETWEEN THE BEOTHUK AND MI'KMAQ IN THE EARLY 1800S

By the early 1800s the Beothuk confined their activities to Notre Dame Bay and the country inland from there, including the watershed of the Exploits River and Red Indian Lake. The permanent Mi'kmaw population, estimated at about 150 people, lived on the west and south coasts. Their most important communities were at Flat Bay (St. George's Bay) and Bay d'Espoir. Other groups lived at Great Codroy River, Bonne Bay and Bay of Islands on the west coast, and at White Bear Bay, Clode Sound and Gander Bay.[134] Although the Newfoundland Mi'kmaq revered some individuals in St. George's Bay, they considered Cape Breton Island their "headquarters." They generally hunted and trapped inland from their coastal communities, and were joined seasonally by hunting parties from Cape Breton Island and Nova Scotia. In 1810, as many as 200-300 Mi'kmaq gathered in Bay d'Espoir.[135] Though the Mi'kmaq recognized that a great portion of the interior was "Red Indian country", so W. E. Cormack reported after his trek across Newfoundland in 1822, some of them moved further inland and were familiar with Beothuk hunting grounds. Mi'kmaq routinely travelled up the Exploits River and camped at Wigwam Point to hunt and trap.[136] Others knew about a Beothuk settlement at South Twin Lake which Cormack later investigated; they complained to him that the Beothuk stole their axes whenever they encamped in "Red Indian country," an indication of trespass. On one occasion a Mi'kmaw party had taken possession of a Beothuk camp.[137] These incursions into Beothuk territory would have created resentment among the Beothuk. Naval officers patrolling the Newfoundland coast repeatedly reported strife between the two native groups, and Governor Duckworth responded by issuing a proclamation asking the Mi'kmaq to live in peace with the "native Indians."[138]

Shanawdithit later told Cormack that "from infancy all her nation were taught to cherish animosity and revenge against all other people; that this was enforced by narrating during the winter evenings, the innumerable wrongs inflicted on the Boeothics by the white men and by the Mik-maks."[139] Elders taught that contact with either group would be punished with death, and by exclusion from the country of the good spirit after death. This shows how the Beothuk deeply resented the losses they had suffered and were intent on keeping animosities alive.

Though hostility was mutual, there is only one story in which Beothuk were said to have killed a Mi'kmaq.[140] As a rule, the Beothuk seem to have fled at the sight of them.[141] In one case a Beothuk couple was so anxious to get away that they left their infant in their canoe; the Mi'kmaq who found it, said he placed food with the child. In another story a gun shot frightened a Beothuk couple from their canoe, which drifted to the river bank where the Mi'kmaq were hiding. Two Beothuk children were still in it but on landing they were said to have quickly disembarked and fled.[142]

Mi'kmaw traditions also describe the kidnapping of Beothuk and their subsequent integration by marriage.[143] The best known case is that of Santu Tony's father who was a "Red Indian," and as a baby, was stained red. He was later "taken" by Mi'kmaq, reared by them, and married a Mi'kmaw woman. Their daughter, Santu, was born around 1837. Santu said that her father was still alive in the late 1840s; he could therefore qualify as the last surviving Beothuk. Another Beothuk who married into a Mi'kmaw family was Gabriel; nothing is known about the circumstances that led him to join them. Gabriel's son married a Newfoundland woman who is said to have been the grandmother of Mrs. White from Stephenville.[144] Other Mi'kmaw and Newfoundland families also claim Beothuk ancestry.

Some Mi'kmaq assert that their ancestors lived in Newfoundland before the eighteenth century, or even before the arrival of Europeans, or of the Beothuk. These statements are based on anthropologist Frank G.

Speck's interviews with Mi'kmaw informants in 1914.[145] Speck reported that the Newfoundland Mi'kmaq referred "to their predecessors as Sa'yewe'djki'k, 'the ancients', speaking of them as though they were the first inhabitants of the island." The Sa'yewe'djki'k families were said to have become completely merged with the later comers. "Ignoring this evidence" Speck concluded that the term Sa'yewe'djki'k referred to earlier Mi'kmaw "colonists" whose numbers were few and whose isolation rendered them distinct in some respects in culture and possibly dialect, though their place names were typical Mi'kmaw terms. Today, representatives of the Conne River Band are of the opinion that the western and southern parts of Newfoundland have always been Mi'kmaw territory, while Beothuk occupancy was always confined to the central and eastern regions.[146]

15

WILLIAM EPPES CORMACK AND THE BOEOTHICK INSTITUTION

There were no further official searches for the Beothuk after Buchan's expeditions. Indeed, when William Eppes Cormack, a businessman with scientific interests and a philanthropic bent, decided to explore the interior and look for the Beothuk, Governor Hamilton prevented Cormack's friend, magistrate Charles Fox Bennett (the later premier), from accompanying him. Cormack was not discouraged, and in the fall of 1822 he crossed the island on foot with his Mi'kmaw guide, Joseph Sylvester.[147] The men started on September 5 from Random Sound, Trinity Bay, and after a harrowing trip, arrived at Flat Bay in St. George's Bay on November 2. Cormack collected information on geological formations and the flora and fauna of the interior, but failed to meet any Beothuk because their route lay too far south.

For a time Cormack's energies and possibly his finances were exhausted, but by 1827 he was ready for another expedition. This time he was better informed about the Beothuk's whereabouts and planned to search the country between Notre Dame Bay and Red Indian Lake. On his way to Exploits Island, he stopped over in Twillingate and founded the "Boeothick Institution" to enlist public support and raise funds. The objective of the institution was to open a communication with, and promote the civilisation of the "Red Indians," to procure an authentic history of the tribe and to learn more about their language, customs and pursuits.[148] Other benefits, such as knowledge about the resources of the country were expected to accure as well. Many prominent citizens joined.[149]

Ingeborg Marshall

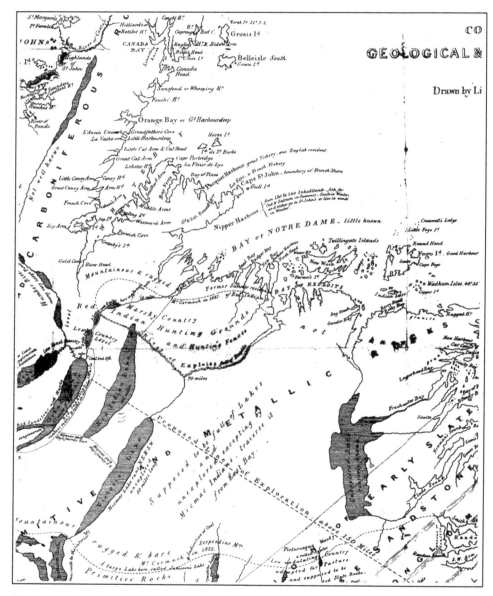

Fig. 16 Former Summer residence of Red Indians; Red Indian Hunting
Grounds and Hunting Fences; Mr. Cormack [his track] in 1822.

(From R.H. Bonnycastle, *Newfoundland in 1842*, vol. 1.)

On 31 October 1827, Cormack and three native guides—an Abenaki, an Innu and a Mi'kmaq—entered the country at the mouth of the Exploits River and from there walked in a westerly direction. At South Twin Lake they found a Beothuk settlement with the remains of eight or ten winter mamateeks, each large enough for 18 or 20 people. There were also vestiges of summer dwellings, a vapour bath and other signs of Beothuk occupancy. The party then trekked to Red Indian Lake where they came across clusters of mamateeks, store houses, an abandoned canoe, caribou fences and a cemetery. But none of these had recently been used and Cormack feared that the Beothuk might no longer exist (Fig.16).[150] They returned to the coast by rafting down the Exploits River, thereby completing a circuit of about 320 kilometres in "Red Indian country." While gliding down the stream, Cormack's attention was arrested by "the Indian fences to entrap the deer [caribou]. They extend from the lake downwards, continuous on the banks of the river at least 30 miles [48 km] . . . connecting these fences with those on the north-side of the lake, is at least 40 miles [64 km] of country, easterly and westerly, prepared to intercept all the deer [caribou] that pass that way in their periodical migrations. It was melancholy to contemplate the gigantic, yet feeble efforts of a whole primitive nation . . . forsaken and going to decay."[151]

In January 1828 Cormack informed the Boeothick Institution about his trip and asked the Institution to employ three native men—Abenaki and Innu—to search for Beothuk survivors in areas which had not yet been investigated. The Institution agreed, and the men spent four months around Grand and Red Indian lakes, but failed to find any recent signs of Beothuk.[152] The same native party, led by John Lewis, an Abenaki, later walked from Croque Harbour to White Bay, and then searched the country to the east. Although old marks of occupation abounded, the Beothuk seemed to have abandoned the area for some time and Cormack concluded that they were dying out.[153] Thus the Beothuk Shanawdithit, captured in 1823, appeared to be the sole survivor of her people and the only person who could give authentic information about them.

16

SHANAWDITHIT

In April 1823, Shanawdithit, together with her mother, Doodebewshet, her father, her older sister (called Easter Eve by the settlers), and possibly others, had come to the coast to look for mussels. When they encountered furriers Shanawdithit's father tried to escape and drowned while crossing a brook. The women surrendered and were brought to the magistrate, John Peyton Jr. on Exploits Island. He took them to St. John's, but after a short visit was asked to return them to the Exploits River. The mother and elder daughter were suffering from a consumptive illness and soon died. Shanawdithit, said to be in better health, was taken into John Peyton Jr.'s household where she acted as a "kind of servant."[154] Peyton's 17-year-old wife, Eleanor, may well have found it difficult to incorporate into her family a native woman several years her senior with whom she could barely communicate, and whose cultural background would have been a mystery to her. Since the Peytons lived in a new house at Exploits Island in summer and at Lower Sandy Point in winter, Shanawdithit would not have lived under the same roof as John Peyton Sr. the known "Indian killer," who, by that time, had retired to his house at Upper Sandy Point.[155]

Usually called Nance or Nancy April, Shanawdithit was about 23 years old and nearly "six feet" (1.82 metres) tall. She had a good figure and handsome features, and although she was said to be pert at times, she was an industrious and intelligent worker, generally affable and affectionate. It may be assumed that the warmth of a growing family, with children who loved her, eased her life in the Peyton household. Bishop John Inglis of Nova Scotia, who visited the Peytons on his tour around the island in 1827, described her "deportment [at a service as] serious and becoming."

He regretted that he could not baptize and confirm her in the Christian faith because she had not been sufficiently instructed. Considering the dramatic events in Shanawdithit's life, such as her capture and subjection to English habits, values and language, it was probably her own traditional beliefs that had sustained her and had helped her to adjust as well as she did. It is therefore unlikely that Shanawdithit would have been willing to accept her captors' religion. Bishop Inglis also recorded that Shanawdithit was fond of Peyton's three young children who would "leave their mother to go to her."[156] Based on this remark some writers have portrayed Eleanor as being jealous of her children's fondness for Shanawdithit or having treated her badly, but there is no evidence for such allegations.[157]

At the founding meeting of the Boeothick Institution, in October 1827, it had been decided that Shanawdithit should be "placed under the paternal care of the Institution," but nothing was done about this until a year later. When it became clear that Shanawdithit alone could provide the information which the Boeothick Institution had pledged to obtain, she was transferred to St. John's, where she arrived on September 20, 1828, and was placed under Cormack's tutelage.[158] One of Cormack's priorities was to help Shanawdithit to improve her English, and she soon was able to communicate, illustrating her narrative on paper. Ten of her sketches are preserved in The Rooms Provincial Museum; the notations were added by Cormack. Working with Shanawdithit he found her to be a lively person with a strong sense of gratitude and great affection for her parents and friends. Although her temper was generally calm, "when some of the servants treated her, as she thought, with disrespect, her fierce Indian spirit kindled—the savage eye darted fire and vengeance" and only Cormack could "subdue the tempest which raged in [her] bosom."[159]

In response to questions about the Beothuk's way of life, Shanawdithit drew food items (see Fig.4), dwellings, store houses, bark dishes, a harpoon, a spear, the "Red Indian devil," a dancing woman (see Fig.3) and six mythological emblems (Fig.17). In one of his letters to Bishop Inglis, Cormack noted that he had "lately discovered the key to the Mythology of her tribe", but Shanawdithit's sketch is the only tangible evidence of such a discovery. Even though the figures on some of the staves can be identified—a whale's tail, a fishing craft and "*Kuus* moon . . ." "which they worship"—with no additional information (other than that one of the staves was owned by a "chief" in the camp that Buchan visited), the meaning and function of these emblems elude us.[160]

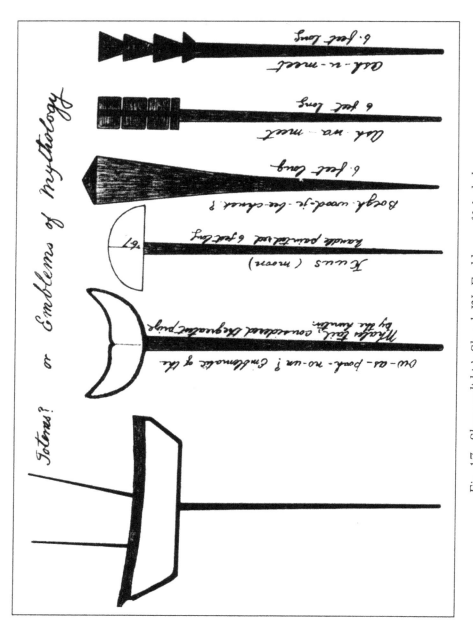

Fig. 17 Shanawdithit's Sketch IX. Emblems of Mythology.

Recalling the story of their origin, Shanawdithit said "the Voice told them that they sprang from an arrow stuck in the ground." She also referred to their belief in life after physical death, on a happy island. "A tradition of old times told that the first white men that came over the great lake were from the good spirit, and that those who came next were sent by the bad spirit; and that if the Boeothics made peace and talked with the white men . . . or with the Mik-mak . . . which belonged to the bad spirit . . . they would not, after they died, go to the happy island, nor hunt, nor fish, nor feast in the country of the good spirit." Presumably due to this injunction, laid down by the elders, Shanawdithit consistently refused to accompany expeditions into Beothuk country, saying that she would be killed.[161]

In view of what is known of other Algonquian hunter-fisher-gatherers, the Beothuk's religious beliefs are likely to have been based on the concept of a multiplicity of animate beings. Accordingly, every conspicuous object in nature, such as the sun, the moon, water and plants, was considered to be animate and had to be regarded with respect which was often expressed in elaborate ritual. Beliefs of this nature would have constituted a pervasive force throughout the Beothuk's lives and have influenced individual as well as communal behaviour. Yet, while Shanawdithit gave much information about her people, she seems to have been reluctant to talk about the Beothuk's world view and belief-related practices, or to explain how they related to (the spirits of) the animal world. Perhaps Cormack did not ask questions that would have prompted her to disclose such knowledge, or maybe she felt uneasy talking about matters that were sacred to her people. It can be assumed nevertheless that rituals accompanied the Beothuk's seasonal activities. Archaeologists suggest that one of these rituals would have been the feast of *mokoshan*, celebrated to honour the caribou spirit and to ensure good luck in hunting, as was the custom among the Labrador Innu. In preparation for the *mokoshan* the Innu crushed and boiled large numbers of caribou longbones to extract the marrow which was then consumed by all members of the community. The feast was accompanied by drumming, singing and dancing. Evidence that the Beothuk may also have celebrated feasts of this nature is provided by the large amounts of caribou bone mash (the residue left after the marrow has been extracted) that have been found on several excavated Beothuk camp sites.[162]

Ingeborg Marshall

While Shanawdithit lived in Cormack's house, she also helped him to make a list of Beothuk words and phrases, including *beothuk*=(Red) Indian, rendered by Cormack in a variety of spellings. Components of this term relate to words in other Algonquian languages that stand for man or human being to which an animate plural ending has been attached. The name Beothuk would therefore denote singular as well as plural. Among the phrases are the Beothuk equivalents for "don't be afraid," "not hurt you," and "we come to be friends," which Cormack might have intended to use in a hoped-for encounter.[163] Shanawdithit's list contains 120 words that are new, or distinct from those previously given by Oubee and Demasduit. This brings the number of known Beothuk terms to 325 plus 21 numerals and the names of the months. Comparisons of Beothuk with the hypothetical Proto-Algonquian language provide evidence that Beothuk could be of Algonquian origin even though its vocabulary is markedly divergent.[164] This no doubt resulted from the splitting of the Beothuk language from its Proto-Algonquin mother language at least 2,500 to 3,000 years ago, and its subsequent development in relative isolation.[165]

By providing a census of her people, citing figures and names, Shanawdithit demonstrated to Cormack the continued decline of her tribe. In 1811 when Captain Buchan came to their principal camp at Red Indian Lake, the Beothuk group had already been reduced to 72 people in all. In the following one or two years 22 members of the tribe died. After this, many succumbed to want and hardship, particularly while inland, and some were shot by settlers. By 1819, when John Peyton Jr.'s party captured Demasduit at Red Indian Lake, the entire population numbered 31. After the death of Demasduit's family, only 27 people were left. No further deaths occurred until early spring 1823 when Shanawdithit's uncle and his daughter were killed, and subsequently eight people in his mamateek perished. By April 1823, when Shanawdithit and her family came to the coast, they left only 12 or 13 of her kin behind. But "being unable to keep up the deer-fences; and being driven from the shore, and from the fish and the oysters, and the nests of water-fowl, their means of existence were completely cut off", and Shanawdithit had little hope that they would survive. She never talked about these facts without tears.[166]

If one leaves aside the human tragedy that unfolds with the figures and names, it is reasonable to suggest that the deaths of 22 Beothuk within two years of contact with Captain Buchan's party was due to the transmission of disease. Dr. William Carson later wrote that "tubercular consumption" was prevalent among the Newfoundland population, and that the four Beothuk women he had seen died of it.[167] It would have taken only one infected individual in Buchan's party to have passed on the disease to the Beothuk. Their lack of immunity to this disease, crowded quarters and lack of food would have constituted optimal conditions for its spread. Tuberculosis may well have invaded the Beothuk population by the early 1800s if not earlier, and played an important role in their demise.[168]

In January 1829, Cormack's business folded and he left Newfoundland. Shanawdithit was moved to the home of Attorney General James Simms, one of the warmest advocates of her people. Most likely she already suffered from tuberculosis at the time of her capture, though her health deteriorated less rapidly than that of her mother and sister. Dr. William Carson's careful attention was in vain, however; the disease gradually worsened, and Shanawdithit died in a St. John's hospital on 6 June 1829.[169] She was buried in a cemetery on the south side of St. John's harbour. A plain stone cairn with a plaque bearing Shanawdithit's name now marks the general area.[170] Although rumours persisted that Beothuk survivors were still at large, with Shanawdithit's death the Beothuk, as a distinct cultural entity, had become extinct.

17
CONCLUSION

In retrospect, the evidence would suggest that environmental factors, the significant reduction of their territory, the increasing difficulty of gaining access to vital food resources, persecution and disease contributed to the Beothuk's demise. However, their persistent withdrawal from contact, and their commitment to revenge, aggravated conflicts and accelerated the process. Valuing their independence, traditions and cultural integrity above all, the Beothuk seem to have been prepared to face increasing hostilities in defence of these values.

Many Newfoundlanders today are interested in the history and culture of the Beothuk and are anxious to preserve their memory. The Beothuk Historic Site at Boyd's Cove, with its attractive interpretation centre and Gerald Squires' "The Spirit of the Beothuk," have therefore enjoyed much support and appreciation (Fig.18). The statue was commissioned by the Beothuk Institute, which was founded in 1997 for this purpose and for developing a better public knowledge of the Beothuk and other aboriginal peoples of the province. Searches for the identity of the Beothuk and attempts at coming to terms with the Beothuk's demise have inspired an increasing amount of artistic expression in the form of poetry, fiction, plays, songs, a musical, paintings, prints and sculpture. Contributions of this nature, combined with continued scholarly investigations, will further an appreciation of this unique native group and add to our understanding of this tragic phase in Newfoundland's history.

Fig. 18 *"The Spirit of the Beothuk," a bronze sculpture, created by Newfoundland artist Gerald Squires, commissioned by the Beothuk Institute.*

(Photograph by Ingeborg Marshall, reproduced with permission of the artist)

ENDNOTES

Abbreviations used in the reference notes:

BL   = British Library, London, UK.

CNS = Centre for Newfoundland Studies, Queen Elizabeth II Library, Memorial University of Newfoundland, St. John's, NL.

NAC = National Archives of Canada, Ottawa.

PANL = Provincial Archives of Newfoundland and Labrador, St. John's, NL.

PRO   = Public Record Office, Kew, UK.

PRRL = Provincial Research and Reference Library, St. John's, NL.

USPG = United Society for the Propagation of the Gospel, London, UK.

[1] Major source materials for this study were information given by Beothuk captives, including ten drawings by the Beothuk woman Shanawdithit; Beothuk artifacts and reports of archaeological investigations; Colonial Office correspondence; unpublished and published contemporary records; newspaper accounts and maps.

Many contemporary reports are published in J.P. Howley's *The Beothucks or Red Indians* (Cambridge 1915), which is a classic in the field of Beothuk studies.

For more detailed information on the Beothuk see Ingeborg Marshall, *A History and Ethnography of the Beothuk* (Montreal 1996).

[2] James A. Tuck, *Newfoundland and Labrador Prehistory* (Ottawa 1976), 54-58; M.A.P. Renouf and Trevor Bell, "Gould Site, Port au Choix, 1999 Report of Field Activities," ms. report prepared for Parks Canada, 2000:8.

[3] Ibid; Shaun J. Austin, "Maritime Archaic and Recent Indian Evidence from Cape Cove Beach, Newfoundland," in *Canadian Journal of Archaeology*, Vol. 8 (No.2) 1984:119.

[4] Tuck, *Newfoundland and Labrador Prehistory*, 79-100.

[5] James A. Tuck, "Some Speculations on Language and Prehistory in Newfoundland and Labrador," Paper presented at the Atlantic Canada Studies Conference in St. John's, 1992, 14.

6 M.A.P. Renouf, Trevor Bell, Michael Teal, "Making Contact: Recent Indians and Palaeo-Eskimos on the Island of Newfoundland," in Martin Appelt, Joel Berglund and Hans Christian Gullov (eds.) *Identities and Cultural Contacts in the Arctic* (Proceedings from a Conference at the Danish National Museum, Copenhagen,1999). New carbon dates have established that in some areas the Cow Head material was replaced by Beaches forms earlier than was originally assumed—but every field season might change the present dates again.

7 Renouf and Bell, "Gould Site," 12; latest research tends to indicate that the Cow Head people were neither directly related to the Maritime Archaic Indians nor to the Beaches people who gradually replaced them.

8 James A. Tuck, *Anthropology 3290: Prehistory of Atlantic Canada* (St. John's, n.d.), 160; Renouf, Bell, Teal, "Making Contact" (Copenhagen 1999), 107.

9 William W. Fitzhugh, "Winter Cove 4 and the Point Revenge Occupation of the Central Labrador Coast," *Arctic Anthropology* 15, no.2, 1978:170. While stone tools from different prehistoric groups can be similar, projectiles usually differ and are considered diagnostic for a specific group.

10 Gerald Penney, "The Prehistory of the Southwest Coast of Newfoundland" (MA thesis, Memorial University of Newfoundland, 1984), 40. Little Passage material was first identified by Penney at the L'Anse à Flamme site.

11 Ralph T. Pastore, *Shanawdithit's People, The Archaeology of the Beothuks* (St. John's 1992), 11; Tuck, *Atlantic Canada*, 153.

12 Pastore, *Shanawdithit's People*, 12; Ralph T. Pastore, "Excavations at Boyd's Cove, 1984: A Preliminary Report," in J. Sproull Thomson and C. Thomson (eds.), *Archaeology in Newfoundland and Labrador 1984* (St. John's 1985), 323.

13 For detailed references see Marshall, *History and Ethnography*, 265-78.

14 Leo English, "Some Aspects of Beothuk Culture," *Newfoundland Quarterly* 59:2, 1960,11-13 [population of 20,000]; Keith Winter, *Shananditti* (Vancouver 1975),1 [population of 50,000].

15 James Mooney, *The Aboriginal Population of North America, North of Mexico* (Washington DC. 1928), 23-4; James A. Tuck, "The Beothucks" in *Micropaedia* (Chicago 1991), 116.

16 A. L. Kroeber, *Cultural and Natural Areas of Native North America* (Berkeley 1939),141, 171—listing population densities for Montagnais-Naskapi and Tête de Boule.

17 David B. Quinn, *New American World* (5 vols., New York 1979), I:95, in Howley, *Beothucks*, 12-13; Ralph T. Pastore, "Excavations at Boyd's Cove: The 1985 Field Season, a Preliminary Report," in J. Sproull Thomson and C. Thomson (eds.), *Archaeology in Newfoundland and Labrador 1985* (St. John's 1986), 223.

18 Frank G. Speck, *Beothuk and Micmac* (New York 1922), 62-64.

19 Tuck, *Newfoundland and Labrador Prehistory*, 23; Chrestien LeClerq, *New Relation of Gaspesia* . . . (ed. W.I. Ganong, Toronto 1910; reprint, New York 1968), 97.

20 Wm. Avalonus (pen name of Magistrate William Sweetland of Bonavista), "Aborigines of Newfoundland," *Royal Gazette,* 7 Jan. 1862, in Howley, *Beothucks,* 287.

21 Howley, *Beothucks*, 227-9.

22 Ingeborg Marshall, *Reports and Letters by George Christopher Pulling* (St. John's 1989), 132; Lieut. John Cartwright, "Remarks on the situation of the Red Indians, natives of Newfoundland; with some account of their manner of living; together with such descriptions as are necessary to the explanation of the sketch of the country they inhabit: taken on the spot in the year 1768," PRRL, 971.8 C24, in Howley, *Beothucks*, 29-41, here 33; George Cartwright, *A Journal of Transactions and Events During a Residence of Nearly Sixteen Years on the Cost of Labrador* (3 vols. Newark 1792), I:10, in Howley, *Beothucks*, 48.

23 Howley, *Beothucks*, 230.

24 Ibid. 230.

25 Henry S. Burrage (ed.), *Early English and French Voyages, Chiefly from Hakluyt 1534-1608* (2nd edn. New York 1967), 392.

26 John Cartwright, "Remarks...1768," in Howley, *Beothucks*, 40.

27 Ibid., in Howley, *Beothucks*, 30-31.

28 George Cartwright, *Journal*, I:9; John Cartwright, "Remarks . . . 1768," in Howley, *Beothucks*, 33; Howley, *Beothucks*, 212, 230; Speck, *Beothuk and Micmac*, 61-2.

29 W.E. Cormack," Report of Mr. W.E. Cormack's Journey in search of the Red Indians in Newfoundland," in *Edinburgh New Philosophical Journal*, 20:6, 1829, 318-29, in Howley, *Beothucks*, 189-97, here 194.

30 W.E. Cormack, "Account of a journey across the Island of Newfoundland, by W.E. Cormack, Esq. in a Letter addressed to the Right Hon. Earl Bathurst, Secretary of State for the Colonies, &&—with a map of Mr. Cormack's journey across the Island of Newfoundland," *Edinburgh Philosophical Journal* 10:19, 1824, 156-62; "Substance of the Narrative of Wm. Cull, Fogo," 22 July 1810, PANL, CSOC, GN 2/I/A, vol.21, f.27-30, in Howley, *Beothucks*, 69; Marshall, *Reports and Letters*, 125, 127, 131; Lieut. David Buchan's Diary of his journey up the Exploits River in search of the Red Indians, in the winter of 1810-11, PRO, CO 194/50, f.153-88, in Howley, *Beothucks*, 72-90, here 75, 84, 87.

31 Cormack, "Journey in search," 324-5, in Howley, *Beothucks*, 193-4.

32 Gillian T. Cell, *Newfoundland Discovered* (London1982), 193; Marshall, *Reports and Letters*, 132.

33 Marshall, *History and Ethnography*, 412-14.

34 Wallis, Wilson D. and Ruth Sawtell Wallis, *The Micmac Indians of Eastern Canada*, (Minneapolis 1955), 266.

35 Cormack, "Journey in search," 324-25, in Howley, *Beothucks*, 193.

36 Howley, *Beothucks*, 331, Plates XXX, XXXI, XXXIII.

37 Anonymous, "Sketches of Savage Life: Shaa-naan-dithit," *Fraser's Magazine for Town and Country* 13:75, No. LXXV (March 1836), 323 [the information was collected by W.E. Cormack; the author was his friend, John McGregor].

38 Henry P. Biggar, *The Precursors of Jacques Cartier, 1497-1534* (Ottawa 1911), 13-15.

39 James Alexander Williamson, *The Cabot Voyages and Bristol Explorations under Henry VII* (Cambridge 1962),266-70; letters from Alberto Cantino to Duke of Ferrara, 17 October 1501, and Pietro Pasqualigo to the Signory of Venice, 18 October 1501, in Biggar, *Precursors*, 63-67.

40 Quinn, *New World*, IV:64, doc. 560.

41 Cell, *Newfoundland Discovered*, 4-6. In recent years remains of this settlement have been excavated and can now be visited; artifacts from the site are on exhibit in the Cupids Museum.

42 William Gilbert and Ken Reynolds, "A Report of an Archaeological Survey: The

Come by Chance River and Dildo Pond," 1989, Ts. The Rooms Provincial Museum.
John Guy, "A journall of the voiadge discoverie made in a barke builte in Newfoundland
called the Indeavour, begunne the 7 of october 1612, & ended the 25th. of November
following," Lambeth Palace Library, Fulham Papers, Letters from Newfoundland,
vol. I-XVII, MS 250, in Cell, *Newfoundland Discovered*, 68-78.

[43] Marshall, *History and Ethnography*, 344-49.

[44] Ibid. 32-3; Henry Crout to Sir Percival Willoughby, 8 September 1612,
Nottingham University, UK, MMSS, Mix 1/20, transcript by Dr. Robert Barakat,
CNS.

[45] R. J. Lahey, "The Role of Religion in Lord Baltimore's Colonial
Enterprise," *Maryland Historical Magazine* 72:4, 1977, 501 [Sir Arthur Aston];
Cell, *Newfoundland Discovered*, 117 [Capt. Richard Whitbourne].

[46] Reply by Archbishop Laud, 29 September 1639, PRO, CO 1/10, f.97-115,
abbreviated in Howley, *Beothucks*, 23.

[47] Speck, *Beothuk and Micmac*, 119-20.

[48] Penney, "Prehistory", 19, 64, 166; Gerald Penney, "Results of Six Historic
Resources Overview Assessments in Newfoundland and Labrador—1986," in C.
Thomson and J. Sproull Thomson (eds.), *Archaeology in Newfoundland and
Labrador 1986* (St. John's 1989), 12-26; Howley, *Beothucks*, 292-4, 334.

[49] Howley, *Beothucks*, 25, 183; J. B. Jukes, *Excursions in and about
Newfoundland during the Years 1839 and 1840* (2 vols. London 1842, reprint
Toronto 1969), I:172, in Howley, *Beothucks*, 26; *ibid.* II:129-30; Speck, *Beothuk
and Micmac*, 28 ["the Red Indians were beaten and driven out"], 65, 121-2.

[50] Peter Pope, "A True and Faithful Account: Newfoundland in 1680,"
Newfoundland Studies 12:1-2,1996, 34; W.E. Cormack, Esq., *Narrative of a Journey
across the Island of Newfoundland, the Only Ever Performed by a European* (St.
John's 1856), in Howley, *Beothucks*, 130-68, here 152.

[51] Jukes, *Excursions*, I:172, II:130.

[52] Bishop John Inglis, Diary, 2 July 1827, NAC, Microfilm A 713.

[53] Jerry Wetzel, Pat Anderson, Douglas Sanders, *Freedom To Live Our Own
Way In Our Own Land* (Peter Usher, ed., Conne River 1980),13; Michael G.
Wetzel, "Decolonizing Ktaqmkuk Mi'kmaw History" (Master of Law thesis,
Dalhousie University, 1995),110.

54 Denis Bartels, "Time Immemorial? A Research Note on Micmacs in Newfoundland," *Newfoundland Quarterly* 75:3, 1979, 6-9.

55 The French did offer a reward for the heads of the English and their Indian allies. In1749 Mi'kmaq from Isle Royale who were wintering in Newfoundland took advantage of the offer and captured 23 Newfoundland settlers; the following spring 12 of them escaped, but the Mi'kmaq claimed rewards for the scalps of the remaining 11 from the French in Quebec, E.B. O'Callaghan and B. Fernow, *Documents Related to the Colonial History of the State of New York* (15 vols., Albany NY 1853-87), X:174-5.

56 Bishop John Inglis, Diary, 4 July 1827, USPG, C/Can/NS 9, doc. 57-8, in Howley, *Beothucks*, 297; Jukes, *Excursions*, II:130-1.

57 Wm. Taverner to Commissioners of Trade and Plantations, 2 February 1733/34, PRO, CO 194/23, f.184; Charles de la Morandière, *Histoire de la pêche française de la morue dans l'Amérique septentrionale* (3 vols. Paris 1962), I:21 [recorded in 1720].

58 Speck, *Beothuk and Micmac*, 126.

59 Morandière, *Histoire*, I:18-19, 21-2; Capt. Wheeler to William Blathwayt, 27 October 1684, PRO, CO 1/55, f.242b.

60 Commander Graydon, 16 October 1701, PRO, CO 195/3, f.11,13.

61 John Cartwright, "Remarks . . . 1768," in Howley, *Beothucks*, 35.

62 Pierre Francois-Xavier de Charlevoix, *History and General Description of New France* (6 vols., New York 1780, rpt. Chicago 1962), I:144.

63 Commodore J. Percy to Council of Trade and Plantations, 13 Oct. 1720, CSPC 1720, Vol. 3, doc. 260; Answer to Heads of Enquiry by Commodore Bowler, 9 October 1724, PRO, CO 194/7, f.240.

64 V.R. Taylor, *The Early Atlantic Salmon Fishery in Newfoundland and Labrador* (Ottawa 1985), 52-8, Table A3.

65 John Cartwright, "Remarks . . . 1768," and George Cartwright, Journal, I:14, in Howley, *Beothucks*, 33, 49.

66 Marshall, *Reports and Letters*, 120, 128.

67 Harold S. Peters and Thomas D. Burleigh, *The Birds of Newfoundland* (St. John's 1951), 246-9.

68 George Cartwright, *Journal*, I:6, in Howley, *Beothucks*, 47.

69 *Encyclopedia of Newfoundland and Labrador* (5 vols, St. John's 1981), I:89.

70 Levi George Chafe, *Chafe's Sealing Book* (3rd edn., St. John's 1923), 18; Burd Journal, 1726, PANL, MG 231.

71 Today the harbour seal population in Newfoundland is inconsiderable, Boulva and I.A. McLaren, *Biology of the Harbour Seal, Phoca vitulina, in Eastern Canada* (Ottawa1979), 3.

72 Answer to HoE by Commander Bowler, 1727, PRO, CO 194/8, f.151-66.

73 Answer to HoE by Commander Falkingham, 4 October 1732, PRO, CO 194/9, f.215.

74 George Cartwright, *Journal*, I:6, in Howley, *Beothucks*, 47.

75 Marshall, *History and Ethnography*, pp. 80-81, Table 5.1.

76 John Cartwright, "Remarks...1768," in Howley, *Beothucks*, 30-1; Buchan's "Diary," 1811, in Howley, *Beothucks*, 74,75; Cormack, *Narrative*, 38, in Howley, *Beothucks*, 152; Cormack, "Journey in search", 327, in Howley, *Beothucks*, 195.

77 Ralph T. Pastore, "Fishermen, Furriers, and Beothuks: The Economy of Extinction," *Man in the Northeast* 33, 1987, 48.

78 Howley, *Beothucks*, 91-2 fn.1, 93.

79 Great Britain, Parliament, House of Commons, *First, Second and Third Reports of the Committee appointed to enquire into the State of Trade to Newfoundland, 1793. First Series Reports*, Vol. 10, Miscell. 1785-1808, 392-503, in Howley, *Beothucks*, 54.

80 Lewis Amadeus Anspach, *A History of the Island of Newfoundland* (London 1819), 181, in Howley, *Beothucks*, 27.

81 John Cartwright, "Remarks . . . 1768," in Howley, *Beothucks*, 29-41; Lieut. John Cartwright to Governor Hugh Palliser, 19 September 1768, PRRL, 971.8 C24, in Howley, *Beothucks*, 41-44; Cartwright's report "Remarks . . . 1768" and his letter to Palliser were first published by his niece D.F. Cartwright in 1826; she sent the original manuscripts to Bishop Feild in Newfoundland in the 1850s and they are now in the Provincial Reference and Research Library (PRRL), St. John's.

82 Lieut. John Cartwright, "A Sketch of the River Exploits the East End of Lieutenants Lake, 1768," PANL, Cartwright Collection, MG 100; Lieut. John Cartwright, "A Sketch of the River Exploits and the East End of Lieutenants Lake in Newfoundland" (submitted 1773), NAC, NMC 27; Lieut. John Cartwright, "A map of the Island of Newfoundland," NAC, NMC 14033.

83 The term "sewels" is a variant of shewel or scarecrow, *Compact Edition of the Oxford English Dictionary* (Oxford 1979), II:2756:575.

84 For more details on Beothuk canoes see Ingeborg Marshall, *Beothuk Bark Canoes: An Analysis and Comparative Study* (Ottawa 1985).

85 [McGregor], "Sketches," 322.

86 Marshall, *Reports and Letters*, 123, 125, 127-28, 130, 132-33, 135-40; Howley, *Beothucks*, 271, 275.

87 Marshall, *Reports and Letters*, 123, 125, 130,138, 140; Howley, *Beothuks*, 267.

88 Marshall, *Reports and Letters*, 121-2.

89 Howley, *Beothucks*, 271.

90 Ibid. 275.

91 Ibid. 27, 51; Marshall, *Reports and Letters*, 128.

92 Peter Bakker and Lynn Drapeau. "Adventures with the Beothuks in 1787: A Testimony from Jean Conan's Autobiography," in William Cowan (ed.), *Actes du vingt-cinquième congrès des Algonquinistes* (Ottawa 1994), 32-45.

93 Marshall, *Reports and Letters*, 134.

94 Ibid. 138, 140.

95 Howley, *Beothucks*, 97, 181, 269. The theme of a person having killed a large number of enemies, or wishing to kill more to achieve a personal quota, is one that recurs in folk tales in many places.

96 Marshall, *Reports and Letters*, 122, 123; Howley, Beothucks, 267.

97 John Bland to J.P. Rance, 1 September 1797, PRO, CO 194/39, f. 218, in Howley, *Beothucks*, 56 (Howley erroneously has 1790).

98 Marshall, *Reports and Letters*, 135-37.

99 Ibid. 123-7.

100 Howley, *Beothucks*, 51.

101 Ibid. 230.

102 George Cartwright, "The Case of the Wild or Red Indians," probably submitted in 1784, PRO, CO 194/35, 1780-84 miscell. f.338-42.

103 A proposal submitted by G.C. Pulling in 1786, BL, Liverpool Papers, Add. Mss. 38347, f. 348-9, in Marshall, *Reports and Letters*, 50.

104 Pulling sent a preliminary report, entitled "Facts relating to the Native Indians of Newfoundland collected from the Salmon Catchers and Furriers, who reside near those parts frequented by the Indians," to Chief Justice Reeves, PRO, CO 194/39, f.221b-229; his final report is entitled "A few facts by G.C. Pulling respecting the native Indians of the Isle of newfoundland, anno Domini 1792," BL., Liverpool Papers, Add.Ms.38352,f.18-47, in Marshall, *Reports and Letters*, 119-143.

105 G.C. Pulling to John Reeves, 2 April 1793, BL, Liverpool Papers, Add.Ms.38352, f.49b, in Marshall, *Reports and Letters*, 60.

106 John Reeves, "State of the Wild Indians in the Interior Parts of Newfoundland," to the Right Honourable Henry Dundas [secretary of state for Colonial Affairs], 5 December 1792, BL, Add.Ms.38351, f.338-41, in Howley, *Beothucks*, 54-6.

107 State of Trade to Newfoundland 1793, *First Series Reports*, vol. 10, pg. 479. [See n. 79.]

108 Bland to Rance, 1 Sept. 1797, in Howley, *Beothucks*, 56 (Howley erroneously has 1790).

109 William Waldegrave to Duke of Portland, 25 October 1797, PRO, CO 194/39, f.214-29; "Minutes relative to proposed alterations for the benefits of the Island of Newfoundland," PRO, CO 194/23, f.420-25.

110 Avalonus, "Aborigines of Newfoundland," 28 Jan. 1862, in Howley, *Beothucks*, 288.

[111] Marshall, *Reports and Letters*, 129, 141; Marshall, *History and Ethnography*, 124-26; Bland to Rance, 1 Sept. 1797, in Howley, *Beothucks*, 56 (Howley erroneously has 1790).

[112] Governor Charles Morice Pole to Duke of Portland, 25 October 1800, PRO, CO 194/42, f.213-17; Governor Erasmus Gower "Observations on the Return of the Fishery for 1804," 18 March 1806, PRO, CO 194/45, f.29-30.

[113] Edward Chappell R.N., *Voyage of His Majesty's Ship "Rosamond" to Newfoundland and the Southern Coast of Labrador* (London 1818), 182-3.

[114] Gower, "Observations . . . for 1804," 18 March 1806; John McGregor, *British America*, (2 vols., 2nd edition, Edinburgh and London 1833), I:256.

[115] Governor John Holloway to Viscount Castlereagh, 25 November 1809, PRO, CO 194/48, f.59.

[116] Buchan's "Diary," 1811, in Howley, *Beothucks*, 72-85; Duckworth's proclamations to the Mi'kmaq, 10 August 1810, PRO, ADM 80/122, f.29, and to the inhabitants of Newfoundland,1 August 1810, PRO, CO 194/49, f.26, in Howley, *Beothuks*, 70, 71.

[117] Howley, *Beothucks*, 180, 226-27, 229.

[118] Commander Buchan's "Memorandum of the Cruize of HM Schr. *Adonis* from Augt. 13th to 19th Octr. 1811," NAC, Duckworth Papers, MG 24 A 45, f. 4918-20, and Buchan to Duckworth, 25. July 1812, ibid., f. 5032-35.

[119] Buchan's "Diary," 1811, in Howley, *Beothucks*, 77,85; added are a few details from the description of Beothuk dwellings by E.S. (presumed to be a member of the Slade family), printed in the *Liverpool Mercury*, 1829, in Howley, *Beothucks*, 100.

[120] Cormack, "Journey in search," 323, in Howley, *Beothucks*, 192.

[121] Shanawdithit's Sketch V, in Marshall, *History and Ethnography*, 152; Howley, *Beothucks*, 97.

[122] [McGregor], "Sketches," 323.

[123] "Capt. David Buchan's Track into the Interior of Newfoundland, 1820," BL, Mss.51222, ADD.57703 f.1 and 2.

[124] Howley, *Beothucks*, 91-92, 96.

125 Ibid. 96.

126 E.S., *Liverpool Mercury*, 1829, in Howley, *Beothucks*, 92-101.

127 Grand Jury Room, 25 May 1819, PANL, CSOC, GN 2/1/A, vol. 30, f.125, in Howley, *Beothucks*, 105; Chief Justice Forbes to Governor Hamilton, 29 June 1819, PANL, CSOC, GN 2/1/A, vol.30, f.181.

128 Hercules Robinson, "Private Journal Kept on Board HMS 'Favorite,' 1820", *Royal Geographical Society Journal*, 1834, 4:216, in Howley, *Beothucks*, 128.

129 The portrait is now in the National Archives of Canada, Ottawa, Picture Div., neg. C-87698.

130 *The Mercantile Journal*, St. John's, 27 May 1819.

131 Commander Buchan to Governor Hamilton, 10 March 1820, report of his second expedition to Red Indian Lake, PRO, CO 194/63, f.64-77, in Howley, *Beothucks*, 121-26.

132 Buchan to Hamilton, 4 June 1820, PRO, CO 194/63, f.79.

133 Hamilton to Lord Bathurst, 28 June 1820, PANL, CSOC, GN 2/1/A, vol.32, f.209.

134 Cormack, *Narrative*, 37-8, in Howley, *Beothucks*, 151-2.

135 Capt. Parker to Governor Duckworth, 28 September 1810, NAC, Duckworth Papers, MG 24 A 45, f.4684-7.

136 Buchan's "Diary," 1811, in Howley, *Beothucks*, 73; Howley, *Beothucks*, 176, 224; Cormack, "Account of a Journey", 161.

137 Ibid.; Cormack, *Narrative*, 38, in Howley, Beothucks, 152; Speck, *Beothuk and Micmac*, 48; Buchan to Duckworth, 17 July 1812, NAC, Duckworth Papers MG 24 A 45, f.5021-3.

138 Capt. H.F. Edgell to Governor Pole, 28 August 1801, NAC, Pole Papers, MG 205; Governor Holloway to Viscount Castlereagh, 18 November 1808, PRO, CO 194/47, f. 61-9; *ibid.* 25 November 1809, PRO, CO 194/48, f. 59; Parker to Duckworth, 28 September 1810, NAC, Duckworth Papers, MG 24 A 45, f.4684-7; Robinson, "Private Journal," 216, in Howley, *Beothucks*, 127; Proclamation by Governor Duckworth, 1 August 1810, PRO, ADM 80/122, f.29, in Howley, *Beothucks*, 70.

139 [McGregor] "Sketches," 322.

140 Howley, *Beothucks*, 280 and fn.1.

141 Ibid. 285.

142 Speck, *Beothuk and Micmac*, 51; Howley, *Beothucks*, 279.

143 E.C. Parsons, "Micmac Folklore," *Journal of American Folklore*, 38:147, 1925, 100; Speck, *Beothuk and Micmac*, 55-60.

144 Harry Cuff, "I interviewed the great-grandchild of a Beothuk," *Newfoundland Quarterly* 65:2, 1966, 25.

145 Speck, *Beothuk and Micmac*, 26, 123-24.

146 Wetzel et al, *Freedom*, 13; Wetzel, "Decolonizing," 110.

147 Cormack, *Narrative*, 3-4, Howley, *Beothucks*, 130, n.3. There is considerable evidence that the name of Cormack's guide was Joseph Sylvester, for example, see Joseph Sylvester's signature in a catechism and prayer book in Mi'kmaw hieroglyph (dated 1820s), Fortress of Louisbourg, National Historic Site of Canada, curatorial collection.

148 "Boeothick Institution," *Royal Gazette*, 13 November 1827, in Howley, *Beothucks*, 182-87.

149 Patron: The Lord Bishop of Nova Scotia, Dr. John Inglis; Vice Patron: The Hon. Augustus Wallet Des Barres; President: W.E. Cormack; Vice President: John Dunscomb; Secretary: John Stark; Hon. Vice Patron: Prof. Robert Jameson, Edinburgh; Resident Agent: John Peyton Jr.; plus 13 (or more) Corresponding Members from among Newfoundland professionals and merchants.

150 Cormack, "Journey in search," 318-29, in Howley, *Beothucks*, 189-97.

151 Cormack, "Journey in search," 237, in Howley, *Beothucks*, 195.

152 Cormack, "Journey in search," 329, in Howley, *Beothucks*, 196-197, and 217.

153 Howley, *Beothucks*, 217-20.

154 Ibid. 175, 180, 181.

155 Amy Louise Peyton, *River Lords, Father and Son* (St. John's 1987), 35, 74, 80; Inglis Diary, 2 July 1827, NAC.

156 Inglis Diary, 4 July 1827, USPG.

157 Annamarie Beckel, All Gone Widdun (St. John's, 1999) 162-3, 194.

158 Two letters from John Stark to Cormack, 16 September 1828, in Howley, *Beothucks*, 202-3; Howley, *Beothucks*, 225.

159 Ibid.; [McGregor], "Sketches," 323.

160 Cormack to Bishop Inglis, 26 October 1828, in Howley, *Beothucks*, 208-9; Buchan's "Diary," 1811, in Howley, *Beothucks*, 79; Marshall, *Reports and Letters*, 141, 2nd entry in the vocabulary.

161 Avalonus, *Royal Gazette*, 7 Jan. 1862, in Howley, *Beothucks*, 288; [McGregor] "Sketches," 322; Howley, *Beothuks*, 184.

162 Raymond Le Blanc, "The Wigwam Brook Site and the Historic Indians" (MA thesis, Memorial University 1973), 83; Pastore, "Boyd's Cove, 1985 Field Season," 221.

163 John Hewson, *Beothuk Vocabularies* (St. John's 1978), 126.

164 Ibid. 138-40.

165 Ives Goddard, "Eastern Algonquian Languages," and "Central Algonquian Languages," in Bruce G. Trigger (ed.), *Northeast* (vol. 15 of *Handbook of North American Indians*, Washington DC, 1978), 70, 583-7.

166 Howley, *Beothucks*, 226-9; [McGregor], "Sketches", 323.

167 Dr. William Carson, "Answers to questions . . .", 1830, PRO, CO 194/81, f.59.

168 Ingeborg Marshall, "Disease as a factor in the demise of the Beothuk Indians," in *Change and Continuity*, ed Carol Wilton (Toronto 1992) 138-49.

169 Shanawdithit's obituary in *The Public Ledger*, St. John's, 12 June 1829, in Howley, *Beothucks*, 231.

170 Marshall, *History and Ethnography*, 220-21.

SELECT BIBLIOGRAPHY

Cell, Gillian T. *Newfoundland Discovered*. London: Hakluyt Society, 1982. This book includes a transcript of: John Guy, "A Iournall of the voiadge of discoverie . . .,"1612. Lambeth Palace Library, London, Fulham Papers, Letters from Newfoundland, vol. I-XVII, Ms. No. 250, f.406-12 - see pg. 68-78.

Howley, James P. *The Beothucks or Red Indians*. Cambridge: Cambridge University Press, 1915. Reprint, Toronto: Coles Publ. Co. Ltd, 1974, 1982; Reprint Toronto: Prospero Books, Canadian Collection, 2000. This book includes transcripts of:

John Cartwright, "Remarks on the Situation of the Red Indians, natives of Newfoundland, . . ." and a letter to Governor Hugh Palliser, 19 Sept. 1768, originals in Provincial Reference and Resource Library, St. John's, NL, 971.8 C24, in Howley, pp. 29-44.

David Buchan, "Narrative of Lieut. Buchan's Journey up the Exploits River in search of the Red Indians, . . ." 12-29 Jan. 1811, and concluding Remarks, in Provincial Reference and Resource Library, St. John's, NL, 917.18 B85 (a copy in the Public Record Office, London, CO 194/50, f.153-88 includes Buchan's diary from 4th to 19th March 1811), complete set in Howley pp. 72-90.

David Buchan to Governor Hamilton, 10 March 1820, report of his second expedition to Red Indian Lake, PRO, CO 194/63, f. 64-77, in Howley pp. 121-26.

William Eppes Cormack, "Narrative of a Journey across the Island of Newfoundland, the Only Ever Perfomed by a European", St. John's: *Morning Post and Commercial Journal*, 1856, in Howley pp. 130-68.

William Eppes Cormack, "Report of Mr. W.E. Cormack's journey in search of the Red Indians in Newfoundland." *Edinburgh New Philosophical Journal* 20:6, 1829, 318-29, in Howley, pp. 189-197.

[McGregor, John—published anonymously]. "Sketches of Savage Life: Shaa-naan-dithit," *Fraser's Magazine for Town and Country* 13: 75, No. LXXV (March 1836), 316-23. This article can be consulted on Dr. Hans Rollmann's website: http://www.mun.ca/rels/native/index.html.

Marshall, Ingeborg. *A History and Ethnography of the Beothuk*. Montreal: McGill-Queen's University Press, 1996.

— *Reports and Letters by George Christopher Pulling*. St. John's: Breakwater Books, 1989.

Pastore, Ralph T. "Fishermen, Furriers, and Beothucks: The Economy of Extinction," *Man in the Northeast* 33 (Spring 1987), 47-62.

— *Shanawdithit's People*. St. John's: Atlantic Archaeology, 1992.

Renouf, M.A.P. *Ancient Cultures, Bountiful Seas*. St. John's: Historic Sites Association, 1999.

Speck, Frank G. *Beothuk and Micmac*. Indian Notes and Monographs. New York: Museum of the American Indian, Heye Foundation, 1922.

Tuck, James A. *Newfoundland and Labrador Prehistory*. Ottawa: National Museum of Man, National Museums of Canada, 1976.